# The Army of Northern Virginia: The History of the Most Famous Confederate Army during the American Civil War
## By Charles River Editors

# About Charles River Editors

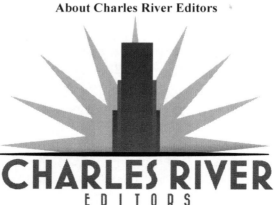

**Charles River Editors** was founded by Harvard and MIT alumni to provide superior editing and original writing services, with the expertise to create digital content for publishers across a vast range of subject matter. In addition to providing original digital content for third party publishers, Charles River Editors republishes civilization's greatest literary works, bringing them to a new generation via ebooks.

Sign up here to receive updates about free books as we publish them, and visit Our Kindle Author Page to browse today's free promotions and our most recently published Kindle titles.

# Introduction

Americans have long been fascinated by the Civil War, marveling at the size of the battles, the leadership of the generals, and the courage of the soldiers. Since the war's start over 150 years ago, the battles have been subjected to endless debate among historians and the generals themselves. The Civil War was the deadliest conflict in American history, and had the two sides realized it would take 4 years and inflict over a million casualties, it might not have been fought. Since it did, however, historians and history buffs alike have been studying and analyzing the biggest battles ever since.

Of course, the most famous battles of the war involved the Army of the Potomac facing off against Robert E. Lee's Army of Northern Virginia at places like Antietam and Gettysburg. Antietam was the bloodiest day of the war and forced Lee out of Maryland, allowing Lincoln to issue the Emancipation Proclamation. The following summer would see the biggest and most famous battle at Gettysburg. Lee would try and fail to dislodge the Union army with attacks on both of its flanks during the second day and Pickett's Charge right down the center of the line on the third and final day. Meade's stout defense held, barely, repulsing each attempted assault, handing the Union a desperately needed victory that ended up being one of the Civil War's turning points.

At the Battle of the Wilderness (May 5-7, 1864), Ulysses S. Grant and Robert E. Lee fought to a standstill in their first encounter, failing to dislodge each other despite incurring nearly 30,000 casualties between the Union Army of the Potomac and the Confederate Army of Northern Virginia. Despite the fierce fighting, Grant continued to push his battered but resilient army south, hoping to beat Lee's army to the crossroads at Spotsylvania Court House, but Lee's army beat Grant's to Spotsylvania and began digging in, setting the scene for on and off fighting from May 8-21 that ultimately inflicted more casualties than the Battle of the Wilderness. In fact, with over 32,000 casualties among the two sides, it was the deadliest battle of the Overland Campaign.

After the last major pitched battle of the Overland Campaign was fought at Cold Harbor in early June, Ulysses S. Grant's Army of the Potomac had suffered more casualties during the campaign than Robert E. Lee had in his entire Army of Northern Virginia at the start of May. Understandably, the American public was shocked by the carnage, and to this day Grant has been accused of being a butcher, but attrition had become a vital war aim for the North, and Grant remained undeterred.

Refusing to attack Lee in frontal assaults, and aware that Lee dared not venture out to counterattack, Grant nearly captured Richmond in mid-June by stealing a march on Lee's army and crossing the James River. The fog of war, poor luck, and a skillful impromptu defense by P.G.T. Beauregard stopped Grant from taking Petersburg, which was a critical railroad hub and supply line for Richmond, before Lee's army could confront, thereby saving the Confederacy for the time being.

The two armies began to dig in around Petersburg, and unbeknownst to them they would be there for the next 9 months, constructing elaborate trenches and engaging in the kind of warfare that would be the forerunner of World War I. Both sides engaged in innovative and unique attempts at mining underneath the enemy's siege lines, as well as countermining, which led to the famous Battle of the Crater that turned an ingenious engineering feat into a Union debacle. Lee's attempts to break the siege by threatening Washington and trying to fight Grant's army proved just as futile.

Though the North couldn't have known it at the time, the siege of Petersburg was the beginning of the end. Grant would pin Lee's army down around that vital railroad hub for nearly 10 months, slowly extending the siege lines and overstretching the Confederates before finally breaking their line in early April. That would send Lee on the retreat that would bring the armies to Appomattox a week later.

Although the surrender of the Army of Northern Virginia to Grant and the Army of the Potomac at Appomattox Courthouse did not officially end the long and bloody Civil War, the surrender is often considered the final chapter of the war. For that reason, Appomattox has captured the popular imagination of Americans ever since Lee's surrender there on April 9, 1865.

Lee is remembered today for constantly defeating the Union's Army of the Potomac in the Eastern theater from 1862-1865, considerably frustrating Lincoln and his generals. His leadership of his army led to him being deified after the war by some of his former subordinates, especially Virginians, and he came to personify the Lost Cause's ideal Southern soldier. His reputation was secured in the decades after the war as a general who brilliantly led his men to amazing victories against all odds. Despite his successes and his legacy, Lee wasn't perfect. And of all the battles Lee fought in, he was most criticized for Gettysburg, particularly his order of Pickett's Charge on the third and final day of the war.

*The Army of Northern Virginia: The History of the Most Famous Confederate Army during the American Civil War* chronicles the famous army's campaigns and battles. Along with pictures and a bibliography, you will learn about the Army of Northern Virginia like never before.

## Preparing the Peninsula Campaign

After First Manassas, the Confederate army under General Joseph E. Johnston stayed camped near the outskirts of Washington D.C., while the North reorganized the Army of the Potomac under Johnston's acquaintance, George B. McClellan. McClellan was widely considered a prodigy thanks to his West Point years, his service in Mexico, his observation during the Crimean War, and his oft-forgotten campaign in Western Virginia against Robert E. Lee in 1861. Though he is best known for his shortcomings today, McClellan had nearly ended Lee's Civil War career before it started, as General Lee was blamed throughout the South for losing western Virginia after his defeat at the Battle of Cheat Mountain. Lee would eventually be reassigned to constructing coastal defenses on the East Coast, and when his men dug trenches in preparation for the defense of Richmond, he was derisively dubbed the "King of Spades". That Lee was even in position to assume command of the Army of Northern Virginia the following year during the Peninsula Campaign was due more to his friendship with Jefferson Davis than anything else.

**McClellan**

**Johnston**

During the Civil War, one of the tales that was often told among Confederate soldiers was that Joseph E. Johnston was a crack shot who was a better bird hunter than just about everyone else in the South. However, as the story went, Johnston would never take the shot when asked to, complaining that something was wrong with the situation that prevented him from being able to shoot the bird when it was time. The story is almost certainly apocryphal, used to demonstrate the Confederates' frustration with a man who everyone regarded as a capable general. Johnston began the Civil War as one of the senior commanders, leading (ironically) the Army of the Potomac to victory in the Battle of First Bull Run over Irvin McDowell's Union Army. But Johnston would become known more for losing by not winning. Johnston was never badly beaten in battle, but he had a habit of "strategically withdrawing" until he had nowhere else to go.

Meanwhile, as he was reorganizing the Army of the Potomac, McClellan vastly overestimated the strength of Johnston's army, leading him to plan an amphibious assault on Richmond that avoided Johnston's army in his front. In response, Johnston moved his army toward Culpeper

Court House, which angered President Davis because it signified a retreat. For that reason, Davis brought Lee to Richmond as a military adviser, and he began to constrain Johnston's authority by issuing direct orders himself.

Despite Confederate misgivings, Johnston's movement had disrupted McClellan's anticipated landing spot, and McClellan had already faced a number of issues in planning the campaign even before reaching the jump-off point. The first option for the landing spot (Urbana) had been scrapped, and there was bickering over the amount of troops left around Washington without the Army of the Potomac fighting on the Overland line. Moreover, McClellan had to deal with politics; the Joint Committee on the Conduct of the War (which included Senators Wade, Chandler, and Johnson, the future Vice President grew increasingly leery of his intentions and insisted on knowing why, after five months of intense training, McClellan's troops had still not engaged the enemy. "General," Wade stated, "you have all the troops you have called for, and if you haven't enough, you shall have more. They are well organized and equipped, and the loyal people of this country expect that you will make a short and decisive campaign. To this McClellan responded haughtily that "we must bear in mind the necessity of having everything ready in case of a defeat…" Dismissing McClellan, Chandler turned to Wade and scoffed, "I don't know much about war, but it seems to me that this is infernal, unmitigated cowardice!"

The Joint Committee began demanding that Lincoln replace the problematic McClellan, fearing that McClellan's impotence would lead to the capture of Washington. Increasingly disturbed by his new commanding officer's indolence (and receiving unrelenting pressure from Secretary of War Edwin W. Stanton and the Joint Committee), on January 27, 1862, Lincoln issued his famed General War Order No. 1, which called for the forward movement of all Union armies by February 22, 1862 (a move in part intended to derail any reluctance from other field generals who may attempt to pull similar delay strategies). Undeterred, McClellan was able to convince Lincoln to postpone the order for two months to allow his men to better prepare. He then persuaded Lincoln to change his strategy for the planned offensive against Richmond, convincing him that the attack would be more effective if launched from the peninsula between the York and James rivers rather than by the proposed Overland north-south route. Ultimately, McClellan would abandon this plan before launching the Peninsula Campaign at a different landing.

On March 8, Lincoln, nearly at the end of his patience, sought to appease McClellan, the Joint Committee, and his twelve division commanders by allowing McClellan to present his proposed "Urbanna Plan" for military evaluation. To Lincoln's surprise, the plan was accepted by a vote of eight to four, thus leaving him no choice but do what was possible to push the plan forward. Following the Committee's recommendation to break the Army of the Potomac into individually-commanded corps, each headed by a specially-chosen corps commander, Lincoln called for McClellan to select corps leaders. McClellan, however, balked at the idea, citing that he did not yet know his men well enough to know their strengths and weaknesses. Feeling he was left with no choice, Lincoln issued General War Order No. 2, appointing McDowell, Edwin "Bull" Sumner, S. P. Heintzelman, and E. D. Keyes to corps command, effective immediately. To McClellan's dismay, and fuelling his belief that his superiors wanted him to fail, three of those appointed had opposed the plan.

Heintzelman

**Sumner**

**Keyes**

Later that same day, Lincoln sent word for McClellan to meet with him after breakfast. At that meeting, Lincoln reluctantly repeated rumors of charges that were circulating among his staff; charges that touched his honor as a soldier. Lincoln said reluctantly, "There is a very ugly matter . . . a rumor that the Urbanna Plan was conceived with the traitorous intent of removing its defenders from Washington, and thus giving over to the enemy the capital and government, thus left defenseless." Incensed, McClellan stood and stated emphatically, "I will permit no one to couple the word treason with my name!" Apologizing, Lincoln let the matter go at that, dismissing McClellan. A short time later, however, McClellan returned to the President's office with his twelve division commanders in tow to compel them to voice their support of his plan in front of the President. By this point, McClellan had resigned himself to having to outmaneuver Lincoln when need be.

Three days later, on March 11, 1862, McClellan received word that President Lincoln had issued another War Order (No. 3), relieving him as General-in-Chief but allowing him to retain his position as commander of the Army of the Potomac, the biggest of seven armies in the Eastern theater. With time passing and the pieces of McClellan's Urbanna Plan now falling apart, Lincoln had done what he had to do to maintain order.

Finally, in March 1862, after nine months in command, General McClellan began his invasion of Virginia, initiating what would become known as the Peninsula Campaign. Showing his proclivity for turning movement and grand strategy, McClellan completely shifted the theater of operations; rather than march directly into Richmond and use his superior numbers to assert domination, he opted to exploit the Union naval dominance and move his army via an immense naval flotilla down the Potomac into Chesapeake Bay and land at Fort Monroe in Hampton, Virginia, at the southern tip of the Virginia Peninsula. In addition to his 130,000 thousand men, he moved 15,000 thousand horses and mules by boat as well. There he planned for an additional 80,000 men to join him, at which time he would advance westward to Richmond. One of the European observers likened the launch of the campaign to the "stride of a giant."

**Moving Towards Richmond**

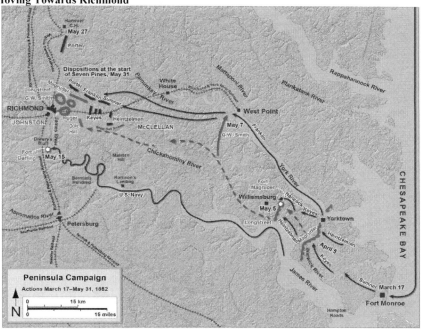

**A map or the armies' marches towards Richmond**

McClellan's Peninsula Campaign has been analyzed meticulously and is considered one of the grandest failures of the Union war effort, with McClellan made the scapegoat. In actuality, there was plenty of blame to go around, including Lincoln and his Administration, which was so concerned about Stonewall Jackson's army in the Shenandoah Valley that several Union armies were left in the Valley to defend Washington D.C., and even more were held back from McClellan for fear of the capital's safety. The Administration also micromanaged the deployment of certain divisions, and with Stanton's decision to shut down recruiting stations in early 1862, combined with the Confederacy concentrating all their troops in the area, the Army of the Potomac was eventually outnumbered in front of Richmond.

At the beginning of the campaign, however, McClellan had vastly superior numbers at his disposal, with only about 70,000 Confederate troops on the entirety of the peninsula and fewer than 17,000 between him and Richmond. McClellan was unaware of this decisive advantage, however, because of the intelligence reports he kept receiving from Allen Pinkerton, which vastly overstated the number of available Confederate soldiers.

As Johnston marched his army to oppose McClellan, he was fully aware that he was severely outnumbered, even if McClellan didn't know that. For that reason, he was in constant communication with the leadership in Richmond, and in April he continued trying to persuade Davis and Lee that the best course of action would be to dig in and fight defensively around Richmond. President Davis would have none of it.

From the beginning, McClellan's caution and the narrow width of the Peninsula worked against his army. At Yorktown, which had been the site of a decisive siege during the Revolution, McClellan's initial hopes of surrounding and enveloping the Confederate lines through the use of the Navy was scuttled when the Navy couldn't promise that it'd be able to operate in the area. That allowed General John Magruder, whose Confederate forces were outmanned nearly 4-1, to hold Yorktown for the entire month of April. Magruder accomplished it by completely deceiving the federals, at times marching his men in circles to make McClellan think his army was many times larger. Other times, he spread his artillery batteries across the line and fired liberally and sporadically at the Union lines, just to give the impression that the Confederates had huge numbers. The ruse worked, leaving the Union command thinking there were 100,000 Confederates.

**Magruder**

As a result of the misimpressions, McClellan chose not to attack Yorktown in force, instead opting to lay siege to it. In part, this was due to the decisive advantage the Union had in siege equipment, including massive mortars and artillery. The siege successfully captured Yorktown in early May with only about 500 casualties, but Magruder bought enough time for Johnston to march south and confront McClellan on the Peninsula.

After taking Yorktown, McClellan sent George Stoneman's cavalry in pursuit and attempted to move swiftly enough to cut off Johnston's retreat by use of Navy ships. At the battle of Williamsburg, which the Confederates fought as a delaying action to retreat, Winfield Scott Hancock led his brigade in a successful flanking attack against General Longstreet's Confederates and quickly occupied two abandoned Confederate strongholds. Hancock's brigade then sharply repulsed a Confederate assault by the 24th Virginia regiment.

At this point, Hancock had been ordered by General Edwin "Bull" Sumner to pull back his men to Cub Creek, but he instead decided to hold his ground, and his men repulsed an assault by the 5th North Carolina regiment in short order. As Confederate General D.H. Hill scrambled to stop that regiment's assault, Hancock's men counterattacked and drove them off the field, inflicting nearly 1,000 casualties on the two regiments that had attacked his brigade and losing just 100.

The Battle of Williamsburg was ultimately inconclusive, with the Confederates suffering 1600 casualties and the Army of the Potomac suffering 2200, but McClellan labeled it a "brilliant victory" over superior forces. While that was inaccurate, the press accounts of Hancock's performance fairly earned him national renown, and McClellan telegraphed Washington to report, "Hancock was superb today." Hancock had just won the nickname "Hancock the Superb."

Hancock

### Planning for Battle

As Johnston pulled back, he decided to have his army dig in with the Chickahominy River in front of it, which he could use as a natural barrier. Meanwhile, McClellan stretched his line further to the northeast so that McDowell's I Corps, which was supposed to march south and join the Army of the Potomac, would have its transportation lines covered by Union forces. Once his men were in position, McClellan began to have his army dig in to make it almost unassailable.

In fact, McDowell's corps was not on the way to McClellan, but Johnston believed he was and changed the Confederate dispositions to attack McClellan before McDowell arrived. Confederate general James Longstreet explained in his memoirs, "On the 27th, General Johnston received information that General McDowell's corps was at Fredericksburg, and on the march to reinforce McClellan's right at Mechanicsville. He prepared to attack McClellan before McDowell could reach him. To this end he withdrew Smith's division from the Williamsburg road, relieving it by the division of D. H. Hill; withdrew Longstreet's division from its position, and A. P. Hill's from Ashland. The fighting column was to be under General G. W. Smith, his next in rank, and General Whiting was assigned command of Smith's division,--the column to consist of A. P. Hill's, Whiting's, and D. R. Jones's divisions. The latter was posted between the Mechanicsville pike and Meadow Bridge road. A. P. Hill was to march direct against McClellan's outpost at Mechanicsville, Whiting to cross the river at Meadow Bridge, and D. R. Jones at Mechanicsville, thus completing the column of attack on the east side. I was to march by the Mechanicsville road to the vicinity of the bridge, and to strike down against the Federal right, west of the river, the march to be made during the night; D. H. Hill to post a brigade on his right on the Charles City road to guard the field to be left by his division, as well as the line left vacant by Longstreet's division."

**Longstreet**

In reality, Washington had become so skittish about Stonewall Jackson's actions in the Shenandoah Valley, where the Confederate general had confounded three different Union armies, that the administration ultimately ordered McDowell to the Valley. This was almost certainly unnecessary in the first place, and it was even more pointless when Jackson's army left the Valley in June to link up with the Army of Northern Virginia outside Richmond.

On the 27th, the Confederates learned that McDowell was not marching south, but many of the generals still believed an attack was prudent, and that the Confederates couldn't win a siege. Longstreet explained, "At nightfall the troops took up the march for their several assigned positions. Before dark General Johnston called a number of his officers together for instructions,--viz., Smith, Magruder, Stuart, and Longstreet. When we were assembled, General Johnston announced later information: that McDowell's line of march had been changed,--that he was going north. Following the report of this information, General Smith proposed that the plan for battle should be given up, in view of the very strong ground at Beaver Dam Creek.1 I urged that the plan laid against the concentrating columns was made stronger by the change of direction of McDowell's column, and should suggest more prompt and vigorous prosecution. In this Magruder and Stuart joined me. The pros and cons were talked over till a late hour, when at last General Johnston, weary of it, walked aside to a separate seat. I took the opportunity to draw near him, and suggested that the Federal position behind Beaver Dam Creek, so seriously objected to by General Smith, could be turned by marching to and along the high ground between the Chickahominy and Pamunkey Rivers; that the position of the enemy when turned would be abandoned without a severe struggle, and give a fair field for battle; that we should not lose the opportunity to await another possible one."

The most notable aspect of the Union line in the Confederates' opinion was that it had a concave shape, and as a result, the Army of the Potomac's left flank was not on the same side of the Chickahominy as the rest of the army. Thus, if the Confederates could successfully attack the Union left on its side of the river, they would be isolated from help and could possibly be destroyed in detail. In his memoirs, Johnston explained:

"Longstreet, as ranking officer of the three divisions to be united near Hill's camp, was instructed, verbally, to form his own and Hill's division in two lines crossing the Williamsburg road at right angles, and to advance to the attack in that order; while Huger's division should march along the Charles City road by the right flank, to fall upon the enemy's left flank as soon as our troops became engaged with them in front. It was understood that abatis, or earthworks, that might be encountered, should be turned. General Smith was to engage any troops that might cross the Chickahominy to assist Heintzelman's and Keyes's corps; or, if none came, he was to fall upon the right flanks of those troops engaged with Longstreet. The accident of location prevented the assignment of this officer to the command of the principal attack, to which he was entitled by his rank. As his division was on the left of all those to be engaged, it was apprehended that its transfer to the right might cause a serious loss of time.

"The rain began to fall violently in the afternoon, and continued all night; and, in the morning, the little streams near our camps were so much swollen as to make it seem probable that the Chickahominy was overflowing its banks, and cutting the communication between the two parts of the Federal army.

"Being confident that Longstreet and Hill, with their forces united, would be successful in the earlier part of the action against an enemy formed in several lines, with wide intervals between them, I left the immediate control, on the Williamsburg road, to them, under general instructions, and placed myself on the left, where I could soonest learn the approach of Federal reenforcements from beyond the Chickahominy. From this point scouts and reconnoitering parties were sent forward to detect such movements, should they be made."

Longstreet was also confident in the plan's success, as he noted in his memoirs:

"The plan settled upon was that the attack should be made by General D. H. Hill's division on the Williamsburg road, supported by Longstreet's division. Huger's division, just out of garrison duty at Norfolk, was to march between Hill's right and the swamp against the enemy's line of skirmishers, and move abreast of the battle;

G. W. Smith's division, under Whiting, to march by the Gaines road to Old Tavern, and move abreast of the battle on its left. The field before Old Tavern was not carefully covered by the enemy's skirmishers north of Fair Oaks, nor by parties in observation.

"Experience during the discussion of the battle ordered for the 28th caused me to doubt of effective work from the troops ordered for the left flank, but the plan seemed so simple that it was thought impossible for any one to go dangerously wrong; and General Johnston stated that he would be on that road, the better to receive from his troops along the crest of the Chickahominy information of movements of the enemy on the farther side of the river, and to look to the co-operation of the troops on the Nine Miles road.

To facilitate marches, Huger's division was to have the Charles City road to the head of White Oak Swamp, file across it and march down its northern margin; D. H. Hill to have the Williamsburg road to the enemy's front; Longstreet's division to march by the Nine Miles road and a lateral road leading across the rear of General Hill on the Williamsburg road; G. W. Smith by the Gaines road to Old Tavern on the Nine Miles road."

Longstreet wrote that he didn't think it was possible to suffer a serious hitch in the plans, but the planning required coordination among numerous Confederate divisions on multiple roads, which could only make timing a problem. As the events of May 31 would prove, things would go awry from the beginning.

# The Battle of Seven Pines

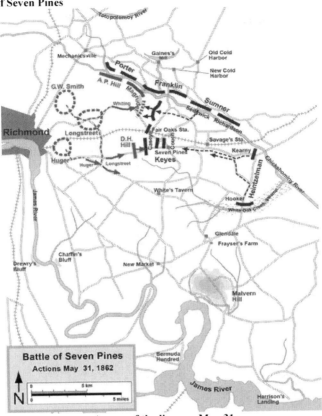

**A map of the lines on May 31**

    Johnston intended for the Confederate attack to start as early as possible on May 31, but those wishes would never come close to fruition. Part of this was due to the vague orders he gave his division commander Huger, which failed to fix a time for attack:

> "The reports of Major-General D. H. Hill give me the impression that the enemy is in considerable strength in his front. It seems to me necessary that we should increase our force also; for that object I wish to concentrate the troops of your division on the Charles City road, and to concentrate the troops of Major-General Hill on the Williamsburg road. To do this it will be necessary for you to move, as early in the morning as possible, to relieve the brigade of General Hill's division now on the Charles City road. I have desired General Hill to send you a guide. The road is the second large one diverging to the right from the Williamsburg road. The first turns off near the tollgate. On reaching your position on the Charles City road,

learn at once the route to the main roads, to Richmond on your right and left, especially those to the left, and try to find guides. Be ready, if an action should begin on your left, to fall upon the enemy's left flank.

"Most respectfully your obedient servant, J. E. Johnston.

P. S.--It is necessary to move very early."

**Huger**

Due to those orders, Huger had no idea what was going on during the early morning until another Confederate division was passing by his own on the road. Moreover, from the beginning of the day, the use of different roads confounded various Confederate generals, and the problems were exacerbated by flooding in the area as a result of heavy rainfall over the previous few days. Longstreet explained some of the early trouble: "Subsequent events seem to call for mention just here that General Smith, instead of moving the troops by the route assigned them, marched back to the Nine Miles road near the city, rode to Johnston's Headquarters about six in the morning, and reported that he was with the division, but not for the purpose of taking command from

General Whiting. As General Johnston did not care to order him back to his position as commander of the left wing, he set himself to work to make trouble, complained that my troops were on the Nine Miles road in the way of his march, and presently complained that they had left that road and were over on the Williamsburg road, and induced General Johnston to so far modify the plans as to order three of my brigades down the Nine Miles road to the New Bridge fork."

Unfortunately for the Confederates, those orders wouldn't reach the front because the courier rode into Union lines and was captured before reporting the information. While this compelled the Union generals to (mistakenly) think the attack would come down the Nine Miles Road, it caused severe congestion and mix-ups among the Confederates on the right side of their line.

Even at this point, with confusion about orders and roads, and flooding delaying movements, Longstreet believed by 9:00 a.m. that the marches and dispositions could be straightened out enough to deliver an overwhelming attack on the Union left: "My march by the Nine Miles and lateral roads leading across to the Williamsburg road was interrupted by the flooded grounds about the head of Gillis Creek. At the same time this creek was bank full, where it found a channel for its flow into the James. The delay of an hour to construct a bridge was preferred to the encounter of more serious obstacles along the narrow lateral road, flooded by the storm. As we were earlier at the creek, it gave us precedence over Huger's division, which had to cross after us. The division was prepared with cooked rations, had wagons packed at six o'clock, and rested in the rear of General Hill's at nine A. M. Meanwhile, General G. W. Smith's division had marched by the Nine Miles road and was resting near the fork of the New Bridge road at Old Tavern. Upon meeting General Huger in the morning, I gave him a succinct account of General Johnston's plans and wishes; after which he inquired as to the dates of our commissions, which revealed that he was the ranking officer, when I suggested that it was only necessary for him to take command and execute the orders. This he declined. Then it was proposed that he should send two of his brigades across to join on the right of the column of attack, while he could remain with his other brigade, which was to relieve that of General Hill on the Charles City road. Though he expressed himself satisfied with this, his manner was eloquent of discontent. The better to harmonize, I proposed to reinforce his column by three of my brigades, to be sent under General Wilcox, to lead or follow his division, as he might order. Under this arrangement it seemed that concert of action was assured. I gave especial orders to General Wilcox to have care that the head of his column was abreast the battle when it opened, and rode forward to join General Hill, my other three brigades advancing along the Williamsburg road."

**Smith**

While the Confederates were moving along the roads, the Union was able to see the marches thanks to the efforts of Thaddeus Lowe's observation balloon. Around noon, Lowe was hovering above the area and was able to relay news of Confederate battle formations back to the Union headquarters. Unfortunately for the Army of the Potomac, McClellan was ill, but news of an imminent Confederate attack made its way around camp in the early afternoon, several hours after Johnston had hoped to begin the assault.

**A picture of Lowe using an observation balloon at Seven Pines**

As it turned out, the fighting began around 1:00 p.m. mostly because Confederate division commander D.H. Hill, one of the South's most competent generals, was tired of the delays. Hill's division was to be the vanguard of the attack, and since his men were in the front, they had avoided some of the confusion on the roads behind them and were thus in position by early morning. Hill bristled as he waited for men from Longstreet and Huger's commands, and eventually, he decided to fire off a signal gun around noon. With that, the time for an attack by his division was set for about 1:00 p.m., about five hours after Johnston had originally planned, and as fate would have it, acoustics in the area prevented Johnston from hearing the signal gun and being aware of his own army's attack. Indeed, Johnston would not learn of the ongoing engagement until about 4:00 p.m. that day, and he incorrectly asserted in his memoirs that the Confederate assault started around 3:00.

When Hill started the attack around 1:00 p.m. that day, he was hurling four brigades against Silas Casey's Union division in his front, and even though Hill's men accounted for less than

1/3rd of the anticipated attacking force, his men immediately began to push the inexperienced federals back. At this early moment in the battle, Hill was still waiting for Huger's men to join the attack, and he eventually got so tired of waiting that he decided to try to turn the Union flank with just one of his own brigades. Longstreet discussed the early part of the action by Hill's division: "He had four brigades, and was ordered to advance in columns of brigades, two on each side of the road. Garland's and G. B. Anderson's brigades in columns, preceded by skirmishers, advanced on the left of the road at the sound of the guns, and engaged after a short march from the starting. As Rodes's brigade was not yet in position, some little time elapsed before the columns on the right moved, so that Garland's column encountered more than its share of early fight, but Rodes, supported by Rains's brigade, came promptly to his relief, which steadied the advance. The enemy's front was reinforced and arrested progress of our skirmishers, but a way was found by which the enemy was turned out of position, and by and by the open before the intrenched camp was reached."

**Casey**

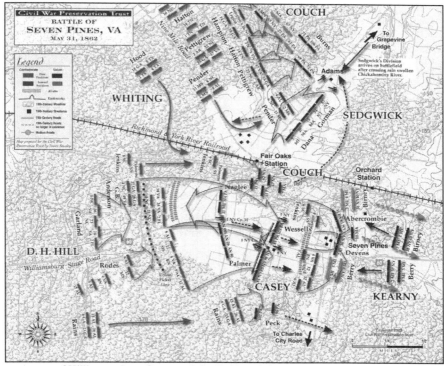

**A map of Hill's attack on Casey and the Union reinforcements arriving under Phil Kearny**

As Casey's men found themselves suddenly in a desperate fight for control of their fortifications, the division commander sent word back to his corps commander Keyes that he needed reinforcements. For unknown reasons, Keyes was slow to respond, and all the while, McClellan remained bedridden and generally unaware of the danger posed to his army's left flank. Even as late as 2:30, nearly 90 minutes after the fighting had started, Union headquarters remained in the dark about the situation across the Chickahominy.

As Casey's division fell back to a second line of defenses, they were bolstered by Couch's division in Keyes' IV Corps, but this coincided with Hill finally receiving reinforcements from behind him. This led to savage fighting across the second line of defenses by the middle of the afternoon, as Longstreet explained, "The battle moved bravely on. R. H. Anderson's brigade was ordered to support its left at Fair Oaks, and Pickett's, on the railroad, was drawn near. Hill met Casey's troops rallying, and reinforcements with them coming to recover the lost ground, but they were forced back to the second intrenched line (Couch's), where severe fighting ensued, but the line was carried at two o'clock, cutting Couch with four regiments and two companies of infantry, and Brady's six-gun battery, off at Fair Oaks Station. Finding that he could not cut his way back to his command, Couch stood back from the railroad and presently opened his battery fire across our advancing lines. As he was standing directly in front of Smith's division, we thought that he would soon be attacked and driven off. Nevertheless, it was not prudent to leave that point on our flank unguarded until we found Smith's division in action. The force was shut off from our view by the thick pine wood, so that we could know nothing of its strength, and only knew of its position from its artillery fire. We could not attack it lest we should fall under the fire of the division in position for that attack. Anderson's other regiments, under the gallant Colonel M. Jenkins, were ordered into Hill's forward battle, as his troops were worn. Jenkins soon found himself in the van, and so swiftly led on that the discomfited troops found no opportunity to rally. Reinforcements from the Third Corps came, but in the swampy wood Jenkins was prompt enough to strike their heads as their retreating comrades passed. Right and left and front he applied his beautiful tactics and pushed his battle. "

With the fighting becoming more severe, commanders on both sides could hear the noise of the battle, but the wooded nature of the terrain often concealed views of what was going on, and in the case of the Army of the Potomac, most of the soldiers were across a river that had been swollen by rain. While Phil Kearny's division from Heintzelman's III Corps was able to easily march to the battle because they were south of the river, any other potential Union reinforcements would have to cross the river, a logistical feat made more difficult by the rushing torrents and the fact most of the bridges in the area had been destroyed by the retreating Confederates earlier.

**Kearny**

On the other side, Johnston finally learned of Hill's initial assault due to communications from Longstreet, but he only learned about it right around the time Hill was preparing to assault the second line of defense, which consisted of Casey's battered division, Couch's division, and reinforcements from Kearny. Longstreet explained the dispositions once Kearny's men joined the mix: "General Kearny, finding that he could not arrest the march, put Berry's brigade off to the swamp to flank and strike it, and took part of Jamison's brigade to follow. They got into the swamp and followed it up to the open near the Couch intrenchment, but Jenkins knew that there was some one there to meet them, and pushed his onward battle. General Hill ordered Rains's brigade to turn this new force, while Rodes attacked, but the latter's men were worn, and some of them were with the advance. Kemper's brigade was sent to support the forward battle, but General Hill directed it to his right against Berry, in front of Rains, and it seems that the heavy, swampy ground so obstructed operations on both sides as to limit their work to infantry fusillades until six o'clock."

By this time, Johnston had surmised that the Chickahominy was impassable as a result of the flooding, and he was mostly right, so he prepared to funnel Smith's men into the fight instead of having them guard the Confederate left flank, figuring the river would protect that flank. He wrote in his memoirs, "When the action began on the right, the musketry was not heard at my position on the Nine-miles road, from the unfavorable condition of the air to sound. I supposed, therefore, that the fight had not begun, and that we were hearing an artillery duel. However, a staff-officer was sent to ascertain the fact. He returned at four o'clock, with intelligence that our infantry as well as artillery had been engaged for an hour, and that our troops were pressing forward with vigor. As no approach of Federal troops from the other side of the Chickahominy had been discovered or was suspected, I hoped strongly that the bridges were impassable. It seemed to me idle, therefore, to keep General Smith longer out of action, for a contingency so remote as the coming of reenforcements from the Federal right. He was desired, therefore, to direct his division against the right flank of Longstreet's adversaries."

Johnston personally led three brigades from Whiting's division down the Nine Mile Road and into the fray on the right flank of Keyes' defenders near Fair Oaks Station (which would lend an alternative name to the entire battle itself), but unfortunately for the Confederates, the addition of most of Whiting's division was offset by the only Union reinforcements that would cross the Chickahominy that day. Once the fighting grew desperate, McClellan ordered Bull Sumner to attempt to send some reinforcements across the swollen Chickahominy, a treacherous assignment that mostly fell upon John Sedgwick's division. Israel Richardson, in command of another one of Sumner's divisions, came up to a bridge only to find that Union soldiers were waist deep in water while attempting to use it, so he was only able to get Oliver O. Howard's brigade across. Sumner proved luckier with Sedgwick's division; when met with general reluctance by Sedgwick's men at the proposition of crossing the one remaining bridge (the already damaged Grapevine Bridge), Sumner scoffed, "Impossible!? Sir, I tell you I can cross! I am ordered!" It turned out Sumner was right, but just barely, because shortly after Sedgwick's division got across, the bridge was swept away by the river.

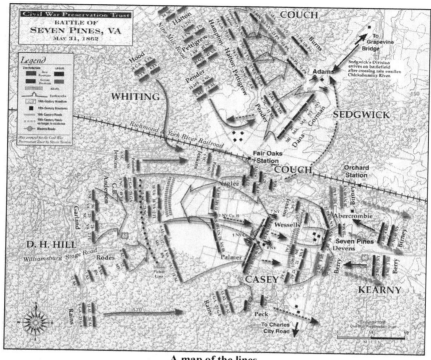

**A map of the lines**

As Johnston was leading men down the Nine Mile Road, he saw some of Sumner's reinforcements arriving, but he mistakenly concluded that it was only a brigade instead of an entire division and a brigade. He explained, "On my way to Longstreet's left, to combine the action of the two bodies of Confederate troops, I passed the head of General Smith's column near Fair Oaks, and saw the camp of a body of infantry of the strength of three or four regiments, apparently in the northern angle between the York River Railroad and the Nine-miles road, and the rear of a body of infantry moving in quick time from that point toward the Chickahominy, by the road to the Grape-vine Ford… I had passed the railroad some little distance with Hood's brigade, when the action commenced, and stopped to see its termination. But, being confident that the Federal troops opposing ours were those whose camps I had just seen, and therefore not more than a brigade, I did not doubt that General Smith was quite strong enough to cope with them."

As early evening was setting in, the battle had reached its fevered pitch, but both sides could not dislodge the enemy. In the fighting, Whiting's division lost three of brigade leaders, and Oliver O. Howard was seriously wounded on the Union side. Further south, on the Confederates' far right flank, more confusion reigned. Longstreet explained, "Our battle on the Williamsburg road was in a sack. We were strong enough to guard our flanks and push straight on, but the front was growing heavy. It was time for Wilcox's brigades under his last order, but nothing was heard of them. I asked General Stuart, who had joined me, if there were obstacles to Wilcox's march between the Charles City and Williamsburg roads. He reported that there was nothing more than swamp lands, hardly knee-deep. He was asked for a guide, who was sent with a courier bearing orders for them to remain with General Wilcox until he reported at my headquarters."

As darkness set in, it was apparent that the day's fighting was just about over, but it was at this point that the Confederates suffered one of the most important casualties of the Civil War. In his memoirs, Johnston described the end of the fighting that day, and how he was one of the last ones wounded in the fray:

"This condition of affairs existed on the left at half-past 6 o'clock, and the firing on the right seemed then to be about Seven Pines. It was evident, therefore, that the battle would not be terminated that day. So I announced to my staff-officers that each regiment must sleep where it might be standing when the contest ceased for the night, to be ready to renew it at dawn next morning.

"About seven o'clock I received a slight wound in the right shoulder from a musket-shot, and, a few moments after, was unhorsed by a heavy fragment of shell which struck my breast. Those around had me borne from the field in an ambulance; not, however, before the President, who was with General Lee, not far in the rear, had heard of the accident, and visited me, manifesting great concern, as he continued to do until I was out of danger.

The firing ceased, terminated by darkness only, before I had been carried a mile from the field."

If anything, Johnston was understated about his injuries, which included a broken shoulder blade and a chest wound that had knocked him unconscious. Since he had to be removed from the field, G.W. Smith took over as the highest ranking officer, but aside from asserting his rank (as he had done to Longstreet earlier), he was decisive about little else. Longstreet described the Confederates' attempts to untangle themselves and prepare to renew the attack in the morning: "The brigades were so mixed up through the pines when the battle closed that there was some delay in getting the regiments to their proper commands, getting up supplies, and arranging for the morning. D. H. Hill's was put in good order and in bivouac near the Casey intrenchment; those of Longstreet between the Williamsburg road and railroad. Wilcox's brigade took position on the right, in place of the detachment under Jenkins; Pryor's brigade next on the left; Kemper, Anderson, and Colston near the stage road (Williamsburg). They made blazing fires of pine-knots to dry their clothing and blankets, and these lighted reinforcing Union troops to their lines behind the railroad."

In fairness to Smith, it might not have mattered whether he had been more aggressive, since the Union defenders were able to use the break in fighting to both strengthen their defensive line and get more men across the Chickahominy. According to Longstreet, news about the Army of the Potomac throwing up pontoon bridges unnerved Smith, and the new commander subsequently came up with an unworkable attack plan:

"Major-General G. W. Smith was of the highest standing of the West Point classes, and, like others of the Engineers, had a big name to help him in the position to which he had been suddenly called by the incapacitation of the Confederate commander. I found his Headquarters at one o'clock in the morning, reported the work of the commands on the Williamsburg road on the 31st, and asked for part of the troops ordered up by General Johnston, that we might resume battle at daylight. He was disturbed by reports of pontoon bridges, said to be under construction for the use of other reinforcements to join the enemy from the east side, and was anxious lest the enemy might march his two corps on the east side by the upper river and occupy Richmond. But after a time these notions gave way, and he suggested that we could renew the battle on the Williamsburg road, provided we would send him one of our brigades to help hold his position and make the battle by a wheel on his right as a pivot.

"The enemy stood: Sedgwick's division in front of Smith; Richardson's division in column of three brigades parallel to the railroad and behind it, prepared to attack my left; on Richardson's left was Birney's brigade behind the railroad, and under the enemy's third intrenched line were the balance of the Third and all of the Fourth Corps. So the plan to wheel on Smith's right as a pivot, my right stepping out on the wheel, would have left the Third and Fourth Corps to attack our rear as soon as we moved.

"Besides, it was evident that our new commander would do nothing, and we must look to accident for such aid as might be drawn to us during the battle.

"The plan proposed could only be considered under the hypothesis that Magruder would come in as the pivotal point, and, upon having the enemy's line fully exposed, would find the field fine for his batteries, and put them in practice without orders from his commander, and, breaking the enemy's line by an enfilade fire from his artillery, would come into battle and give it cohesive power."

Smith should've been right to be concerned about his left flank, as reconnaissance reports provided to McClellan indicated little Confederate activity in front of the Union's right. Nonetheless, McClellan didn't order a counterattack, no doubt partly out of fear that he was outnumbered.

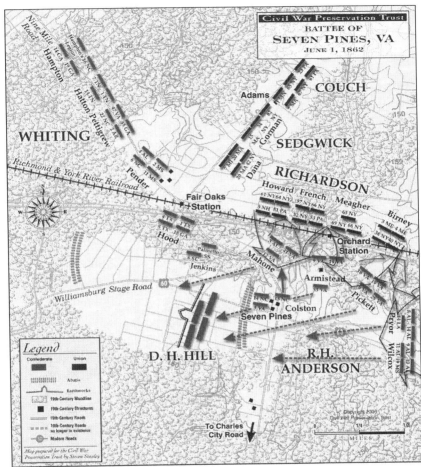

BATTLE OF
**SEVEN PINES, VA**
JUNE 1, 1862

**A map of the fighting on June 1**

Longstreet remembered things quite differently. As the fighting recommenced that morning, Longstreet's wing found itself in a dogged battle, but as he and Whiting pushed Smith to reinforce them, the new commander wavered. Whiting wrote back to Smith that morning, "I am going to try a diversion for Longstreet, and have found, as reported, a position for artillery. The enemy are in full view and in heavy masses. I have ordered up Lee with four pieces. The musketry firing in advance is tremendous." However, when he didn't hear from Smith, he sent back word that without orders to the contrary, he would begin withdrawing the men from the line.

Thus, as Longstreet noted, "Whiting's position, instead of being pivotal, began its rearward move at the opening fire at daybreak, and continued in that line of conduct until it reached a point of quiet. General Smith was informed that the brigade called for by him would not be sent over; that his troops were doing nothing, while all of mine were in severe battle, except a single brigade, and the enemy was massing his fighting force against me; that the grounds were so flooded that it was difficult to keep up our supply of ammunition; that with the aid of his troops the battle would be ours."

Longstreet eventually sent a dispatch back to Smith that read, ""Can you reinforce me The entire enemy seems to be opposed to me. We cannot hold out unless we get help. If we can fight together, we can finish the work to-day, and Mac's time will be up. If I cannot get help, I fear that I must fall back." By this point, however, Smith had been persuaded by other generals back at headquarters not to continue an assault. Longstreet wrote in his memoirs, "[Smith] held a council with Generals McLaws and Whiting and Chief Engineer Stevens, and submitted the question, 'Must the troops be withdrawn, or the attack continued?' All voted in favor of the former except McLaws. In a letter, since written, he has said, 'I alone urged that you be reinforced and the attack continued, and the question was reconsidered, and I was sent to learn your views.'"

As a result of the hesitation, the Confederates now found themselves in the prickly position of having to pull back in an orderly fashion during the middle of the battle. Given the relative inexperience of Civil War generals and soldiers in 1862, it's little surprise that this nearly proved disastrous for the Confederates, and a rout was staved off by just one Confederate brigade, led by George Pickett. Though he was no longer present on the field, Johnston wrote in his memoirs about Pickett's fighting: "Next morning, Brigadier-General Pickett, whose brigade was near the left of Longstreet's and Hill's line, learned that a strong body of Federal troops was before him and near. He moved forward and attacked it, driving it from that ground. Very soon, being reinforced apparently, the Federals (several brigades) assumed the offensive, and attacked him. In the mean time General Hill had sent two regiments of Colston's brigade to him. Although largely outnumbered, Pickett met this attack with great resolution, and after a brisk but short action repulsed the enemy, who disappeared, to molest him no more."

Johnston also pointed out that aside from the action in Longstreet's front that morning, there were no serious attempts by the Army of the Potomac to assault the Confederates. This was a point echoed by Longstreet as he concluded his account of the battle:

"The failure of the enemy to push the opportunity made by the precipitate retreat of General Wilcox, and Pickett's successful resistance, told that there was nothing in the reports of troops coming over from the east side to take part in the battle, and we were convinced that the river was not passable. I made an appeal for ten thousand men, that we might renew our battle without regard to General Smith and those about him. It received no more consideration than the appeal made through General McLaws.

Then General Lee, having been assigned to command, came upon the field after noon by the Nine Miles road, and, with General Smith, came over to the Williamsburg road. A similar proposition was made General Lee, but General Smith protested that the enemy was strongly fortified. At the time the enemy's main battle front was behind the railroad, fronting against me but exposed to easy enfilade fire of batteries to be posted on his right flank on the Nine Miles road, while his front against me was covered by the railway embankment. It is needless to add that under the fire of batteries so posted his lines would have been broken to confusion in twenty minutes. General Holmes marched down the Williamsburg road and rested in wait for General Lee. Like General Huger, he held rank over me. General Lee ordered the troops back to their former lines. Those on the Williamsburg road were drawn back during the night, the rear-guard, Pickett's brigade, passing the Casey works at sunrise on the 2d unmolested. Part of Richardson's division mistook the camp at Fair Oaks for the Casey camp, and claimed to have recovered it on the afternoon of the 1st, but it was not until the morning of the 2d that the Casey camp was abandoned.

The Confederate losses in the two days fight were 6134; the Union losses, 5031."

Given his lackluster performance on the night of June 30 and the morning of June 1, not to mention the serious challenges facing the Confederates, it should perhaps come as little surprise that Smith's command of the Army of Northern Virginia had officially lasted less than 18 hours. Longstreet sarcastically wrote about Smith's career after being removed from command: "He reported sick on the 2d and left the army. When ready for duty he was assigned about Richmond and the seaboard of North Carolina. He applied to be restored to command of his division in the field, but the authorities thought his services could be used better elsewhere. He resigned his commission in the Confederate service, went to Georgia, and joined Joe Brown's militia, where he found congenial service, better suited to his ideas of vigorous warfare."

**The Aftermath of the Battle**

From his first day in command, Lee faced a daunting, seemingly impossible challenge. McClellan had maneuvered nearly 100,000 troops to within seven miles of Richmond, three Union units were closing in on General Jackson's Confederates in Virginia's Shenandoah Valley, and a fourth Union army was camped on the Rappahannock River ostensibly ready to come to McClellan's aid.

Moreover, as Longstreet indicated in his memoirs, Lee had a mixed record by this time in the war and was not beloved by the Army of Northern Virginia: "The assignment of General Lee to command the army of Northern Virginia was far from reconciling the troops to the loss of our beloved chief, Joseph E. Johnston, with whom the army had been closely connected since its earliest active life. All hearts had learned to lean upon him with confidence, and to love him dearly. General Lee's experience in active field work was limited to his West Virginia campaign against General Rosecrans, which was not successful. His services on our coast defences were known as able, and those who knew him in Mexico as one of the principal engineers of General Scott's column, marching for the capture of the capital of that great republic, knew that as military engineer he was especially distinguished; but officers of the line are not apt to look to the staff in choosing leaders of soldiers, either in tactics or strategy. There were, therefore, some misgivings as to the power and skill for field service of the new commander. The change was accepted, however, as a happy relief from the existing halting policy of the late temporary commander."

Of course, Lee would quickly demonstrate he was the opposite of indecisive. With Stonewall Jackson having bottled up the Union in the Shenandoah Valley, Lee wrote to him on June 11, "Your recent successes have been the cause of the liveliest joy in this army as well as in the country. The admiration excited by your skill and boldness has been constantly  mingled with solicitude for your situation. The practicability of reinforcing you has been the subject of earnest consideration. It has been determined to do so at the expense of weakening this army. Brigadier-General Lawton, with six regiments from Georgia, is on the way to you, and Brigadier-General Whiting, with eight veteran regiments, leaves here to-day. The object is to enable you to crush the forces opposed to you. Leave your enfeebled troops to watch the country and guard the passes covered by your cavalry and artillery, and with your main body, including Ewell's division and Lawton's and Whiting's commands, move rapidly to Ashland by rail or otherwise, as you may find most advantageous, and sweep down between the Chickahominy and Pamunkey, cutting up the enemy's communications, etc., while this army attacks General McClellan in front. He will thus, I think, be forced to come out of his intrenchments, where he is strongly posted on the Chickahominy, and apparently preparing to move by gradual approaches on Richmond. Keep me advised of your movements, and, if practicable, precede your troops, that we may confer and arrange for simultaneous attack."

**Jackson**

On June 12, as McClellan sat on Richmond's eastern outskirts waiting for reinforcements, Lee began to ring the city with troop entrenchments. Realizing that McClellan's flank appeared to be exposed and hoping to hit it with Jackson's army, Lee tasked J.E.B. Stuart with assessing whether the Union army had any real protection north and west of the exposed flank. Stuart suggested that his men circumnavigate McClellan's army, to which Lee responded with deference that would become his trademark and a symbol of his trust in his subordinates. Lee gave Stuart vague orders: "You will return as soon as the object of your expedition is accomplished, and you must bear constantly in mind, while endeavoring to execute the general purpose of your mission, not to hazard unnecessarily your command or to attempt what your judgment may not approve; but be content to accomplish all the good you can without feeling it necessary to obtain all that might be desired. I recommend that you take only such men as can stand the expedition, and that you take every means in your power to save and cherish those you take. You must leave sufficient cavalry here for the service of this army, and remember that one of the chief objects of your expedition is to gain intelligence for the guidance of future operations."

**Lee**

**Stuart**

With that, Stuart embarked with 1200 troopers on a spectacular three-day, 150 mile ride in the rear of and around the entire Army of the Potomac, a mission that would require him to keep just ahead of pursuing horsemen led by Union Brig. General Philip St. George Cooke, Stuart's father-in-law. Though daunting and dangerous, Stuart and his men successfully completed the historic ride, with Stuart returning to Richmond to report to Lee on June 14 and most of his cavalry returning the following day. Stuart was able not only to report that McClellan's flank was indeed completely unguarded, he delivered 165 captured Union soldiers, 260 horses and mules, and a collection of quartermaster and ordinance supplies as well. The "ride around McClellan" proved to be a public relations sensation for Stuart, resulting in dramatic newspaper accounts, hordes of women cheering and strewing flower petals in his path when he rode through the streets of Richmond, and his face appearing on the front pages of most newspapers in both the North and South. The flamboyant officer relished every second of his ride, later writing, "There was something of the sublime in the implicit confidence and unquestioning trust of the rank and file in a leader guiding them straight, apparently, into the very jaws of the enemy, every step appearing to them to diminish the faintest hope of extrication."

Although the Battle of Seven Pines was tactically inconclusive, McClellan's resolve to keep pushing forward seemed to all but vanish. He confided in a letter to his wife, "I am tired of the sickening sight of the battlefield, with its mangled corpses & poor suffering wounded! Victory has no charms for me when purchased at such cost."

McClellan maneuvered his army so that it was all south of the Chickahominy, but as he settled in for an expected siege, Lee went about preparing Richmond's defenses and devising his own aggressive attacks. With more Confederate troops swelling the ranks, Lee's army was McClellan's equal by late June, and on June 25, Lee commenced an all-out attempt to destroy McClellan's army in a series of fierce battles known as the Seven Days Battles.

After a stalemate in the first fighting at Oak Grove, Lee's army kept pushing ahead, using Stonewall Jackson to attack McClellan's right. Although Stonewall Jackson was unusually lethargic during the week's fighting, the appearance of his "foot cavalry" spooked McClellan even more, and McClellan was now certain he was opposed by 200,000 men, more than double the actual size of Lee's army. It also made McClellan think that the Confederates were threatening his supply line, forcing him to shift his army toward the James River to draw supplies.

On June 26, the Union defenders sharply repulsed the Confederate attacks at Mechanicsville, in part due to the fact that Stonewall Jackson had his troops bivouac for the night despite the fact heavy gunfire indicating a large battle was popping off within earshot. When the Confederates had more success the next day at Gaines' Mills, McClellan continued his strategic retreat, maneuvering his army toward a defensive position on the James River and all but abandoning the siege.

McClellan managed to keep his forces in tact, ultimately retreating to Harrison's Landing on the James River and establishing a new base of operation. Feeling increasingly at odds with his superiors, in a letter sent from Gaines' Mills, Virginia dated June 28, 1862, a frustrated McClellan wrote to Secretary of War Stanton, "If I save the army now, I tell you plainly that I owe no thanks to any other person in the Washington. You have done your best to sacrifice this army." McClellan's argument, however, flies in the face of common knowledge that he had become so obsessed with having sufficient supplies that he'd actually moved to Gaines' Mill to accommodate the massive amount of provisions he'd accumulated. Ultimately unable to move his cache of supplies as quickly as his men were needed, McClellan eventually ran railroad cars full of food and supplies into the Pamunkey River rather than leave them behind for the Confederates.

Despite the fact all of Lee's battle plans had been poorly executed by his generals, particularly Stonewall Jackson, he ordered one final assault against McClellan's army at Malvern Hill. Incredibly, McClellan was not even on the field for that battle, having left via steamboat back to Harrison's Landing. Biographer Ethan Rafuse notes McClellan's absence from the battlefield was inexcusable, literally leaving the Army of the Potomac leaderless during pitched battle, but McClellan often behaved coolly under fire, so it is likely not a question of McClellan's personal courage.

Ironically, Malvern Hill was one of the Union army's biggest successes during the Peninsula Campaign. Union artillery had silenced its Confederate counterparts, but Lee still ordered an infantry attack by D.H. Hill's division, which never got within 100 yards of the Union line. After the war, Hill famously said of Malvern Hill, "It wasn't war. It was murder." Later that evening, General Isaac Trimble, best known for leading a division during Pickett's Charge at Gettysburg, began moving his troops forward as if to attack, only to be stopped by Stonewall Jackson, who asked "What are you going to do?" When Trimble replied that he was going to charge, Jackson countered, "General Hill has just tried with his entire division and been repulsed. I guess you'd better not try it."

After Malvern Hill, McClellan withdrew his army to Harrison's Landing, where it was protected by the Union Navy along the James River and had its flanks secured by the river itself. At this point, the bureaucratic bickering between McClellan and Washington started flaring up again, as McClellan refused to recommence an advance without reinforcements. After weeks of indecision, the Army of the Potomac was finally ordered to evacuate the Peninsula and link up with John Pope's army in northern Virginia, as the administration was more comfortable having their forces fighting on one line instead of exterior lines.

Making things all the worse, McClellan's delays would allow Lee to swing his army into Northern Virginia to face the threat posed by John Pope's army. Upon his arrival in Washington, McClellan told reporters that his failure to defeat Lee in Virginia was due to Lincoln not sending sufficient reinforcements.

## John Pope and the Army of Virginia

Lee and his army had pushed McClellan's Army of the Potomac away from Richmond, but there was little time for celebration in July 1862. While McClellan was trying to extricate his army from a tricky spot on the Virginian Peninsula, about 50,000 Union soldiers were menacing the Confederates in Northern Virginia, outnumbering Lee's army. If McClellan's Army of the Potomac linked up with the army now being gathered in Northern Virginia, they would vastly outnumber Lee and begin yet another drive toward Richmond. For Lee, the best option (and it was hardly a good one) was to try to prevent the two Union armies from linking up, and the only way to do that would be to inflict a decisive defeat upon the army in Northern Virginia before it was joined by McClellan's men.

Thus, even before McClellan had completely withdrawn his troops, Lee sent Jackson northward to intercept the new army President Abraham Lincoln had placed under Maj. General John Pope, which was formed out of the scattered troops in the Virginia area, including those who Stonewall Jackson had bedeviled during the Valley Campaign. Pope had successfully commanded Union soldiers in victories at Island No. 10 and during the Siege of Corinth, earning himself a promotion to Major General in March 1862.

However, Pope was also uncommonly brash, and he got off to a bad start with his own men by issuing one of the most notorious messages of the Civil War:

"Let us understand each other. I have come to you from the West, where we have always seen the backs of our enemies; from an army whose business it has been to seek the adversary and to beat him when he was found; whose policy has been attack and not defense. In but one instance has the enemy been able to place our Western armies in defensive attitude. I presume that I have been called here to pursue the same system and to lead you against the enemy. It is my purpose to do so, and that speedily. I am sure you long for an opportunity to win the distinction you are capable of achieving. That opportunity I shall endeavor to give you. Meantime I desire you to dismiss from your minds certain phrases, which I am sorry to find so much in vogue amongst you. I hear constantly of 'taking strong positions and holding them,' of 'lines of retreat,' and of 'bases of supplies.' Let us discard such ideas. The strongest position a soldier should desire to occupy is one from which he can most easily advance against the enemy. Let us study the probable lines of retreat of our opponents, and leave our own to take care of themselves. Let us look before us, and not behind. Success and glory are in the advance, disaster and shame lurk in the rear. Let us act on this understanding, and it is safe to predict that your banners shall be inscribed with many a glorious deed and that your names will be dear to your countrymen forever."

**Pope**

Pope's arrogance and patronization of soldiers in the Eastern theater turned off many of the men in his new command, and it even caught the notice of Lee, who uncharacteristically called his opponent a "miscreant".

Pope's Army of Virginia was officially consolidated on June 26, 1862, comprised of soldiers in various war departments who had been engaged in Northern Virginia earlier in the year. The army, about 50,000 strong, included three corps under Franz Sigel, Nathaniel Banks, and Irvin McDowell. Sigel replaced John Frémont, who outranked Pope and thus refused to be Pope's subordinate, while Banks had been bested in the Shenandoah Valley by Jackson and McDowell had lost the First Battle of Bull Run. Soldiers of the IX Corps under Ambrose Burnside, who would lead men disastrously at Antietam and Fredericksburg, would eventually link up with Pope's army ahead of the Second Battle of Bull Run

Each corps in Pope's army also had their own cavalry brigade, instead of centralizing the cavalry under one command, an organizational mistake that would not be fixed until after the battle. Conversely, Lee's cavalry were organized into one division under JEB Stuart and attached to Stonewall Jackson's wing of the Army of Northern Virginia. As a result of the Union army's organization, the smaller brigades of cavalry were both ineffective at traditional cavalry duties like screening the army's movements and performing reconnaissance, and their force was diluted in actual battle.

In addition to threatening Lee's army and Richmond, Pope's army was an immediate threat to the Virginian civilians in the area, and Pope's army began employing methods of appropriating resources that infuriated the Confederacy. Pope's General Order No. 5 instructed his men to "subsist upon the country," giving them the ability to take civilian supplies in exchange for vouchers that "loyal citizens of the United States" could turn in after the Civil War for reimbursement. General Orders 7 and 11 instructed soldiers to destroy any building that Confederate soldiers or partisans used to shoot at Union soldiers, and Pope also ordered his army to "arrest all disloyal male citizens within their lines or within their reach." While these policies were tame in comparison to the total warfare and scorched earth used in 1864 by William Tecumseh Sherman and Phil Sheridan, in the early years of the war they were still considered unconventional, and Lee was so incensed by them that he stated Pope "ought to be suppressed."

After the war, Pope would write about the campaign in a way that sought to defend his conduct, and he portrayed himself as far less arrogant in taking command of the Army of Virginia:

"It became apparent to me at once that the duty to be assigned to me was in the nature of a forlorn-hope, and my position was still further embarrassed by the fact that I was called from another army and a different field of duty to command an army of which the corps commanders were all my seniors in rank. I therefore strongly urged that I be not placed in such a position, but be permitted to return to my command in the West, to which I was greatly attached and with which I had been closely identified in several successful operations on the Mississippi. It was not difficult to forecast the delicate and embarrassing position in which I should be placed, nor the almost certainly disagreeable, if not unfortunate, issue of such organization for such a purpose.

It was equally natural that the subordinate officers and the enlisted men of those corps should have been ill-pleased at the seeming affront to their own officers, involved in calling an officer strange to them and to the country in which they were operating, and to the character of the service in which they were engaged, to supersede well-known and trusted officers who had been with them from the beginning, and whose reputation was so closely identified with their own. How far this feeling prevailed among them, and how it influenced their actions, if it did so at all, I am not able to tell."

Of course, if Pope had truly felt that way in 1862, it's unclear why he would have issued the patronizing message he had upon taking command.

### Cedar Mountain

Lee had taken a risk by sizing up McClellan and splitting his forces while the Army of the Potomac was still in the vicinity, but it was calculated and ultimately proved correct. With that, Lee decided upon trying to strike and hopefully destroy Pope's army before McClellan sailed his army back toward Washington D.C. However, shortly after sending Jackson north to take up a defensive stance against Pope near Gordonsville, Lee learned of intelligence suggesting Burnside's command was heading to unite with Pope, so he ordered A.P. Hill's 12,000 man

"Light Division" to join Jackson. Despite the fact Lee now had only about 30,000 men at most opposing McClellan, the Union general continued to believe he was outnumbered and informed the Lincoln Administration he would need 50,000 more men to advance again. Then, despite having his request rejected and being given orders on August 3 to begin withdrawing his men from the Peninsula and head back to join Pope's army, McClellan protested before putting the withdrawal in motion on August 14.

McClellan has since been accused of intentionally delaying his evacuation out of spite and his disdain for Pope. McClellan was not in command at Second Bull Run, but he generated substantial controversy over whether he moved with speed to come to Pope's aid. What is unmistakable is that McClellan would feel vindicated if and when Pope was embarrassed, at one point mentioning that one possibility for the campaign is to let Pope attempt to get out of "his scrape." Lincoln would later accuse McClellan flat out of "acting badly" during the campaign.

On June 26, General Pope deployed his forces in an arc across Northern Virginia; its right flank (Sigel's corps) was around Sperryville on the Blue Ridge Mountains, the center consisted of Banks's corps at Little Washington, and its left flank (McDowell's corps) was outside Fredericksburg along the Rappahannock River. As Lee had anticipated, on August 6 Pope marched his forces south to capture the rail junction at Gordonsville, which meant to both threaten the Confederates from the north and distract Lee from McClellan's withdrawal from the Peninsula.

Just like in the Valley, Jackson's men were outnumbered by Pope's army, but Pope's corps were divided in three locations and none of them outnumbered Jackson individually. Jackson was thus determined to try to deal with them all separately before they could overwhelm him collectively.

Setting out on August 7, Jackson began marching his men toward the Union's isolated center, which consisted of about 8,000 men under Banks. However, his march was immediately hampered by a severe heat wave, which slowed his progress. On top of that, Jackson's insistence on keeping his marching plans secret messed up coordination among his principal subordinates, who were confused over which route they were supposed to take themselves. The delays allowed Pope to start shifting Sigel's corps to link up with Banks and form a defensive line around Cedar Run.

On August 9, Jackson's advancing column came into contact with the Union defenders posted on a ridge around Cedar Run, and they began forming a battle line while engaging in a general artillery duel with the Union forces. Jubal Early, whose brigade was in Jackson's vanguard, later explained, "No infantry had yet been seen, but the boldness with which the cavalry confronted us and the opening of the batteries, satisfied me that we had come upon a heavy force, concealed behind the ridge on which the cavalry was drawn up, as the ground beyond was depressed. I therefore halted the brigade, causing the men to cover themselves as well as they could by moving back a little and lying down, and then sent word for General Winder to come up."

However, the tempo of the battle changed on a dime after the mortal wounding of Confederate General Charles Winder, whose absence from the battlefield left the command of his division disorganized. A gap in the Confederate line opened up due to a misunderstanding by William Taliaferro, who had succeeded Winder, and that provided a chance for Banks to launch an attack. As Union soldiers came crashing down on the Confederates' right flank, another advance flanked the Confederates on their left and began rolling up their line.

Worried about losing control of his men and determined to inspire them, Jackson suddenly rode into the battlefield and attempted to brandish his sword, but the man who had once warned his VMI cadets to be ready to throw the scabbards of their swords away found that due to the infrequency with which he had used it, it had rusted in its scabbard. Waving his sword in its scabbard above his head, the Stonewall Brigade headed forward to reinforce the line.

However, the day wasn't saved for the Confederates until A.P. Hill's Light Division stabilized the Confederates' left flank and launched a counterattack. Jackson, who had not reconnoitered properly, was in danger of being beaten back by the vanguard of Banks's force when Hill came rushing in and changed the course of the battle, leading to a collapse of the Union right. Though outsiders thought Hill and Jackson worked like a "well oiled war machine," in reality, the two were maintaining an increasingly contentious relationship. The fact the two generals were at each other's throats was somewhat ironic, given that both of them were stern men. One of the men in his regiment recalled Hill's actions during the battle:

"I saw A.P. Hill that day as he was putting his "Light Division" into battle, and was very much struck with his appearance. In his shirtsleeves and with drawn sword he sought to arrest the stragglers who were coming to the rear, and seeing a Lieutenant in the number, he rode at him and fiercely inquired: "Who are you, sir, and where are you going?" The trembling Lieutenant replied: "I am going back with my wounded friend." Hill reached down and tore the insignia of rank from his collar as he roughly said: "You are a pretty fellow to hold a commission -- deserting your colors in the presence of the enemy, and going to the rear with a man who is scarcely badly enough wounded to go himself. I reduce you to the ranks, sir, and if you do not go to the front and do your duty, I'll have you shot as soon as I can spare a file of men for the purpose." And then clearing the road, he hurried forward his men to the splendid service which was before them."

**A.P. Hill**

The Confederates had won the battle, but at a surprisingly staggering cost. Banks, who had attempted to take the offensive despite being outnumbered 2-1, lost over a quarter of his command, while Jackson had suffered nearly 1500 casualties himself. Jackson knew not to attempt the offensive anymore since Pope's army was beginning to link up, while the Lincoln

Administration was ordering Pope to cancel his thrust towards Gordonsville.

Once certain McClellan was in full retreat, Lee began the process of reuniting his own army, still hoping to strike Pope before McClellan's troops could arrive as reinforcements. Lee wrote in his official post-campaign report:

"The victory at Cedar Run effectually checked the progress of the enemy for the time, but it soon became apparent that his army was being largely increased. The corps of Major-General Burnside fromNorth Carolina, which had reached Fredericksburg, was reported to have moved up the Rappahannock a few days after the battle to unite with General Pope, and a part of General McClellan's army was believed to have left Westover for the same purpose. It therefore seemed that active operations on the James were no longer contemplated, and that the most effectual way to relieve Richmond from any danger of attack from that quarter would be to re-enforce General Jackson and advance upon General Pope.

Accordingly on August 13 Major-General Longstreet, with his division and the two brigades under General Hood, were ordered to proceed to Gordonsville. At the same time General Stuart was directed to move with the main body of his cavalry to that point, leaving a sufficient force to observe the enemy still remaining in Fredericksburg and to guard the railroad. General R. H. Anderson was also directed to leave his position on James River and follow Longstreet."

Meanwhile, Pope was apparently now convinced that he did not have enough strength to take the offensive, despite the fact his numbers were at least equal to the Army of Northern Virginia and he was being promised further reinforcements from Burnside's corps and McClellan's army. After the war, he wrote, "It is only necessary to say that the course of these operations made it plain enough that the Rappahannock was too far to the front, and that the movements of Lee were too rapid and those of McClellan too slow to make it possible, with the small force I had, to hold that line, or to keep open communication with Fredericksburg without being turned on my right flank by Lee's whole army and cut off altogether from Washington."

Lee was determined to attack Pope, Pope was being ordered to cancel his forward movements, and Pope was apparently of the mind that he had to take the defensive. The ball was now in Lee's court, and it would lead the two armies to very familiar ground.

**Moving Toward Manassas**

Once Lee had united his army in mid-August, he was initially determined to try to slip around Pope's left flank, not his right. Lee explained in his post-campaign report:

"On the 16th the troops began to move from the vicinity of Gordonsville toward the Rapidan, on the north side of which, extending along the Orange and Alexandria Railroad in the direction of Culpeper CourtHouse, the Federal Army lay in great force. It was determined with the cavalry to destroy the railroad bridge over the Rappahannock in rear of the enemy, while Longstreet and Jackson crossed the Rapidan and attacked his left flank. The movement, as explained in the accompanying order, was appointed for August 18, but the necessary preparations not having been completed, its execution was postponed to the 20th. In the interval the enemy, being apprised of our design, hastily retired beyond the Rappahannock. General Longstreet crossed the Rapidan at Raccoon Ford and, preceded by Fitzhugh Lee's cavalry brigade, arrived early in the afternoon near Kelly's Ford, on the Rappahannock, where Lee had a sharp and successful skirmish with the rear guard of the enemy, who held the north side of the river in strong force. Jackson passed the Rapidan at Somerville Ford and moved toward Brandy Station, Robertson's brigade of cavalry, accompanied by General Stuart in person, leading the advance. Near Brandy Station a large body of the enemy's cavalry was encountered, which was gallantly attacked and driven across the Rappahannock by Robertson's command."

Whether Lee's initial plan could have been successful if not for bad luck is unclear, but his plan was intercepted during a Union cavalry raid and brought to Pope, who used the news to withdraw to a tighter defensive line around the Rappahannock River. Rising waters made it far more dangerous for the Confederates to attempt to cross the Rappahannock with Union artillery on the other side of it. Moreover, Pope was biding his time in the hopes of receiving reinforcements from the Army of the Potomac that would greatly swing the numbers to the Union's advantage. He explained, "On the 21st of August, being then at Rappahannock Station, my little army confronted by nearly the whole force under General Lee, which had compelled the retreat of McClellan to Harrison's Landing, I was positively assured that two days more would see me largely enough reënforced by the Army of the Potomac to be not only secure, but to assume the offensive against Lee, and I was instructed to hold on "and fight like the devil."

Lee's next strategic shift was also a result of luck. Cavalry leader JEB Stuart had been concocting a plan to ride around Pope's army, just like he had done to McClellan's, only to be almost captured in the Union cavalry raid that had not only stolen Lee's orders but also one of his famous plumed hats. On August 22, Stuart's men conducted a raid on Pope's camp that bagged a bunch of valuables, as Longstreet explained in his memoirs:

"General Stuart was ordered over, with parts of his brigades, to investigate and make trouble in the enemy's rear. He crossed at Waterloo and Hunt's Mill with fifteen hundred troopers and Pelham's horse artillery, and rode to Warrenton. Passing through, he directed his ride towards Catlett's Station to first burn the bridge over Cedar Creek.

Before reaching Catlett's a severe storm burst upon him, bogging the roads and flooding the streams behind him. The heavy roads delayed his artillery so that it was after night when he approached Catlett's. He caught a picket-guard and got into a camp about General Pope's Headquarters, took a number of prisoners, some camp property, and, meeting an old acquaintance and friend in a colored man, who conducted him to General Pope's tents, he found one of the general's uniform coats, a hat, a number of official despatches, a large amount of United States currency, much of the general's personal equipments, and one of the members of his staff, Major Goulding. He made several attempts to fire the bridge near Catlett's, but the heavy rains put out all fires that could be started, when he sought axes to cut it away. By this time the troops about the camps rallied and opened severe fire against him, but with little damage. The heavy rainfall admonished him to forego further operations and return to the army while yet there was a chance to cross Cedar Creek and the Rappahannock before the tides came down. On the night of the 23d he reached Sulphur Springs, where he met General Jackson's troops trying to make comfortable lodgement on the east bank, passed over, and resumed position outside General Lee's left. The despatch-book of General Pope gave information of his troops and his anxiety for reinforcements, besides mention of those that had joined him, but General Stuart's especial pleasure and pride were manifested over the possession of the uniform coat and hat of General Pope. Stuart rode along the line showing them, and proclaiming that he was satisfied with the exchange that made even his loss at Verdierville before the march; but the despatch lost at Verdierville [Lee's orders] was the tremendous blow that could not be overestimated."

With information about Pope's dispositions, his strategic thinking, and the news about impending reinforcements, Lee now changed tack and decided to try to turn Pope's right, as he explained in his report:

"As our positions on the south bank of the Rappahannock were commanded by those of the enemy, who guarded all the fords, it was determined to seek a more favorable place to cross higher up the river, and thus gain the enemy's right. Accordingly, General Longstreet was directed to leave Kelly's Ford on the 21st and take the position in front of the enemy in the vicinity of Beverly Ford and the Orange and Alexandria Railroad bridge, then held by Jackson, in order to mask the movement of the latter, who was instructed to ascend the river.

On the 22d Jackson crossed Hazel River at Welford's Mill and proceeded up the Rappahannock, leaving Trimble's brigade near Freeman's Ford to protect his trains. In the afternoon Longstreet sent General Hood, with his own and Whiting's brigade, under Colonel Law, to relieve Trimble. Hood had just reached the position when he and Trimble were attacked by a considerable force which had crossed at Freeman's Ford. After a short but spirited engagement the enemy was driven precipitately over the river with heavy loss. General Jackson arrived at the Warrenton Springs Ford in the afternoon, and immediately began to cross his troops to the north side, occupying the Springs and the adjacent heights. He was interrupted by a heavy rain, which caused the river to rise so rapidly that the ford soon became impassable for infantry and artillery."

While Lee was sending Jackson stealthily past Pope's right, the two armies skirmished around the Rappahannock River from August 22-25, which preoccupied Pope and helped keep his army in place and vulnerable to Jackson's turning movement. Meanwhile, Jackson's wing of the Army of Northern Virginia was heading toward Bristoe Station and the railroad junction at Manassas, where he would be positioned not only to destroy Pope's supply lines but also potentially cut off Pope's line of retreat.

Pope learned about Jackson's turning movement on August 26, and his initial response was to try to coordinate the dispositions of the reinforcements he thought he was due to receive imminently:

"I accordingly held on till the 26th of August, when, finding myself to be outflanked on my right by the main body of Lee's army, while Jackson's corps having passed Salem and Rectortown the day before were in rapid march in the direction of Gainesville and Manassas Junction, and seeing that none of the reënforcements promised me were likely to arrive, I determined to abandon the line of the Rappahannock and communications with Fredericksburg, and concentrate my whole force in the direction of Warrenton and Gainesville, to cover the Warrenton pike, and still to confront the enemy rapidly marching to my right.^

Stonewall Jackson's movement on Manassas Junction was plainly seen and promptly reported, and I notified General Halleck of it. He informed me on the 23d of August that heavy reënforcements would begin to arrive at Warrenton Junction on the next day (24th), and as my orders still held me to the Rappahannock I naturally supposed that these troops would be hurried forward to me with all speed. Franklin's corps especially, I asked, should be sent rapidly to Gainesville. I also telegraphed Colonel Herman Haupt, chief of railway transportation, to direct one of the strongest divisions coming forward, and to be at Warrenton Junction on the 24th, to be put in the works at Manassas Junction. A cavalry force had been sent forward to observe the Thoroughfare Gap early on the morning of the 26th, but nothing was heard from it."

By the time Pope was aware of Jackson's move on his right, the Confederates were well into his rear. On the night of August 26, Jackson's men slipped through Thoroughfare Gap and headed for the railroad at Bristoe Station, cutting up the line. The following morning, Jackson moved on the Union supplies stored at Manassas Junction, where he met one sole Union brigade led by George W. Taylor and easily pushed it aside, mortally wounding Taylor in the process. McClellan would later cite the defeat of Taylor's force as justification for not sending more infantry reinforcements to Pope without corresponding artillery and cavalry for their protection.

However, by the end of August 27, Jackson's men were being chased by a Union division under the command of "Fighting Joe" Hooker, forcing Jackson to conduct a rearguard action while he retreated and dug in behind an unfinished railroad near Bull Run creek. Jackson had posted his men about a mile away from where he had become a Confederate hero the year before during First Manassas, when his brigade had rallied the Confederates on Henry Hill and turned the tide of that battle. Now he was digging in right on a spot that Union soldiers opposing him had stood on 13 months earlier. Lee later reported, "General Jackson's force being much inferior to that of General Pope, it became necessary for him to withdraw from Manassas and take a position west of the turnpike road from Warrenton to Alexandria, where he could more readily unite with the approaching column of Longstreet. Having fully supplied the wants of his troops, he was compelled, for want of transportation, to destroy the rest of the captured property. This was done during the night of the 27th, and 50,000 pounds of bacon, 1,000 barrels of corned beef, 2,000 barrels of salt pork, and 2,000 barrels of flour, besides other property of great value, were burned."

On August 27, Jackson routed a Union brigade near Union Mills (Bull Run Bridge), inflicting several hundred casualties and mortally wounding Union Brig. Gen. George W. Taylor. Maj. Gen. Richard S. Ewell's Confederate division fought a brisk rearguard action against Maj. Gen. Joseph Hooker's Union division at Kettle Run, resulting in about 600 casualties. Ewell held back Union forces until dark. That night, Jackson marched his divisions north to the Bull Run battlefield, where he took position behind an unfinished railroad grade. Pope explained the outlook on the night of August 27, "The movement of Jackson presented the only opportunity which had offered to gain any success over the superior forces of the enemy. I determined, therefore, on the morning of the 27th of August to abandon the line of the Rappahannock and throw my whole force in the direction of Gainesville and Manassas Junction, to crush any force of the enemy that had passed through Thoroughfare Gap, and to interpose between Lee's army and Bull Run. Having the interior line of operations, and the enemy at Manassas being inferior in force, it appeared to me, and still so appears, that with even ordinary promptness and energy we might feel sure of success."

**Picture of a train derailed near Manassas Junction by the raiding Confederates**

With the Confederate army divided and Pope's army inbetween them, Pope was now positioned to prevent them from linking up by blocking the Thoroughfare Gap. Ultimately he opted not to, later claiming that when he saw smoke from the flames shooting near Manassas, he figured he had Jackson in trouble and could annihilate the Confederates before Longstreet reunited with them. In fact, those flames were coming from his own supplies, after Jackson's men began torching what they couldn't carry. As a result, Longstreet's wing of the army would suffer only a slight harassment from Union cavalry and one Union division before they gave way at Thoroughfare Gap.

With the path established for Longstreet's wing to march and reunite with Jackson's wing, the race was now on. Could Pope's army fall on Jackson's wing and destroy it before Longstreet rejoined it?

**August 28**

Although Pope was now planning to thrust at Jackson's army, the Second Battle of Bull Run actually began on the evening of August 28 with Jackson's men taking the offensive. Pope was in the process of gathering all his men at Centreville, just above Bull Run and a few miles away from Jackson's men, because he thought Jackson's men were at Centreville itself. As Jackson's men kept their defensive line along the unfinished railroad cut, they watched a Union column marching along the Warrenton Turnpike near Brawner's farm, and it turned out to be soldiers from Brig. Gen. Rufus King's division (of McDowell's corps) marching toward Centreville to meet up with the rest of Pope's army and hopefully discover Jackson. Unbeknownst to the column, they were actually marching right past Jackson's entire wing of the army.

Emboldened by the news that Longstreet was passing through Thoroughfare Gap around the same time, Jackson got characteristically aggressive, and figuring that this Union column was retreating behind Bull Run to link up with Pope's army and perhaps even reinforcements from the Army of the Potomac, he decided to try to annihilate the column.

In the late afternoon, Jackson ordered his principal officers, "Bring out your men, gentlemen." With that, he ordered his artillery to open up on the column marching conspicuously across their front. As fate would have it, the part of the column in Jackson's front at this time was John Gibbon's brigade, which could be identified by their Black Hats. This "Black Hat Brigade" was destined to become one of the most famous Union brigades of the war after being christened the Iron Brigade by McClellan during the subsequent Maryland Campaign and fighting heroically at Gettysburg, but they had never seen action before Jackson's grizzled veterans opened fire on them that night around 6:30 p.m.

John Hatch's brigade of King's division had already marched past Jackson's front, so Gibbon worked to get reinforcements from Abner Doubleday's brigade and formed a battle line. Due to Pope's belief that Jackson was at Centreville, Gibbon mistakenly thought that the artillery being fired at them was coming from JEB Stuart's cavalry, and that two brigades could sweep them aside and end the harassment of their march. The Black Hat Brigade had never fought before, and now they were about to make a general advance against half of the Army of Northern Virginia.

**Gibbon**

While Gibbon formed his line along the turnpike, he used the 2nd Wisconsin regiment to advance through woods on the Confederates' right flank. In fact, when Gibbon convened with the regiment in the woods, he instructed them to capture the artillery. In reality, he was posting a lone regiment on the right flank of Richard S. Ewell's entire division, which was supported in the rear by William Taliaferro's division.

With his line formed, Gibbon's previously untested men began moving forward, only to come face to face with Confederates at nearly point blank range in Brawner's farm. Major Rufus Dawes, who would become a hero on Day 1 at Gettysburg in command of the 6th Wisconsin, described the fighting the 6th Wisconsin endured that night, "Our men on the left loaded and fired with the energy of madmen, and the 6th worked with equal desperation. This stopped the rush of the enemy and they halted and fired upon us their deadly musketry. During a few awful moments, I could see by the lurid light of the powder flashes, the whole of both lines. The two ... were within ... fifty yards of each other pouring musketry into each other as fast as men could load and shoot."

Meanwhile, the 2nd Wisconsin came through the woods and found themselves squarely on the Confederates' right flank at an angle that also happened to expose their own right flank. Thankfully for the Union, the 2nd Wisconsin was one of the few veteran regiments on the field that night, and they stood firm even after the Stonewall Brigade unleashed the first volley, firing a volley of their own and thus starting a general musketry exchange. Out of the nearly 430 men fighting for the 2nd Wisconsin, nearly 60% would become casualties.

The fact that daylight was running out likely contributed to the confusion that induced Gibbon to stand firm against the artillery assault, but it would also prove to be his saving grace. Gibbon shored up the right of his line with men from Doubleday's brigade and kept plugging in gaps in his line, and the fighting was so hot that Jackson actually started directing single regiments into the fighting. While Jackson was ordering multiple regiments into the fray, the unwitting Gibbon was countering by ordering up single regiments. Jackson described the fighting, "In a few moments our entire line was engaged in a fierce and sanguinary struggle with the enemy. As one line was repulsed another took its place and pressed forward as if determined by force of numbers and fury of assault to drive us from our positions."

By the time Jackson ordered up Isaac Trimble's brigade, it was so dark that all semblance of command coordination vanished. The Confederates started making piecemeal assaults instead of a general advance, allowing the heavily outnumbered Union regiments to repulse the attacks one at a time. By 9:00, the Union soldiers fought a gradual retreat back to the turnpike, leaving the field to Jackson's men. The fighting had produced a remarkable number of casualties in just 2 hours, with 1,150 Union and 1,250 Confederate casualties. Nevertheless, the Union soldiers had held their ground despite being outnumbered 3-1, and furthermore the Confederate casualties included Ewell and Taliaferro, two of Jackson's division commanders.

**Ewell**

Pope later wrote about where he was and what he was thinking when he heard about the fighting on the night of the 28th.

"The engagement of King's division was reported to me about 10 o'clock at night near Centreville. I felt sure then, and so stated, that there was no escape for Jackson. On the west of him were McDowell's corps (I did not then know that he had detached Ricketts *, Sigel's corps, and Reynolds's division, all under command of McDowell. On the east of him, and with the advance of Kearny nearly in contact with him on the Warrenton pike, were the corps of Reno and Heintzelman. Porter was supposed to be at Manassas Junction, where he ought to have been on that afternoon.

"I sent orders to McDowell (supposing him to be with his command), and also direct to General King, several times during that night and once by his own staff-officer, to hold his ground at all hazards, to prevent the retreat of Jackson toward Lee, and that at daylight our whole force from Centreville and Manassas would assail him from the east, and he would be crushed between us. I sent orders also to General Kearny at Centreville to move forward cautiously that night along the Warrenton pike; to drive in the pickets of the enemy, and to keep as closely as possible in contact with him during the night, resting his left on the Warrenton pike and throwing his right to the north, if practicable, as far as the Little River pike, and at daylight next morning to assault vigorously with his right advance, and that Hooker and Reno would certainly be with him shortly after daylight. I sent orders to General Porter, who I supposed was at Manassas Junction, to move upon Centreville at dawn, stating to him the position of our forces, and that a severe battle would be fought that morning (the 29th).

With Jackson at or near Groveton, with McDowell on the west, and the rest of the army on the east of him, while Lee, with the mass of his army, was still west of Thoroughfare Gap, the situation for us was certainly as favorable as the most sanguine person could desire, and the prospect of crushing Jackson, sandwiched between such forces, were certainly excellent. There is no doubt, had General McDowell been with his command when King's division of his corps became engaged with the enemy, he would have brought forward to its support both Sigel and Reynolds, and the result would have been to hold the ground west of Jackson at least until morning brought against him also the forces moving from the direction of Centreville.

To my great disappointment and surprise, however, I learned toward daylight the next morning (the 29th) that King's division had fallen back toward Manassas Junction, and that neither Sigel nor Reynolds had been engaged or had gone to the support of King. The route toward Thoroughfare Gap had thus been left open by the wholly unexpected retreat of King's division, due to the fact that he was not supported by Sigel and Reynolds, and an immediate change was necessary in the disposition of the troops under my command."

However, as Longstreet noted in his memoirs, Pope actually had it backwards. Longstreet's wing of the army was already on its way through Thoroughfare Gap after pushing aside relatively light resistance, and Jackson's men could actually see the musket smoke and hear the artillery produced by Longstreet's soldiers in the Gap. Longstreet wrote, "During the night the Federal commander reported to his subordinates that McDowell had 'intercepted the retreat of Jackson, and ordered concentration of the army against him,' whereas it was, of course, Jackson who had intercepted McDowell's march. He seems to have been under the impression that he was about to capture Jackson, and inclined to lead his subordinates to the same opinion."

Sure enough, Pope was operating under the mistaken assumption that Jackson's men had engaged King's division as it was retreating from Centreville, clearly unaware that Jackson had taken up that position the night before and was biding his time until Longstreet joined him. That night, Pope told Phil Kearny, who commanded a division in the Army of the Potomac, "General McDowell has intercepted the retreat of the enemy and is now in his front ... Unless he can escape by by-paths leading to the north to-night, he must be captured." In actuality, when King's division extricated itself from the fighting at Brawner's farm and continued east to meet up with the rest of Pope's army, there were no longer any Union forces between Jackson and Longstreet.

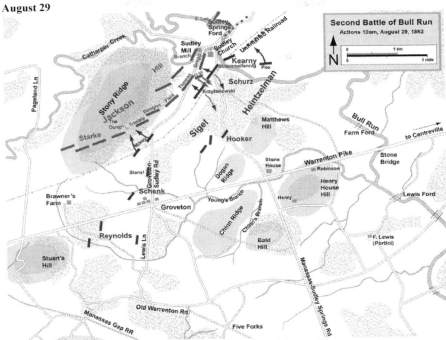

**The battle lines on the morning of August 29**

Pope would begin operations on August 29 laboring under an entirely faulty premise, and his various orders to different subordinates would result in a completely uncoordinated general attack on Jackson's defensive line.

"About daylight, therefore, on the 29th of August, almost immediately after I received information of the withdrawal of King's division toward Manassas Junction, I sent orders to General Sigel, in the vicinity of Groveton, to attack the enemy vigorously at daylight and bring him to a stand if possible. He was to be supported by Reynolds's division. I instructed Heintzelman to push forward from Centreville toward Gainesville on the Warrenton pike at the earliest dawn with the divisions of Kearny and Hooker, and gave orders also to Reno with his corps to follow closely in their rear. They were directed to use all speed, and as soon as they came up with the enemy to establish communication with Sigel, and to attack vigorously and promptly. I also sent orders to General Porter at Manassas Junction to move forward rapidly with his own corps and King's division of McDowell's corps, which was there also, upon Gainesville by the direct route from Manassas Junction to that place. I urged him to make all possible speed, with the purpose that he should come up with the enemy or connect himself with the left of our line near where the Warrenton pike is crossed by the road from Manassas Junction to Gainesville.

Shortly after sending this order I received a note from General McDowell, whom I had not been able to find during the night of the 28th, dated Manassas Junction, requesting that King's division be not taken from his command. I immediately sent a joint order, addressed to Generals McDowell and Porter, repeating the instructions to move forward with their commands toward Gainesville, and informing them of the position and movements of Sigel and Heintzelman."

**Heintzelman**

Thus, with Longstreet marching his 26,000 soldiers toward Jackson at dawn that morning, it would fall upon Jackson and his nearly 20,000 men to hold out for at least the entire morning against potentially all of Pope's army.

Luckily for the Confederates, Pope's unfamiliarity with the Confederate dispositions and his convoluted attack orders would ruin his plans. Pope intended to strike both of Jackson's flanks that morning, and Sigel began the fighting around 7:00 a.m. on Jackson's left with Robert Schenck's division, Carl Schurz's division, and Robert Milroy's brigade. His line also had John Reynolds's division from Heintzelman's corps in reserve, and he anticipated being supported by Kearny's division as well.

Sigel advanced his men without knowing exactly where Jackson's flank was, and as it turned out A.P. Hill had extended Jackson's left until it was nearly touching Bull Run creek, and Stuart's cavalry was posted on the other side of the creek crossing to provide artillery support. While Stuart's horse artillery was engaged, the cavalrymen fastened logs and dragged them on the dirt road behind their horses, kicking up a cloud of dust that was meant to confuse Union commanders into thinking Jackson had more men than he actually did.

**Franz Sigel**

For the next three hours, Sigel threw his corps at A.P. Hill's Light Division in a series of attacks that were not properly coordinated with the supporting elements from the other corps of the army. At the same time, even though Jackson was essentially fighting a delaying action intended to buy time for Longstreet, Hill's men couldn't help but charge forward and counterattack Sigel's men after repulsing each attack. In addition to Sigel's divisions fighting piecemeal, those divisions had their brigades fighting piecemeal. Making matters worse, Sigel made one last assault around 10:00 a.m. in the belief that Phil Kearny's division was making the attack with them. To Sigel's horror, Kearny's division didn't move as he had expected. Historians have attributed Kearny's failure to move for his disdain for Sigel, but Kearny insisted in his post-battle report, "On the 29th, on my arrival, I was assigned to the holding of the right wing, my left on Leesburg road. I posted Colonel Poe, with Berry's brigade, in first line, General Robinson, First Brigade, on his right, partly in line and partly in support, and kept Birney's most disciplined regiments reserved and ready for emergencies. Toward noon I was obliged to occupy a quarter of a mile additional on left of said road, from Schurz' troops being taken elsewhere."

Despite being repulsed, Pope wasn't done attacking Jackson's left. Hooker's division (from Heintzelman's corps) now came up, as did a brigade from Burnside's IX Corps led by Isaac Stevens. Kearny's division was also still ready to make an assault on the left. Pope arrived at the scene around noon, just in time to watch this next wave of attacks on Jackson's left.

As those attacks were starting, the first elements of Longstreet's wing were coming up on Jackson's right, as were some of Stuart's cavalry, which had been employed in guiding Longstreet's men to Jackson's line. As Longstreet's men began arriving, Longstreet recounted an exchange between he and Lee over whether to conduct an attack on Pope's left flank, which was at that time was concentrating its efforts on Jackson: "When I reported my troops in order for battle, General Lee was inclined to engage as soon as practicable, but did not order. All troops that he could hope to have were up except R. H. Anderson's division, which was near enough to come in when the battle was in progress. I asked him to be allowed to make a reconnoissance of the enemy's ground, and along his left. After an hour's work, mounted and afoot, under the August sun, I returned and reported adversely as to attack, especially in view of the easy approach of the troops reported at Manassas against my right in the event of severe contention. We knew of Ricketts's division in that quarter, and of a considerable force at Manassas Junction, which indicated one corps." Lee acquiesced to Longstreet's advice, which some Lost Cause advocates would later claim gave Longstreet the confidence to go against Lee's wishes. Considering Longstreet's disobedience of General Lee's wishes to be nearly insubordination, Lee's most famous biographer, Douglas Southall Freeman, later wrote: "The seeds of much of the disaster on July 2, 1863, at the Battle of Gettysburg were sown in that instant—when Lee yielded to Longstreet and Longstreet discovered that he would." However, Longstreet's men had marched about 30 miles and briefly fought at Thoroughfare Gap the day before, so Longstreet was well aware that his men were anything but fresh.

One of the sources of Longstreet's apprehension that day was Fitz-John Porter's corps, one of the few commands from the Army of the Potomac that would engage in substantial fighting during the battle. Porter, along with McDowell's corps, were on the left of the Union line and were advancing northwest toward what they thought would be Jackson's right when they encountered Stuart's cavalry. In fact, Stuart's cavalry had just escorted Longstreet's men to the field, and as they engaged in skirmishing, orders from Pope for Porter and McDowell arrived.

**Porter**

The orders, now known as the "Joint Order", essentially ordered Porter to perform the impossible. The order suggested that Porter and McDowell move along the Manassas-Gainesville Road (as they had been doing) toward Gainesville while also maintaining contact with the rest of the Union line, which at the time had John Reynolds's division on the left flank. At the same time, the order stated "as soon as communication is established [with the other divisions] the whole command shall halt. It may be necessary to fall back behind Bull Run to Centreville tonight." Finally, Pope's order added a caveat: "If any considerable advantages are to be gained from departing from this order it will not be strictly carried out."

Historian John J. Hennessy, who wrote a history on the campaign, has since labeled Pope's order "masterpiece of contradiction and obfuscation that would become the focal point of decades of wrangling." To start, it was not possible for this column to continue marching toward Gainesville and maintain contact with the left of the Union line at the same time. And in addition to the incredibly murky and contradictory suggestions, Pope gave the men on his left this order without realizing that Longstreet's wing of the army had arrived on the battlefield to Jackson's left, a deployment that induced Porter to widely choose not to make an attack on the 29th. Despite the wisdom of the decision, it was one that would lead to Porter being court-martialed and effectively ending his military career.

Somehow, even in the years after the Civil War, Pope remained mistaken about Longstreet's dispositions on the afternoon of the 29th, and he continued to direct his vitriol at Porter, who he believed had disobeyed his orders out of loyalty to McClellan, writing:

"From 1:30 to 4 o'clock P. M. very severe conflicts occurred repeatedly all along the line, and there was a continuous roar of artillery and small-arms, with scarcely an intermission. About two o'clock in the afternoon three discharges of artillery were heard on the extreme left of our line or right of the enemy's, and I for the moment, and naturally, believed that Porter and McDowell had reached their positions and were engaged with the enemy. I heard only three shots, and as nothing followed I was at a loss to know what had become of these corps, or what was delaying them, as before this hour they should have been, even With ordinary marching, well up on our left. Shortly afterward I received information that McDowell's corps was advancing to join the left of our line by the Sudley Springs road, and would probably be up within two hours. At 4:30 o'clock I sent a peremptory order to General Porter, who was at or near Dawkins's Branch, about four or five miles distant from my headquarters, to push forward at once into action on the enemy's right, and if possible on his rear, stating to him generally the condition of things on the field in front of me. At 5:30 o'clock, when General Porter should have been going into action in compliance with this order, I directed Heintzelman and Reno to attack the enemy's left. The attack was made promptly and with vigor and persistence, and the left of the enemy was doubled back toward his center. After a severe and bloody action of an hour Kearny forced the position on the left of the enemy and occupied the field of battle there."

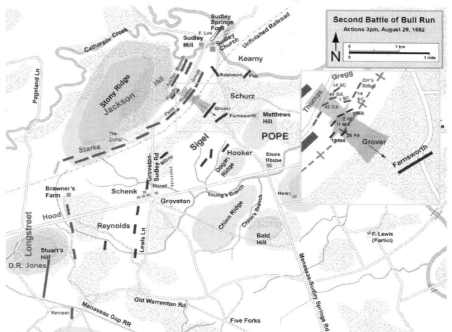

As Pope's account indicates, his failure to understand the situation on his left resulted in the mistaken belief that the afternoon would include attacks on both of Jackson's flanks instead of just one desperate assault on Jackson's left yet again. The highlight of that attack came when a brigade led by Brig. Gen. Cuvier Grover successfully marched into a gap in the Confederate line, only to be repulsed because Kearny's division did not support it. Furthermore, Pope had expected the attack to be a diversionary tactic while his left surprised Jackson's right, still unaware of Longstreet's position. Eventually Brig. Gen. Dorsey Pender's brigade sealed the gap in A.P. Hill's line.

While this was going on, Pope ordered John Reynolds to advance on the left, during which Reynolds ran into Longstreet's wing and immediately called off the advance. When Reynolds reported this to Pope, Pope refused to believe it could be Longstreet and somehow thought Reynolds had mistaken Porter's corps for Confederates. The next attack was made by Jesse Reno's division of Burnside's IX Corps, which saw one brigade attack the very center of Jackson's line without support. Once again, that attack was eventually repulsed.

With every attack having been repulsed thus far, Pope continued to hold out hope that Porter's corps would deliver him a victory, even as he remained confused as to why he hadn't heard any fighting or accounts of fighting on his left. At 4:30 p.m., Pope sent orders to Porter to attack, but Porter did not get that message until it was dusk, and he still had Longstreet in his front, making an attack on Jackson's right impossible. But Pope ordered Kearny's division to attack Jackson's left in conjunction with his order to Porter, so Kearny's division surged forward around 5:00, crashing into A.P. Hill's division, which had already taken most of the Union attacks during the day.

Kearny reported what went wrong with this new wave:

"During the first hours of combat General Birney, on tired regiments in the center falling back, of his own accord rapidly pushed across to give them a hand to raise themselves to a renewed fight. In early after noon General Pope's order, per General Roberts, was to send a pretty strong force diagonally to the front to relieve the center in the woods from pressure. Accordingly I detached for that purpose General Robinson, with his brigade; the Sixty-third Pennsylvania Volunteers, Colonel Hays; the One hundred and fifth Pennsylvania Volunteers, Captain Craig; the Twentieth Indiana, Colonel Brown, and, additionally, the Third Michigan Marksmen, under Colonel Champlin. General Robinson drove forward for several hundred yards, but the center of the main battle being shortly after driven back and out of the woods, my detachment, thus exposed, so considerably in front of all others, both flanks in air, was obliged to cease to advance, and confine themselves to holding their own. At 5 o'clock, thinking-- though at the risk of exposing my fighting line to being enfiladed--that I might drive the enemy by an unexpected attack through the woods, I brought up additionally the most of Birney's regiments---the Fourth Maine, Colonel Walker and Lieutenant-Colonel Carver: the Fortieth New York, Colonel Egan; First New York, Major Burr, and One hundred and first New York, Lieutenant-Colonel Gesner--and changed front to the left, to sweep with a rush the first line of the enemy. This was most successful. The enemy rolled up on his own right. It presaged a victory for us all. Still our force was too light. The enemy brought up rapidly heavy reserves, so that our farther progress was impeded. General Stevens came up gallantly in action to support us, but did not have the numbers."

Despite launching a fierce attack, Kearny's division could only do so much for so long until Jackson reinforced Hill's line by pulling Early's brigade from his right and sending Lawrence Branch's brigade into the fight.

Although the Union assaults had finally come to an end, Lee was still entertaining thoughts about launching an attack with Longstreet's men. Once again, Longstreet successfully argued against it, insisting that a reconnaissance and an attack in the morning was a better option. John Bell Hood's division conducted the reconnaissance in force, but nightfall brought his skirmishing with the Union left to an end.

As August 29 was drawing to a close, Pope had clearly failed to bag Jackson's wing of the army, but the battle was not a debacle either. Moreover, two of McClellan's corps from the Army of the Potomac were now nearby at Alexandria, comprising about 25,000 men. Although Pope clearly couldn't count on McClellan to actually order them forward as reinforcements anymore, he still had the option of pulling his own army back to Alexandria, uniting with McClellan's army, and then figuring out a new course of action.

Instead, Pope continued to talk himself into believing that he had Jackson on the ropes, and that Lee's army was in the process of retreating. Years later, he was still trying to justify his belief that Lee was retreating, writing:

"Every indication during the night of the 29th and up to 10 o'clock on the morning of the 30th pointed to the retreat of the enemy from our front. Paroled prisoners of our own army, taken on the evening of the 29th, who came into our lines on the morning of the 30th, reported the enemy retreating during the whole night in the direction of and along the Warrenton pike (a fact since confirmed by Longstreet's report).| Generals McDowell and Heintzelman, who reconnoitered the position held by the enemy's left on the evening of the 29th, also confirmed this statement. They reported to me the evacuation of these positions by the enemy, and that there was every indication of their retreat in the direction of Gainesville. On the morning of the 30th, as may be easily believed, our troops, who had been marching and fighting almost continuously for many days, were greatly exhausted. They had had little to eat for two days, and artillery and cavalry horses had been in harness and under the saddle for ten days, and had been almost out of forage for the last two days. It may be readily imagined how little these troops, after such severe labors and hardships, were in condition for further active marching and fighting."

Given Pope's mistaken beliefs, the one man who might have been able to extricate him from the mistake he was about to make happened to be the one man least inclined to help. For several days, George McClellan had at least 25,000 men within two days' march of Pope's army, yet he continued to insist that he couldn't move toward Manassas without the necessary cavalry and artillery. Pope might not have gotten much right in his writings about the battle after the war, but he rightly ridiculed McClellan's stance:

"On the 28th I had telegraphed General Halleck our condition, and had begged of him to have rations and forage sent forward to us from Alexandria with all speed; but about daylight on the 30th I received a note from General Franklin, written by direction of General McClellan, informing me that rations and forage would be loaded into the available wagons and cars at Alexandria as soon as I should send back a cavalry escort to guard the trains. Such a letter, when we were fighting the enemy and when Alexandria was full of troops, needs no comment. Our cavalry was well-nigh broken down completely, and certainly we were in no condition to spare troops from the front, nor could they have gone to Alexandria and returned within the time by which we must have had provisions and forage or have fallen back toward supplies; nor am I able to understand of what use cavalry could be to guard railroad trains."

Understandably, supporters of Pope and critics of McClellan would heavily criticize the inaction and accuse McClellan of intentionally making Pope's life more difficult. It seems they were right; McClellan bragged in a private letter to his wife weeks earlier, "Pope will be badly thrashed within two days & ... they will be very glad to turn over the redemption of their affairs to me. I won't undertake it unless I have full & entire control." Even as Pope was launching a series of assaults against Jackson on August 29, McClellan suggested to Lincoln that they should "leave Pope to get out of his scrape, and at once use all our means to make the capital perfectly safe."

### August 30

One of the most ill-conceived attacks of the entire war would be made on August 30, and one of the best executed attacks of the entire war would follow it.

On the morning of August 30, Pope held a council of war at his headquarters, where he was unmistakably informed of Longstreet's position and that Jackson's men had not moved during the night. But as it turned out, some of Longstreet's men, a division under Richard Anderson, had arrived on the field late at night and woke up to find that they were dangerously close to the Union line. With that, they countermarched to link back up with the rest of Longstreet's wing, and when Pope heard of that movement it seemed to confirm to him that the Confederates were retreating, and he even telegraphed back to Washington that "the enemy was retreating to the mountains". Thus, even though Jackson's men were still in place and Longstreet was still posted on the Union army's left with about 25,000 men, Pope remained determined to attack what he believed was a retreating Confederate army.

Around noon, Pope ordered Porter to attack once again, this time in conjunction with Hatch's division and Reynolds's division on the Union left, up the Manassas-Gainesville turnpike. On the Union right, the divisions of Ricketts, Kearny, and Hooker, all of whom had fought hard the day before, were ordered to attack as well. Pope believed he was conducting a pincers attack on a retreating Confederate army, when in fact he was about to march Porter's corps right across Longstreet's front, all but exposing the left flank of Porter's 10,000 men to Longstreet's 25,000 Confederates. And far from retreating, Lee was going about bolstering Jackson's defenses, including posting artillery that could sweep the field in Jackson's front. Lee himself could not have drawn up a more favorable plan for the Confederates than Pope had.

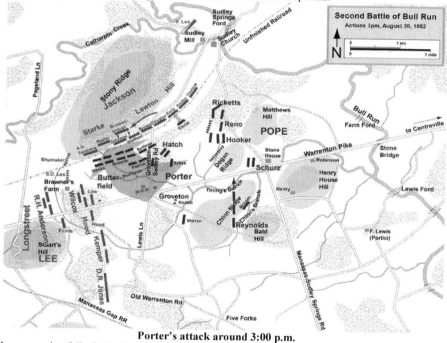

**Porter's attack around 3:00 p.m.**

In a campaign full of mistakes, the Union attacks managed not to be properly coordinated. Due to delays in getting his corps up, Porter would not make his assault until about an hour after the attack launched by the Union right. Jackson described how fierce the fighting was on his left in his report:

"About 2 p. m. the Federal infantry in large force advanced to the attack of our left, occupied by the division of Gen. Hill. It pressed forward, in defiance of our fatal and destructive fire, with great determination, a portion of it crossing a deep cut in the railroad track and penetrating in heavy force an interval of nearly 175 yards, which separated the right of Gregg's from the left of Thomas brigade. For a short time Gregg's brigade, on the extreme left, was isolated from the main body of the command; but the Fourteenth South Carolina Regiment, then in reserve, with the Forty-ninth Georgia, left of Col. Thomas, attacked the exultant enemy with vigor, and drove them back across the railroad track with great slaughter. Gen. McGowan reports that the opposing forces at one time delivered their volleys into each other at the distance of 10 paces. Assault after assault was made on the left, exhibiting on the part of the enemy great pertinacity and determination, but every advance was most successfully and gallantly driven back.

Gen. Hill reports that six separate and distinct assault were thus met and repulsed by his division, assisted by Hays' brigade, Col. Forno commanding.

By this time the brigade of Gen. Gregg, which from its position on the extreme left was most exposed to the enemy's attack, had nearly expended its ammunition. It had suffered severely in its men, and all its field officers except two were killed or wounded."

Porter's attack would be made under even more trying circumstances, since the division on his far left under Daniel Butterfield would have to cross about 600 yards in an open field in front of Jackson's men, who were posted behind a natural fortification in an unfinished railroad cut. On Butterfield's right was Hatch's division, which would have to march across land exposed to the batteries Lee had dutifully directed earlier in the day, not to mention Jackson's infantry. Even still, Hatch's division created a breach in Jackson's line, forcing the Stonewall Brigade to reinforce the line. The fighting was so heavy that some Confederates ran out of ammunition and began throwing rocks at the nearest Union soldiers, members of the 24th New York, which induced the Union men to throw some back.

Seeing no breakthroughs and still wary of Longstreet on his left, Porter kept his other division in reserve, but his entire command was now north of the Warrenton Turnpike and so far out in front of Longstreet that Porter's cautious alignment was still in no position to defend against the now impending flank attack. To top it off, McDowell ordered Reynolds to move his division up to support Porter's right, pulling even more Union soldiers from south of the Warrenton Turnpike and bringing them north of the Turnpike. That decision would only make it that much easier for Longstreet's assault to roll up the entire Union line, and by having only about 2,000 men still south of the Turnpike in front of Longstreet, Pope's army had inadvertently placed itself in serious danger of being trapped along Bull Run with the only roads of retreat being covered by Jackson near Sudley Springs Ford and Longstreet advancing east across the Warrenton Turnpike.

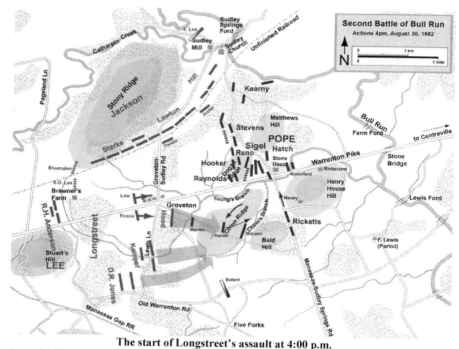

### The start of Longstreet's assault at 4:00 p.m.

Around 4:00, Longstreet's assault started with the objective of reaching Henry Hill, the exact same spot McDowell's Union army had desperately sought to reach in the First Battle of Bull Run. As Longstreet explained, the advantageous positioning for his flank attack was so apparent to the men under his command that they were all but able to start the assault perfectly without even being commanded:

"Porter's masses were in almost direct line from the point at which I stood, and in enfilade fire. It was evident that they could not stand fifteen minutes under the fire of batteries planted at that point, while a division marching back and across the field to aid Jackson could not reach him in an hour, more time probably than he could stand under the heavy weights then bearing down upon him. Boldness was prudence! Prompt work by the wing and batteries could relieve the battle. Reinforcements might not be in time, so I called for my nearest batteries. Ready, anticipating call, they sprang to their places and drove at speed, saw the opportunity before it could be pointed out, and went into action. The first fire was by Chapman's battery, followed in rolling practice by Boyce's and Reilly's. Almost immediately the wounded began to drop off from Porter's ranks; the number seemed to increase with every shot; the masses began to waver, swinging back and forth, showing signs of discomfiture along the left and left centre.

In ten or fifteen minutes it crumbled into disorder and turned towards the rear. Although the batteries seemed to hasten the movements of the discomfited, the fire was less effective upon broken ranks, which gave them courage, and they made brave efforts to rally; but as the new lines formed they had to breast against Jackson's standing line, and make a new and favorable target for the batteries, which again drove them to disruption and retreat. Not satisfied, they made a third effort to rally and fight the battle through, but by that time they had fallen back far enough to open the field to the fire of S. D. Lee's artillery battalion. As the line began to take shape, this fearful fire was added to that under which they had tried so ineffectually to fight. The combination tore the line to pieces, and as it broke the third time the charge was ordered. The heavy fumes of gunpowder hanging about our ranks, as stimulating as sparkling wine, charged the atmosphere with the light and splendor of battle. Time was culminating under a flowing tide. The noble horses took the spirit of the riders sitting lightly in their saddles. As orders were given, the staff, their limbs already closed to the horses' flanks, pressed their spurs, but the electric current overleaped their speedy strides, and twenty-five thousand braves moved in line as by a single impulse. My old horse, appreciating the importance of corps headquarters, envious of the spread of his comrades as they measured the green, yet anxious to maintain his role, moved up and down his limited space in lofty bounds, resolved to cover in the air the space allotted his more fortunate comrades on the plain.

Leaving the broken ranks for Jackson, our fight was made against the lines near my front. As the plain along Hood's front was more favorable for the tread of soldiers, he was ordered, as the column of direction, to push for the plateau at the Henry House, in order to cut off retreat at the crossings by Young's Branch. Wilcox was called to support and cover Hood's left, but he lost sight of two of his brigades,--Featherston's and Pryor's, --and only gave the aid of his single brigade. Kemper and Jones were pushed on with Hood's right, Evans in Hood's direct support. The batteries were advanced as rapidly as fields were opened to them, Stribling's, J. B. Richardson's, Eshleman's, and Rogers's having fairest field for progress."

As Longstreet came crashing down from the west and south, sweeping the field before him in just 15 minutes, it became clear to Pope how tenuous his position was. Like the Confederates at First Bull Run, Pope ordered all available reinforcements to take up a defensive line on Henry Hill, and he wrote about the desperate resistance put up by some of the men under his command:

"The main attack of the enemy was made against our left, but was met with stubborn resistance by the divisions of Schenck and Reynolds, and the brigade of Milroy, who were soon reënforced on the left by Ricketts's division. The action was severe for several hours, the enemy bringing up heavy reserves and pouring mass after mass of his troops on our left. He was able also to present at least an equal force all along our line of battle. Porter's corps was halted and reformed, and as soon as it was in condition it was pushed forward to the support of our left, where it rendered distinguished service, especially the brigade of regulars under Colonel (then Lieutenant-Colonel) Buchanan.

McLean's brigade of Schenck's division, which was posted in observation on our left flank, and in support of Reynolds, became exposed to the attack of the enemy on our left when Reynolds's division was drawn back to form line to support Porter's corps, then retiring from their attack, and it was fiercely assailed by Hood and Evans, in greatly superior force. This brigade was commanded in person by General Schenck, the division commander, and fought with supreme gallantry and tenacity. The enemy's attack was repulsed several times with severe loss, but he returned again and again to the assault.

It is needless for me to describe the appearance of a man so well known to the country as General R. C. Schenck. I have only to say that a more gallant and devoted soldier never lived, and to his presence and the fearless exposure of his person during these attacks is largely due the protracted resistance made by this brigade. He fell, badly wounded, in the front of his command, and his loss was deeply felt and had a marked effect on the final result in that part of the field."

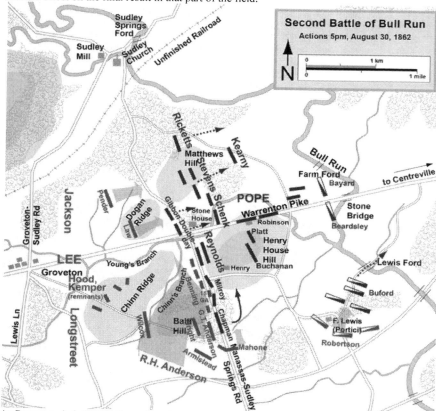

As Pope marshaled more forces into the vacuum around Henry Hill, nightfall became his best friend. By holding out on Henry Hill long enough, Pope kept the Warrenton Turnpike open so that he could retreat east across Bull Run. He was aided in this by the fact that Jackson's wing of the army was too slow to cut off that avenue of retreat, certainly a byproduct of the fact that they had been submitted to the heaviest marching and fighting of the past week. Still, Jackson has been criticized for having the slows, just like during the Seven Days' Battles; John Hennessy considered Jackson's action (or lack of it) "one of the battle's great puzzles" and "one of the most significant Confederate failures".

Though Pope's army didn't scramble back toward Washington in as much disorder as McDowell's army had during the First Battle of Bull Run, the result was ultimately the same. And as if to antagonize Pope even more, around the same time he began retreating across the Warrenton Turnpike toward Centreville, Franklin's corps from McClellan's Army of the Potomac was marching into Centreville, about 5 miles east of Bull Run. Had Franklin been allowed to march even a day earlier, there's no telling how differently the battle might have gone.

Darkness granted Pope the respite Longstreet would not, as Longstreet noted in his memoirs: "When the last guns were fired the thickening twilight concealed the lines of friend and foe, so that the danger of friend firing against friend became imminent. The hill of the Henry House was reached in good time, but darkness coming on earlier because of thickening clouds hovering over us, and a gentle fall of rain closely following, the plateau was shut off from view, and its ascent only found by groping through the darkening rainfall. As long as the enemy held the plateau, he covered the line of retreat by the turnpike and the bridge at Young's Branch. As he retired, heavy darkness gave safe-conduct to such of his columns as could find their way through the weird mists."

The losses at the Second Battle of Bull Run were staggering, especially since the battle took place before Antietam and Gettysburg. About 10,000 soldiers, or nearly 16% of Pope's army, was killed, wounded, or captured, while Lee's army lost nearly 8,500, almost the same percentage of his forces.

**Lee Decides to Invade Maryland**

After two days' fighting, Lee had achieved another major victory, and he now stood unopposed in the field 12 miles away from Washington D.C. While Joseph Johnston and P.G.T. Beauregard had stayed in this position in the months after the First Battle of Bull Run, Lee determined upon a more aggressive course: taking the fight to the North.

In early September, convinced that the best way to defend Richmond was to divert attention to Washington, Lee had decided to invade Maryland after obtaining Jefferson Davis's permission. On September 3, the famous general reported to the Confederate president:

HEADQUARTERS ALEXANDRIA AND LEESBURG ROAD,

Near Dranesville, September 3, 1862.

His Excellency President DAVIS,

Richmond, Va.:

Mr. PRESIDENT: The present seems to be the most propitious time since the commencement of the war for the Confederate Army to enter Maryland. The two grand armies of the United States that have been operating in Virginia, though now united, are much weakened and demoralized. Their new levies, of which I understand 60,000 men have already been posted in Washington, are not yet organized, and will take some time to prepare for the field. If it is ever desired to give material aid to Maryland and afford her an opportunity of throwing off the oppression to which she is now subject, this would seem the most favorable.

After the enemy had disappeared from the vicinity of Fairfax Court House, and taken the road to Alexandria and Washington, I did not think it would be advantageous to follow him farther. I had no intention of attacking him in his fortifications, and am not prepared to invest them. If I possessed the necessary munitions, I should be unable to supply provisions for the troops. I therefore determined, while threatening the approaches to Washington, to draw the troops into Loudoun, where forage and some provisions can be obtained, menace their possession of the Shenandoah Valley, and, if found practicable, to cross into Maryland. The purpose, if discovered, will have the effect of carrying the enemy north of the Potomac, and, if prevented, will not result in much evil.

The army is not properly equipped for an invasion of an enemy's territory. It lacks much of the material of war, is feeble in transportation, the animals being much reduced, and the men are poorly provided with clothes, and in thousands of instances are destitute of shoes. Still, we cannot afford to be idle, and though weaker than our opponents in men and military equipments, must endeavor to harass if we cannot destroy them. I am aware that the movement is attended with much risk, yet I do not consider success impossible, and shall endeavor to guard it from loss. As long as the army of the enemy are employed on this frontier I have no fears for the safety of Richmond, yet I earnestly recommend that advantage be taken of this period of comparative safety to place its defense, both by land and water, in the most perfect condition. A respectable force can be collected to defend its approaches by land, and the steamer Richmond, I hope, is now ready to clear the river of hostile vessels.

Should General Bragg find it impracticable to operate to advantage on his present frontier, his army, after leaving sufficient garrisons, could be advantageously employed in opposing the overwhelming numbers which it seems to be the intention of the enemy now to concentrate in Virginia.

I have already been told by prisoners that some of Buell's cavalry have been joined to General Pope's army, and have reason to believe that the whole of McClellan's, the larger portion of Burnside's and Cox's, and a portion of Hunter's, are united to it.

What occasions me most concern is the fear of getting out of ammunition. I beg you will instruct the Ordnance Department to spare no pains in manufacturing a sufficient amount of the best kind, and to be particular, in preparing that for the artillery, to provide three times as much of the long-range ammunition as of that for smooth-bore or short-range guns. The points to which I desire the ammunition to be forwarded will be made known to the Department in time. If the Quartermaster's Department can furnish any shoes, it would be the greatest relief. We have entered upon September, and the nights are becoming cool.

I have the honor to be, with high respect, your obedient servant,

R. E. LEE, General.

A few days later, Jefferson Davis responded to Lee's suggestion by approving an invasion of Maryland subject to a number of conditions:

General R. E. LEE, Commanding, &c.:

SIR: It is deemed proper that you should, in accordance with established usage, announce, by proclamation to the people of Maryland, the motives and purposes of your presence among them at the head of an invading army, and you are instructed in such proclamation to make known--

1st. That the Confederate Government is waging this war solely for self-defense; that it has no design of conquest, or any other purpose than to secure peace and the abandonment by the United States of their pretensions to govern a people who have never been their subjects, and who prefer self-government to a union with them.

2d. That this Government, at the very moment of its inauguration, sent commissioners to Washington to treat for a peaceful adjustment of all differences, but that these commissioners were not received, nor even allowed to communicate the object of their mission; and that, on a subsequent occasion, a communication from the President of the Confederacy to President Lincoln remained without answer, although a reply was promised by General Scott, into whose hands the communication was delivered.

3d. That among the pretexts urged for continuance of the war, is the assertion that the Confederate Government desires to deprive the United States of the free navigation of the Western rivers, although the truth is that the Confederate Congress, by public act, prior to the commencement of the war, enacted that "the peaceful navigation of the Mississippi River is hereby declared free to the citizens of any of the States upon its boundaries, or upon the borders of its navigable tributaries," a declaration to which this Government has always been, and is still, ready to adhere.

4th. That now, at a juncture when our arms have been successful, we restrict ourselves to the same just and moderate demand that we made at the darkest period of our reverses, the simple demand that the people of the United States should cease to war upon us, and permit us to pursue our own path to happiness, while they in peace pursue theirs.

5th. That we are debarred from the renewal of formal proposals for peace by having no reason to expect that they would be received with the respect mutually due by nations in their intercourse, whether in peace or in war.

6th. That, under these circumstances, we are driven to protect our own country by transferring the seat of war to that of an enemy, who pursues us with a relentless and, apparently, aimless hostility; that our fields have been laid waste, our people killed, many homes made desolate, and that rapine and murder have ravaged our frontiers; that the sacred right of self-defense demands that, if such a war is to continue, its consequences shall fall on those who persist in their refusal to make peace.

7th. That the Confederate army, therefore, comes to occupy the territory of their enemies, and to make it the theater of hostilities; that with the people themselves rests the power to put an end to this invasion of their homes, for, if unable to prevail on the Government of the United States to conclude a general peace, their own State government, in the exercise of its sovereignty, can secure immunity from the desolating effects of warfare on the soil of the State by a separate treaty of peace, which this Government will ever be ready to conclude on the most just and liberal basis.

8th. That the responsibility thus rests on the people of ------- continuing an unjust and oppressive warfare upon the Confederate States--a warfare which can never end in any other manner than that now proposed. With them is the option of preserving the blessings of peace by the simple abandonment of the design of subjugating a people over whom no right of dominion has ever been conferred, either by God or man.

In conjunction with giving Lee his approval, Davis wrote a public proclamation to the Southern people and, ostensibly, the Europeans whose recognition he hoped to gain. Recognizing the political sensitivity of appearing to invade the North instead of simply defending the home front, Davis cast the decision as one of self-defense, and that there was "no design of conquest", asserting, "We are driven to protect our own country by transferring the seat of war to that of an enemy who pursues us with a relentless and apparently aimless hostility."

Once he had his president's approval, Lee actually issued orders to be proclaimed before citizens of Maryland, acutely aware that the border state had plenty of Confederate sympathizers who might not look kindly toward having their state invaded by the Confederate army:

TO THE PEOPLE OF MARYLAND:

It is right that you should know the purpose that has brought the army under my command within the limits of your State, so far as that purpose concerns yourselves.

The people of the Confederate States have long watched with the deepest sympathy the wrongs and outrages that have been inflicted upon the citizens of a Commonwealth allied to the States of the South by the strongest social, political, and commercial ties.

They have seen with profound indignation their sister-State deprived of every right and reduced to the condition of a conquered province.

Under the pretense of supporting the Constitution, but in violation of its most valuable provisions, your citizens have been arrested and imprisoned upon no charge and contrary to all forms of law; the faithful and manly protest against this outrage made by the venerable and illustrious Marylander to whom in better days no citizen appealed for right in vain was treated with scorn and contempt; the government of your chief city has been usurped by armed strangers; your legislature has been dissolved by the unlawful arrest of its members; freedom of the press and of speech has been suppressed; words have been declared offences by an arbitrary decree of the Federal executive, and citizens ordered to be tried by a military commission for what they may dare to speak.

Believing that the people of Maryland possessed a spirit too lofty to submit to such a government, the people of the South have long wished to aid you in throwing off this foreign yoke, to enable you again to enjoy the inalienable rights of freemen and restore independence and sovereignty to your State.

In obedience to this wish our army has come among you, and is prepared to assist you with the power of its arms in regaining the rights of which you have been despoiled.

This, citizens of Maryland, is our mission, so far as you are concerned. No constraint upon your free will is intended ; no intimidation will be allowed. Within the limits of this army at least, Marylanders shall once more enjoy their ancient freedom of thought and speech. We know no enemies among you, and will protect all, of every opinion. It is for you to decide your destiny freely and without constraint.

This army will respect your choice, whatever it may be; and, while the Southern people will rejoice to welcome you to your natural position among them, they will only welcome you when you come of your own free will.

Today the decision to invade Maryland is remembered through the prism of Lee hoping to win a major battle in the North that would bring about European recognition of the Confederacy, potential intervention, and possible capitulation by the North, whose anti-war Democrats were picking up political momentum. However, Lee also hoped that the fighting in Maryland would relieve Virginia's resources, especially the Shenandoah Valley, which served as the state's "breadbasket". And though largely forgotten today, Lee's move was controversial among his own men. Confederate soldiers, including Lee, took up arms to defend their homes, but now they were being asked to invade a Northern state. An untold number of Confederate soldiers refused to cross the Potomac River into Maryland.

Lee hinted at all of this in his report after the campaign while justifying his decision to make the invasion:

"Although not properly equipped for invasion, lacking much of the material of war, and feeble in transportation, the troops poorly provided with clothing, and thousands of them destitute of shoes, it was yet believed to be strong enough to detain the enemy upon the northern frontier until the approach of winter should render his advance into Virginia difficult, if not impracticable. The condition of Maryland encouraged the belief that the presence of our army, however inferior to that of the enemy, would induce the Washington Government to retain all its available force to provide against contingencies, which its course toward the people of that State gave it reason to apprehend. At the same time it was hoped that military success might afford us an opportunity to aid the citizens of Maryland in any efforts they might be disposed to make to recover their liberties. The difficulties that surrounded them were fully appreciated, and we expected to derive more assistance in the attainment of our object from the just fears of the Washington."

For his part, General Longstreet also held the same view as Lee, believing an invasion of Maryland had plenty of advantages. He wrote of the decision in his memoirs, "The Army of Northern Virginia was afield without a foe. Its once grand adversary, discomfited under two commanders, had crept into cover of the bulwarks about the national capital. The commercial, social, and blood ties of Maryland inclined her people to the Southern cause. A little way north of the Potomac were inviting fields of food and supplies more plentiful than on the southern side; and the fields for march and manoeuvre, strategy and tactics, were even more inviting than the broad fields of grain and comfortable pasture-lands. Propitious also was the prospect of swelling our ranks by Maryland recruits."

Lee had also no doubt taken stock of the North's morale, both among its people and the soldiers of Pope's army and McClellan's army. In the summer of 1862, the Union had suffered more than 20,000 casualties, and Northern Democrats, who had been split into pro-war and anti-war factions from the beginning, increasingly began to question the war. As of September 1862, no progress had been made on Richmond; in fact, a Confederate army was now about to enter Maryland. And with the election of 1862 was approaching, Lincoln feared the Republicans might suffer losses in the Congressional midterms that would harm the war effort.

With all of that in mind, he restored General McClellan and removed General Pope after the second disaster at Bull Run. McClellan was still immensely popular among the Army of the Potomac, and with a mixture of men from his Army of the Potomac and Pope's Army of Virginia, he began a cautious pursuit of Lee into Maryland.

Although McClellan had largely stayed out of the political fray through 1862, McClellan's most ardent supporters could not deny that he actively worked to delay reinforcing Pope during the Second Manassas campaign once the Army of the Potomac was evacuated from the Peninsula. Nevertheless, McClellan ultimately got what he wanted out of Pope's misfortune. Though there is some debate on the order of events that led to McClellan taking command, Lincoln ultimately restored McClellan to command, likely because McClellan was the only administrator who could reform the army quickly and efficiently.

**McClellan**

Naturally, McClellan's ascension to command of the armies around Washington outraged the Republicans in Congress and the Lincoln Administration, some of whom had all but branded him a traitor for his inactivity in early 1862 and his poor performance on the Peninsula. This would make it all the more ironic that McClellan's campaign into Maryland during the next few weeks would bring about the release of the Emancipation Proclamation.

**Initial Movements**

The most fateful decision of the Maryland Campaign was made almost immediately, when early on Lee decided to divide his army into four parts across Maryland. Lee ordered Longstreet's men to Boonsboro and then to Hagerstown, Stonewall Jackson's forces to Harpers Ferry, and Stuart's cavalry and D.H. Hill's division to screen the Army of Northern Virginia's movements and cover its rear.

**D.H. Hill**

Why Lee chose to divide his army is still heavily debated among historians, who have pointed to factors like the importance of maintaining his supply lines through the Shenandoah Valley. Lee was also unaware what kind of resistance he might face at places like Frederick and Harpers Ferry, and it's also possible that he simply assumed McClellan's caution would allow him to take and keep the initiative and dictate the course of the campaign. With McClellan now assuming command of the Northern forces, Lee probably expected to have plenty of time to assemble his troops and bring his battle plan to fruition.

This time, however, McClellan was better prepared to face Lee. He had beaten Lee in a campaign through western Virginia in 1861 and had clearly underestimated Lee as a result during the Peninsula Campaign, but now he realized that Lee was not the timid, indecisive general McClellan initially thought.

Though it was clear in early September that Lee had crossed the Potomac, the Army of Northern Virginia decided to use ridges, mountains and cavalry to screen their movements. McClellan believed the most realistic goal was to drive the Confederates out of Maryland and aimed to do so, but his 85,000 strong Army of the Potomac moved conservatively into Maryland during the early portion of the campaign while still dealing with logistics. A report from the infamous intelligence chief Allan Pleasanton reached McClellan and estimated the Rebel force at 100,000, while other reports couldn't ascertain the nature of the that army's movements or motives. McClellan told the Administration on September 10 that the estimates of the Army of Northern Virginia put it somewhere between 80,000-150,000 men, which obviously had a huge effect on the campaign.

With the benefit of hindsight, historians now believe that Lee's entire Army of Northern Virginia had perhaps 50,000 men at most and possibly closer to 30,000 during the Maryland campaign. It's unclear how Lee's army, which numbered 55,000 before the Maryland Campaign, suffered such a steep drop in manpower, but historians have cited a number of factors, including disease and soldiers' refusal to invade the North. Lee clearly felt the pinch too, ordering his officers to keep straggling to a minimum and calling stragglers "unworthy members of an army that has immortalized itself". And far from Longstreet's hope that an invasion of Maryland would swell the Confederate ranks with sympathizers, it's estimated that only a few dozen at most latched on with the invading army in Maryland. Union general John Gibbon, who commanded the famed Iron Brigade, also admitted his surprise with the people of Maryland, later writing, "I did not believe before coming here that there was so much Union feeling in the state... The whole population [of Frederick] seemed to turn out to welcome us. When Genl McClellan came thro the ladies nearly eat him up, they kissed his clothing, threw their arms around his horse's neck and committed all sorts of extravagances."

**Gibbon**

In his post-campaign report, Lee summarized the initial movements of his army leading up to September 12:

"It was decided to cross the Potomac east of the Blue Ridge, in order, by threatening Washington and Baltimore, to cause the enemy to withdraw from the south bank, where his presence endangered our communications and the safety of those engaged in the removal of our wounded and the captured property from the late battlefields. Having accomplished this result, it was proposed to move the army into Western Maryland, establish our communications with Richmond through the Valley of the Shenandoah, and, by threatening Pennsylvania, induce the enemy to follow, and thus draw him from his base of supplies.

It had been supposed that the advance upon Fredericktown would lead to the evacuation of Martinsburg and Harper's Ferry, thus opening the line of communication through the Valley. This not having occurred, it became necessary to dislodge the enemy from those positions before concentrating the army west of the mountains. To accomplish this with the least delay, General Jackson was directed to proceed with his command to Martinsburg, and, after driving the enemy from that place, to move down the south side of the Potomac upon Harper's Ferry. General McLaws, with his own and

R. H. Anderson's division, was ordered to seize Maryland Heights, on the north side of the Potomac, opposite Harper's Ferry, and Brigadier-General Walker to take possession of Loudoun Heights, on the east side of the Shenandoa, where it unites with the Potomac. These several commands were directed, after reducing Harper's Ferry and clearing the Valley of the enemy, to join the rest of the army at Boonsborough or Hagerstown.

The march of these troops began on the 10th, and at the same time the remainder of Longstreet's command and the division of D. H. Hill crossed the South Mountain and moved toward Boonsborough. General Stuart, with the cavalry, remained east of the mountains, to observe the enemy and retard his advance.

A report having been received that a Federal force was approaching Hagerstown from the direction of Chambersburg, Longstreet continued his march to the former place, in order to secure the road leading thence to Williamsport, and also to prevent the removal of stores which were said to be in Hagerstown. He arrived at that place on the 11th, General Hill halting near Boonsborough to prevent the enemy at Harper's Ferry from escaping through Pleasant Valley, and at the same time to support the cavalry. The advance of the Federal Army was so slow at the time we left Fredericktown as to justify the belief that the reduction of Harper's Ferry would be accomplished and our troops concentrated before they would be called upon to meet it. In that event, it had not been intended to oppose its passage through the South Mountains, as it was desired to engage it as far as possible from its base.

General Jackson marched very rapidly, and, crossing the Potomac near Williamsport on the 11th, sent A. P. Hill's division directly to Martinsburg, and disposed the rest of his command to cut off the retreat of the enemy westward. On his approach, the Federal troops evacuated Martinsburg, retiring to Harper's Ferry on the night of the 11th, and Jackson entered the former place on the 12th, capturing some prisoners and abandoned stores."

**The Lost Order**

On September 12, Stonewall Jackson's men were making their way to the outskirts of Harpers Ferry, whose garrison McClellan had unsuccessfully requested to have evacuated and added to his army. Meanwhile, the Union army was on the verge of entering Frederick, still unaware of Lee's dispositions but less than 20 miles behind the fragmented Confederate army.

It was around Frederick that the North was about to have one of the greatest strokes of luck during the Civil War. For reasons that are still unclear, Union troops in camp at Frederick came across a copy of Special Order 191, wrapped up among three cigars. The order contained Lee's entire marching plans for Maryland, making it clear that the Army of Northern Virginia had been divided into multiple parts, which, if faced by overpowering strength, could be entirely defeated in detail and bagged separately before they could regather into one fighting force. The Lost Order had been issued on September 9, and it read:

HDQRS. ARMY OF NORTHERN VIRGINIA,

September 9, 1862.

I. The citizens of Fredericktown being unwilling, while overrun by members of his army, to open their stores, in order to give them confidence, and to secure to officers and men purchasing supplies for benefit of this command, all officers and men of this army are strictly prohibited from visiting Fredericktown except on business, in which case they will bear evidence of this in writing from division commanders. The provost-marshal in Fredericktown will see that his guard rigidly enforces this order.

II. Major Taylor will proceed to Leesburg, Va., and arrange for transportation of the sick and those unable to walk to Winchester, securing the transportation of the country for this purpose. The route between this and Culpeper Court-House east of the mountains being unsafe will no longer be traveled. Those on the way to this army already across the river will move up promptly; all others will proceed to Winchester collectively and under command of officers, at which point, being the general depot of this army, its movements will be known and instructions given by commanding officer regulating further movements.

III. The army will resume its march tomorrow, taking the Hagerstown road. General Jackson's command will form the advance, and, after passing Middletown, with such portion as he may select, take the route toward Sharpsburg, cross the Potomac at the most convenient point, and by Friday morning take possession of the Baltimore and Ohio Railroad, capture such of them as may be at Martinsburg, and intercept such as may attempt to escape from Harper's Ferry.

IV. General Longstreet's command will pursue the main road as far as Boonsborough, where it will halt, with reserve, supply, and baggage trains of the army.

V. General McLaws, with his own division and that of General R. H. Anderson, will follow General Longstreet. On reaching Middletown will take the route to Harper's Ferry, and by Friday morning possess himself of the Maryland Heights and endeavor to capture the enemy at Harper's Ferry and vicinity.

VI. General Walker, with his division, after accomplishing the object in which he is now engaged, will cross the Potomac at Cheek's Ford, ascend its right bank to Lovettsville, take possession of Loudoun Heights, if practicable, by Friday morning, Keys' Ford on his left, and the road between the end of the mountain and the Potomac on his right. He will, as far as practicable, co-operate with Generals McLaws and Jackson, and intercept retreat of the enemy.

VII. General D. H. Hill's division will form the rear guard of the army, pursuing the road taken by the main body. The reserve artillery, ordnance, and supply trains, &c., will precede General Hill.

VIII. General Stuart will detach a squadron of cavalry to accompany the commands of Generals Longstreet, Jackson, and McLaws, and, with the main body of the cavalry, will cover the route of the army, bringing up all stragglers that may have been left behind.

IX. The commands of Generals Jackson, McLaws, and Walker, after accomplishing the objects for which they have been detached, will join the main body of the army at Boonsborough or Hagerstown.

X. Each regiment on the march will habitually carry its axes in the regimental ordnance wagons, for use of the men at their encampments, to procure wood, &c.

By command of General R. E. Lee:

R. H. CHILTON,

Assistant Adjutant-General.

The "Lost Order" quickly made its way to General McClellan, who took several hours to debate whether or not it was intentional misinformation or actually real. McClellan is usually faulted for not acting quickly enough on these orders, but much of the instructions are vague and seemingly contradicted recent Rebel movements. Moreover, McClellan was rightly concerned that the orders could be false misinformation meant to deceive the Union, since the manner in which the orders were lost was bizarre and could not be accounted for. After about 18 hours, McClellan was confident enough that they were accurate and famously boasted to General Gibbon, "Here is a paper with which if I cannot whip *Bobby Lee,* I will be willing to go home."

McClellan also wired Lincoln, "I have the whole rebel force in front of me, but I am confident, and no time shall be lost. I think Lee has made a gross mistake, and that he will be severely punished for it. I have all the plans of the rebels, and will catch them in their own trap if my men are equal to the emergency… Will send you trophies."

Though having Lee's marching plans offered McClellan an incredible advantage, the Lost Order may also have reinforced McClellan's belief that Lee's army had a significant advantage in manpower through its vague wording of "commands."

**Harpers Ferry**

**Harpers Ferry in the 1860s**

As General Lee marched his Army of Northern Virginia down the Shenandoah Valley into Maryland, he planned to capture the garrison and arsenal at Harpers Ferry to secure his supply line back to Virginia. But even before they were far into Maryland, Jackson and Hill were getting on each other's nerves, and after one scolding from Jackson on September 3, witnesses noticed Hill responded to the reprimand "rather sullenly, his face flushing up."

During another march, Hill became furious after finding that Jackson had directly ordered his division to halt without informing Hill of the change in plans. When Hill asked his subordinates why they halted, and he was informed that it was Jackson's orders, he confronted Jackson and offered him his sword, telling him, "If you take command of my troops in my presence, take my sword also." Jackson responded, "Put up your sword and consider yourself in arrest." Another Confederate soldier remembered afterward that Hill "marched on foot with the rear guard all the day through Maryland, an old white hat slouched over his eyes, his coat off and wearing an old flannel shirt, looking mad as a bull."

Eventually, both of the generals cooled their tempers, and by September 10 Hill was asking to be restored to command ahead of battle, a request Jackson granted. A Confederate noted that after being restored to command, Hill " mounted his horse and dashed to the front of his troops, and looking like a young eagle in search of his prey, took command of his division to the delight of all his men."

The Confederates were completely unaware of the Army of the Potomac's luck as they began to carry out Lee's plans, and Stonewall Jackson was already in the process of forcing the capitulation of Harpers Ferry.

To Stonewall Jackson's advantage, Col. Dixon S. Miles, Union commander at Harpers Ferry, had insisted on keeping most of his troops near the town instead of taking up commanding positions on the most important position, Maryland Heights. On September 12, Confederate forces engaged the Union's marginal defenses on the heights, but only a brief skirmish ensued. Then on September 13, two Confederate brigades arrived and easily drove the Union troops from the heights, even as critical positions to the west and south of town remained heavily defended.

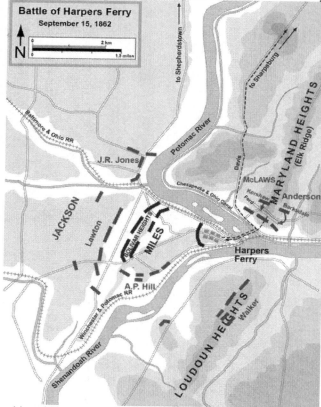

On September 14, as the Army of the Potomac was bearing down on the Confederates around

South Mountain several miles away, Jackson had methodically positioned his artillery around Harpers Ferry and ordered Maj. Gen. A. P. Hill to move down the west bank of the Shenandoah River in preparation for a flank attack on the Union left the next morning. While Miles suggested surrendering, several officers among the garrison argued that they should attempt a breakout. When Miles suggested it was a "wild and impractical" idea, Benjamin "Grimes" Davis made clear that he would attempt it with men from the 12th Illinois Cavalry, the Loudoun Rangers, and other small units. Eventually, Davis successfully led about 1,400 men out of Harpers Ferry and inadvertently ran into the wagon train carrying Longstreet's ordnance. Porter Alexander, the chief artillerist of Longstreet's corps, explained, "My reserve ordnance train, of about 80 wagons, had accompanied Lee's headquarters to Hagerstown, and had also followed the march back to Boonsboro. I was now ordered to cross the Potomac at Williamsport, and go thence to Shepherdstown, where I should leave the train and come in person to Sharpsburg. The moon was rising as I started, and about daylight I forded the Potomac, unaware of having had a narrow escape from capture, with my train, by Gregg's brigade of cavalry. This brigade had escaped that night from Harper's Ferry, and crossed our line of retreat from Boonsboro. It had captured and destroyed the reserve ordnance train, of 45 wagons of Longstreet's corps."

By the following morning, September 15, Jackson had positioned nearly fifty guns on Maryland Heights and at the base of Loudoun Heights. Then he began a fierce artillery barrage from all sides, followed by a full-out infantry assault. Realizing the hopelessness of the situation, Col. Miles raised the white flag of surrender, enraging some of the men, one of whom beseeched him, "Colonel, don't surrender us. Don't you hear the signal guns? Our forces are near us. Let us cut our way out and join them." Miles dismissed the suggestion, insisting, "They will blow us out of this place in half an hour." Almost on cue, an exploding artillery shell mortally wounded Miles, and some historians have argued Miles was fragged by Union soldiers.

Jackson had lost less than 300 casualties while forcing the surrender of nearly 12,500 Union soldiers at Harpers Ferry, the largest number of Union soldiers to surrender at once during the entire war. For the rest of the day, the Confederates helped themselves to supplies in the garrison, including food, uniforms, and more, as Jackson sent a letter to Lee informing him of the success, "Through God's blessing, Harper's Ferry and its garrison are to be surrendered." Already a legend, Jackson earned the attention of the surrendered Union troops, who tried to catch a glimpse of him only to be surprised at his rather disheveled look. One of the men remarked, "Boys, he isn't much for looks, but if we'd had him we wouldn't have been caught in this trap."

Jackson had little time to celebrate before hearing back from Lee ordering him to quickly march to Sharpsburg as soon as he could. But the surrender of Harpers Ferry still needed to be fully processed, so Jackson ordered A.P. Hill's Light Division to remain at Harpers Ferry and carry out all the necessities, including the parole of the Union prisoners. Jackson would recount in his post-battle report, "By a severe night's march we reached the vicinity of Sharpsburg on the morning of the 16th."

### South Mountain

It's unclear when Lee realized that McClellan had found a copy of his marching orders, and it's even possible that he knew almost right away. But that still gave Lee, who only had about 18,000 men at his disposal in the vicinity, little time to regroup. On the night of September 13 McClellan's army began moving at an uncharacteristically quick pace, and the following day, the advancing Union army began pushing in on the Confederate forces at several mountain passes at South Mountain: Crampton's Gap, Turner's Gap, and Fox's Gap. If McClellan's men could successfully push their way through these gaps, they would have an even greater chance of falling upon the different pieces of Lee's army. Lee explained this in his report to Jefferson Davis after the campaign:

"Mr. PRESIDENT: My letter to you of the 13th instant informed you of the positions of the different divisions of this army. Learning that night that Harper's Ferry had not surrendered, and that the enemy was advancing more rapidly than was convenient from Fredericktown, I determined to return with Longstreet's command to the Blue Ridge, to strengthen D. H. Hill's and Stuart's divisions, engaged in holding the passes of the mountains, lest the enemy should fall upon McLaws' rear, drive him from the Maryland Heights, and thus relieve the garrison at Harper's Ferry."

Despite being significantly outnumbered, Lee's army had the advantage of fighting defensively on higher terrain. At Crampton's Gap, Union General William Franklin's nearly 13,000 strong VI Corps crashed down on about 2,000 Confederates led by Howell Cobb who were part of Lafayette McLaws' division. McClellan had ordered Franklin's corps to set out for Crampton's Gap on the morning of September 14, wasting nearly 11 hours in the process, and Franklin delayed his assault for 3 more hours while arranging his lines for what turned out to be a short fight. Though Franklin's men eventually took Crampton's Gap, his failure to follow it up by pursuing the Confederates not only spared McLaws' division but also allowed Stonewall Jackson's forces to rejoin Lee's men near Sharpsburg early on September 16.

Meanwhile, it fell upon Confederates under Maj. Gen. D.H. Hill to defend Turner's Gap and Fox's Gap, thus stretching just 5,000 Confederates across two gaps separated by several miles. At Turner's Gap, the Union's Iron Brigade earned its first glory and its eternal nickname for attacking uphill against the Confederate brigade under Colonel Alfred H. Colquitt. The Iron Brigade's comrades in Union General Joseph Hooker's I Corps were also positioned on opposite sides of the gap, forcing Confederate Brig. Gen. Robert E. Rodes to retreat from his exposed position. However, the rearguard action resulted in the Union running out of daylight on September 14, with Confederates still holding Turner's Gap.

Meanwhile, to the south of Turner's Gap, other troops from D.H. Hill's division defended Fox's Gap against Union General Jesse Reno's IX Corps. Despite attacking at 9:00 a.m., fierce fighting took place as reinforcements on both sides swept in across the lines. Reno himself was killed during the fighting, and Confederates continued to hold the gap at the close of the fighting. Lee later reported about the fighting at South Mountain:

"The effort to force the passage of the mountains had failed, but it was manifest that without re-enforcements we could not hazard a renewal of the engagement, as the enemy could easily turn either flank. Information was also received that another large body of Federal troops had during the afternoon forced their way through Crampton's Gap, only 5 miles in rear of McLaws. Under these circumstances, it was determined to retire to Sharpsburg, where we would be upon the flank and rear of the enemy should he move against McLaws, and where we could more readily unite with the rest of the army. This movement was efficiently and skillfully covered by the cavalry brigade of General Fitzhugh Lee, and was accomplished without interruption by the enemy, who did not appear on the west side of the pass at Boonsborough until about 8 a.m. on the following morning. The resistance that had been offered to the enemy at Boonsborough secured sufficient time to enable General Jackson to complete the reduction of Harper's Ferry."

Thus, despite the fact the Confederates had clung to two of the three passes, their precarious position left the defenders at each exposed, and by withdrawing them all, Lee had no choice but to give McClellan a chance to bring battle before his entire army was together. South Mountain was the first major pitched battle between the two sides in September, and the Union had given as good as it got, prompting *The New York World* to write that the battle at South Mountain would "turn back the tide of rebel successes" and report that "the strength of the rebels is hopelessly broken."

Ambrose Burnside, who would play a controversial role at Antietam, believed that South Mountain had been a "brilliant" success, writing in his post-campaign report:

"Early on the morning of the 14th, General Pleasonton commenced his reconnaissance of Turner's Gap and South Mountain, assisted by Cox's division, supported by Willcox's division, of General Reno's corps, and found the enemy in force. General Pleasonton had reconnoitered the ground fully, and, after posting Benjamin's and Gibson's batteries on the high grounds immediately in front of the gap, indicated to Cox's division the road that should be taken in order to turn the enemy's right. This division and Willcox's division became engaged immediately.

Soon after, I arrived on the ground with General Reno, and directed him to order up General Rodman's and General Sturgis' division to sup port Cox's division, which had passed up to the left of the main gap by the Sharpsburg road over the South Mountain. After these divisions had passed on to the front, General Reno moved on and took the immediate command of his corps. Soon after, General Hooker's corps arrived, composed of the divisions of Generals Meade, Ricketts, Hatch, and Doubleday, and I ordered it to move up to the right of the main pike, by the Old Hagerstown road, and, if possible, turn the enemy's left and get in his rear. At the same time I detached from his corps General Gibbon's brigade, with Captain Campbell's battery, for the purpose of making a demonstration upon the enemy's center, up the main pike, as soon as the movements of Generals Hooker and Reno had sufficiently progressed. At the same time I sent orders to General Reno, whose corps had been sharply engaged all the morning, to move upon the enemy's position with his whole three as soon as I informed him that General Hooker was well advanced up the crest of the mountain on our right.

About this time the general commanding arrived on the ground, and I repeated to him my dispositions, which he fully approved. He remained at my headquarters during the remainder of the engagement, and I reported to him, personally, all the orders that I gave from that time.

The orders given to both Generals Hooker and Reno were most skillfully and successfully executed, after which General Gibbon was ordered forward just before sunset, and succeeded in pushing his command up the main road to within a short distance of the crest of the main pass, during which movement he had a most brilliant engagement after night-fall, our forces gradually driving the enemy before them.

At this time, say 8 p.m., the enemy had been driven from their strong positions, and the firing ceased, except upon our extreme left, where General Reno's division, then under command of General Cox (General Reno having been killed about 7 p.m.), were partially engaged till 10 o'clock.

My command, having been engaged for a greater part of the day upon the crests of the mountain without water, and many without food, were very much exhausted. Nevertheless they maintained their positions, and were ready on the following morning for an advance on the enemy, who had retreated in the direction of Sharpsburg during the night."

**Hooker**

## Dispositions Before the Battle of Antietam

Lee braced himself for renewed hostilities on September 15, but McClellan remained cautious and did not attack the Confederates that day, allowing Jackson to finish off the garrison at Harpers Ferry and make his way back to Lee on September 16. By that point, Lee had already decided to pull back his army to Sharpsburg, with its back to the Potomac River and its front along Antietam Creek, affording his army at least one natural obstacle separating his army from McClellan's.

McClellan's lead elements arrived around Sharpsburg on the night of September 15, and the rest of the army came up on September 16, but McClellan did not order a general attack that day out of fear that he was still heavily outnumbered. Had he done so, he would not only have had an overwhelming advantage but would not have had to deal with A.P. Hill's Light Division, which was still busy at Harpers Ferry. Lee explained McClellans movements on the 16th:

"On the 16th the artillery fire became warmer, and continued throughout the day. The enemy crossed the Antietam beyond the reach of our batteries and menaced our left. In anticipation of this movement, Hood's two brigades had been transferred from the right and posted between D. H. Hill and the Hagerstown road. General Jackson was now directed to take position on Hood's left, and formed his line with his right resting upon the Hagerstown road and his left extending toward the Potomac, protected by General Stuart with the cavalry and horse artillery. General Walker, with his two brigades, was stationed on Longstreet's right. As evening approached, the enemy opened more vigorously with his artillery, and bore down heavily with his infantry upon Hood, but the attack was gallantly repulsed. At 10 p.m. Hood's troops were relieved by the brigades of Lawton and Trimble, of Ewell's division, commanded by General Lawton. Jackson's own division, under General J. R. Jones, was on Lawton's left, supported by the remaining brigades of Ewell."

With McClellan's men all in position on the night of the 16th, McClellan decided to give general battle on the 17th. Longstreet described the scene before the battle commenced: "The blue uniforms of the federals appeared among the trees that crowned the heights on the eastern bank of the Antietam. The number increased, and larger and larger grew the field of blue until is seemed to stretch as far as the eye could see, and from the tops of the mountains down to the edge of the stream gathered the great army of McClellan."[1]

Still operating under the belief that he was outnumbered, McClellan's plan was to break Lee's left flank in the northern sector, because the crosses that he knew about over Antietam Creek (Burnside's Bridge and the bridge leading to Boonsboro) were held on the other side by Confederates who could operate along the high ground. McClellan's cavalry had not scouted other passes along Antietam Creek, and he and his officers seemed to be unaware that the Antietam Creek was so shallow in places around those bridges that the men could have waded across without trying to squeeze across bridges.

Worried about being outnumbered, McClellan's plan called for an assault with only half his army, starting with two corps along the Confederate left, and the support of perhaps a third or fourth corps. Meanwhile, he initially planned to launch diversionary attacks in the center and the Confederate right. However, the late night skirmishing and probing conducted by men of Hooker's I Corps on the night of the 16th suggested to Lee that they would attack there in force on the morning of the 17th, and before the battle he bolstered his left flank. He also sent word to A.P. Hill and Lafayette McLaws to force march with all haste to Sharpsburg.

---

[1]   Gaffney, P., and D. Gaffney. *The Civil War: Exploring History One Week at a Time.* Page 179.

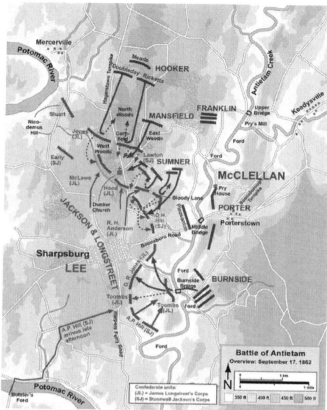

**The dispositions at Antietam and the action during the 17th**

## The Beginning of the Battle

As Lee had guessed, and as McClellan intended, the Battle of Antietam began near dawn on the morning of the 17th, with the advance of Hooker's I Corps down the Hagerstown Turnpike toward the small white Dunker Church, a small one room building that served as a church for a small group of German Baptists. Initially opposing Hooker's 8,500 man Corps were Stonewall Jackson's men, which numbered just under 8,000. Jackson's defenders were deployed across the Turnpike in the West Woods on the left, and a cornfield on the right.

**The Dunker Church in the background**

Hooker decided to start the fighting with an artillery bombardment due to the fact that the nature of the terrain made it unclear what his corps would be facing in the cornfield and the West Woods. Hooker's men could see the Confederates' bayonets shining in the cornfield, but the corn was high enough to conceal their number. During the artillery duel, infantry pushed forward until there was a fierce pitched battle in the cornfield, including hand-to-hand fighting. Colonel Benjamin Cook of the 12th Massachusetts later recalled his experience in the cornfield as "the most deadly fire of the war. Rifles are shot to pieces in the hands of the soldiers, canteens and haversacks are riddled with bullets, the dead and wounded go down in scores."

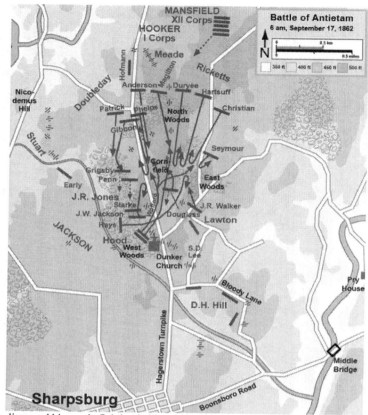

Battle of Antietam
6 am, September 17, 1862

350 ft 400 ft 450 ft 500 ft

Jackson discussed his men's fighting in his post-battle report:

"About sunrise the Federal infantry advanced in heavy force to the edge of the wood on the eastern side of the turnpike, driving in our skirmishers. Batteries were opened in front from the the wood with shell and canister, and our troops became exposed for near an hour to a terrific storm of shell, canister, and musketry. Gen. Jones having been compelled to leave the field, the command of Jackson's division devolved upon Gen. Starke. With heroic spirit our lines advanced to the conflict, and maintained their position, in the face of superior numbers, with stubborn resolution, sometimes driving the enemy before them and sometimes compelled to fall back before their well-sustained and destructive fire. Fresh troops from time to time relieved the enemy's ranks, and the carnage on both sides was terrific.

At this early hour Gen. Starke was killed. Col. Douglass, commanding Lawton's brigade, was also killed. Gen. Lawton, commanding division, and Col. Walker, commanding brigade, were severely wounded. More than half of the brigades of

Lawton and Hays were either killed or wounded, and more than a third of Trimble's, and all the regimental commanders in those brigades, except two, were killed or wounded. Thinned in their ranks and exhausted of their ammunition, Jackson's division and the brigades of Lawton, Hays, and Trimble retired to the rear, and Hood, of Longstreet's command, again took the position from which he had been before relieved.

In the mean time Gen. Stuart moved his artillery to a position nearer to the main command, and more in our rear. Early, being now directed, in consequence of the disability of Gen. Lawton, to take command of Ewell's division, returned with his brigade (with the exception of the Thirteenth Virginia Regiment, which remained with Gen. Stuart) to the piece of wood where he had left the other brigades of his division when he was separated from them. Here he found that the enemy had advanced his infantry near the wood in which was the Dunkard church, and had planted a battery across the turnpike near the edge of the wood and an open field, and that the brigades of Lawton, Hays, and Trimble had fallen back some distance to the rear. Finding here Cols. Grigsby and Stafford, with a portion of Jackson's division, which formed on his left, he determined to maintain his position there if re-enforcements could be sent to his support, of which he was promptly assured. Col. Grigsby, with his small command, kept in check the advance of the enemy on the left flank, while Gen. Early attacked with great vigor and gallantry the column on his right and front."

Abner Doubleday, though wrongly credited for inventing baseball, led the division making the attack on the Confederates' far left. He would later report about the fierce fighting in the vicinity of the West Woods:

"The general order of battle was for two regiments of Patrick's brigade to precede the main body, deployed as skirmishers, and supported by Patrick's two remaining regiments; these to be followed by Phelps' brigade, 200 paces in the rear, and this in turn by Doubleday's brigade, with the same interval. In accordance with this disposition, General Patrick deployed the Twenty-first New York, under Colonel Rogers, as skirmishers on the right, and the Thirty-fifth New York, under Colonel Lord, on the left, supporting the former with the Twentieth New York Militia, Lieutenant-Colonel Gates, and the latter with the Twenty-third New York, Colonel Hoffman.

By General Hatch's order, Phelps' brigade advanced in column of divisions at half distance, preserving the intervals of deployment. My brigade advanced in the same order. On reaching a road part way up the mountain, and parallel to its summit, each brigade deployed in turn and advanced in line of battle. Colonel Phelps' brigade, owing to an accidental opening, preceded for a while our line of skirmishers, but soon halted, and advanced in line some 30 paces in their rear. General Patrick rode to the front with his skirmishers, drew the fire of the enemy, and developed their position. They lay behind a fence on the summit running north and south, fronted by a woods and backed by a corn-field, full of rocky ledges. Colonel Phelps now ordered his men to advance, and General Hatch rode through the lines, pressing them forward. They went in with a cheer, poured in a deadly fire, and drove the enemy from his position behind the fence, after a short and desperate conflict, and took post some yards beyond.

Here General Hatch was wounded and turned over the command to me, and as during the action Colonel Wainwright, Seventy-sixth New York Volunteers, was also wounded, the command of my brigade subsequently devolved upon Lieutenant-Colonel Hermann, Fifty-sixth Pennsylvania Volunteers. Phelps' brigade being few in number, and having suffered severely, I relieved them just at dusk with my brigade, reduced by former engagements to about 1,000 men, who took position beyond the fence referred to, the enemy being in heavy force some 30 or 40 paces in our front. They pressed heavily upon us, attempting to charge at the least cessation of our fire. At last I ordered the troops to cease firing, lie down behind the fence, and allowed the enemy to charge to within about 15 paces, apparently under the impression that we had given way. Then, at the word, my men sprang to their feet and poured in a deadly volley, from which the enemy fled in disorder, leaving their dead within 30 feet of our line.

I learned from a wounded prisoner that we were engaged with 4,000 to 5,000, under the immediate command of General Pickett, with heavy masses in their vicinity. He stated also that Longstreet in vain tried to rally the men, calling them his pets, and using every effort to induce them to renew the attack. The firing on both sides still continued, my men aiming at the flashes of the enemy's muskets, as it was too dark to see objects distinctly, until our cartridges were reduced to two or three rounds.

General Ricketts now came from the right and voluntarily relieved my men at the fence, who fell back some 10 paces and lay down on their arms. A few volleys from Ricketts ended the contest in about thirty minutes, and the enemy withdrew from the field--not, however, until an attempt to flank us on our left, which was gallantly met by a partial change of front of the Seventy-sixth New York Volunteers, under Colonel Wainwright, and the Seventh Indiana, under Major Grover. In this attempt the enemy lost heavily, and were compelled to retreat in disorder.

While the main attack was going on at the fence referred to, Colonel Rogers, with his own and Lieutenant-Colonel Gates' regiments (the Twentieth New York State Militia and Twenty-first New York Volunteers, of Patrick's brigade), rendered most essential service by advancing his right and holding a fence bounding the northeast side of the same corn-field, anticipating the enemy, who made a furious rush to seize this fence, but were driven back. Colonel Rogers was thus enabled to take the enemy in flank, and also to pick off their cannoneers and silence a battery which was at the right and behind their main body."

Despite Jackson's valiant defense, the Union advance kept pushing forward along the West Woods and the Turnpike, and Jackson's line was on the verge of collapse by 7:00 a.m. In one of the most legendary parts of the battle, John Bell Hood's Texans had come up to the field and had not eaten breakfast, so they were held in reserve and allowed to start preparing a meal. Just before they could eat, however, they were called into action, infuriating his men. Thankfully for the Confederates, it would be the Union who felt the brunt of their fury. Hood explained:

"The extreme suffering of my troops for want of food induced me to ride back to General Lee, and request him to send two or more brigades to our relief, at least for the night, in order that the soldiers might have a chance to cook their meagre rations. He said that he would cheerfully do so, but he knew of no command which could be spared for the purpose; he, however, suggested I should see General Jackson and endeavor to obtain assistance from him. After riding a long time in search of the latter, I finally discovered him alone, lying upon the ground, asleep by the root of a tree. I aroused him and made known the half-starved condition of my troops; he immediately ordered Lawton's, Trimble's and Hays's brigades to our relief. He exacted of me, however, a promise that I would come to the support of these forces the moment I was called upon. I quickly rode off in search of my wagons, that the men might prepare and cook their flour, as we were still without meat; unfortunately the night was then far advanced, and, although every effort was made amid the darkness to get the wagons forward, dawn of the morning of the 17th broke upon us before many of the men had had time to do more than prepare the dough. Soon thereafter an officer of Lawton's staff dashed up to me, saying, "General Lawton sends his compliments with the request that you come at once to his support." "To arms" was instantly sounded and quite a large number of my brave soldiers were again obliged to march to the front, leaving their uncooked rations in camp.

Still, indomitable amid every trial, they moved off by the right flank to occupy the same position we had left the night previous. As we passed, about sunrise, across the pike and through the gap in the fence just in front of Dunkard Church, General Lawton, who had been wounded, was borne to the rear upon a litter, and the only Confederate troops, left on that part of the field, were some forty men who had rallied round the gallant Harry Hays. I rode up to the latter, and, finding that his soldiers had expended all their ammunition, I suggested to him to retire, to replenish his cartridge boxes, and reassemble his command.

My command remained near the church, with empty cartridge boxes, holding aloft their colors whilst Frobel's batteries rendered most effective service in position further to the right, where nearly all the guns of the battalion were disabled. Upon the arrival of McLaws's Division, we marched to the rear, renewed our supply of ammunition, and returned to our position in the wood, near the church, which ground we held till a late hour in the afternoon, when we moved somewhat further to the right and bivouacked for the night."

Hood's division had helped the Confederates stave off the first major assault in the West Woods, and Hooker's attack fizzled out in part because Hooker was seriously injured during the fighting. Hooker had been seemingly everywhere during the fighting, and many of his comrades believed that Antietam would have turned out differently had he not been injured. Before his injury, Hooker said of the cornfield, "every stalk of corn in the northern and greater part of the field was cut as closely as could have been done with a knife, and the slain lay in rows precisely as they had stood in their ranks a few moments before."

Hooker was replaced by George Meade, who would ironically also replace Hooker as commander of the Army of the Potomac before Gettysburg, and Meade explained to his wife after the battle:

"Yesterday and the day before my division commenced the battle, and was in the thickest of it. I was hit by a spent grape-shot, giving me a severe contusion on the right thigh, but not breaking the skin. Baldy [Meade's horse] was shot through the neck, but will get over it. A cavalry horse I mounted afterwards was shot in the flank. When General Hooker was wounded, General McClellan placed me in command of the army corps, over General Ricketts's head, who ranked me. This selection is a great compliment, and answers all my wishes in regard to my desire to have my services appreciated. I cannot ask for more, and am truly grateful for the merciful manner I have been protected, and for the good fortune that has attended me. I go into the action to-day as the commander of an army corps. If I survive, my two stars are secure, and if I fall, you will have my reputation to live on. God bless you all! I cannot write more. I am well and in fine spirits. Your brother Willie is up here, but was not in action yesterday."

As the I Corps' attack fizzled out, Jackson explained what happened next:

The force in front was giving way under this attack when another heavy column of Federal troops were seen moving across the plateau on his left flank. By this time the expected re-enforcements (consisting of Semmes' and Anderson's brigades and a part of Barksdale's, of McLaws' division) arrived, and the whole, including Grigsby's command, now united, charged upon the enemy, checking his advance, then driving him back with great slaughter entirely from and beyond the wood, and gaining possession of our original position. No further advance, beyond demonstrations, was made by the enemy on the left."

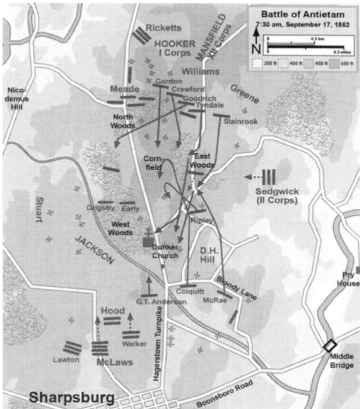

Jackson was referring to the Union's uncoordinated attacks from the East Woods, east of the cornfield. Hooker's I Corps was relieved by the XII Corps under Joseph Mansfield, who had been promoted to Corps command just a few days earlier and was so new to command and unfamiliar with the terrain that he advanced his men in a file that was 10 ranks deep instead of the normal 2-rank-deep battle line. On top of that, Mansfield got confused by Confederate fire from the cornfield, mistakenly believing that it was friendly fire. And once he got all the necessary information and the delays sorted out, he was mortally wounded, with one of his men explaining, "The general, tottering in his saddle, goaded the bleeding horse north along the Smoketown Road, away from the 10th Maine, until he came upon the right company of the 125th Pennsylvania. Captain Gardner (K Co.), who noticed that the general seemed ill, immediately called for some men to help the general dismount. Sergeant John Caho (K Co.) and Privates Sam Edmunson (K Co.) and E.S. Rudy (H Co.), with two stragglers, gently eased the bleeding officer from his horse. Forming a chair with their muskets, the five men picked up Mansfield and carried him to a lone tree in the rear of their line, where they left him to await the arrival of a surgeon."

**Mansfield**

As the XII Corps struggled, Edwin Sumner's II Corps began an unsupported and uncoordinated attack from the east, entering the East Woods in confusion. Like Mansfield, Sumner's battle line was comprised unusually and made an inviting target for Confederate artillery. The Corps suffered over 2,000 casualties in half an hour, with division commander John Sedgwick suffering a serious injury. Sumner has long been criticized for the lack of coordination and the unusual battle formation.

By 10:00 a.m., over 13,000 men had become casualties in just 4 hours, and two Union corps commanders were out of the fight.

**The Center**

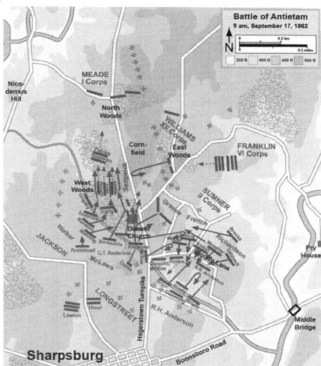

As if the fighting in the north wasn't fierce enough, the fighting at midday would turn one sunken road into "Bloody Lane". Having been repulsed in the north, the next Union attacks focused on the center of the Confederate line, beginning ironically with a division of Sumner's II Corps which had gotten lost in the East Woods during the attack in the north and ventured south. With Sumner's II Corps advancing in a disorderly fashion and being badly repulsed, Sumner initially asked French's lost division to make a diversionary attack on the center.

There French's men found D.H. Hill's division, which after South Mountain was reduced to only about 2,500 men itself. On top of that, some of Hill's brigades had reinforced Jackson's men during the morning, meaning French had veered right into the most lightly defended part of the Confederate line. However, Hill's men were protected by the features of the "sunken road", a dirt road that had been worn down over the years by wagons and thus formed a sort of trench that made defensive warfare much safer.

General Longstreet reported after the battle:

"Hood was not strong enough to resist the masses thrown against him. Several of Maj. Gen. D. H. Hill's brigades re-enforced the position; but even with these our forces seemed but a handful when compared with the hosts thrown against us. The commands engaged the enemy, however, with great courage and determination, and, retiring very slowly, delayed him until the forces of Generals Jackson and Walker came to our relief. D.R. Jones' brigade, under Col. G. T. Anderson, came up about the same moment; soon after this the divisions of Major-Generals McLaws and R. H. Anderson. Col. S. D. Lee's reserve artillery was with General Hood, and took a distinguished part in the attack on the evening of the 16th, and in delaying that of the 17th. General Jackson soon moved off to our left for the purpose of turning the enemy's right flank, and the other divisions, except Walker's, were distributed at other points of the line. As these movements were made, the enemy again threw forward his masses against my left. This attack was met by Walker's division, two pieces of Captain Miller's battery, of the Washington Artillery, and two pieces of Captain Boyce's battery, and was driven back in some confusion. An effort was made to pursue, but our line was too weak. Colonel Cooke, of the Twenty-seventh North Carolina, very gallantly charged with his own regiment, but, his supply of ammunition being exhausted and he being unsupported, he was obliged to return to his original position in the line.

From this moment our center was extremely weak, being defended by but part of Walker's division and four pieces of artillery; Cooke's regiment, of that division, being without a cartridge. In this condition, again the enemy's masses moved forward against us. Cooke stood with his empty guns, and waved his colors to show that his troops were in position. The artillery played upon their ranks, with canister. Their lines began to hesitate."

**The dead in the Bloody Lane**

Longstreet was referencing Anderson's division, which arrived at 10:30 a.m. and represented the last reserve Lee currently had at his disposal. But as Anderson's men fortified the line, 4,000 Union soldiers from Maj. Gen. Israel B. Richardson's division of Sumner's II Corps took up the fight on French's left. He was soon joined by another attack against the center of the line by Thomas F. Meagher's famous Irish Brigade, easily recognizable thanks to their emerald green flags. Although the Confederate line had a strong vantage point, one Union soldier noted of their predicament, "We were shooting them like sheep in a pen. If a bullet missed the mark at first it was liable to strike the further bank, angle back, and take them secondarily."

As the fighting in the center raged, Col. Francis C. Barlow and 350 men from two New York regiments took a commanding position that oversaw the sunken road and allowed them to pour in a deadly flanking fire that enfiladed the Confederate line. Miscommunication by the Confederates over how to face this threat inadvertently resulted in an entire brigade marching toward the rear back toward Sharpsburg, breaking the Confederate line.

At this point, it was about 1:00 p.m., and in the middle another 5,500 casualties had been incurred. As the broken Confederate line started retreating, Franklin's VI Corps, comprised of 12,000 men, were ready to advance on the center. In the field, Franklin's request to advance was denied by Edwin Sumner, who in addition to commanding the II Corps was in command of the "grand division", making him responsible for that wing of the army thanks to the unwieldy structure of the Army of the Potomac's leadership. Franklin thus had to attempt to make the request to McClellan himself, whose headquarters were over a mile to the rear, costing precious time. McClellan personally rode to the area, listened to both men's arguments, and decided to hold Franklin's men in place, still clearly concerned that he was outnumbered.

**Burnside's Attack**

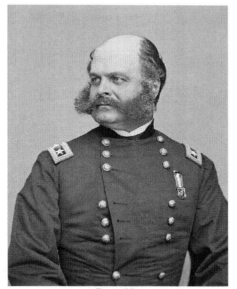

**Burnside**

Lee's army may ultimately have been saved by the Northern army's inability to cross the creek near "Burnside's Bridge". Ambrose Burnside had been given command of the "Right Wing" of the Army of the Potomac (the I Corps and IX Corps) at the start of the Maryland Campaign for the Battle of South Mountain, but McClellan separated the two corps at the Battle of Antietam, placing them on opposite ends of the Union battle line. However, Burnside continued to act as though he was a wing commander instead of a corps commander, so instead of directly commanding his IX corps, he funneled orders through General Jacob D. Cox. This poor organization contributed to the corps's hours-long delay in attacking and crossing what is now called "Burnside's Bridge" on the right flank of the Confederate line.

Making matters worse, Burnside did not perform adequate reconnaissance of the area, which afforded several easy fording sites of the creek out of range of the Army of Northern Virginia. Instead of unopposed crossings, his troops were forced into repeated assaults across the narrow bridge which was dominated by Confederate sharpshooters on high ground across the bridge. On top of that, Burnside's failure to have his men wade across meant that they were easily repulsed a couple of times trying to force their way across the bridge. McClellan got so fed up that he began sending couriers, and at one point he ordered an aide, "Tell him if it costs 10,000 men he must go now." Burnside reacted angrily, "McClellan appears to think I am not trying my best to carry this bridge; you are the third or fourth one who has been to me this morning with similar orders." As Confederate staff officer Henry Kyd Douglas later pointed out, "Go and look at [Burnside's Bridge], and tell me if you don't think Burnside and his corps might have executed a hop, skip, and jump and landed on the other side. One thing is certain, they might have waded it that day without getting their waist belts wet in any place."

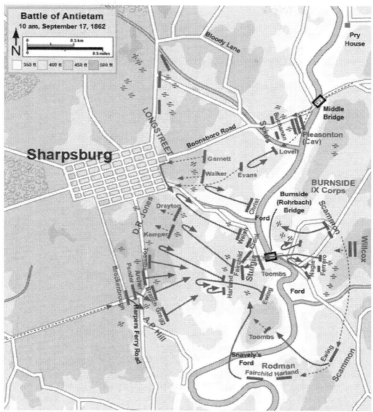

Burnside discussed his dispositions in his post-battle report, as well as describing the now famous "Burnside's Bridge" and the terrain near where he was ordered to attack:

General Cox was still retained in temporary command of the Ninth Army Corps, which was the only portion of my command then with me, and my orders were to a great extent given directly to him, and I would respectfully refer the general commanding to his very excellent and minute report. The distribution of the forces was as follows: On the crest of the hill immediately in front of the bridge was Benjamin's battery of six 20-pounders, with the remaining batteries in rear of the crest under partial cover; in rear of Benjamin's battery on the extreme right, joining on to General Sykes' division, was General Crook's brigade, with General Sturgis' division in his rear; on the left, and in rear of Benjamin's battery, was Rodman's division, with Scammon's brigade in support; General Willcox's division was held in reserve. The whole command bivouacked in these positions in three lines on the night of the 16th.

On the morning of the 17th the enemy opened a heavy artillery fire on our lines, but did us little harm. Our batteries were soon brought to bear on their batteries, which were soon silenced and two of his caissons blown up.

About this time I received an order from the general commanding to make my dispositions to carry the stone bridge over the Antietam nearly opposite our center, but to await further orders before making the attack. I accordingly threw my lines forward.

The disposition of the troops at this time was as follows: General Crook's brigade and General Sturgis' division immediately in front of the bridge and the ford, a short distance above, their front covered by the Eleventh Connecticut, Col. H. W. Kingsbury, thrown out as skirmishers; General Rodman's division, with Scammon's brigade in support, opposite the ford, some three-quarters of a mile below the bridge; General Willcox's division in the woods at the left of Benjamin's battery, in rear of the other lines. Benjamin's battery retained its original position, and the following batteries were placed in advance on his right and left, those on the left overlooking the bridge and the heights above it; Clark's and Durell's on the right; Muhlenberg's, Cook's, and McMullin's on the left, and one section of Simmonds' with Crook's brigade and one section with Benjamin's battery. The battery of Dahlgren boat howitzers, attached to the Ninth New York, covered the crossing of Rodman's division at the ford below.

At 10 o'clock I received an order from the general commanding to make the attack. I directed Colonel Kingsbury, of the Eleventh Connecticut, to move forward with his line of skirmishers, and directed General Cox to detail General Crook's brigade to make the assault. General Rodman was directed to cross over at the ford below the bridge, and join on to the left of the command, which was to be thrown over the bridge. From General Crook's position it was found to be almost impossible to carry the bridge, and General Sturgis was ordered to make a detail from his division for that purpose. He immediately sent forward the Second Maryland (Lieutenant-Colonel Duryea) and the Sixth New Hampshire (Colonel Griffin), which regiments made several successive attacks in the most gallant style, but were driven back by the galling fire of the enemy. I then directed the batteries on the left to concentrate their fire on the woods above the bridge, and sent word to General Sturgis to detail the Fifty-first Pennsylvania (Colonel Hartranft) and the Fifty-first New York (Colonel Potter) to assault the bridge and carry it at all hazards. In the mean time Colonel Crook had brought a section of his battery to bear upon the heights just above the bridge. General Sturgis, by a judicious posting of these two regiments in rear of a spur which fronted the bridge, succeeded in protecting them from the enemy's fire until they reached the crest of the spur, at which point they commenced their charge and carried the bridge at the point of the bayonet at about 1 o'clock, the whole division following immediately.

The regiments separated at the head of the bridge to the right and left, and moved up the steep bank crowning the heights immediately beyond. Our loss at this place was fearful, the enemy being posted in rifle-pits and behind barricades, within easy musket range of our men, and almost entirely concealed and covered from our shots. We lost at this point some of our most valuable officers. Among them was Col. H. W. Kingsbury, of the Eleventh Connecticut, and Lieutenant-Colonel Bell, of the Fifty-first Pennsylvania.

Colonel Crook's brigade crossed immediately after Sturgis' division, and took its position in support in rear. General Rodman's division succeeded in crossing the fords below, after a sharp fight of musketry and artillery, and joined on to the left of Sturgis,

Scammon's brigade crossing after him and taking his position in rear and in support. General Willcox's division was ordered across to take position on the right of General Sturgis. In describing the ground here and the bridge, I cannot do better than to copy that contained in the excellent report of General Cox:

'The bridge itself is a stone structure of three arches, with stone parapet above, this parapet to some extent flanking the approach to the bridge at either end. The valley in which the stream runs is quite narrow, the steep slope on the right bank approaching quite to the water's edge. On this slope the roadway is scarped, running both ways from the bridge end, and, passing to the higher lands above by ascending through ravines above and below, the other ravine being some 600 yards above the bridge was a strong stone fence, running parallel to the stream; the turns of the roadway were covered by rifle-pits and breastworks made of rails and stone, all of which defenses, as well as the woods which covered the slope, were filled with the enemy's infantry and sharpshooters. Besides the infantry defenses, batteries were placed to enfilade the bridge and all its approaches. The crest of the first hill above the bridge is curved toward the stream at the extremes, forming a sort of natural tete-de-pont. The next ridge beyond rises somewhat higher, though with less regularity, the depression between the two being but slight, and the distance varying in places from 300 to 700 yards.'

The dispositions being completed, about 3 o'clock, in accordance with instructions received from the general commanding, I directed General Cox to move forward with the whole command, except Sturgis' division, which was left in reserve, in the order in which they were formed, and attack the town of Sharpsburg and the heights on the left.

Eventually, after about three hours and several attempts, the Union men pushed their way across, but once they were on the other side of the Antietam they delayed yet again to regroup. After two hours attempting to get ammunition across the bridge, Burnside's men began another general advance against the Confederate right, which by now had been reinforced by every conceivable unit Lee could muster. Meanwhile, A.P. Hill's men were on the march and nearing the vicinity. They had intended to be brought up to the Confederate left, but Lee ordered him to come up on the Confederate right instead.

As Hill's men neared Boteler's Ford, the best available route across the Potomac for the Confederates, Burnside began shifting his men around the Confederate right even though he heavily outnumbered them, in the hopes that a move on Boteler's Ford would cut Lee's army off and trap it along the Potomac. Around 3:00 p.m., Burnside ordered nearly 8,000 fresh soldiers to push west, and meanwhile the streets of Sharpsburg were filled with retreating Confederates. Lee's army was disorganized and on the verge of being broken.

As Burnside's men pushed in on his right flank, Lee turned to see dust from a unit marching from the southwest. Had they been Union men, his entire army may have been bagged at Sharpsburg, and when Lee asked whose troops they were, one of his aides assured him, "They are flying the Virginia flags." Lee excitedly announced, "It is A.P. Hill from Harpers Ferry!" One of Jackson's aides recalled Hill's arrival just in the nick of time:

"But then, just then, A.P. Hill, picturesque in his red battleshirt, with 3 of his brigades, 2500 men, who had marched 17 miles from Harpers Ferry and had waded the Potomac, appeared upon the scene. Tired and footsore, the men forgot their woes in that supreme moment, and with no breathing time braced themselves to meet the coming shock. They met it and stayed it. The blue line staggered and hesitated, and hesitating, was lost. At the critical moment A.P. Hill was always at his strongest. ... Again A.P. Hill, as at Manassas, Harper's Ferry, and elsewhere had struck with the right hand of Mars. No wonder both Lee and Jackson, when, in the delirium of their last moments on earth, they stood again to battle saw the form of A.P. Hill leading his columns on; but it is a wonder and a shame that the grave of this valiant Virginian has not a stone to mark it and keep it from oblivion."

Writer William Allan would note of Hill's performance:

"It was at this critical moment that A. P. Hill, who had marched seventeen miles from Harper's Ferry that morning, and had waded the Potomac, reached the field upon the flank of Burnside's victorious column. With a skill, vigor and promptness, which cannot be too highly praised, A. P. Hill formed his men in line, and threw them upon Burnside's flank. Toombs, and the other brigades of D. R, Jones's division, gave such aid as they were able. The Confederate artillery was used with the greatest courage and determination to check the enemy, but it was mainly A. P. Hill's attack which decided the day at this point, and drove Burnside in confusion and dismay back to the bridge. There is no part of General James Longstreet's article more unworthy than the single line in which he obscurely refers to the splendid achievement of a dead comrade, whose battles, like Ney's, were all for his country, and none against it, and who crowned a brilliant career by shedding his life's blood to avert the crowning disaster. A.P. Hill's march was a splendid one. He left Harper's Ferry sixteen hours after McLaws, but reached the battle-field only five hours behind him. McLaws had, however, the night to contend with. The vigor of Hill's attack, with hungry and march worn men, is shown by the fact that he completely overthrew forces twice as numerous as his own. Though his force of from two thousand to three thousand five hundred men was too small to permit of an extended aggressive, his arrival was not less opportune to Lee than was that of Blucher to Wellington at Waterloo, nor was his action when on the field in any way inferior to that of the Prussian field-marshal."

With Hill crashing down on his left flank, Burnside lost his nerve, even though the IX Corps still heavily outnumbered Hill's Light Division even after incurring 20% casualties during the day already. Burnside ordered a general retreat back to Antietam Creek and waited there while requesting more reinforcements from McClellan, who informed him, "I can do nothing more. I have no infantry." When told he had repulsed men under the command of Burnside, his West Point friend, Hill was reportedly asked if he knew his old classmate, to which he responded, "Ought to! He owes me eight thousand dollars!" Hill had allegedly loaned the money to Burnside in their friendlier antebellum days.

Of course, McClellan's assertion that he had no infantry was not entirely true. By the end of the afternoon, Union attacks on the flanks and the center of the line had been violent but eventually unsuccessful. Aware that his army was badly bloodied but fearing Lee had many more men than he did, McClellan refused to commit fresh reserves from Franklin's VI Corps or Fitz-John Porter's V Corps. McClellan's decision was probably sealed by Fitz John Porter telling him, "Remember, General, I command the last reserve of the last Army of the Republic." Thus, the day ended in a tactical stalemate, with the Union suffering nearly 12,500 casualties (including over 2,000 dead) and the Confederates suffering over 10,000 casualties (including over 1,500 dead). Nearly 1/4th of the Army of the Potomac had been injured, captured or killed, and the same could be said for nearly 1/3rd of Lee's Army of Northern Virginia. It was the deadliest and bloodiest day in American history.

After the battle, McClellan wrote to his wife, "Those in whose judgment I rely tell me that I fought the battle splendidly and that it was a masterpiece of art. ... I feel I have done all that can be asked in twice saving the country. ... I feel some little pride in having, with a beaten & demoralized army, defeated Lee so utterly. ... Well, one of these days history will I trust do me justice." Historians have generally been far less kind with their praise, criticizing McClellan for not sharing his battle plans with his corps commanders, which prevented them from using initiative outside of their sectors. McClellan also failed to use cavalry in the battle; had cavalry been used for reconnaissance, other fording options might have prevented the debacle at Burnside's Bridge. As historian Stephen Sears would point out in his seminal book about the Maryland Campaign, "In making his battle against great odds to save the Republic, General McClellan had committed barely 50,000 infantry and artillerymen to the contest. A third of his army did not fire a shot. Even at that, his men repeatedly drove the Army of Northern Virginia to the brink of disaster, feats of valor entirely lost on a commander thinking of little beyond staving off his own defeat."

### Lee's Retreat and the Aftermath

On the morning of September 18, Lee's army prepared to defend against a Union assault that ultimately never came. Finally, an improvised truce was declared to allow both sides to exchange their wounded. That evening, Lee's forces began withdrawing across the Potomac to return to Virginia.

McClellan made one push against Lee's army at nearby Shepherdstown. Shortly before dusk on September 19, Union Brig. General Charles Griffin sent 2,000 infantry and sharpshooters from Maj. General Fitz-John Porter's V Corps across the Potomac River at Boteler's Ford (also known as Shepardstown Ford) in pursuit, only to pull them back the following day when Stonewall Jackson's men entered the fray. However, Union General Adelbert Ames had mistakenly received orders to advance across the Potomac into Virginia, so he sent the 20th Maine regiment wading into the water, which actually encountered retreating Union troops as they did, and they were promptly fired upon by a barrage of Confederate artillery.

The 20th Maine would become famous at Gettysburg, but here they had no fighting chance. Just as soon as Joshua Lawrence Chamberlain's 20th had crossed, their bugles sounded retreat. Remaining calm atop his horse, Chamberlain redirected his men back across the river, "steadying his men through a deep place in the river where several of the Fifth New York were drowned in his presence." And although Lieutenant Colonel Chamberlain had his horse shot out from under him, he succeeded in returning his regiment safely back to shore with only three casualties suffering minor wounds, his ability to remain calm under pressure now apparent.

As the Battle of Shepherdstown indicated, Lee's rear guard was formidable enough that officers throughout the Army of the Potomac concurred with McClellan's actions not to go after the Army of Northern Virginia. Lee's army then moved toward the Shenandoah Valley while the Army of the Potomac hovered around Sharpsburg.

Although Antietam ended as a tactical draw, the Maryland Campaign is now widely considered a turning point in the Civil War. It resulted in forcing Lee's army out of Maryland and back into Virginia, making it a strategic victory for the North and an opportune time for President Abraham Lincoln to issue the Emancipation Proclamation. James McPherson would summarize the critical importance of the Maryland Campaign: "No other campaign and battle in the war had such momentous, multiple consequences as Antietam. In July 1863 the dual Union triumphs at

Gettysburg and Vicksburg struck another blow that blunted a renewed Confederate offensive in the East and cut off the western third of the Confederacy from the rest. In September 1864 Sherman's capture of Atlanta reversed another decline in Northern morale and set the stage for the final drive to Union victory. These also were pivotal moments. But they would never have happened if the triple Confederate offensives in Mississippi, Kentucky, and most of all Maryland had not been defeated in the fall of 1862."

Although McClellan is often criticized for the way he conducted the fighting at Antietam, Lee has not gone without criticism either. Longstreet's artillery chief, Porter Alexander, who would be tasked with conducting the artillery bombardment before Pickett's Charge at Gettysburg, was extremely critical of Lee for the Maryland Campaign, writing in his memoirs:

"Lee's hopes were by no means so exaggerated as McClellan's fears. He counted upon no hope from Maryland, until his own army should have demonstrated its ability to maintain itself within the state. He hardly hoped for more than 'to detain the enemy upon the northern frontier until the approach of winter should render his advance into Virginia difficult, if not impracticable.' But he did entertain hopes of a decisive victory here on a field more remote from a safe place of refuge for the enemy than his victories of the Seven Days and of 2d Manassas had been. The hope would have been reasonable had his army been larger and his armament better, but under all the circumstances and conditions it was as improbable of realization as the chance of an earthquake would have been. He did, indeed, win a complete victory over all the infantry which the enemy engaged, but their position was more favorable to prevent his making a counter-stroke than was his to resist their attack. Their heavy guns across the Antietam gave him protection, just as at Fredericksburg the Federal artillery on the Stafford heights, afterward in two battles, safely covered the Federal infantry on the opposite shore.

Briefly, Lee took a great risk for no chance of gain except the killing of some thousands of his enemy with the loss of, perhaps, two-thirds as many of his own men. That was a losing game for the Confederacy. Its supply of men was limited; that of the enemy was not. That was not war! Yet now, who would have it otherwise? History must be history and could not afford to lose this battle from its records. For the nation is immortal and will forever prize and cherish the record made that day by both sides, as actors in the boldest and the bloodiest battle ever fought upon this continent."

**Lincoln and McClellan meeting after Antietam**

McClellan had successfully removed Lee's army from Maryland, but he had failed to knock Lee's army out while it was on the ropes. When Lee escaped back to Virginia without pursuit, the Lincoln Administration was greatly frustrated.

Despite heavily outnumbering the Southern army and badly damaging it during the battle of Antietam, McClellan never did pursue Lee across the Potomac, citing shortages of equipment and the fear of overextending his forces. General-in-Chief Henry W. Halleck wrote in his official report, "The long inactivity of so large an army in the face of a defeated foe, and during the most favorable season for rapid movements and a vigorous campaign, was a matter of great disappointment and regret." Lincoln sardonically referred to the Army of the Potomac as General McClellan's bodyguard, and in one October message to McClellan, Lincoln didn't bother trying to conceal his disgust, writing, "I have just read your dispatch about sore-tongued and fatigued horses, Will you pardon me for asking what the horses of your army have done since the Battle of Antietam that fatigues anything?"

Some of Lincoln's assertions make clear his lack of familiarity with military matters. McClellan still had to deal with the logistical reorganization of his army and the rehabilitation after having suffered about 10,000 casualties in one day. And as Lincoln grew more disenchanted with McClellan, specifically the state of inertia along the Potomac, JEB Stuart rode around McClellan's army for the second time in early October, displaying just how unable the Union forces were to cover the Potomac crossings.

McClellan also faced growing public pressure and pressure from the Administration to advance before the midterm elections. McClellan wished to wait until Spring of 1863 to resume active campaigning, hoping once again to use the Peninsula, but he was compelled to move by mid-October. McClellan saw the campaign as merely a temporary way of placating the Administration before positioning his army around Fredericksburg to plan for the following Spring.

Lincoln had finally had enough of McClellan's "slows", and his constant excuses for not taking forward action. Lincoln relieved McClellan of his command of the Army of the Potomac on November 7, 1862, effectively ending the general's military career. Once again using the media to deflect his inadequacies, McClellan blamed Washington for having not sent more men and equipment before mounting the Antietam offensive. Lincoln reportedly responded, "Sending reinforcements to McClellan is like shoveling flies across a barn."[2] McClellan's military career was essentially over, having ended in disgrace.

Ironically, when McClellan was removed, the army was at a highpoint in terms of morale, and McClellan was starting to understand that if the Administration wouldn't allow a transfer of his army onto the Peninsula, he would have to continue sliding east along the overland route using available railroads, which is similar in scope to Ulysses S. Grant's 1864 Overland Campaign. But it was not to be for another 2 years, and on November 7, 1862, McClellan was replaced by Ambrose Burnside, one of the subordinates most responsible for the shortcomings of the Maryland campaign.

---

[2]  Lanning, Michael Lee. *The Civil War 100.* Page 189. Pages 189--190.

## Moving Toward Fredericksburg

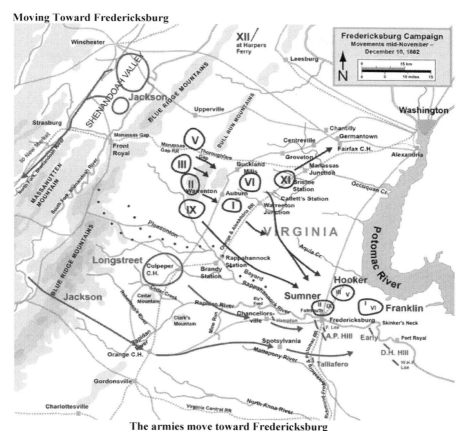

**The armies move toward Fredericksburg**

Given the way McClellan was sacked, Burnside understood he was under pressure from the Lincoln Administration to be aggressive, but instead of going for Lee's army, which was split with Stonewall Jackson's men covering their supply lines in the Shenandoah, Burnside made his objective Richmond. After deliberating for a few days, Burnside relayed to the Administration that he would try to keep Lee in place by feigning movements in the Army of Northern Virginia's vicinity before shifting his army southeast and crossing the Rappahannock River to Fredericksburg. Burnside preferred this movement because it protected his flank from Stonewall Jackson's corps, in no small part due to the havoc Jackson had wreaked in his Valley Campaign earlier that year.

**Stonewall Jackson**

Thus, instead of striking out at Lee's nearby army, Burnside began moving the Army of the Potomac southeast on November 15 toward the Rappahannock River. But even as he was moving his army, problems with his army's logistics cropped up, specifically with pontoon bridges. The bridges were needed to cross the Rappahannock River, and had they been there on time, the Army of the Potomac would have beaten Lee's Army of Northern Virginia to Fredericksburg, forcing the Confederates to take up a defensive line closer to Richmond and allowing Burnside's men an unopposed crossing. Instead, the Administration had failed to provide the bridges on time at Falmouth, a few miles west and across river from Fredericksburg, on November 17. Instead of sending Edwin "Bull" Sumner's corps across as an advance, Burnside cautiously kept his army together out of concern rising waters from rains might make it impossible for the rest of the army to ford the river.

The Army of the Potomac's failure to cross the Rappahannock in mid-November allowed Lee to reach Fredericksburg with General James Longstreet's corps on November 23, where they were posted to the west of the town on the imposing Marye's Heights. By the end of November, Stonewall Jackson's corps had arrived in the vicinity, and Lee posted him to Longstreet's right to defend against crossing sites downstream from Fredericksburg.

Longstreet described the terrain in his memoirs:

"At the west end of the ridge where the river cuts through is Taylor's Hill (the

Confederate left), which stands at its highest on a level with Stafford Heights. From that point the heights on the south side spread, unfolding a valley about a mile in width, affording a fine view of the city, of the arable fields, and the heights as they recede to the vanishing limits of sight. Next below Taylor's is Marye's Hill, rising to half the elevation of the neighboring heights and dropping back, leaving a plateau of half a mile, and then swelling to the usual altitude of the range. On the plateau is the Marye mansion. Along its base is a sunken road, with retaining walls on either side. That on the east is just breast-high for a man, and just the height convenient for infantry defence and fire. From the top of the breast-work the ground recedes gradually till near the canal, when it drops off three or four feet, leaving space near the canal of a rod or two of level ground. The north end of the sunken road cuts into the plank or Gordonsville road, which is an extension of Hanover Street from near the heart of the town. At the south end it enters the Telegraph road, extending out from the town limits and up over the third, or Telegraph Hill, called, in its bloody baptismal, "Lee's Hill." An unfinished railroad lies along the Telegraph road as far as the highlands. The Fredericksburg and Potomac Railroad lies nearly parallel with the river four miles, and then turns south through the highlands. The old stage road from the city runs about half-way between the river and the railroad four miles, when it turns southwest and crosses the railroad at Hamilton's Crossing. The hamlet of Falmouth, on the north side of the river, was in front of the right centre of the Federal position, half a mile from Fredericksburg."

Longstreet's artillery chief, Porter Alexander, explained just how strong a defensive position Marye's Heights afforded:

"There was, however, one natural feature which proved of great value. The Confederate line occupied a range of low hills nearly parallel to the river and a few hundred yards back from the town. The Telegraph road, sunken from three to five feet below the surface, skirted the bottom of these hills for about 800 yards, until it reached the valley of Hazel Run, into which it turned. This sunken road was made part of the line of battle for McLaws's infantry. It not only formed a parapet invisible to the enemy until its defenders rose to fire over it, but it afforded ample space for several ranks to load and fire, and still have room behind them for free communication along the line. In easy canister range, nine guns on the hills above could fire over the heads of the infantry."

While Longstreet's men started to approach Fredericksburg, the town itself received a surrender request from Edwin Sumner on November 21, citing the fact that Confederates had been shooting at them from locations inside the town. Longstreet's chief artillerist, Porter Alexander, explained how this led to the evacuation of many of the town's citizens:

"On the 21st Sumner sent a formal demand for the surrender of the town, basing it upon the statement that his troops had been fired upon from under cover of the houses, and that mills and manufactories in the town were furnishing provisions and clothing to the enemy. He demanded an answer by 5 P. M., and said that if the surrender was not immediate at nine next morning, he would shell the town, the intermediate 16 hours being allowed for the removal of women and children.

This note, only received by the Mayor at 4.40 P. M., was referred to Longstreet, who authorized a reply to be made that the city would not be used for the purposes complained of, but that the Federals could only occupy the town by force of arms. Mayor Slaughter pointed out that the civil authorities had not been responsible for the firing which had been done, and, further, that during the night it would be impossible to remove the noncombatants. During the night Sumner sent word that in consideration of the pledges made, and, in view of the short time remaining for the removal of women and children, the batteries would not open as had been proposed.

But the letter left it to be inferred that the purpose to shell was only postponed, and Lee, who had now arrived, advised the citizens to vacate the town. This advice was followed by the greater part of the population. It was pitiable to see the refugees endeavoring to remove their possessions and encamping in the woods and fields, for miles around, during the unusually cold weather which soon followed."

By the time Burnside had all the bridges he needed, Longstreet's corps had been on the high ground outside of Fredericksburg for days, and Stonewall Jackson's corps had arrived. At this point, there was a lull in action on both sides for several days, leaving Lee to wonder what Burnside intended to do with his nearly 115,000 man army. On December 6, Lee wrote a dispatch to President Jefferson Davis back in Richmond:

"The enemy still maintain his position north of the Rappahannock. I can discover no indications of his advancing, or of transferring his troops to other positions. Scouts on both of his flanks north of the Rappahannock report no movement, nor have those stationed on the Potomac discovered the collection of transport or the passage of troops down that river.

Gen. Burnside's whole army appears to be encamped between the Rappahannock and Potomac. His apparent inaction suggests the probability that he is waiting for expected operations elsewhere, and I fear troops may be collecting south of James River. Yet I get no reliable information of organized or tried troops being sent to that quarter, nor am I aware of any of their general officers in whom confidence is placed being there in command. There is an evident concentration of troops hitherto disposed in other parts of Virginia, but whether for the purpose of augmenting Gen. Burnside's army or any other I cannot tell…

I have heard that, on the 30th ultimo, ten regiments from Virginia had reached the Baltimore depot, in Washington, their destination unknown. Should Gen. Cox have withdrawn from the Kanawha Valley, I should think the State troops, under Gen. Floyd, could protect that country, and would recommend that the Confederate troops be brought at once to Staunton, to operate in the Shenandoah Valley, if necessary, or south of James River. I think the strength of the enemy south of James River is greatly exaggerated, but have no means of ascertaining the fact.

From the reports forwarded to me by Gen. G. W. Smith, the officers serving there seem to be impressed with its magnitude. If I felt sure of our ability to resist the advance of the enemy south of that river, it would relieve me of great embarrassment, and I should feel better able to oppose the operations which may be contemplated by Gen. Burnside. I presume that the operations in the Department of the West and South will require all the troops in each, but, should there be a lull of the war in these departments, it might be advantageous to leave a sufficient covering force to conceal the movement, and draw an active, when the exigency arrives, to the vicinity of Richmond. Provisions and forage in the mean time could be collected in Richmond. When the crisis shall have passed, these troops could be returned to their departments with re-enforcements.

I need not state to you the advantages of a combination of our troops for a battle, if it can be accomplished, and, unless it can be done, we must make up our minds to fight with great odds against us.

I hope Your Excellency will cause me to be advised when, in your judgment, it may become necessary for this army to move nearer Richmond. It was never in better health or in better condition for battle than now. Some shoes, blankets, arms, and accouterments are still wanting, but we are occasionally receiving small supplies, and I hope all will be provided in time.

There was quite a fall of snow yesterday, which will produce some temporary discomfort.

I have the honor to be, with great respect, your obedient servant,

R. E. LEE"

One of the reasons Burnside hadn't moved is because Burnside himself wasn't sure if Lee knew of his strategy. Burnside had intended to cross the Army of the Potomac east of Fredericksburg downriver, but Lee had positioned Jackson's men to prevent just such a crossing. When Union gunboats were attacked by men under Jackson's command, including Jubal Early's division and D.H. Hill's division, Burnside believed that Lee had correctly anticipated where he intended to move. At the same time, it also made him assume that Lee's right was strengthened to the east of Fredericksburg, and that the Army of Northern Virginia's center and/or left would be weakened as a result. That assumption ultimately induced Burnside to attempt the crossing of the Rappahannock directly in front of Fredericksburg itself, as he explained in a December 9 dispatch to Union general-in-chief Henry Halleck, "I think now the enemy will be more surprised by a crossing immediately in our front than any other part of the river. ... I'm convinced that a large force of the enemy is now concentrated at Port Royal, its left resting on Fredericksburg, which we hope to turn."

Burnside would explain what he hoped to accomplish in his official report after the campaign:

"During my preparations for crossing at the place I had at first selected, I discovered that the enemy had thrown a large portion of his force down the river and elsewhere, thus weakening his defenses in front; and also thought I discovered that he did not anticipate the crossing of our whole force at Fredericksburg; and I hoped, by rapidly throwing the whole command over at that place, to separate, by a vigorous attack, the forces of the enemy on the river below from the forces behind and on the crests in tile rear of the town, in which case we should fight him with great advantages in our favor. To do this we had to gain a height on the extreme right of the crest, which height commanded a new road, lately built by the enemy for purposes of more rapid communication along his lines; which point gained, his positions along the crest would have been scarcely tenable, and he could have been driven from them easily by an attack on his front, in connection with a movement in rear of the crest."

**Crossing the Rappahannock**

**The pontoon bridges used by William Franklin's "Grand Division" to cross the Rappahannock**

In the early morning hours of December 11, with all of the necessary supplies on hand and his artillery situated on the commanding Stafford Heights in his rear, Burnside ordered the Union's engineers to begin building half a dozen pontoon bridges at several points along the Rappahannock, with two of them near the center of the town, one on the southern part of the town, and three more downriver. The orders would bring about some of the most unique fighting of the Civil War.

**The locations of the pontoon bridges are marked as black lines across the river**

Fully aware that the Army of the Potomac would have to cross the river somewhere at some time, Lafayette McLaws's division, representing the left of the Army of Northern Virginia's line, had men posted all along the front in a way that would allow the Confederate defenders to contest a crossing. That included several regiments along the river bank and some in the town of Fredericksburg itself. As soon as Confederates in these advanced positions noted the Union movements, a Confederate battery sounded a signal alert by firing twice around 4:00 a.m. The Army of Northern Virginia was already aware of Burnside's attempts to cross the river before they'd barely begun.

One of the engineers, Wesley Brainerd of the 50th New York Engineers, recalled, "A long line of arms moving rapidly up and down was all I saw, for a moment later they were again obscured by the fog. But I knew too well that line of arms was ramming cartridges and that the crisis was near." Sure enough, the engineers were met by a strong volley that Brainerd described, "The bullets of the enemy rained upon my bridge. They went whizzing and zipping by and around me, pattering on the bridge, splashing into the water and thugging through the boats."

McLaws explained his dispositions as the Union engineers began building pontoon bridges in his front:

"One brigade was constantly on duty in the city to guard the town and defend the river crossings as far down as a quarter of a mile below Deep Run Creek. Two regiments from General Anderson's division picketed the river bank above the town, reporting to the brigadier-general in charge of the brigade on duty in the city. The orders were that two guns should be fired from one of my batteries in a central position, which would be the signal that the enemy were attempting to cross. These were the positions of my command and the orders governing them up to the 10th instant. On that day the brigade of General Barksdale, composed of the Mississippi troops, were on duty in the city.

About 2 a.m. on the 11th, General Barksdale sent me word that the movements of the enemy indicated they were preparing to lay down their pontoon bridges, and his men were getting into position to defend the crossing. About 4.30 o'clock he notified me that the bridges were being placed, and he would open fire so soon as the working parties came in good range of his rifles. I gave the order, and the signal guns were fired about 5 a.m.

I had been notified from your headquarters the evening previous (the 10th instant) to have all the batteries harnessed up at daylight on the 11th, and I had given orders that my whole command should be under arms at the same time.

General Barksdale kept his men quiet and concealed until the bridges were so advanced that the working parties were in easy range, when he opened fire with such effect the bridges were abandoned at once. Nine separate and desperate attempts were made to complete the bridges under fire of their sharpshooters and guns on the opposite banks, but every attempt being attended with such severe loss from our men--posted in rifle-pits, in the cellars of the houses along the banks, and from behind whatever offered concealment--that the enemy abandoned their attempts for the time and opened a terrific fire from their numerous batteries concentrated along the hills just above the river."

**Barksdale**

As McLaws indicated, the defenseless Union engineers were more than a little skittish about being exposed to Confederate fire as they defenselessly tried to construct pontoon bridges across the river. In response, the Army of the Potomac's artillery opened up on the town with about 150 guns, trying to force the Confederate defenders out of the town and thus out of range of the pontoon bridges, but the Confederate defenders were able to hide in cellars and maintain their positions. One of Brainerd's comrades in the 50th New York Engineers, surgeon Clark Raum, described the bombardment, "When the artillery fairly opened the roar was terrific – dreadful – I know of no words to express it. The screeching of the shells thru the air the whiz of the solid shot, the boom, boom, boom of the cannon, the sharp ring of the rifles and rattle of the musketry all commingles made one's ears tingle.

Despite the artillery fire, Barksdale's brigade continued to employ sharpshooters from buildings in town, completely frustrating the attempts to construct the pontoon bridges near the town. Around 2:00, a completely flustered Burnside complained, "The army is held by the throat by a few sharpshooters!" Eventually, Henry Hunt concocted a new plan to help the crossings. Hunt suggested to Burnside that infantry should be ferried across the river and then spread out to establish a line on the western bank of the river, pushing forward to fight the Confederate defenders in town while the engineers completed the pontoon bridges. Burnside initially hesitated, believing that it would result in "death to most of those who should undertake the voyage", but the men of Colonel Norman Hall's brigade let off three cheers in response to Hall's suggestion that his men be given the assignment. With that, the order was given, and by now the Confederates' use of the town had so enraged the Union officers that the men now set to ferry across were ordered to give no quarter and take no prisoners among the Confederates they found in the town.

Around 3:00 p.m., now nearly 12 hours since the attempt to cross had started, about 130 men from the 7th Michigan and 19th Massachusetts were ferried across the river in small boats, but this was no pleasure cruise. One Union soldier looking on at the scene watching it unfold explained,

"An oarsman would be seen relinquishing his oar and falling down dead or wounded in the bottom of his boat or overboard into the river. Then another would drop while not a few of their partners with rifles in hand were suffering a similar fate by their side…It may have been the saddest sight during my life in the army."

Once they made it, they formed a skirmish line for the purposes of fighting the Confederates in town. As they engaged in running street battles to clear Fredericksburg one street at a time, the engineers were able to complete the pontoon bridges less than 90 minutes later. To help secure the landing zones, the Army of the Potomac fired thousands of artillery shells at the city and the Confederates positioned on the ridges to the west of Fredericksburg. One Confederate officer described the scene as a "line of angry blazing guns firing through white clouds of smoke & almost shaking the earth with their roar. Over & in the town the white winkings of the bursting shells reminded one of a countless swarm of fire-flies. Several buildings were set on fire, & their black smoke rose in remarkably slender, straight, & tall columns for two hundred feet, perhaps, before they began to spread horizontally & unite in a great black canopy." One of Barksdale's men from the 17th Mississippi described the kind of fighting going on all throughout Fredericksburg, "There were six men in the basement of [a] two-story house, and any one of them now living will testify to the fact that the house was torn to pieces, the chimney falling down in the basement among us; .... A few moments after the batteries opened, several regiments of Union infantry came yelling down the hill toward the river, laying hold of the boats and coming over toward where we were stationed. As they came up the bank we tried to get out at the end of the house."

From his position along the left of the Confederate line, Porter Alexander described his view of the shelling of Fredericksburg:

"The city, except its steeples, was still veiled in the mist which had settled in the valleys. Above it and in it incessantly showed the round white clouds of bursting shells, and out of its midst there soon rose three or four columns of dense black smoke from houses set on fire by the explosions. The atmosphere was so perfectly calm and still that the smoke rose vertically in great pillars for several hundred feet before spreading outward in black sheets. The opposite bank of the river, for two miles to the right and left, was crowned at frequent intervals with blazing batteries, canopied in clouds of white smoke.

Beyond these, the dark blue masses of over 100,000 infantry in compact columns, and numberless parks of white-topped wagons and ambulances massed in orderly ranks, all awaited the completion of the bridges. The earth shook with the thunder of the guns, and, high above all, a thousand feet in the air, hung two immense balloons. The scene gave impressive ideas of the disciplined power of a great army, and of the vast resources of the nation which had sent it forth."

As the 7th Michigan and 19th Massachusetts struggled in their fight in Fredericksburg, the 20th Massachusetts crossed into town and bolstered them, advancing house by house. One of the men of the 20th Massachusetts later noted the "Michigan men made a rush at the nearest houses and took quite a number of prisoners. The orders to the whole Brigade were to bayonet every armed man found firing from a house ..., but it was not of course obeyed.... In fact no prisoners were taken but the few the Michigans took and the wounded who lay about struck by our shells. The 7th Michigan were deployed on the left and a short distance up the street at the foot of which we landed, and the 19th on the right, both holding houses, fences, etc., and exchanging shots with the Rebels who were a little farther back .... When a good many troops had got over, we were advanced up the street."

The Confederates had taken up such strong positions in houses that many of the Union soldiers in town found themselves being fired upon by an invisible enemy, often seeing nothing but a muzzle flash. One soldier in the 20th Massachusetts explained, "Here we cleared the houses near us, but shot came from far and near – we could see no one and were simply murdered…every shot of the enemy took effect. How I escaped I cannot say, as more than a dozen actually fell on me."

With the pontoon bridges completed, the first to cross were advanced elements of Edwin Sumner's Grand Division. Burnside had organized the Army of the Potomac into three "Grand Divisions", which gave the Grand Division commanders control over several corps. McClellan had used a similar organization during the Maryland Campaign, and it caused him serious problems at Antietam when Burnside continued acting like a Grand Division commander instead of simply a corps commander, needlessly causing delays in orders being passed down the chain of command. Sumner's Grand Division consisted of Darius Couch's II Corps (which included divisions led by Winfield S. Hancock, Oliver O. Howard, and William H. French), Orlando B. Willcox's IX Corps (which included divisions led by William W. Burns, Samuel D. Sturgis, and George W. Getty), and a cavalry division led by Alfred Pleasonton.

**Sumner**

Barksdale's brigade retreated by fighting a delaying defense in depth that prevented the Union from fully taking Fredericksburg until night began to fall. In the process of crossing and clearing the town, the Army of the Potomac had suffered more than 350 casualties, inflicting about 240 on the Confederates themselves. The crossing and fighting in Fredericksburg that day were unprecedented. It was the first time the U.S. Army had intentionally bombarded an American city, the first time American soldiers crossed a body of water under enemy fire, and the first major urban combat of the Civil War.

When the Union soldiers had taken complete control of the town, they exacted their vengeance with a fury by looting buildings throughout the town. Lee would later liken their activities at

Fredericksburg to the Vandals, but it's no surprise that the Union soldiers were enraged by the tactics of the Confederate sharpshooters, who had hidden in private homes to take potshots at them and make December 11 a miserable day. The Union soldiers wreaked such havoc that one news correspondent in Fredericksburg wrote, "In some cases the whole side of a house has been shot away, roofs and chimneys have tumbled in, window frames smashed to atoms, and doors jarred from the hinges." One Union soldier noted, "Furniture of all sorts is strewn along the streets.... Every namable household utensil or article of furniture, stoves, crockery and glass-ware, pots, kettles and tins, are scattered, and smashed and thrown everywhere, indoors and out, as if there had fallen a shower of them in the midst of a mighty whirlwind."

**The Market House at the edge of Fredericksburg was Barksdale's headquarters on December 11**

The construction of pontoon bridges to the south went much more smoothly, thanks to the protection of artillery. Of course, that didn't mean there were no delays. Despite the fact the bridges south of town were completed by 11:00 a.m. and William Franklin's Grand Division was ordered to cross at 4:00 p.m., only one brigade made the crossing that day, and the rest wouldn't be across until 1:00 p.m. on December 12. As a result, Stonewall Jackson was able to recall Early's division and D.H. Hill's division, both of which were posted further downriver, in the early morning hours of December 13 without suffering any consequences.

**Franklin**

Franklin's Grand Division was the rule rather than the exception. The Army of the Potomac spent most of December 12 crossing the river and planning to align for battle on December 13. But despite having all of December 12 to concoct a battle plan, Burnside managed to do no more than pass on vague instructions to his officers. Burnside conducted a personal reconnaissance south of Fredericksburg on the afternoon of December 12, but when Franklin asked him for orders, he held off on issuing any concrete orders during the day. Franklin's 60,000 man Grand Division, responsible for the entire left wing of Burnside's army, would not be given a battle plan for December 13 until after 7:00 a.m. on the 13th itself.

## Fighting South of Fredericksburg

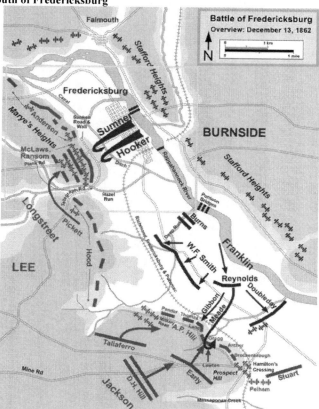

"My God, General Reynolds, did they think my division could whip Lee's whole army?" – George Meade

The Battle of Fredericksburg has long been remembered as a Union debacle, and a decisive Confederate victory, based almost entirely on the fighting that took place in the late afternoon of December 13. Before the assaults on Marye's Heights, however, Burnside hoped to turn the Confederates' position by pushing Stonewall Jackson's corps back on the Confederate right and thus flanking Longstreet's well-defended position on Marye's Heights outside of town. Given that the Army of the Potomac vastly outnumbered the Confederates, by upwards of 50,000 soldiers, the plan had a decent chance of success if executed properly.

The problem is the plan was never executed properly because it was unclear just what Burnside's plan was. On December 12, Burnside had told Franklin that he was envisioning that Franklin's Grand Division would attack Jackson's corps while being supported by Hooker's Grand Division, but the orders Franklin received on the morning of December 13 instructed

Franklin to hold his position while sending "a division at least" to seize Prospect Hill, the highest ground in the area. Naturally, Sumner expected that the attack would consist of his entire Grand Division, but apparently Burnside thought a demonstration by one division of one corps would convince Lee to withdraw toward Richmond.

Given the confusing orders, Franklin decided to follow the letter of the orders. On the morning of December 13, a dense fog hung in the valley Fredericksburg is located in, keeping the armies hidden from each other, and while the armies bided their time Franklin instructed I Corps commander John Reynolds to choose one of his divisions to make the attack. Reynolds tapped George Meade's 4,500 man division, to be supported by John Gibbon's division. Abner Doubleday's division was to cover the advance's left flank by facing south and combating JEB Stuart's cavalry, which had situated itself at a nearly 90 degree angle on the Confederates' right flank to offer enfilading fire.

**Meade**

Meade's men began their advance forward in heavy fog around 8:30 a.m. with Gibbon's division in back of them, and as they reached Richmond Road, they began receiving enfilading fire from JEB Stuart's artillery, being manned by the young "gallant" Major John Pelham, who opened on them with 2 guns. As Union artillery tried to silence Pelham's guns from their dangerous position, Stuart told Pelham he could withdraw, to which Pelham responded, "Tell the General I can hold my ground." The 24th Michigan Infantry, a brand new regiment full of raw recruits, was ordered to deal with Pelham, but they were unable to stop Pelham's battery until it began to run low on ammunition after about an hour. Lee would later praise the young Major, stating, "It is glorious to see such courage in one so young."

**"Gallant John Pelham"**

Once the fog started to lift around 10:30, Jackson's artillery began raining down on the advancing Union soldiers from Prospect Hill, stopping Meade's division in its tracks about 600 yards from the hill around 11:00 a.m. Meade described the fighting to his wife, "On the 13th it was determined to make an attack from both positions, and the honor of leading this attack was assigned to my division. I cannot give you all the details of the fight, but will simply say my men went in beautifully, carried everything before them, and drove the enemy for nearly half a mile, but finding themselves unsupported on either right or left, and encountering an overwhelming force of the enemy, they were checked and finally driven back. As an evidence of the work they had to do, it is only necessary to state that out of four thousand five hundred men taken into action, we know the names of eighteen hundred killed and wounded. There are besides some four hundred missing, many of whom are wounded."

Meade was more detailed in his official report:

"Early on the morning of the 13th, I accompanied the general commanding the First Corps to the headquarters of the left grand division, where the commanding general indicated the point he was instructed to attack, and I was informed my division had been selected to make the attack.

The point indicated was on the ridge, or rather range of heights, extending from the Rappahannock, in the rear of Fredericksburg, to the Massaponax, and was situated near the left of this ridge, where it terminated in the Massaponax Valley. Between the heights to be attacked and the plateau on which the left grand division was posted, there was a depression or hollow of several hundred yards in width, through which, and close to the foot of the heights, the Richmond railroad ran. The heights along the crest were wooded. The slope to the railroad from the extreme left for the space of 300 or 400 yards was clear; beyond this it was wooded, the woods extending across the hollow and in front of the railroad. The plateau on our side was level and cultivated ground up to the crest of the hollow, where there was quite a fall to the railroad. The enemy occupied the wooded heights, the line of railroad, and the wood in front. Owing to the wood, nothing could be seen of them, while all our movements on the cleared ground were exposed to their view. Immediately on receiving orders, the division was moved forward across the Smithfield ravine, advancing down the river some 700 or 800 yards, when it turned sharp to the right and crossed the Bowling Green road, which here runs in a parallel direction with the railroad. Some time was consumed in removing the hedge fences on this road, and bridging the drains on each side for the passage of the artillery.

Between 9 and 10 o'clock the column of attack was formed as follows: The First Brigade in line of battle on the crest of the hollow, and facing the railroad, with the Sixth Regiment deployed as skirmishers; the Second Brigade in rear of the First 300 paces; the Third Brigade by the flank, its right flank being a few rods to the rear of the First Brigade, having the Ninth Regiment deployed on its flank as skirmishers and flankers, and the batteries between the First and Second Brigades. This disposition had scarcely been made when the enemy opened a brisk fire from a battery posted on the Bowling Green road, the shot from which took the command from the left and rear.

Apprehending an attack from this quarter, the Third Brigade was faced to the left, thus forming, with the First, two sides of a square. Simpson's battery was advanced to the front and left of the Third Brigade, and Cooper's and Ransom's batteries moved to a knoll on the left of the First Brigade. These batteries immediately opened on the enemy's battery, and, in conjunction with some of General Doubleday's batteries in our rear, on the other side of the Bowling Green road, after twenty minutes' firing, silenced and compelled the withdrawal of the guns. During this artillery duel the enemy advanced a body of sharpshooters along the Bowling Green road, and under cover of the hedges and trees on the roadside."

As Meade's men stayed in place under heavy fire from Jackson's corps on Prospect Hill, Meade got ever more desperate about finding someone, anyone, to support his division in the attack. He explained the action in his report:

"As soon as the enemy's guns were silenced, the line of infantry was ordered to the attack. The First Brigade, on the right, advanced several hundred yards over cleared ground, driving the enemy's skirmishers before them, till they reached the woods previously described as being in front of the railroad, which they entered, driving the enemy out of them to the railroad, where they were found strongly posted in ditches and behind temporary defenses. The brigade (First) drove them from there and up the heights in their front, though, owing to a heavy fire being received on their right flank, they obliqued over to that side, but continued forcing the enemy back till they had crossed the crest of the hill; crossed a main road which runs along the crest, and reached open ground on the other side, where they were assailed by a severe fire from a large force in their front, and, at the same time, the enemy opened a battery which completely enfiladed them from the right flank. After holding their ground for some time, no support arriving, they were compelled to fall back to the railroad. The Second Brigade, which advanced in rear of the First, after reaching the railroad, was assailed with so severe a fire on their right flank that the Fourth Regiment halted and formed, faced to the right, to repel this attack. The ether regiments, in passing through the woods, being assailed from the left, inclined in that direction and ascended the heights, the Third going up as the One hundred and twenty-first of the brigade was retiring. The

Third continued to advance, and reached nearly the same point as the First Brigade, but was compelled to withdraw for the same reason. The Seventh engaged the enemy to the left, capturing many prisoners and a stand of colors, driving them from their rifle-pits and temporary defenses, and continuing the pursuit till, encountering the enemy's reenforcements, they were in turn driven back. The Third Brigade had not advanced over 100 yards, when the battery on the height on its left was remanned, and poured a destructive fire into its ranks. Perceiving this, I dispatched my aide-de-camp, Lieutenant Dehon, with orders for General Jackson to move by the right flank till he could clear the open ground in front of the battery, and then, ascending the height through the woods, swing around to the left and take the battery. Unfortunately Lieutenant Dehon fell just as he reached General Jackson, and a short time afterward the latter officer was killed. The regiments, however, did partially execute the movement by obliquing to the right, and advancing across the railroad, a portion ascending the heights in their front. The loss of their commander, and the severity of the fire from both artillery and infantry to which they were subjected, compelled them to withdraw, when those on their right withdrew."

One of the reasons Meade was so desperate for help is because a Confederate mistake had given the Union an opening right in his front, so long as enough soldiers were pushed forward. Despite the fact Jackson's men had been in the area for two weeks, Jackson's line had only been formed the day before when all of his divisions were recalled from the various crossing points downriver of Fredericksburg. When they formed a line, A.P. Hill's Light Division had a 600 yard gap in it near a small, swampy patch of woods. If the Confederates thought Union men would not hit the gap, they were unpleasantly surprised when Meade's 1st brigade poured into the gap and hit one of the brigades in A.P. Hill's division right on its flank. Confederate brigadier Maxcy Gregg was so taken by surprise that he initially thought Meade's men were Confederate comrades and ordered his men not to fire. When he rode to the front of his own line, his mistake cost him his life when one of the advancing Union soldiers shot him through the spine.

Fortunately for the Confederates, they were able to plug their gap by sending forth Jubal Early's division and William Taliaferro's division at just the right time. Early described the action:

"Shortly after noon we heard in our front a very heavy musketry fire, and soon a courier from General Archer came to the rear in search of General A. P. Hill, stating that General Archer was very heavily pressed and wanted reinforcements. Just at that moment, a staff officer rode up with an order to me from General Jackson, to hold my division in readiness to move to the right promptly, as the enemy was making a demonstration in that direction. This caused me to hesitate about sending a brigade to Archer's assistance, but to be prepared to send it if necessary, I ordered Colonel Atkinson to get his brigade ready to advance, and the order had been hardly given, before the adjutant of Walker's battalion of artillery came galloping to the rear with the information that the interval on Archer's left (an awful gulf as he designated it) had been penetrated by heavy columns of the enemy, and that Archer's brigade and all our batteries on the right would inevitably be captured unless there was instant relief. This was so serious an emergency that I determined to act upon it at once notwithstanding the previous directions from General Jackson to hold my division in readiness for another purpose, and I accordingly ordered Atkinson to advance with his brigade.

I was then entirely unacquainted with the ground in front, having been able when I first got up to take only a hasty glance at the country to our right, and I asked Lieutenant Chamberlain, Walker's adjutant, to show the brigade the direction to advance. In reply he stated that the column of the enemy which had penetrated our line was immediately in front of the brigade I had ordered forward, and that by going right ahead there could be no mistake. The brigade, with the exception of one regiment, the 13th Georgia, which did not hear the order, accordingly moved off in handsome style through the woods, but as it did so Lieutenant Chamberlain informed me that it would not be sufficient to cover the entire gap in our line, and I ordered Colonel Walker to advance immediately with my own brigade on the left of Atkinson.

The enemy's column in penetrating the interval mentioned had turned Archer's left and Lane's right, while they were attacked in front, causing Archer's left and Lane's entire brigade to give way, and one column had encountered Gregg's brigade, which, being taken somewhat by surprise, was thrown into partial confusion, resulting in the death of General Gregg, but the brigade was rallied and maintained its ground. Lawton's brigade advancing rapidly and gallantly under Colonel Atkinson, encountered that column of the enemy which had turned Archer's left, in the woods on the hill in rear of the line, and by a brilliant charge drove it back down the hill, across the railroad, and out into the open plains beyond, advancing so far as to cause a portion of one of the enemy's batteries to be abandoned. The brigade, however, on getting out into the open plain came under the fire of the enemy's heavy guns, and the approach of a fresh and heavy column on its right rendered it necessary that it should retire, which it did under orders from Colonel Evans, who had succeeded to the command by reason of Atkinson's being severely wounded.

Two of Brockenborough's regiments from the right participated in the repulse of the enemy. Colonel Walker advanced, at a double quick, further to the left, encountering one of the columns which had penetrated the interval, and by a gallant and resolute charge he drove it back out of the woods across the railroad into the open plains beyond, when, seeing another column of the enemy crossing the railroad on his left, he fell back to the line of the road, and then deployed the 13th Virginia Regiment to the left, and ordered it to advance under cover of the timbers to attack the advancing column on its flank. This attack was promptly made and Thomas' brigade, attacking in front at the same time, the enemy was driven back with heavy loss.

As soon as Atkinson and Walker had been ordered forward, Hoke was ordered to move his brigade to the left of Hays, but before he got into position, I received a message stating that Archer's brigade was giving way and I ordered Hoke to move forward at once to Archer's support, obliquing to the right as he moved. Just as Hoke started, I received an order from General Jackson, by a member of his staff, to advance to the front with the whole division, and Hays' brigade was at once ordered forward in support of Hoke. The 13th Georgia Regiment which had been left behind on the advance of Lawton's brigade was ordered to follow Hoke's brigade and unite with it.

Hoke found a body of the enemy in the woods in rear of Archer's line on the left, where the regiments on that flank, which had been attacked in rear, had given way, but Archer still held the right with great resolution, though his ammunition was exhausted. Upon a gallant charge, by the brigade under Hoke, the enemy was driven out of the woods upon his reserves posted on the railroad in front, and then by another charge, in which General Archer participated, the railroad was cleared and the enemy was pursued to a fence some distance beyond, leaving in our hands a number of prisoners, and a large number of small arms on the field.

The movements of the three brigades engaged have been described separately from the necessity of the case, but they were all engaged at the same time, though they went into action separately and in the order in which they have been mentioned, and Lawton's brigade had advanced further out into the plains than either of the others.

On riding to the front, I directed Lawton's brigade, which was retiring, to be re-formed in the woods-Colonel Atkinson had been left in front severely wounded and he fell into the enemy's hands. Captain E. P. Lawton, Assistant Adjutant General of the brigade, a most gallant and efficient officer, had also been left in front at the extreme point to which the brigade advanced, mortally wounded, and he likewise fell into the enemy's hands.

I discovered that Hoke had got too far to the front where he was exposed to the enemy's artillery, and also to a flank movement on his right, and I sent an order for him to retire to the original line, which he did, anticipating the order by commencing to retire before it reached him. Two of his regiments and a small battalion were left to occupy the line of the railroad where there was cover for them and his other two regiments, along with the 13th Georgia, which had not been engaged, were put in the slight trenches previously occupied by Archer's brigade. Walker continued to hold the position on the railroad which he had taken after repulsing the enemy. Lawton's brigade was sent to the rear for the purpose of resting and replenishing its ammunition. Hays' brigade, which had advanced in rear of Hoke, had not become engaged, but in advancing to the front it had been exposed to a severe shelling which the enemy began, as his attacking columns were retiring in confusion before my advancing brigades. Hays was posted in rear of Hoke for the purpose of strengthening the right in the event of another advance. When I had discovered Lawton's brigade retiring, I sent to General D. H. Hill for reinforcements for fear that the enemy might again pass through the unprotected interval, and he sent me two brigades, but before they arrived Brigadier General Paxton, who occupied the right of Taliaferro's line, had covered the interval by promptly moving his brigade into it.

The enemy was very severely punished for this attack, which was made by Franklin's grand division, and he made no further attack on our right. During this engagement and subsequently there were demonstrations against A. P. Hill's left and Hood's right which were repulsed without difficulty.."

As Meade's men fought desperately to exploit the Confederate mistake and keep a gap open, officers in the rear vacillated over how to proceed. Gibbon refused to let any of his brigades support Meade's assault, operating under the belief that he was supposed to maintain a support position. One of his brigades would not move forward to Meade's help until 1:30 p.m., more than 2 hours after Meade's men had started the assault. 2 more brigades followed, but all three of these were sharply repulsed. Yet another supporting brigade was thrown into the fray, but the Confederates drove them back in fierce hand-to-hand fighting that drove the disorganized Union soldiers back. Simply put, the supporting brigades had made their attacks too late to help Meade's breakthrough in Jackson's line. An enraged Meade complained to his corps commander, "My God, General Reynolds, did they think my division could whip Lee's whole army?"

As the Union soldiers were pushed back, Early had trouble controlling his own men, and some of them led a counterattack without orders, continuing forward in a chase after the retreating Union men. This brought them through an open field, allowing Union artillery to unleash grapeshot canister blasts on them. Early's counterattack also coincided with an advance by General David Birney's division of the Union III Corps, which finally began moving forward after Meade singlehandedly ordered them forward with profanity that one staffer said "almost makes the stones creep." Birney's men were far too late to help Meade's attack, but they stopped the Confederate advance. Stonewall Jackson's men withdrew back to their defensive positions on the high ground, bringing the fighting south of Fredericksburg to an end. Franklin had lost 5,000 casualties, and Stonewall Jackson had lost nearly 3,500 casualties.

With the fighting ending around the middle of the afternoon, Burnside had already concentrated on trying to dislodge Longstreet from Marye's Heights, and when he learned that his men had failed to force Stonewall Jackson's withdrawal, he apparently did not have contingency plans or decide on a new plan. When he ordered Franklin to "advance his right and front," the kind of general attack that very well could have been successful hours earlier, Franklin refused on the grounds that all of his men had already been engaged and were battered. In reality, Franklin still had about 20,000 men at his disposal, comprised of the VI Corps and Doubleday's division, who had not fought in the infantry battle at all.

Meade was bitter for weeks, and he described the effect the fighting had on his division:

"It will be seen from the foregoing that the attack was for a time perfectly successful.' The enemy was driven from the railroad, his rifle-pits, and breastworks, for over half a mile. Over 300 prisoners were taken and several standards, when the advancing line encountered the heavy re-enforcements of the enemy, who, recovering from the effects of our assault, and perceiving both our flanks unprotected, poured in such a destructive fire from all three directions as to compel the line to fall back, which was executed without confusion. Perceiving the danger of the too great penetration of my line, without support, I dispatched several staff officers both to General Gibbon's command and General Birney's (whose division had replaced mine at the batteries from whence we advanced), urging an advance to my support, the one on my right, the other on my left. A brigade of Birney's advanced to our relief just as my men were withdrawn from the wood, and Gibbon's division advanced into the wood on our right in time to assist materially in the safe withdrawal of my broken line.

An unsuccessful effort was made to reform the division in the hollow in front of the batteries. Failing in this, the command was reformed beyond the Bowling Green road and marched to the ground occupied the night before, where it was held in reserve till the night of the 15th, when we recrossed the river.

Accompanying this report is a list giving the names of the killed, wounded, and missing, amounting in the aggregate to 179 killed, 1,082 wounded, and 509 missing. When I report that 4,500 men is a liberal estimate of the strength of the division taken into action, this large loss, being 40 per cent., will fully bear me out in the expression of my satisfaction at the good conduct of both officers and men. While I deeply regret the inability of the division, after having successfully penetrated the enemy's lines, to remain and hold what had been secured, at the same time I deem their withdrawal a matter of necessity. With one brigade commander killed, another wounded, nearly half their number hors du combat, with regiments separated from brigades, and companies from regiments, and all the confusion and disorder incidental to the advance of an extended line through wood and other obstructions, assailed by a heavy fire, not only of infantry but of artillery--not only in front but on both flanks--the best troops would be justified in withdrawing without loss of honor."

The fighting conducted by Meade's division was one of the most talked-about aspects of the battle among Civil War veterans after the war, so much so that Longstreet went out of his way in his memoirs to discuss the fact that it had been compared to Pickett's Charge:

"The charge of Meade's division has been compared with that of Pickett's, Pettigrew's, and Trimble's at Gettysburg, giving credit of better conduct to the former. The circumstances do not justify the comparison.

When the fog lifted over Meade's advance he was within musket-range of A. P. Hill's division, closely supported on his right by Gibbon's, and guarded on his left by Doubleday's division. On Hill's right was a fourteen-gun battery, on his left eight guns. Meade broke through Hill's division, and with the support of Gibbon forced his way till he encountered part of Ewell's division, when he was forced back in some confusion. Two fresh divisions of the Third Corps came to their relief, and there were as many as fifty thousand men at hand who could have been thrown into the fight. Meade's march to meet his adversary was half a mile,--the troops of both sides fresh and vigorous.

Of the assaulting columns of Pickett, Pettigrew, and Trimble, only four thousand seven hundred under Pickett were fresh; the entire force of these divisions was only fifteen thousand strong. They had a mile to march over open field before reaching the enemy's line, strengthened by field-works and manned by thrice their numbers. The Confederates at Gettysburg had been fought to exhaustion of men and munitions. They lost about sixty per cent. of the assaulting forces,--Meade about forty. The latter had fresh troops behind him, and more than two hundred guns to cover his rallying lines. The Confederates had nothing behind them but field batteries almost exhausted of ammunition. That Meade made a brave, good fight is beyond question, but he had superior numbers and appointments. At Gettysburg the Confederate assault was made against intrenched lines of artillery and infantry, where stood fifty thousand men."

## It Is Well That War Is So Terrible

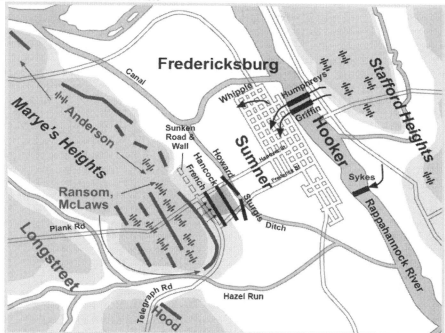

Although the Union almost broke the Confederate lines in the South, they were ultimately repulsed, and the battle is mostly remembered for the piecemeal attacks the Union army made on heavily fortified positions Longstreet's men took up on Marye's Heights. With the massacre at Antietam still fresh in his mind (partially caused by the Confederates having not constructed defensive works), Longstreet ordered trenches, abatis (obstacles formed by felled trees with sharpened branches), and fieldworks to be constructed, which to Longstreet's credit helped set a precedent for all future defensive battles of the Army of Northern Virginia. To his thinking, if the artillery didn't keep Union forces at bay, the 2500 Confederates lined up four-deep behind a quarter-mile long four-foot stone wall would deter even the most foolhardy.

Colonel Alexander kept busy re-positioning Longstreet's artillery. Captain Sam Johnston, Lee's engineer in charge of the Army of Northern Virginia, accompanied Alexander on his reconnoitering to supervise the positioning of Lee's gun pits: Lee said the guns were to be placed on the brow or reverse slope of the heights so they might square-off with Union artillery on Stafford Heights. Alexander, however, had a much different strategy in mind. Expecting the Union attack to fall on their far-left flank, Alexander positioned the gun pits to fire directly into the advancing Union infantry and sweep the battlefield, essentially disagreeing with General Lee's assessment that the Confederate ordnance could not duel effectively with the enemy's guns at such a distance. After some verbal disagreement, Lee walked away, leaving the gun pits' positioning unchanged. Upon General Longstreet's inspection of the artillery, Alexander reported proudly, "General, we cover that ground now so well that we will comb it as with a fine-tooth comb. A chicken could not live on that field when we open on it!"

During the time the two armies jockeyed for optimal position, Colonel Alexander received the nickname "the cuss with the spy glass" from Union troops, the result of his precise shelling of Union sharpshooters with a 24-pound howitzer, said to be his favorite gun. In one case, Alexander was able to target a building hidden from view by low hills and trees containing Union sharpshooters, lobbing a shell containing 175 mini-balls that nearly brushed the grass as it curved the hill but still hit the building dead center. Confederates along the line shouted, "That got 'em! That got 'em! You can hear 'em just a hollerin' and a groanin' in there!"

As the fog lifted across Fredericksburg around 10:30, Burnside's first attack against Marye's Heights was getting ready to move forward. Operating under the mistaken belief that Franklin's division would be the decisive attack that forced Lee to withdraw to a new defensive line, Burnside ordered Edwin Sumner to send "a division or more" to take the Confederate left, essentially giving him the same kind of vague instructions Franklin had received. In an army composed of over 100,000 men, Burnside had effectively given his two subordinates discretionary orders to push forward as few as 10,000 men against Lee's nearly 70,000 strong Army of Northern Virginia.

Thus, William H. French's division of Darius Couch's II Corps began moving forward through town, dodging Confederate shells while passing obstacles like houses, fences, and gardens that broke up the line in places and forced them to reform under fire. Couch explained what his men had to go through just to approach the Heights in his official report: In rear of the town the ground is a broken plain, traversed about midway by a canal or ditch, running from right to left. Across this plain, some 600 yards from the outer edge of town, commences the first rise of hills on which the enemy had erected his batteries. Two roads cut the plain nearly at right angles with the canal--the one a plank road, leading to Culpeper, to the right; the other, to the left, the Telegraph road leading to Richmond." Longstreet's guns had that whole space covered, and any Union soldier "lucky enough to survive the artillery would have to meet 2,000 of McLaws's men at the front of the Heights near the sunken road and 7,000 men situated on the crest of the Heights.

**The wall along the sunken road offered the Confederate defenders invaluable protection.**

On top of having to push one of his divisions forward, Couch also received orders to help General Willcox link up with the right of Franklin's Grand Division, necessarily keeping some of his men out of the assault: "The major-general commanding directs me to say to you that General Willcox has been ordered to extend to the left, so as to connect with Franklin's right. You will extend your right so far as to prevent the possibility of the enemy occupying the upper part of the town. You will then form a column of a division for the purpose of pushing in the direction of the Plank and Telegraph roads, for the purpose, of seizing the height in rear of the town. This column will advance in three lines, with such intervals as you may Judge proper, this movement to be covered by a heavy line of skirmishers in front and on both flanks. You will hold another division in readiness to advance in support of this movement, to be formed in the same manner as the leading division. Particular care and precaution must be taken to prevent collision with our own troops in the fog. The movement will not commence until you receive orders. The watchword will be 'Scott.'"

French's division began pushing toward the Heights, with Winfield Scott Hancock's division about 200 yards behind him to support the assault, and French's men were cut down en masse. Moreover, French's men stopped to fire their own volleys at the Confederate defenders, which made them sitting targets and delayed their advance. Most of the division was stopped about 125 yards from the wall of the sunken road. Those that got closer found that their only protection was to stay completely down on the ground and/or hide behind their comrades' corpses. 50% of French's division was wounded, killed or captured in the assault. Those who were still alive and hugging the ground actually grabbed at the legs and feet of their advancing comrades, urging and begging them to withdraw instead of get themselves killed.

Longstreet described what his men did to Hancock's advancing division in his memoirs: "Hancock, coming speedily with his division, was better organized and in time to take up the fight as French was obliged to retire. This advance was handsomely maintained, but the galling fire they encountered forced them to open fire. Under this delay their ranks were cut up as rapidly as they had collected at the canal, and when within a hundred yards of the stone wall they were so thinned that they could do nothing but surrender, even if they could leap to the road-bed. But they turned, and the fire naturally slackened, as their hurried steps took them away to their partial cover. The troops behind the stone wall were reinforced during this engagement by two of Cooke's regiments from the hill-top, ordered by General Ransom, and General McLaws ordered part of Kershaw's brigade in on their right."

Having seen hundreds of his men cut down in the first hour, French realized the strategy was hopeless, so he used his last division to try a flank attack: "Seeing shortly that this could not be done, the men falling by hundreds, Howard was directed to move his division to the right of the Telegraph road, and turn the enemy's left, the ground presenting some favorable features for such an attack." Furthermore, Sumner sent in one of the IX Corps' divisions, led by Samuel Sturgis.

Howard described the fate of his men in his post-battle report:

"At about 12.55 p.m. I was ordered to move to the right of Hancock and attack the works there, debouching on the right of the Plank road, where I had already located a company of sharpshooters, of General Sully's command, to pick off the enemy's cannoneers within range. This order was immediately countermanded by General Couch, and I was sent to support General Hancock. My command was moved out, Colonel Owen's brigade in front. He was ordered by me cross the bridge over the mill-race, which is just outside of the town, moving on Hanover street by the flank, left in front. As soon as he reached a plowed field on the left of the road, he was to deploy and move forward in line of battle. This he did in fine style. He moved, without breaking his line, to the vicinity of a small brick house, where he halted, because unsupported, and, fearing he should lose ground, caused the men to lie down. He was now within 100 yards of the enemy's first line. I sent him word to hold what he had got, and to push forward the first opportunity, and not to fire, except when he had something to fire at. Colonel Hall, meanwhile, following Colonel Owen by the flank, was ordered by General Couch, both directly and through me, to deploy to the right of Hanover street, which he did. He made several bold attempts to storm the enemy's rifle-pits, but the concentrated fire of artillery and infantry was too much to carry men through. He kept what ground he got. I held General Sully in the outskirts of the town, ready to support or relieve either brigade. Colonel Hall sent for re-enforcements, stating that his ammunition was getting low. General Sully sent him two regiments, which prolonged his line to the right. Another of General Sully's was deployed on the left of the road, and afterward endeavored to re-enforce Colonel Owen.

This, then, was the condition of things at 4 p.m.: Owen extending from the road which prolonged Hanover street to General Willcox's command; Hall extending from the same road to the right. Now a brigade of General Humphreys' division formed in my rear. Hazard's battery (Company B, Rhode Island Artillery) was sent forward across the mill-race, took position just in rear of Owen's line, and fired briskly. Captain Hazard's conduct was equal to anything I ever saw on a field of battle. With the loss of

16 men hors de combat, he drove up cowardly reluctance to help him move and serve his guns. General Humphreys desired him to cease firing, when the general gallantly led forward his men. They reached my line, a portion passed it a little, met a tremendous volley of musketry and grape, and fell back. One of my regiments, the One hundred and twenty-seventh Pennsylvania, went with him. All were rallied at the millrace ravine. As soon as the battery ceased it was withdrawn, as also was Captain Frank's New York Battery, which had followed Hazard's, and did good service near the same advanced ground."

Neither Howard nor Sturgis could make any headway. In the span of a few hours, Couch's II Corps had lost over 4,000 men, and Sturgis had lost over 1,000. Longstreet, one of the most grizzled generals on either side of the war, was amazed by what he was seeing on the Heights. As Union soldiers threw themselves at his heavily fortified position along the high ground, they were mowed down again and again. General Longstreet compared the near continuous fall of soldiers on the battlefield to "the steady dripping of rain from the eaves of a house." At one point, Lee raised concerns to Longstreet about his line being broken, to which Longstreet replied, "General, if you put every man on the other side of the Potomac on that field to approach me over the same line, and give me plenty of ammunition, I will kill them all before they reach my line."

By the middle of the afternoon, 4 divisions had failed to make any headway against Marye's Heights, but Burnside stubbornly decided to stick with the plan, and he next ordered Hooker's entire Grand Division to cross the Rappahannock and attack the Heights. After performing his own reconnaissance in the front, Hooker returned across the river to urge Burnside not to make the attack. Burnside, who remained behind the river throughout the day and never conducted his own reconnaissance on the 13th, refused Hooker's advice. Given the fact that Burnside despised Hooker, the rejection probably came as no surprise to the disgusted commander of the Central Division.

Adding to the Army of the Potomac's problem, the lull in the charges against the Heights allowed some of Longstreet's men to arrive as reinforcements, including George Pickett's division and John Bell Hood's division. Inexplicably, the movement of these Confederates led some of the Federals to mistakenly (and optimistically) believe that the Confederates were retreating, inducing the V Corps division led by Andrew A. Humphreys to "exploit" the situation. Aware of what had happened before, Humphreys ordered his men to empty their muskets so that they would not stop to shoot, but as his men moved forward, the line was broken by Confederate fire and the fact that injured soldiers on the field started grabbing at their legs and pleading with them not to push forward. Humphreys's men made it to within 50 yards of the wall before hitting the ground, and they were followed by another V Corps division, this one led by George Sykes, which added to Humphreys's problems by stopping and firing at the Confederates, leaving Humphreys's men to dodge the crossfire coming from both sides.

Hooker returned from the meeting with Burnside around 4:00 p.m. and ordered forward Getty's division of the IX Corps. Getty was to attempt a flank attack on the far left of Marye's Heights, and they tried to do so undetected even as night started to fall. When they were discovered, however, they were sharply repulsed.

In the end, a recorded 14 assaults were made on Marye's Heights by elements of 7 Union divisions, resulting in upwards of 8,000 soldiers killed, wounded, or missing, all despite the fact Burnside originally intended for a diversionary attack on the Heights while Franklin made the main attack south of town. Despite all their efforts, not one Union soldier got within 100 feet of the wall at Marye's Heights before being shot or forced to withdraw or drop to the ground. The Confederates had suffered just 1,200 casualties near the heights. Watching the assaults against the Heights at one point during the battle, Lee turned to Longstreet and made one of his most famous remarks of the war: "It is well that war is so terrible, otherwise we should grow too fond of it."

With night falling, the Union assaults stopped, and as Longstreet put it, "The charges had been desperate and bloody, but utterly hopeless." Still, that didn't bring an end to the misery. After all, it was the dead of winter, and those who had survived the assaults were now forced to freeze on the battlefield still hugging the ground, knowing full well that even the slightest move might result in Confederates firing at them. On top of that, the cries of the wounded, and the inability of the soldiers to help for fear of getting shot, added to the misery.

One of the most popular legends of the battle is that one Confederate soldier, Richard Rowland Kirkland, risked his life to bring water to the wounded strewn across the field in front of Marye's Heights. When his commanding officer, Joseph B. Kershaw, denied his request to use a white handkerchief to avoid being shot, Kirkland allegedly replied, "All right, sir, I'll take my chances." With that, Kirkland is said to have gathered canteens, filled them with water, and walked around the battlefield offering aid to the wounded, and soldiers on both sides watched and let him do it unharmed for more than 90 minutes. Kershaw later wrote that when it became clear what Kirkland was doing, wounded soldiers across the battlefield cried for water, and Kirkland stopped to help every single one. For his actions, Kirkland was branded the "Angel of Marye's Heights", and a monument at Fredericksburg commemorates the story.

If the story sounds too good to be true, that's because it almost certainly is. While Kershaw wrote about it well after the war, no official report makes mention of Kirkland's actions, not even the commander of his own regiment. There are no accounts by Union soldiers in the field that night substantiating the legend either. Casting even more doubt on the story, one of the men in Kershaw's brigade tells a similar story in his history of the brigade without mentioning Kirkland:

"In one of the first charges made during the day a Federal had fallen, and to protect himself as much as possible from the bullets of his enemies, he had by sheer force of will pulled his body along until he had neared the wall. Then he failed through pure exhaustion. From loss of blood and the exposure of the sun's rays, he called loudly for water.... To go to his rescue was to court certain death... But one brave soldier from Georgia dared all, and during the lull in the firing leaped the walls, rushed to the wounded soldier, and raising his head in his arms, gave him a drink of water, then made his way back and over the wall amid a hail of bullets knocking the dirt up all around him."

One thing that did make an appearance that night was the Northern Lights, a rare phenomenon that at the time had no scientific explanation. Southern soldiers took it as a divine omen and wrote about it frequently in their diaries. The Union soldiers saw less divine inspiration in the Northern Lights and mentioned it less in their own.

## The Aftermath of the Battle of Fredericksburg

"A stunning defeat to the invader, a splendid victory to the defender of the sacred soil." – *Richmond Examiner*

During the night of December 13, Burnside continued to insist on assaulting Marye's Heights, even vowing to lead the IX Corps himself, which had been his old command at Antietam. His subordinates vigorously argued against that or any other assault, even as the commanding general made the wild claim that the failure to take the Heights had been the fault of poorly executed orders on the behalf of his officers.

Meanwhile, there was still the issue of the men stuck on the field. As one Union soldier from Sykes' division, Lt. Colonel Robert C. Buchanan, noted, "At daylight firing commenced between the pickets, and it was soon found that my position was completely commanded, so that if an individual showed his head above the crest of the hill he was picked off by the enemy's sharpshooters immediately…" Buchanan also accused Confederates of shooting at Union hospital attendants trying to reach and help the wounded, writing, "The enemy shot my men after they were wounded, and also the hospital attendants as they were conveying the wounded off the ground, in violation of every law of civilized warfare." Another Union soldier wrote, "Our line was now about 80 yards in front of a stone wall, behind which the enemy was posted in great numbers… To move even was sure to draw the fire of the enemy's sharpshooters, who were posted in the adjacent houses and in tree-tops, and whose fire we were unable to return. Thus the troops remained for twelve long hours, unable to eat, drink, or attend to the calls of nature, for so relentless were the enemy that not even a wounded man or our stretcher-carriers were exempted from their fire."

Finally, on the afternoon of December 14, Burnside and Lee agreed to a temporary truce that would allow each side to tend to their wounded. With the armies still in position throughout that day, Burnside finally withdrew back across the Rappahannock River on December 15. Although Lee had accomplished a decisive victory over Burnside's forces, the Union general had positioned his reserves and supply line so strategically that he could easily fall back without breaking lines of communication--while Lee had no such reserves or supplies. And since Lee didn't have the men to pursue and completely wipe out Burnside's army, Lee chose not to give chase. Some have contended that this was a military blunder, but given the positioning of the Union artillery on Stafford Heights across the river, a Confederate advance might have met the kind of fate those unfortunate enough to charge Marye's Heights did on December 13.

Either way, the fighting in 1862 was done, and the decisive Confederate victory buoyed the Confederacy's hopes. Lee was described by the *Charleston Mercury* as "jubilant, almost off-balance, and seemingly desirous of embracing everyone who calls on him." The results of the Maryland Campaign from 3 months earlier were apparently old news or forgotten by the *Mercury*, which boasted, "General Lee knows his business and the army has yet known no such word as fail."

Naturally, Fredericksburg represented one of the low points of the Civil War for the North, with the Army of the Potomac having suffered an almost unheard of 8:1 ratio in losses compared to Lee's army. Lincoln reacted to the news by writing, "If there is a worse place than hell, I am in it." It showed too, as noted by Pennsylvania Governor Andrew Curtin, who told Lincoln after touring the battlefield, "It was not a battle, it was a butchery". Curtin noted the president was "heart-broken at the recital, and soon reached a state of nervous excitement bordering on insanity." Radical Republicans frustrated at the prosecution of the war took it out on the generals and the Lincoln Administration; Michigan Senator Zachariah Chandler claimed, "The President is a weak man, too weak for the occasion, and those fool or traitor generals are wasting time and yet more precious blood in indecisive battles and delays." Perhaps the *Cincinnati Commercial* summed up the battle best in reporting, "It can hardly be in human nature for men to show more valor or generals to manifest less judgment, than were perceptible on our side that day."

Although there was jubilant talk in the South of the North giving up the fight imminently after Fredericksburg, it was clearly premature. Lee had concluded an incredibly successful year for the

Confederates in the East, but the South was still struggling. The Confederate forces in the West had failed to win a major battle, suffering defeat at places like Shiloh in Tennessee and across the Mississippi River. As the war continued into 1863, the southern economy continued to deteriorate. Southern armies were suffering serious deficiencies of nearly all supplies as the Union blockade continued to be effective as stopping most international commerce with the Confederacy. Moreover, the prospect of Great Britain or France recognizing the Confederacy had been all but eliminated by the Emancipation Proclamation.

Given the unlikelihood of forcing the North's capitulation, the Confederacy's main hope for victory was to win some decisive victory or hope that Abraham Lincoln would lose his reelection bid in 1864, and that the new president would want to negotiate peace with the Confederacy. Understandably, this colored Confederate war strategy, and unquestionably Lee's, in 1863, which goes a long way toward explaining what happened at Chancellorsville and Gettysburg.

As for those battles, Burnside would not be with the Army of the Potomac during them. In January, a month removed from Fredericksburg, Lincoln fired the man who believed he was not up to the job of commanding the Army of the Potomac but took it anyway to prevent Joe Hooker from becoming the commanding general. As fate would have it, Burnside was replaced by Joe Hooker.

### Preparing for the Chancellorsville Campaign

"My plans are perfect. May God have mercy on General Lee for I will have none." – Joseph Hooker

After the Union debacle at the Battle of Fredericksburg, the fighting in the Eastern theater of the Civil War during 1862 was done, and the decisive Confederate victory buoyed the Confederacy's hopes. Confederate commander Robert E. Lee was described by the *Charleston Mercury* as "jubilant, almost off-balance, and seemingly desirous of embracing everyone who calls on him." The results of Antietam and the Maryland Campaign from 3 months earlier were apparently old news or forgotten by the *Mercury*, which boasted, "General Lee knows his business and the army has yet known no such word as fail."

Naturally, Fredericksburg represented one of the low points of the Civil War for the North, with the Army of the Potomac having suffered an almost unheard of 8:1 ratio in losses compared to Lee's army. Lincoln reacted to the news by writing, "If there is a worse place than hell, I am in it." It showed too, as noted by Pennsylvania Governor Andrew Curtin, who told Lincoln after touring the battlefield, "It was not a battle, it was a butchery". Curtin noted the president was "heart-broken at the recital, and soon reached a state of nervous excitement bordering on insanity." Radical Republicans frustrated at the prosecution of the war took it out on the generals and the Lincoln Administration; Michigan Senator Zachariah Chandler claimed, "The President is a weak man, too weak for the occasion, and those fool or traitor generals are wasting time and yet more precious blood in indecisive battles and delays." Perhaps the *Cincinnati Commercial* summed up the battle best in reporting, "It can hardly be in human nature for men to show more valor or generals to manifest less judgment, than were perceptible on our side that day."

Although there was jubilant talk in the South of the North giving up the fight imminently after Fredericksburg, it was clearly premature. Lee had concluded an incredibly successful year for the Confederates in the East, but the South was still struggling. The Confederate forces in the West had failed to win a major battle, suffering defeat at places like Shiloh in Tennessee and across the Mississippi River. As the war continued into 1863, the southern economy continued to deteriorate. Southern armies were suffering serious deficiencies of nearly all supplies as the Union blockade continued to be effective as stopping most international commerce with the

Confederacy. Moreover, the prospect of Great Britain or France recognizing the Confederacy had been all but eliminated by the Emancipation Proclamation.

Given the unlikelihood of forcing the North's capitulation, the Confederacy's main hope for victory was to win some decisive victory or hope that Abraham Lincoln would lose his reelection bid in 1864, and that the new president would want to negotiate peace with the Confederacy. Understandably, this colored Confederate war strategy, and unquestionably Lee's, in 1863, which goes a long way toward explaining what happened at Chancellorsville and Gettysburg.

As for those battles, Burnside would not be with the Army of the Potomac during them. In January, a month removed from Fredericksburg, Lincoln fired the man who believed he was not up to the job of commanding the Army of the Potomac but took it anyway to prevent Joe Hooker from becoming the commanding general. As fate would have it, Burnside was replaced by Joe Hooker.

Darius N. Couch, who was in command of the II Corps during the Chancellorsville campaign, described some of the measures Hooker took to whip his demoralized army back into a strong fighting force:

"For some days there had been a rumor that Hooker had been fixed upon for the place, and on the 26th of January it was confirmed. This appointment, undoubtedly, gave very general satisfaction to the army, except perhaps to a few, mostly superior officers, who had grown up with it, and had had abundant opportunities to study Hooker's military character; these believed that Mr. Lincoln had committed a grave error in his selection. The army, from its former reverses, had become quite disheartened and almost sulky; but the quick, vigorous measures now adopted and carried out with a firm hand had a magical effect in toning up where there had been demoralization and inspiring confidence where there had been mistrust. Few changes were made in the heads of the general staff departments, but for his chief-of-staff Hooker applied for Brigadier-General Charles P. Stone, who, through some untoward influence at Washington, was not given to him. This was a mistake of the war dignitaries, although the officer finally appointed to the office, Major-General Daniel Butterfield, proved himself very efficient. Burnside's system of dividing the army into three grand divisions was set aside, and the novelty was introduced of giving to each army corps a distinct badge, an idea which was very popular with officers and men."

**Couch**

One noteworthy change Hooker also made in his command structure that Couch did not mention is that he organized all of his cavalry into one corps under George Stoneman, instead of continuing to attach separate brigades of cavalry to the individual corps in the army. This had led to uncoordinated uses of the cavalry, diluting the Union cavalry's ability to conduct reconnaissance and also weakening their impact in battle. Hooker was following Lee's lead in placing the cavalry under one command, but he committed what's considered one of the greatest blunders of the Chancellorsville campaign by thereafter sending the entire cavalry on a raid behind enemy lines instead of using them in their traditional roles of screening the army and conducting reconnaissance.

**Joe Hooker**

As Hooker was adding to his army and reorganizing it, Lee was actually detaching some of his army due to a shortage of supplies. In late March 1863, Lee reported, 'The men are cheerful, and I receive but few complaints, still I do not consider it enough to maintain them in health and vigor, and I fear they will be unable to endure the hardships of the approaching campaign. Symptoms of scurvy are appearing among them, and, to supply the place of vegetables, each regiment is directed to send a daily detail to gather sassafras buds, wild onions, garlic, lamb's quarter, and poke sprouts; but for so large an army the supply obtained is very small."

In addition to that hardship, Lee had detached about 15,000 from Longstreet's corps to defend against potential Union assaults made on the Peninsula, as McClellan had done the year before. When supplies became an issue, Lee ordered Longstreet's men to start gathering supplies around the countryside in Virginia and North Carolina, with the hope that the supplies could be gathered in time before the rest of the army had to face a major attack. As it would turn out, two of Longstreet's divisions, John Bell Hood's and George Pickett's, would be over 100 miles away and way too far away to march back in time to join a battle.

Hooker was ready to place his reorganized juggernaut in motion by mid-April, and with that in mind he devised a simple strategy that called on Stoneman's cavalry to conduct a raid deep behind enemy lines, destroying the Confederate supply lines and cutting Lee's communications with Richmond. Hooker figured this would compel Lee to abandon his line along the Rappahannock River and Fredericksburg and withdraw closer to Richmond, at which time the Army of the Potomac would start giving chase. As it turned out, heavy rains forced a delay in the cavalry raid, but as the battle of Chancellorsville itself would suggest, Lee would not have abandoned his current defensive line anyway.

Having witnessed a host of setbacks in 1862 and Burnside's "Mud March" fiasco at the beginning of 1863, President Lincoln was understandably upset, complaining, "I greatly fear it is another failure already." But after Hooker's first plan was scrapped, he came up with an even more ambitious second plan while discussing it with the leaders in Washington in late April. Once again the cavalry would be sent on a raid far to the south of Lee's lines, but this time Hooker planned to demonstrate along Fredericksburg with much of his army in an attempt to keep Lee's attention while also stealthily marching three of his corps across the Rappahannock several miles to the west, positioning them to strike Lee's left and rear. With supply lines and communication lines cut in his rear, Hooker figured Lee would be forced to fall back, and with this plan a large chunk of Hooker's army would already be across the Rappahannock ready to pursue.

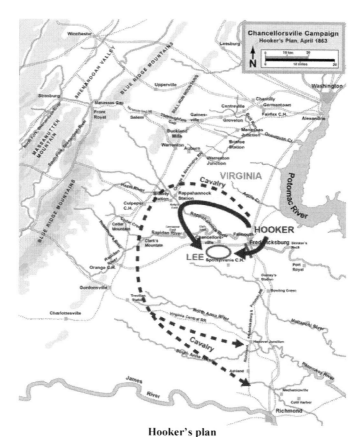

**Hooker's plan**

As Hooker's army prepared to march, he rightly labeled the Army of the Potomac "the finest army on the planet", and historians have largely credited him for his plan. Porter Alexander agreed, writing in his memoirs, "On the whole I think this plan was decidedly the best strategy conceived in any of the campaigns ever set foot against us. And the execution of it was, also, excellently managed, up to the morning of May 1st.

On the other hand, Hooker was taking a major risk by dividing his army, with one part of it across the river and the other part of it on the other side in no position to come to its support. Longstreet noted the predicament this strategy could cause in his memoirs, and he even went so far as to suggest his belief that Lee should've invited the movement and stood ready to fight a defensive battle:

"General Hooker had split his army in two, and was virtually in the condition which President Lincoln afterwards so graphically described in his letter addressed to him June 5 following,--viz.:

'I would not take any risk of being entangled upon the river, like an ox jumped half over a fence and liable to be torn by dogs front and rear, without a fair chance to gore one way or to kick the other.'

My impression was, and is, that General Lee, standing under his trenches, would have been stronger against Hooker than he was in December against Burnside, and that he would have grown stronger every hour of delay, while Hooker would have grown weaker in morale and in confidence of his plan and the confidence of his troops. He had interior lines for defence, while his adversary was divided by two crossings of the river, which made Lee's sixty thousand for defence about equal to the one hundred and thirteen thousand under General Hooker. By the time that the divisions of Pickett and Hood could have joined General Lee, General Hooker would have found that he must march to attack or make a retreat without battle. It seems probable that under the original plan the battle would have given fruits worthy of a general engagement. The Confederates would then have had opportunity, and have been in condition to so follow Hooker as to have compelled his retirement to Washington, and that advantage might have drawn Grant from Vicksburg; whereas General Lee was actually so crippled by his victory that he was a full month restoring his army to condition to take the field. In defensive warfare he was perfect. When the hunt was up, his combativeness was overruling."

### Getting the Jump on Lee

Hooker had designed a grand strategy, and during the first few days he put it in motion, it went nearly flawlessly. On April 27, the column of nearly 40,000 Union soldiers led by Henry Slocum, the XII Corps commander, began marching west to cross the Rappahannock and Rapidan rivers miles upstream and went completely undetected by Lee. In conjunction with that movement, Hooker began demonstrating near Fredericksburg with a large part of his army, as if he was about to force a crossing like Burnside had done in December. Couch explained the dispositions:

In order to confound Lee, orders were issued to assemble the Sixth, Third, and First corps under Sedgwick at Franklin's Crossing and Pollock's Mill, some three miles below Fredericksburg, on the left, before daylight of the morning of the 29th, and throw two bridges across and hold them. This was done under a severe fire of sharp-shooters. The Second Corps, two divisions, marched on the 28th for Banks's Ford, four miles to the right; the other division, Gibbon's, occupying Falmouth, near the river-bank, was directed to remain in its tents, as they were in full view of the enemy, who would readily observe their withdrawal.

**Slocum**

With these distractions, the plan called for the three corps (V, XI and XII) being guided by Slocum to arrive near Chancellorsville around April 30, which consisted of one mansion at a crossroads between the Orange Turnpike and Orange Plank Road. This was essential because the "Wilderness" was directly to the west of Chancellorsville, and it was so tangled that coordinated troop activity in that sector would be all but impossible, as Grant and Lee would find out a year later in May 1864. While they were concentrating there, Stoneman's cavalry set out on April 30 to harry Lee's lines in the south, Couch's II Corps was able to cross on April 30 miles west of Fredericksburg, and the III Corps under Dan Sickles was able to cross the Rappahannock the night of April 30. By the morning of May 1, Hooker had nearly 70,000 men around Chancellorsville, more than Lee's entire army, and Hooker still had John Sedgwick's VI Corps and John Reynolds's I Corps trying to cross in Lee's front a few miles south of Fredericksburg.

As the Army of the Potomac conducted these movements from April 27-30, Lee's army stayed in its defensive line near Fredericksburg, largely unaware of Hooker's intentions. Hooker's movements had worked perfectly, and he had Lee in just the position he had hoped for when concocting the plan. On April 30, Hooker issued General Orders No. 47, prematurely congratulating his army:

"It is with heartfelt satisfaction the commanding general announces to the army that the operations of the last three days have determined that our enemy must either ingloriously fly, or come out from behind his defenses and give us battle on our own ground, where certain destruction awaits him.

The operations of the Fifth, Eleventh, and Twelfth Corps have been a succession of splendid achievements."

## May 1

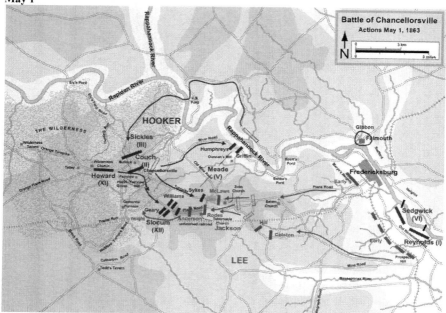

**The action on May 1**

After the war, one of the most famous quotes of the battle allegedly came from Hooker, as reported in a history of the campaign published early in the 20th century. According to author and Civil War veteran John Bigelow Jr., there was a famous exchange between Hooker and division commander Abner Doubleday, in which Doubleday asked Hooker on the march toward Gettysburg, "What was wrong with you at Chancellorsville? Some say you were injured by a shell, and others that you were drunk; now tell us what it was." Hooker allegedly replied, "Doubleday, I was not hurt by a shell, and I was not drunk. For once I lost confidence in Hooker, and that is all there is to it."

Modern historians have strongly disputed that any such exchange took place, and it would certainly be out of character for Hooker, whose arrogance strongly turned off many of his comrades. But in an effort to explain why Hooker conducted such an ambitious campaign only to halt an offensive on May 1 when he had Lee where he wanted, it has often been said that Hooker lost his nerve.

While that has long been an accepted version of what happened, Hooker's General Orders on April 30 indicate that Hooker's plan was to march into a position that would force Lee to retreat or come out of his defenses to attack Hooker. In other words, Hooker's words suggest that he intended to fight a defensive battle all along if Lee would actually give battle, a possibility Hooker largely discounted.

It's also understandable why Hooker figured Lee wouldn't stand his ground and fight. To do so, Lee would have to shift at least part of his army a few miles to the west to face the Union soldiers gathering there, moving his men out of the vicinity of Fredericksburg even while two whole corps of the Army of the Potomac was in their front there. Essentially, Lee would have to split his forces and face the enemy in two fronts, while being heavily outnumbered in both.

Lee had not correctly anticipated what Hooker was doing with the column that set off on April 27 to head to Chancellorsville, but as he explained in his report after the campaign, the fact that Sedgwick and Reynolds were only demonstrating with their corps south of Fredericksburg during those days suggested to him that they were not intended to be the main thrust against his army:

"No demonstration was made opposite any other part of our lines at Fredericksburg, and the strength of the force that had crossed and its apparent indisposition to attack indicated that the principal effort of the enemy would be made in some other quarter. This impression was confirmed by intelligence received from General Stuart that a large body of infantry and artillery was passing up the river. During the forenoon of the 29th, that officer reported that the enemy had crossed in force near Kelly's Ford on the preceding evening. Later in the day he announced that a heavy column was moving from Kelly's toward Germanna Ford, on the Rapidan, and another toward Ely's Ford, on that river. The routes they were pursuing after crossing the Rapidan converge near Chancellorsville, whence several roads lead to the rear of our position at Fredericksburg."

Lee had sent one of the two divisions of Longstreet's corps that had stayed with his army under Richard Anderson toward Chancellorsville on April 29, but that division and the few Confederate forces posted along the Rappahannock crossings in that area would clearly be no match for the several corps Hooker had near Chancellorsville on May 1. Lee had to choose whether he would withdraw as Hooker expected or whether he would stay and fight.

As Longstreet alluded to in his memoirs, Lee was aggressive when he sensed an opportunity, and on May 1 he gambled that Sedgwick and Reynolds were merely a diversionary force that would not cause him trouble if he shifted the vast majority of his army to face the rest of Hooker's men near Chancellorsville. Thus, nearly 80% of Lee's army began marching west toward Chancellorsville in the early morning, leaving about 10,000 Confederates in Marye's Heights outside of Fredericksburg to defend against the 40,000 Union soldiers in their front. The rest of Lee's army, consisting of under 50,000 men, marched to the Zoan and Tabernacle churches along the Orange Turnpike and Orange Plank Road about two miles east of Chancellorsville. With that, the Confederates were outnumbered by 30,000 on their right and about 20,000 on their left.

While the Confederates started digging in along the Turnpike and the Plank Road, Hooker directed two divisions from George Meade's V Corps to head east down the River Road toward Banks's Ford, where they would guard a crossing for the rest of the army, the other division from the V Corps to head east on the Turnpike, and the XII Corps to march down the Plank Road, which meant these divisions would march straight into Confederate positions. Hooker kept Oliver Howard's XI Corps, Couch's II Corps, and Sickles's III Corps in reserve.

Hooker had a sizable numbers advantage, but he was sending three different columns down three different roads, making a coordinated attack practically impossible. As a result, the three roads would see piecemeal actions, beginning with Sykes's division of Meade's Corps hitting Lafayette McLaws's division on the Turnpike. The two sides pushed each other back and forth, while Richard Anderson's division found itself fighting elements of the XII Corps and XI Corps along the Plank Road. While the Union fought along those two roads, Meade's other divisions marched unopposed on the River Road toward Banks's Ford.

When McLaws's division had pushed Sykes's division back along the Turnpike, they got within a mile of Chancellorsville and were able to see the environment Hooker was positioned in. Lee explained in his report:

"At 11 a.m. the troops moved forward upon the Plank and old Turnpike roads, Anderson, with the brigades of Wright and Posey, leading on the former; McLaws, with his three brigades, preceded by Mahone's, on the latter. Generals Wilcox and Perry, of Anderson's division, co-operated with McLaws. Jackson's troops followed Anderson on the Plank road. Colonel Alexander's battalion of artillery accompanied the advance. The enemy was soon encountered on both roads, and heavy skirmishing with infantry and artillery ensued, our troops pressing steadily forward. A strong attack upon General McLaws was repulsed with spirit by Semmes' brigade, and General Wright, by direction of General Anderson, diverging to the left of the Plank road, marched by way of the unfinished railroad from Fredericksburg to Gordonsville, and turned the enemy's right. His whole line thereupon retreated rapidly, vigorously pursued by our troops until they arrived within about 1 mile of Chancellorsville. Here the enemy had assumed a position of great natural strength, surrounded on all sides by a dense forest filled with a tangled undergrowth, in the midst of which breastworks of logs had been constructed, with trees felled in front, so as to form an almost impenetrable abatis. His artillery swept the few narrow roads by which his position could be approached from the front, and commanded the adjacent woods."

While Lee's report makes clear that Hooker was in a strong defensive position, it was also in a position that would make troop movements much more difficult. On the other hand, the ground that the Union divisions were fighting over was high ground with enough openings to place and use artillery. However, instead of pushing his reserves forward, during the middle of the fighting Hooker ordered his advanced divisions to fall back to Chancellorsville, shocking the subordinates who were commanding men in the middle of the fray. As Couch explained:

"Meade was finally pushed out on the left over the Banks's Ford and turnpike roads, Slocum and Howard on the right along the Plank road, the left to be near Banks's Ford by 2 P. M., the right at the junction of its line of movement with the turnpike at 12 M. No opposition was met, excepting that the division marching over the turnpike came upon the enemy two or three miles out, when the sound of their guns was heard at Chancellorsville, and General Hooker ordered me to take Hancock's division and proceed to the support of those engaged. After marching a mile and a half or so I came upon Sykes, who commanded, engaged at the time in drawing back his advance to the position he then occupied. Shortly after Hancock's troops had got into a line in front, an order was received from the commanding general 'to withdraw both divisions to Chancellorsville.' Turning to the officers around me, Hancock, Sykes, Warren, and others, I told them what the order was, upon which they all agreed with me that the ground should not be abandoned, because of the open country in front and the commanding position. An aide, Major J. B. Burt, dispatched to General Hooker to this effect, came back in half an hour with positive orders to return. Nothing was to be done but carry out the command, though Warren suggested that I should disobey, and then he rode back to see the general. In the meantime Slocum, on the Plank road to my right, had been ordered in, and the enemy's advance was between that road and my right flank. Sykes was first to move back, then followed by Hancock's regiments over the same road. When all but two of the latter had withdrawn, a third order came to me, brought by one of the general's staff: 'Hold on until 5 o'clock.' It was then perhaps 2 P. M. Disgusted at the general's vacillation and vexed at receiving an order of such tenor, I replied with warmth unbecoming in a subordinate: 'Tell General Hooker he is too late, the enemy are already on my right and rear. I am in full retreat.'"

Hooker was thus ceding the high ground around the roads and opting to dig in near the Wilderness instead, leaving some of the corps commanders beside themselves. George Meade complained, "My God, if we can't hold the top of the hill, we certainly can't hold the bottom of it!" Couch also considered it the moment the battle was lost, writing, "Proceeding to the Chancellor House, I narrated my operations in front to Hooker, which were seemingly satisfactory, as he said: 'It is all right, Couch, I have got Lee just where I want him; he must fight me on my own ground.' The retrograde movement had prepared me for something of the kind, but to hear from his own lips that the advantages gained by the successful marches of his lieutenants were to culminate in fighting a defensive battle in that nest of thickets was too much, and I retired from his presence with the belief that my commanding general was a whipped man. The army was directed to intrench itself."

On the night of May 1, Lee still had to decide whether to pull his army back or attack Hooker. He was still hoping to destroy the entire portion of Hooker's army at Chancellorsville before Sedgwick and Reynolds began pushing back his sparse defensive line near Fredericksburg. Jackson agreed with him, and as the two met that night to discuss their options. Jackson biographer Robert Lewis Dabney described their meeting:

"When Friday night arrived, Generals Lee and Jackson met, at a spot where the road to the Catharine Iron Furnace turned southwestward from the plank-road, which was barely a mile in front of Hooker's works. Here, upon the brow of a gentle hill, grew a cluster of pine-trees, while the gound was carpeted with the clean, dry sedge and fallen leaves. They selected this spot, with their respective Staffs, to bivouac, while the army lay upon their weapons, a few yards before them, and prepared to sleep upon the ground, like their men. General Stuart had now joined them, and reported the results of his reconnoissances upon the south and west of Hooker's position. He had ascertained that the Federal commander had left a whole corps, under General Reynolds, at Ely's Ford, to guard his communications there, and that he had massed ninety thousand men around Chancellorsville, under his own eye, fortifying them upon the east, south and, southwest, as has been described. But upon the west and northwest his encampments were open, and their movements were watched by Stuart's pickets, who were secreted in the wilderness there. He had also ascertained, that almost all their cavalry had broken through the line of the Rapid Ann in one body, and had invaded the south, followed and watched by the brigade of W. H. Lee, evidently bent upon a grand raid against the Confederate communications. Generals Lee and Jackson now withdrew, and held an anxious consultation. That Hooker must be attacked, and that speedily, was clear to the judgments of both."

**"The Last Meeting" between Lee and Jackson**

As Lee realized, however, "It was evident that a direct attack upon the enemy would be attended with great difficulty and loss, in view of the strength of his position and his superiority of numbers." Thanks to reports from Stuart's cavalry that Hooker's left was well-defended (thanks to Meade's march on River Road) and his right was "in the air" with an open flank, Lee decided "to endeavor to turn his right flank and gain his rear, leaving a force in front to hold him in check and conceal the movement." In other words, having already split his army in two in the face of a larger army, Lee now planned to split his army into three by having some of his command march around Hooker's right, defying all military convention. Dabney explained:

"General Lee had promptly concluded, that while, on the one hand, immediate attack was proper, some more favorable place for assault must be sought, by moving farther toward Hooker's right. The attempt to rout ninety thousand well armed troops, entrenched at their leisure, by a front attack, with thirty-five thousand, would be too prodigal of patriot blood, and would offer too great a risk of repulse. He had accordingly already commanded his troops to commence a movement toward their left, and communicated his views to General Jackson, who warmly concurred in their wisdom. A report was about this time received from General Fitz Hugh Lee, of Stuart's command, describing the position of the Federal army, and the roads which he held with his cavalry leading to its rear. General Jackson now proposed to throw his command entirely into Hooker's rear, availing himself of the absence of the Federal cavalry, and the presence of the Confederate horse, and to assail him from the West, in concert with Anderson and McLaws. Stuart was there with his active horsemen to cover this movement; and he believed that it could be made with comparatively little risk, and, when accomplished, would enable him to crush the surprised enemy. He well knew that he was apparently proposing a 'grand detachment'; a measure pronounced by military science so reprehensible, in the presence of an active adversary."

With that decision, the stage was set for two of the most dramatic days of the Civil War.

**May 2**

Having decided on the night of May 1 to try to turn Hooker's right flank, the Confederates went about getting a guide who could lead Jackson's command on the march. Charles C. Wellford, the man who owned the nearby Catherine Furnace, gave Jackson's mapmaker information about a road near Catherine Furnace that would take them to Brock Road and allow Jackson to march northwest toward Wilderness Tavern, placing them squarely in the flank and rear of Howard's XI Corps. The backwoods route was intended to hide the march from Union pickets, and the lack of Union cavalry to screen the Army of the Potomac made the stealthy march that much likelier to succeed.

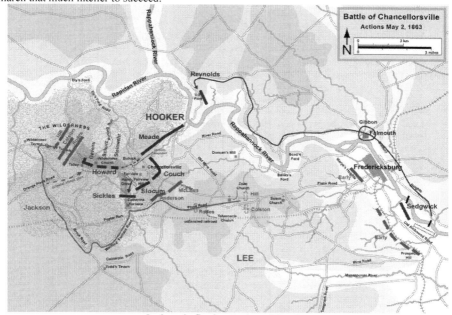

**Jackson's flank attack on May 2**

As Jackson began marching his command that morning along a 12 mile route, Lee started digging in with Anderson's division and McLaws's division in Hooker's front along the Turnpike and the Plank Road. With Jackson's 28,000 men marching around Hooker's right, Lee now had less than 15,000 soldiers holding the line in front of Hooker's 70,000. Meanwhile, Hooker was also still digging in, and to bolster his numbers he ordered Reynolds to leave the Fredericksburg front and march to Chancellorsville to join the right flank. It was a circuitous march that had no hope of reaching Chancellorsville on May 2.

One of the great myths of Stonewall Jackson's legendary flank attack on May 2 is that it came as a complete surprise to the Army of the Potomac when the Confederates came bursting out of the woods on their flank. In fact, despite Stuart's cavalry screening the march in order to hide it to the best of their ability, there were several different times during the day that Union forces spotted the Confederate column and alerted their superiors. As Darius Couch explained:

"On the morning of May 2d our line had become strong enough to resist a front attack unless made in great force; the enemy had also been hard at work on his front, particularly that section of it between the Plank road and turnpike. Sedgwick, the previous night, had been ordered to send the First Corps (Reynolds's) to Chancellorsville. At 7 A. M. a sharp cannonade was opened on our left, followed by infantry demonstrations of no particular earnestness. Two hours later the enemy were observed moving a mile or so to the south and front of the center, and later the same column was reported to the commander of the Eleventh Corps by General Devens, whose division was on the extreme right flank. At 9:30 A. M. a circular directed to Generals Slocum and Howard called attention to this movement and to the weakness of their flanks."

News of Jackson's flank march reached Hooker within hours of its start, and Hooker guessed that it was either a retreat or a flanking march, so at 9:30 he warned XI Corps commander Oliver Howard, "We have good reason to suppose the enemy is moving to our right. Please advance your pickets for purposes of observation as far as may be safe in order to obtain timely information of their approach." Howard claimed later that morning that his corps was "taking measures to resist an attack from the west."

While Hooker was inviting Lee to attack around Chancellorsville, he ordered Sedgwick's VI Corps to "attack the enemy in his front [if] an opportunity presents itself with a reasonable expectation of success". Despite having a 4-1 advantage in manpower, Sedgwick decided to be cautious, possibly remembering what had happened when Union soldiers tried to storm Marye's Heights during the Battle of Fredericksburg the previous December. As a result, Sedgwick decided not to attack the Confederate line, manned by Jubal Early's greatly stretched division. Sedgwick has been heavily criticized by historians ever since, but he rationalized his decision in his post-campaign report:

"The following day, Saturday, May 2, Reynolds' corps was withdrawn from my command, and ordered to proceed to headquarters of the army, at or near Chancellorsville, one division, General Wheaton's, of the Sixth Corps, being sent by General Newton to cover his crossing and take up his bridge. I was also ordered to take up all the bridges at Franklin's crossing and below before daylight. This order was received at 5.25 a.m., after daylight, and could not, of course, be executed without attracting the observation of the enemy, and leaving him free to proceed against the forces under General Hooker."

**Sedgwick**

Lee had divided his army once on May 1 and again on May 2 by betting on Sedgwick's inaction in front of Early, and Sedgwick played right into it. Meanwhile, as Hooker was giving Sedgwick discretionary orders to possibly advance, he decided to try to intercept Jackson's column by moving Sickles's III corps "cautiously toward the road followed by the enemy, and harass the movement as much as possible". This order took the III Corps south past the high ground at Hazel Grove and interposed it between Richard Anderson's division and Jackson's column. By the time the men of the III Corps reached their destination, however, a rearguard conducted by the 23rd Georgia Infantry kept Sickles from harassing Jackson's advance. The 23rd Georgia would lose a majority of its men defending Jackson's rear, and eventually two brigades from A.P. Hill's famous "Light Division" had to reinforce them to cover Jackson.

Around 3:00, Jackson and cavalry officer Fitzhugh Lee were able to scout the Union's lines from high ground near the Plank Road. Despite Howard having told Hooker that he was preparing for the possibility of an attack on his flank, Jackson found Howard's men idling around, completely unprepared for what was about to hit them. In addition to being unprepared, the XI Corps was composed of a bunch of raw recruits who had never seen battle, and those who had seen action performed poorly at Second Manassas. The very reason they were on the far right was because Hooker didn't intend to use them for major combat operations.

As Jackson's men reached the crossroads near Wilderness Tavern, the opening in the area allowed him to form battle lines that straddled the Orange Turnpike in the rear of the XI Corps. They would then be marching through thick underbrush that not only completely obscured them but also scratched them up and tore their clothes. Despite the inevitable noises made by 21,000 men moving forward through a forest, and the scurrying of various animals out of the forest, Howard's corps still remained unprepared, and many of them were mostly concerned with cooking their dinner.

Sometime between 5-6 p.m., Jackson's men came hurdling out of the forest and fell upon Howard's hapless corps, many of whom had stacked unloaded rifles while sitting around campfires. Almost immediately, Jackson's attack rolled up Devens's division, and though Schurz's division tried to form an emergency defensive line in Jackson's front, they were quickly swept aside after finding themselves flanked on both sides. Dabney described the initial moments of the attack:

"With a wild hurrah, the line of Rodes burst upon them from the woods, and the first volley decided their utter rout. The second line, commanded by Colston, unable to restrain their impetuosity, rushed forward at the shout, pressed upon the first, filling up their gaps, and firing over their heads, so that thenceforward the two were almost merged into one, and advanced together, a dense and impetuous mass. For three miles the Federalists were now swept back by a resistless charge. Even the works which confronted the west afforded them no protection; no sooner were they manned by the enemy, than the Confederates dashed upon them with the bayonet, and the defenders were either captured or again put to flight. The battle was but a continued onward march, with no other pause than that required for the rectification of the line, disordered by the density of the woods."

As Dabney's account suggests, the nature of the flank attack ensured that the Confederate officers began losing control of their commands almost immediately as they began rushing forward, but the XI Corps was even more out of control. Howard tried to valiantly rally his routed corps as they began fleeing in a panicked rout eastward, but he was no George H. Thomas and this was no Chickamauga. Most of his soldiers simply ran right past him until they reached Fairview, an open field near Hooker's headquarters at the Chancellor house. The vanguard of Jackson's attack, Robert Rodes's division, chased them the entire way until being brought to heel by the artillery posted there shortly after 7:00. Hooker tried to rally an emergency defensive line by pulling one of Sickles's III Corps divisions, who due to unusual sound acoustics had not heard any of the fighting despite the fact it was going on just 2.5 miles away from them, but it was the fading daylight that would ultimately blunt the Confederate attack.

The greatest resistance Jackson faced in his attack was the temptations that invited his men to stop their pursuit, including food, personal artifacts, guns, and other supplies. Jackson continued to order his subordinates, "Press forward", and he tried to urge the soldiers to keep up what had now become a disorganized pursuit. The XI Corps had lost ¼ of its strength, 2,500 men (nearly half of whom had been captured), in an hour, while its general officers suffered a substantial number of casualties trying to rally their men. By the time the flank attack had petered out, Jackson's men were within sight of Hooker's headquarters at Chancellorsville, and Sickles's III Corps was now positioned between Jackson and the rest of Lee's force.

Lee had not been idle during Jackson's flank attack either, as explained by his nephew, cavalry officer Fitzhugh Lee, after the war: "During the flank march of his great lieutenant, Lee reminded the troops in his front of his position by frequent taps on different points of their lines, and when the sound of cannon gave notice of Jackson's attack, Lee ordered that Hooker's left be strongly pressed to prevent his sending re-enforcements to the point assailed."

Jackson's flank march permanently tarnished Oliver Howard's career and reputation, and he was well aware of it. In his post-campaign report, he took pains to try to explain what happened on the night of May 2:

"At about 6 p.m. I was at my headquarters, at Dowdall's Tavern, when the attack commenced. I sent my chief of staff to the front when firing was heard. General Schurz, who was with me, left at once to take command of his line. It was not three minutes before I followed. When I reached General Schurz's command, I saw that the enemy had enveloped my right, and that the First Division was giving way. I first tried to change the front of the deployed regiments. I next directed the artillery where to go;

then formed a line by deploying some of the reserve regiments near the church. By this time the whole front on the north of the Plank road had given way. Colonel Buschbeck's brigade was faced about, and, lying on the other side of the rifle-pit embankment, held on with praiseworthy firmness. A part of General Schimmelfennig's and a part of General Krzyzanowski's brigades moved gradually back to the north of the Plank road and kept up their fire. At the center and near the Plank road there was a blind panic and great confusion. By the assistance of my staff and some other officers, one of whom was Colonel Dickinson, of General Hooker's staff, the rout was considerably checked, and all the artillery, except eight pieces, withdrawn. Some of the artillery was well served, and told effectively on the advancing enemy. Captain Dilger kept up a continuous fire until we reached General Betty's position.

Now as to the causes of this disaster to my corps:

1. Though constantly threatened and apprised of the moving of the enemy, yet the woods was so dense that he was able to mass a large force, whose exact whereabouts neither patrols, reconnaissances, nor scouts ascertained. He succeeded in forming a column opposite to and outflanking my right.

2. By the panic produced by the enemy's reverse fire, regiments and artillery were thrown suddenly upon those in position.

3. The absence of General Barlow's brigade, which I had previously located in reserve and en echelon with Colonel von Gilsa's, so as to cover his right flank. This was the only general reserve I had. My corps was very soon reorganized near Chancellorsville, and relieved General Meade's corps, on the left of the general line. Here it remained until Wednesday morning, when it resumed its position, as ordered, at the old camp."

Although the flank attack began to lose its steam as the sun went down, Jackson remained active all along his front, and in the process of conducting his own personal reconnaissance during the night, he positioned himself between the lines. Along with some of his staff, Jackson rode so closely to the Union line that some of the horses in his party were shot during a Union musket volley:

"He had now advanced a hundred yards beyond his line of battle, evidently supposing that, in accordance with his constant orders, a line of skirmishers had been sent to the front, immediately upon the recent cessation of the advance. He probably intended to proceed to the place where he supposed this line crossed the turnpike, to ascertain from them what they could learn concerning the enemy. He was attended only by a half dozen mounted orderlies, his signal officer, Captain Wilbourne, with one of his men, and his aide, Lieutenant Morrison, who had just returned to him. General A. P. Hill, with his staff also proceeded immediately after him, to the front of the line, accompanied by Captain Boswell of the Engineers, whom General Jackson had just detached to assist him. After the General and his escort had proceeded down the road a hundred yards, they were surprised by a volley of musketry from the right, which spread toward their front, until the bullets began to whistle among them, and struck several horses."

After that close call, Jackson, Hill, and the staffers started riding back toward their own lines, only to be confused for Union soldiers by their own men, soldiers of the 18th North Carolina:

"General Jackson was now aware of their proximity, and perceived that there was no picket or skirmisher between him and his enemies. He therefore, turned to ride hurriedly back to his own troops; and, to avoid the fire, which was, thus far, limited to the south side of the road, he turned into the woods upon the north side. It so happened that General Hill, with his escort, had been directed by the same motive almost to the same spot.

As the party approached within twenty paces of the Confederate troops, these, evidently mistaking them for cavalry, stooped, and delivered a deadly fire. So sudden and stunning was this volley, and so near at hand, that every horse which was not shot down, recoiled from it in panic, and turned to rush back, bearing their riders toward the approaching enemy. Several fell dead upon the spot, among them the amiable and courageous Boswell; and more were wounded. Among the latter was General Jackson. His right hand was penetrated by a ball, his left forearm lacerated by another, and the same limb broken a little below the shoulder by a third, which not only crushed the bone, but severed the main artery. His horse also dashed, panic-stricken, toward the enemy, carrying him beneath the boughs of a tree which inflicted severe blows, lacerated his face, and almost dragged him from the saddle. His bridle hand was now powerless, but seizing the reins with the right hand, notwithstanding its wound, he arrested his career, and brought the animal back toward his own lines.

General Jackson drew up his horse, and sat for an instant gazing toward his own men, as if in astonishment at their cruel mistake, and in doubt whether he should again venture to approach them."

After personally dressing Jackson's wounds, Hill briefly took command of the Second Corps, until he was himself wounded in the legs, leaving him unable to walk or ride a horse. Hill relinquished command to Rodes, who realized he was over his head and directed JEB Stuart himself to take temporary command of the Second Infantry Corps, a decision Lee seconded when news reached him.

Jackson had been nearly hit by Union gunfire, and after he was injured, a litter started trying to carry him to the rear while coming under Union artillery fire, causing even more troubles:

"The party was now met by a litter, which someone had sent from the rear; and the General was placed upon it, and borne along by two soldiers, and Lieutenants Smith and Morrison. As they were placing him upon it, the enemy fired a volley of canister-shot up the road, which passed over their heads. But they had proceeded only a few steps before the discharge was repeated, with a more accurate aim. One of the soldiers bearing the litter was struck down, severely wounded; and had not Major Leigh, who was walking beside it, broken his fall, the General would have been precipitated to the ground. He was placed again upon the earth; and the causeway was now swept by a hurricane of projectiles of every species, before which it seemed that no living thing could survive. The bearers of the litter, and all the attendants, excepting Major Leigh and the General's two aides, left him, and fled into the woods on either hand, to escape the fatal tempest; while the sufferer lay along the road, with his feet toward the foe, exposed to all its fury.

It was now that his three faithful attendants displayed a heroic fidelity, which deserves to go down with the immortal name of Jackson to future ages. Disdaining to save their lives by deserting their chief, they lay down beside him in the causeway, and sought to protect him as far as possible with their bodies. On one side was Major Leigh, and on the other Lieutenant Smith. Again and again was the earth around them torn with volleys of canister, while shells and minie balls flew hissing over them, and the stroke of the iron hail raised sparkling flashes from the flinty gravel of the roadway.

General Jackson struggled violently to rise, as though to endeavor to leave the road; but Smith threw his arm over him, and with friendly force held him to the earth, saying: "Sir, you must lie still; it will cost you your life if you rise." He speedily acquiesced, and lay quiet; but none of the four hoped to escape alive. Yet, almost by miracle, they were unharmed; and, after a few moments, the Federalists, having cleared the road of all except this little party, ceased to fire along it, and directed their aim to another quarter."

After being painfully carried back behind the Confederate lines, Jackson had his left arm amputated. When Lee heard of Jackson's injuries, he sent his religious leader Chaplain Lacy to Stonewall with the message, "Give him my affectionate regards, and tell him to make haste and get well, and come back to me as soon as he can. He has lost his left arm, but I have lost my right arm."

In a chaotic turn of events, the Confederacy's famous cavalry chief, JEB Stuart, was now in charge of the bulk of Lee's infantry. Making matters even more difficult for a general who had been leading cavalry the entire war, he had to reorganize the corps, which had gotten intermingled and disorganized in the attack. Stuart reported after the battle:

"It was already dark when I sought General Jackson, and proposed, as there appeared nothing else for me to do, to take some cavalry and infantry over and hold the Ely's Ford road. He approved the proposition, and I had already gained the heights overlooking the ford, where was a large number of camp-fires, when Captain [R. H. T.] Adams, of General A. P. Hill's staff, reached me post-haste, and informed me of the sad calamities which for the time deprived the troops of the leadership of both Jackson and Hill, and the urgent demand for me to come and take command as quickly as possible. I rode with rapidity back 5 miles, determined to press the pursuit already so gloriously begun. General Jackson had gone to the rear, but General A. P. Hill was still on the ground, and formally turned over the command to me. I sent also a staff officer to General Jackson to inform him that I would cheerfully carry out any instructions he would give, and proceeded immediately to the front, which I reached at 10 p.m.

I found, upon reaching it, A. P. Hill's division in front, under Heth, with Lane's, McGowan's, Archer's, and Heth's brigades on the right of the road, within half a mile of Chancellorsville, near the apex of the ridge, and Pender's and Thomas' on the left. I found that the enemy had made an attack on our right flank, but were repulsed. The fact, however, that the attack was made, and at night, made the apprehensive of a repetition of it, and necessitated throwing back the right wing, so as to meet it. I was also informed that there was much confusion on the right, owing to the fact that some troops mistook friends for the enemy and fired upon them. Knowing that an advance under such circumstances would be extremely hazardous, much against my inclination, I felt bound to wait for daylight. General Jackson had also sent me word to use my own discretion. The commanding general was with the right wing of the army, with which I had no communication except by a very circuitous and uncertain route. I nevertheless sent a dispatch to inform him of the state of affairs, and rode around the lines restoring order, imposing silence, and making arrangements for the attack early next day. I sent Col. E. P. Alexander, senior officer of artillery, to select and occupy with artillery positions along the line bearing upon the enemy's position, with which duty he was engaged all night."

As if the day hadn't gone poorly enough, Hooker ordered Sickles to make an attack later in the night, only for his men to be mistaken by the XII Corps artillery near Fairview as Confederates. The lone Union assault of the day would be halted by friendly fire.

Around the same time that night, Hooker fired off an order to Sedgwick, still around Fredericksburg, and ordered him to attack with all dispatch. Hooker had now correctly assumed that the Confederates in Sedgwick's front were a skeleton force, and the order to attack was sound, but unfortunately the manner in which he directed Sedgwick to attack required a 14 mile countermarch. Sedgwick reported:

"That night at 11 o'clock I received an order, dated 10.10 p.m., directing me to cross the Rappahannock at Fredericksburg immediately upon receipt of the order, and move in the direction of Chancellorsville until I connected with the major-general commanding; to attack and destroy any force on the road, and be in the vicinity of the general at daylight.

I had been informed repeatedly by Major-General Butterfield, chief of staff, that the force in front of me was very small, and the whole tenor of his many dispatches would have created the impression that the enemy had abandoned my front and retired from the city and its defenses had there not been more tangible evidence than the dispatches in question that the chief of staff was misinformed."

Due to Sedgwick's inaction earlier on May 2 and the nature of the orders that night, Sedgwick's men spent the entire day idle in front of an enemy ¼ their size.

**May 3**

**The morning of May 3**

The Battle of Chancellorsville is best remembered for Stonewall Jackson's legendary flank attack on the night of May 2, but the battle would be decided on May 3. Despite the debacle suffered by the XI Corps, the Army of the Potomac still outnumbered Lee's army in the vicinity, and Jackson's corps (now commanded by Stuart) was still separated from the rest. Lee was determined to ensure Jackson's corps linked up with the rest of the army by attacking Sickles, whose III Corps stood between them along Hazel Grove.

In one of the most fateful decisions of the war, Lee's objective was actually obtained by Hooker's own orders. Early that morning, as the Confederates were preparing an attack despite being outnumbered by nearly 40,000 men, Hooker pulled the III Corps back from Hazel Grove to the Plank Road, covering his flanks and forming a horseshoe defensive line so that Sickles's corps would not be a salient in the line capable of being hit by both wings of the Confederate army around Chancellorsville. With that ground being ceded, Porter Alexander, who had been tasked by Stuart with conducting reconnaissance for placing artillery, was allowed to simply establish about 30 guns on the high ground at Hazel Grove. Alexander explained the consequences of Hooker's poor decision in his memoirs, "Altogether, I do not think there was a more brilliant thing done in the war than Stuart's extricating that command from the extremely critical position in which he found it."

As Hooker abandoned the high ground at Hazel Grove in favor of Fairview, Stuart's artillery began bombarding the Union positions from the high ground, not only forcing General Hooker's troops from Fairview but essentially decimating the Union lines while destroying Hooker's headquarters at Chancellor House. Of this turn of events, Stuart wrote, "As the sun lifted the mist that shrouded the field, it was discovered that the ridge on the extreme right was a fine position for concentrating artillery. I immediately ordered thirty pieces to that point, and, under the happy effects of the battalion system, it was done quickly. The effect of this fire upon the enemy's batteries was superb."

With Stuart's artillery now posted, the Confederates attacked all along the line at dawn, with Stuart's men advancing along the Plank Road from the west while Anderson and McLaws attacked up the Turnpike and Plank Road on the other side of Hooker's army. Stuart launched a savage attack with three divisions all advancing forward together, two of which were in support just a few hundred yards behind. Although many of them had exhausted themselves routing the XI Corps the night before, they were up to the challenge, as Stuart reported:

"At early dawn, Trimble's division composed the second line and Rodes' division the third. The latter had his rations on the spot, and, as his men were entirely without food, was extremely anxious to issue. I was disposed to wait a short time for this purpose; but when, as preliminary to an attack, I ordered the right of the first line to swing around and come perpendicular to the road, the order was misunderstood for an order to attack, and that part of the line became engaged. I ordered the whole line to advance and the second and third lines to follow. As the sun lifted the mist that shrouded the field, it was discovered that the ridge on the extreme right was a fine position for concentrating artillery. I immediately ordered thirty pieces to that point, and, under the happy effects of the battalion system, it was done quickly. The effect of this fire upon the enemy's batteries was superb.

In the meantime the enemy was pressing our left with infantry, and all the re-enforcements I could obtain were sent there. Colquitt's brigade, of Trimble's division, ordered first to the right, was directed to the left to support Pender. Iverson's brigade, of the second line, was also engaged there, and the three lines were more or less merged into one line of battle, and reported hard pressed. Urgent requests were sent for re-enforcements, and notices that the troops were out of ammunition, &c. I ordered that the ground must be held at all hazards; if necessary, with the bayonet. About this time also our right connected with Anderson's left, relieving all anxiety on that subject. I was now anxious to mass infantry on the left, to push the enemy there, and sent every available regiment to that point.

About 8 a.m. the works of the enemy directly in front of our right were stormed, but the enemy's forces retiring from the line facing Anderson, which our batteries enfiladed, caused our troops to abandon these works, the enemy coming in their rear. It was stormed a second time, when I discovered the enemy making a flank movement to the left of the road, for the purpose of dislodging our forces, and hastened to change the front of a portion of our line to meet this attack, but the shortness of the time and the deafening roar of artillery prevented the execution of this movement, and our line again retired. The third time it was taken, I made disposition of a portion of Ramseur's brigade to protect the left flank. Artillery was pushed forward to the crest, sharpshooters were posted in a house in advance, and in a few moments Chancellorsville was ours (10 a.m.). The enemy retired toward Ely's Ford, the road to United States Ford branching one-half mile west of Chancellorsville.

In this hotly contested battle the enemy had strong works on each side of the road, those on the commanding ridge being heavily defended by artillery. The night also had given him time to mass his troops to meet this attack, but the desperate valor of Jackson's corps overcame every obstacle and drove the enemy to his new line of defense, which his engineers had constructed in his rear, ready for occupation, at the intersection of the Ely's Ford and United States Ford roads."

While the Union and Confederate armies fought all along the lines, the Confederate artillery at Hazel Grove became an absolute menace, providing artillerists the opportunity to strike the heart of Hooker's positions. In his seminal history *Lee's Lieutenants*, biographer Douglas Southall Freeman described one artillery exchange during the day: "At Hazel Grove, in short, the finest artillerists of the Army of Northern Virginia were having their greatest day. They had improved guns, better ammunition and superior organization. With the fire of battle shining through his spectacles, William Pegram rejoiced. 'A glorious day, Colonel,' he said to Porter Alexander, 'a glorious day!'"

If Hooker had not regretted his decision to evacuate Hazel Grove earlier in the morning, he probably did around 9:00 a.m., when an artillery shell hit a pillar of the Chancellor house while he was standing near it. Hooker later noted that the shattered pillar struck him "violently... in an erect position from my head to my feet." It's long been speculated that Hooker suffered a concussion, but initially he refused to relinquish command to Couch or any of his staffers. Hooker's injury has long been cited as yet another reason why his generalship became more cautious after May 1.

Even before Hooker was injured, Darius Couch, Hooker's second-in-command, was bewildered not only by the lack of communications coming from Hooker but also the overly cautious timidity that Hooker was displaying:

"Upon the south porch of that mansion General Hooker stood leaning against one of its pillars, observing the fighting, looking anxious and much careworn. After the fighting had commenced I doubt if any orders were given by him to the commanders on the field, unless, perhaps, 'to retire when out of ammunition.' None were received by me, nor were there any inquiries as to how the battle was going along my front. On the right flank, where the fighting was desperate, the engaged troops were governed by the corps and division leaders. If the ear of the commanding general was, as he afterward stated, strained to catch the sound of Sedgwick's guns, it could not have heard them in the continuous uproar that filled the air around him; but as Sedgwick, who was known as a fighting officer, had not appeared at the time set - daylight - nor for some hours after, it was conclusive evidence that he had met with strong opposition, showing that all of Lee's army was not at Chancellorsville, so that the moment was favorable for Hooker to try his opponent's strength with every available man. Moreover, the left wing might at that very time be in jeopardy, therefore he was bound by every patriotic motive to strike hard for its relief. If he had remembered Mr. Lincoln's injunction ('Gentlemen, in your next fight put in all of your men'), the face of the day would have been changed and the field won for the Union arms."

In addition to injuring and likely concussing Hooker, who would spend the next hour in a daze before temporarily relinquishing command, the Confederate artillery ultimately made Fairview untenable for the Union line, the closest open high ground near Hazel Grove and the point at which Lee and Stuart were able to link their forces back together around 10:00 a.m. Stuart had made himself conspicuous during the fighting, as Couch explained:

"In the meanwhile Stuart was pressing the attack. At one time his left was so strongly resisted that his three lines were merged into one. To a notice sent him that the men were out of ammunition, he replied that they must hold their ground with the bayonet. About this time Stuart's right connected with Anderson's left, uniting thus the detached portions of General Lee's army. He then massed infantry on his left and stormed the Federal works. Twice he was repulsed, but the third time Stuart placed himself on horseback at the head of the troops, ordered the charge, carried the intrenchments, and held them, singing with ringing voice, 'Old Joe Hooker, won't you come out of the wilderness?' An eye-witness says he could not get rid of the impression that Harry of Navarre led the charge, except that Stuart's plume was black, for everywhere the men followed his feather. Anderson at the same time moved rapidly upon Chancellorsville, while McLaws made a strong demonstration in his front. At 10 A. M. the position at Chancellorsville was won, and Hooker had withdrawn to another line nearer the Rappahannock. Preparations were at once made by Lee to attack again, when further operations were arrested by intelligence received from Fredericksburg."

Lee's aide-de-camp, Charles Marshall, described the climactic scene:

"Lee's presence was the signal for one of those uncontrollable bursts of enthusiasm which none can appreciate who has not witnessed them. The fierce soldiers, with their faces blackened with the smoke of battle, the wounded crawling with feeble limbs from the fury of the devouring flames, all seemed possessed with a common impulse. One long unbroken cheer, in which the feeble cry of those who lay helpless on the earth blended with the strong voices of those who still fought, rose high above the roar of battle and hailed the presence of a victorious chief. He sat in the full realization of all that soldiers dream of—triumph; and as I looked at him in the complete fruition of the success which his genius, courage, and confidence in his army had won, I thought that it must have been from some such scene that men in ancient days ascended to the dignity of gods."

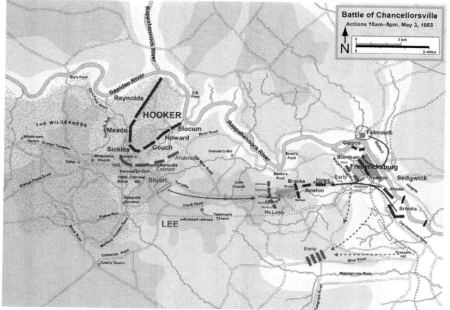

**The action on the afternoon of May 3**

Despite this important success, whatever relief Lee felt upon linking back up with Stuart was almost immediately tempered by news that his right was collapsing against Sedgwick near Fredericksburg. Early had ordered to hold the line unless his men were attacked by "overwhelming numbers," in which case he was to withdraw his men to the south toward Richmond. But if Sedgwick seemed to be withdrawing from in front of him, Early was supposed to shift his men west and join the rest of Lee's army near Chancellorsville.

As it turned out, Early would begin to inadvertently retreat from his defensive line before Sedgwick even attacked on May 3, thanks to miscommunication. Early explained what happened in his memoirs:

"During the morning I rode to Lee's Hill for the purpose of observing the enemy's movements from that point, and I observed a considerable portion of his infantry in motion up the opposite river bank. While I was, in company with Generals Barksdale and Pendleton, observing the enemy's manoeuvre and trying to ascertain what it meant, at about 11 o'clock A. M., Colonel R. H. Chilton, of General Lee's staff, came to me with a verbal order to move up immediately towards Chancellorsville with my whole force, except a brigade of infantry and Pendleton's reserve artillery, and to leave at Fredericksburg the brigade of infantry and a part of the reserve artillery to be selected by General Pendleton, with instructions to the commander of this force to watch the enemy's movements, and keep him in check if possible, but if he advanced with too heavy a force to retire on the road to Spottsylvania Court-House-General Pendleton being required to send the greater part of his reserve artillery to the rear at once.

This order took me very much by surprise, and I remarked to Colonel Chilton that I could not retire my troops without their being seen by the enemy, whose position on Stafford Heights not only overlooked ours, but who had one or two balloons which he was constantly sending up from the heights to make observations, and stated that he would inevitably move over and take possession of Fredericksburg and the surrounding Heights. The Colonel said he presumed General Lee understood all this, but that it was much more important for him to have troops where he was, than at Fredericksburg, and if he defeated the enemy there he could easily retake Fredericksburg; he called my attention to the fact, which was apparent to us all, that there was a very heavy force of infantry massed on the slopes near Falmouth which had moved up from below, and stated that he had no doubt the greater portion of the force on the other side was in motion to reinforce Hooker. He repeated his orders with great distinctness in the presence of General Pendleton, and in reply to questions from us, said that there could be no mistake in his orders.

This was very astounding to us, as we were satisfied that we were then keeping away from the army, opposed to General Lee, a much larger body of troops than my force could engage or neutralize if united to the army near Chancellorsville. It is true that there was the force massed near Falmouth and the indications were that it was moving above, but still there was a much larger force of infantry stationed below, which evinced no disposition to move. While we were conversing, information was brought me that the enemy had abandoned his lower crossing, and that our skirmishers had advanced to the Pratt house, but he still, however, maintained his position at the mouth of Deep Creek with a division of infantry and a number of guns on our side of the river.

The orders as delivered to me left me no discretion, and believing that General Lee understood his own necessities better than I possibly could, I did not feel justified in acting on my own judgment, and I therefore determined to move as directed. It subsequently turned out that Colonel Chilton had misunderstood General Lee's orders, which were that I should make the movement indicated if the enemy did not have a sufficient force in my front to detain the whole of mine, and it was to be left to me to judge of that, the orders, in fact, being similar to those given me at first. It also turned out that the troops seen massed near Falmouth were the 1st corps under Reynolds, moving up to reinforce Hooker, and that the 6th corps, Sedgwick's own, remained behind. "

**Early**

Early was alerted to the mistake in time to form his whole defensive line again by the early morning of May 3, but he was still vastly outnumbered. Early split his forces south of Fredericksburg and west of them, contesting the south while hoping Union fears about Marye's Heights would allow him to hold that position with fewer men. As a result, Marye's Heights, which had been turned into an unassailable fortress by Longstreet's corps in December 1862, was now manned by just two brigades, led by William Barksdale and Harry Hays.

When the fighting started near Marye's Heights that morning, it probably felt like déjà vu to the Union soldiers who knew full well that nearly 8,000 men had fallen in front of the dreaded stone wall at the base of Marye's Heights. And sure enough, the initial two assaults were repulsed by the two hard-pressed Confederate brigades holding it. How much longer they might have held the position against further assaults is unclear, because a flag of truce for the purposes of collecting the dead and wounded allowed Union soldiers to literally walk up to the rifle pit and see how undermanned the Confederates truly were. With that critical information, a third Union charge at the point of bayonets drove the remnants of the two Confederate brigades out of their rifle pits on Marye's Heights in minutes. For the first time in the campaign, one of Lee's lines had been broken by the Union.

**Confederate casualties behind the stone wall at Marye's Heights**

With his position now becoming untenable, Early began to fight while retreating to the south; having been attacked by overwhelming numbers, he was following Lee's orders and pulling his men away from Chancellorsville. Had Lee been at the scene, he almost certainly would have ensured that Early retreated west toward the rest of the army, but instead Early's retreat south would open up Sedgwick's path to Lee's rear at Chancellorsville.

Though Early was retreating away from the rest of the army, his men successfully delayed Sedgwick for hours around Fredericksburg on May 3, helped in large measure by the brigade of Cadmus Wilcox, who explained the nature of the Early's retreat from Fredericksburg:

"Seeing a group of officers near Stansbury's house, I rode to them, and met Generals Barksdale and Hays. The former informed me that the enemy were in considerable force in and below Fredericksburg (this was the first intimation I had of the fact), and expressed some anxiety as to his right flank, and said that he should have reenforcements. I now determined not to move my command up the road until I knew definitely the intention of the enemy, and ordered them in the ravine opposite Dr. Taylor's, where they would be near and yet out of sight. I now rode to the vicinity of the Marye house, to see and confer with General Barksdale. While near the house, I saw great numbers of the enemy in Fredericksburg, and a battery in the street running near the cemetery was firing occasional shots at a battery of ours to the left of the Plank road. I returned to my command without seeing General Barksdale, and, on my return, saw several regiments of the enemy's infantry moving out of the upper edge of the town. I had been with my command but a few minutes when one of General Barksdale's staff reported to me that the general was hard pressed, and wanted me to send him a regiment. I instantly ordered the Tenth Alabama to move in the direction of the Marye house, and rode rapidly in that direction myself, and when in the open field and high ground between Stansbury's and the Plank road, saw Hays' brigade moving over in the direction of the Plank road. This I supposed to be for the support of General Barksdale, but upon inquiry from one of Hays' regiments learned that the enemy had taken Marye's Hill end a portion of two of Barksdale's regiments, and that Hays' brigade was falling back to the Telegraph road. Soon a courier from General Barksdale confirmed this report, and with a suggestion from General Barksdale that I also had better fall back to the Telegraph road. On the left of the Plank road the ground in rear of Marye's Hill is higher, and overlooks and commands well that hill. Believing that my own and Hays' brigade could form in line, extending from near Stansbury's house along the crests of the hills toward the Plank road, and contest the field at least for a time successfully, with the enemy, I asked General Hays not to cross the Plank road, but to remain with me. This he declined doing, having been ordered to fall back to the Telegraph road, and was soon out of sight."

**Wilcox**

As a result of Lee's orders, and much to Wilcox's confusion and chagrin, instead of reforming a defensive line west of Fredericksburg, Hays and Barksdale retreated south and fell back with the rest of Early's division. Thankfully for the Confederates, Wilcox opted to continue fighting a delayed retreat west, buying time for Lee to hurry men east from Chancellorsville to try to stop Sedgwick's advance. Wilcox reported his initial stand:

"Finding myself alone on the left of the Plank road, with the enemy in full view on the crests of the first range of hills in rear of Fredericksburg, and with three times my own force clearly seen and in line, I felt it a duty to delay the enemy as much as possible in his advance, and to endeavor to check him all that I could should he move forward on the Plank road. With this view, I formed my brigade promptly in line along the crests of the hills running near Stansbury's house, at right angles to the Plank road. Two rifled pieces of Lewis' battery were placed in position to the rear of the left of my line, and two slightly in front of my right, which rested some 500 or 600 yards in front of Guest's house. Skirmishers were thrown forward, covering my entire front. As soon as the four pieces of artillery were in position, they opened fire upon the enemy's lines, some 800 or 900 yards to the front. This held the enemy in check for some time. At length they deployed skirmishers to the front and began to advance. This was slow, and, delayed by frequent halts, they seemed reluctant to advance. The enemy now brought a six-gun battery to the front on the left of the Plank road, not far from Marye's house, and opened with a fire of shells upon my line. The enemy's skirmishers now advanced and engaged ours, not nearer, however, than 350 or 400 yards, their solid lines remaining some distance behind the skirmishers. The enemy's battery having fired for some time, both the skirmishers and lines in rear advanced. They had also moved by a flank across the Plank road, and it was reported to me that they were moving up on the far side of the road, and were on a line with my right flank. The artillery was now directed to withdraw; then the skirmishers rejoined their regiments, and all moved to the rear on the River road, half a mile in rear of Dr. Taylor's, where they were halted for a few minutes."

Sedgwick continued pushing west down the Turnpike while Wilcox waited for reinforcements, and around 5:00 p.m., the two lines found themselves just 5 miles away from Lee's rear around Salem Church. Finally, Wilcox was joined by 4 brigades, pulled from McLaws and Anderson, bringing the Confederate forces up to 10,000 men. Wilcox described the climactic finale of the fighting in the east in his post-war report:

The enemy's artillery ceased to fire near 5 p.m. Their skirmishers then advanced; a spirited fire ensued between the skirmishers for some fifteen or twenty minutes. Ours then retired, firing as they fell back. The enemy's skirmishers pursued, followed by their solid lines of infantry and still a third line in rear. On either side of the road, as they advanced from the toll-gate, were open fields, and the ground slightly ascending. These fields continued to within about 250 yards of the church, and then woods, thick, but of small growth. When the front line of the enemy reached this wood, they made a slight halt; then, giving three cheers, they came with a rush, driving our skirmishers rapidly before them. Our men held their fire till their men came within less than 80 yards, and then delivered a close and terrible fire upon them, killing and wounding many and causing many of them to waver and give way. The enemy still press on, surround the school-house, and capture the entire company of the Ninth Alabama stationed in it, and, pressing hard upon the regiment in rear of the school-house, throw it in confusion and disorder, and force it to yield ground. The Ninth Alabama, in rear of this regiment, spring forward as one man, and, with the rapidity of lightning, restore the continuity of our line, breaking the lines of the enemy by its deadly fire and forcing him to give way, and, following him so that he could not rally, retake the school-house, free the captured company, and in turn take their captors. The entire line of the enemy on the right of the road is repulsed, and our men follow in rapid pursuit. The regiment that had given way to the first onset of the enemy now returned to the attack and joined in the pursuit. The enemy did not assail with the same spirit on the left of the road, and were more easily repulsed, and now are followed on either side of the road, which is crowded with a confused mass of the discomfited enemy. With a good battery to play upon this retreating mass, the carnage would have been terrific. There was no rallying or reforming of this line. Another line came up the Plank road at a double-quick, and, filing to the right and left, formed line in front of my brigade. This line was scarcely formed before they were broken by the fire of my men, and fled to the rear.

The pursuit continued as far as the toll-gate. Semmes' brigade and my own were the only troops that followed the retreating enemy. In rear of the gate were heavy reserves of the enemy. Our men were now halted and reformed, it being quite dark, and retired, not pursued by the enemy, leaving pickets far to the front in the open field. The vigor of the enemy's attack at the church was doubtless due to the fact that they believed there was only one brigade to resist them, and that they anticipated an easy affair of it, while the number of dead and wounded left on the field attests the obstinacy of the resistance of our men--200 of the former and more than 150 of the latter, and largely over 200 prisoners not wounded and 1 Federal flag captured.

Thus ended this spirited conflict at Salem Church; a bloody repulse to the enemy, rendering entirely useless to him his little success of the morning at Fredericksburg. The rear of our army at Chancellorsville was now secure and free from danger, and the Sixth Army Corps of the enemy and a part of the Second were now content to remain on the defensive.

Although Wilcox exuberantly described the result as a "bloody repulse", the truth is that Sedgwick was running out of daylight to continue his advance. As a result, Lee's rear was saved. Hooker would later complain that Sedgwick had not advanced as promptly as he should've, no doubt annoyed by what he considered Sedgwick's second straight day of failure: "My object in ordering General Sedgwick forward ...was to relieve me from the position in which I found myself at Chancellorsville...In my judgment General Sedgwick did not obey the spirit of my order, and made no sufficient effort to obey it...When he did move it was not with sufficient confidence or ability on his part to manoeuvre his troops."

Chancellorsville is not the most famous battle of the war, and it's best remembered for the events of May 2, but the action on May 3 may have been the most tactically complex of the war. Lee's army had made assaults on two parts of the Union line at Chancellorsville to ensure that his army linked back up, while still managing to maintain a defensive line and halt Sedgwick's advance on the right, thus conducting a successful offensive on his left and a successful defense on his right. The casualty count attests to the fact that the fighting was just as fierce as it was complex. Over 21,000 men were killed, wounded, or captured on May 3, 1863, making it the second bloodiest day in American history, barely behind the Battle of Antietam.

## Hooker Withdraws

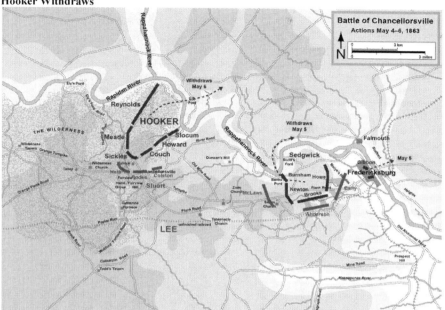

"As to the charge that the battle was lost because [Hooker] was intoxicated, I have always stated that he probably abstained from the use of ardent spirits when it would have been far better for him to have continued in his usual habit in that respect. The shock from being violently thrown to the ground, together with the physical exhaustion resulting from loss of sleep and the anxiety of mind incident to the last six days of the campaign, would tell on any man." – Darius Couch

Lee had managed to win every gamble he took from May 1-3, and he had masterfully defended his right while simultaneously striking at Hooker on his left, but the armies woke up on the morning of May 4 with the Army of the Potomac still heavily outnumbering the Army of Northern Virginia near Chancellorsville and near Salem Church just west of Fredericksburg. Hooker's flanks and Sedgwick's flanks rested on the Rapidan and Rappahannock rivers respectively, which meant they were secure, but with their forces divided and Lee's army between them, Hooker was worried that the advantage of interior lines gave Lee a chance to destroy one of the two separated armies.

Throughout May 4, Hooker dug in, and the lack of offensive activity convinced Lee that he could detach more of Anderson's division to confront Sedgwick to the right. Lee was also able to recall Early's division, which now marched back north and reoccupied Marye's Heights on Sedgwick's left flank, linking up with the men from McLaws's division and Anderson's division opposite Sedgwick. Lee hoped to attack Sedgwick, now slightly outnumbering him, but delays in Anderson's march and hesitation by McLaws resulted in the attack not starting until 6:00 p.m. Sedgwick had spent all day drawing up defensive lines to protect his retreat back across the

Rappahannock, so he was able to repulse the half-hearted offensive that night.

After the Confederate attack stopped and night fell, Sedgwick began extricating his command at Banks's Ford, recrossing the Rappahannock during the night of May 4-5. Hooker had taken a defensive stance and had idled all day near Chancellorsville, yet he now used Sedgwick's withdrawal as the pretext for a withdrawal of his own. Before doing so, however, he called a council of war on the night of May 4 and discussed the matter with his principal subordinates. Couch recounted that night's council of war:

"At 12 o'clock on the night of the 4th - 5th General Hooker assembled his corps commanders in council. Meade, Sickles, Howard, Reynolds, and myself were present; General Slocum, on account of the long distance from his post, did not arrive until after the meeting was broken up. Hooker stated that his instructions compelled him to cover Washington, not to jeopardize the army, etc. It was seen by the most casual observer that he had made up his mind to retreat. We were left by ourselves to consult, upon which Sickles made an elaborate argument, sustaining the views of the commanding general. Meade was in favor of fighting, stating that he doubted if we could get off our guns. Howard was in favor of fighting, qualifying his views by the remark that our present situation was due to the bad conduct of his corps, or words to that effect. Reynolds, who was lying on the ground very much fatigued, was in favor of an advance. I had similar views to those of Meade as to getting off the guns, but said I 'would favor an advance if I could designate the point of attack.' Upon collecting the suffrages, Meade, Reynolds, and Howard voted squarely for an advance, Sickles and myself squarely no; upon which Hooker informed the council that he should take upon himself the responsibility of retiring the army to the other side of the river. As I stepped out of the tent Reynolds, just behind me, broke out, 'What was the use of calling us together at this time of night when he intended to retreat anyhow?'

Thus, during the next day, Hooker began the process of pulling his command back across the river, a delicate process that started with removing the artillery and clearing the roads so that the infantry would not get bottled up. In the early morning hours of May 6, the rest of the corps began crossing the river, with Meade's V Corps protecting the retreat on the south bank. Even still, Couch, who was in command on the south bank of the Rapidan because Hooker was already across, claimed he was tempted to try to fight:

"Near midnight I got a note from Meade informing me that General Hooker was on the other side of the river, which had risen over the bridges, and that communication was cut off from him. I immediately rode over to Hooker's headquarters and found that I was in command of the army, if it had any commander. General Hunt, of the artillery, had brought the information as to the condition of the bridges, and from the reports there seemed to be danger of losing them entirely. After a short conference with Meade I told him that the recrossing would be suspended, and that 'we would stay where we were and fight it out,' returning to my tent with the intention of enjoying what I had not had since the night of the 30th ultimo - a good sleep; but at 2 A. M., communication having been reestablished, I received a sharp message from Hooker, to order the recrossing of the army as he had directed, and everything was safely transferred to the north bank of the Rappahannock."

As a result, the Army of the Potomac was safely back on the other side of the river by May 6, greatly surprising Lee, who was still making plans to attack Hooker in hopes of destroying his command against the Rapidan. Incredibly, upon withdrawing back across the river and retreating, Hooker issued General Orders No. 49, which actually congratulated his army on their recent achievements:

"The major-general commanding tenders to this army his congratulations on its achievements of the last seven days. If it has not accomplished all that was expected, the reasons are well known to the army. It is sufficient to say they were of a character not to be foreseen or prevented by human sagacity or resource.

In withdrawing from the south bank of the Rappahannock before delivering a general battle to our adversaries, the army has given renewed evidence of its confidence in itself and its fidelity to the principles it represents. In fighting at a disadvantage, we would have been recreant to our trust, to ourselves, our cause, and our country.

Profoundly loyal, and conscious of its strength, the Army of the Potomac will give or decline battle whenever its interest or honor may demand. It will also be the guardian of its own history and its own fame.

By our celerity and secrecy of movement, our advance and passage of the rivers were undisputed, and on our withdrawal not a rebel ventured to follow.

The events of the last week may swell with pride the heart of every officer and soldier of this army. We have added new luster to its former renown. We have made long marches, crossed rivers, surprised the enemy in his intrenchments, and whenever we have fought have inflicted heavier blows than we have received.

We have taken from the enemy 5,000 prisoners; captured and brought off seven pieces of artillery, fifteen colors; placed hors de combat 18,000 of his chosen troops; destroyed his depots filled with vast amounts of stores; deranged his communications; captured prisoners within the fortifications of his capital, and filled his country with fear and consternation.

We have no other regret than that caused by the loss of our brave companions, and in this we are consoled by the conviction that they have fallen in the holiest cause ever submitted to the arbitrament of battle."

Whether Hooker truly believed the contents of his orders or not, the rest of his officers and the rank-and-file were well aware of what their retreat meant.

The following day, on May 7, Stoneman's cavalry reentered Union lines east of Richmond on the Peninsula. Hooker's poor use of Stoneman's cavalry had deprived him of necessary reconnaissance on May 2 and made it that much easier for Stuart's cavalry to determine the XI Corps had its right flank in the air. For his part, Stoneman had accomplished nothing of importance, failing to destroy any of the supply lines or communication lines Hooker anticipated he would.

### The Outlook in Early June

In the spring of 1863, General Lee discovered that McClellan had known of his plans and was able to force a battle at Antietam before all of General Lee's forces had arrived in September 1862. General Lee now believed that he could successfully invade the North again, and that his defeat before was due in great measure to a stroke of bad luck. In addition, Lee hoped to supply his army on the unscathed fields and towns of the North, while giving war ravaged northern Virginia a rest.

After Chancellorsville, Longstreet and Lee met to discuss options for the Confederate Army's summer campaign. Longstreet advocated detachment of all or part of his corps to be sent to Tennessee, citing General Grant's advance on Vicksburg, the critical Confederate stronghold on the Mississippi River. Longstreet argued that a reinforced army under Bragg could defeat

Rosecrans and drive toward the Ohio River, compelling Grant to release his hold on Vicksburg. Lee, however, was opposed to a division of his army and instead advocated a large-scale offensive (and raid) into Pennsylvania. In addition, Lee hoped to supply his army on the unscathed fields and towns of the North, while giving war ravaged northern Virginia a rest.

Knowing that victories on Virginia soil meant little to an enemy that could simply retreat, regroup, and then return with more men and more advanced equipment, Lee set his sights on a Northern invasion, aiming to turn Northern opinion against the war and against President Lincoln. With his men already half-starved from dwindling provisions, Lee intended to confiscate food, horses, and equipment as they pushed north--and hopefully influence Northern politicians into giving up their support of the war by penetrating into Harrisburg or even Philadelphia. Given the right circumstances, Lee's army might even be able to capture either Baltimore or Philadelphia and use the city as leverage in peace negotiations.

In the wake of Jackson's death, Lee reorganized his army, creating three Corps out of the previous two, with A.P. Hill and Richard S. Ewell replacing Stonewall. Hill had been a successful division commander, but he was constantly battling bouts of sickness that left him disabled, which would occur at Gettysburg. Ewell had distinguished himself during the Peninsula Campaign, suffering a serious injury that historians often credit as making him more cautious in command upon his return.

**Hill**

**General Ewell**

When Stuart held a full field review of his units on June 5, it impressed the people who watched it, but Lee was there, so he held another one on June 8 when Lee could attend. This one involved about 9,000 mounted troops and four batteries of horse artillery, as well as a mock battle. John Esten Cooke, a Confederate veteran, described the scene in *A Life of General Robert E. Lee*: "A brilliant pageant, succeeded by a dramatic and stirring incident, was now to prelude the march of Lee into the enemy's territory. On the 8th of June, the day of the arrival of Lee's head of column in Culpepper, a review of Stuart's cavalry took place in a field east of the court-house. The review was a picturesque affair. General Lee was present, sitting his horse, motionless, on a little knoll—the erect figure half concealed by the short cavalry-cape falling from his shoulders, and the grave face overshadowed by the broad gray hat—while above him, from a lofty pole, waved the folds of a large Confederate flag. The long column of about eight thousand cavalry was first drawn up in line, and afterward passed in front of Lee at a gallop—Stuart and his staff-officers leading the charge with sabres at tierce point, a species of military display highly attractive to the gallant and joyous young commander. The men then charged in mimic battle the guns of the "Stuart Horse-Artillery," which were posted upon an adjoining hill; and, as the column of cavalry approached, the artillerists received them with a thunderous discharge of blank ammunition, which rolled like the roar of actual battle among the surrounding hills. This sham-fight was kept up for some time, and no doubt puzzled the enemy on the opposite shore of the Rappahannock."

Ironically, Lee described the review in a letter to his wife that was written on the very day Brandy Station was being fought: "I reviewed the cavalry in this section yesterday. It was a splendid sight. The men and horses looked well. They had recuperated since last fall. Stuart was in all his glory. Your sons and nephews are well and flourishing. The country here looks very green and pretty, notwithstanding the ravages of war. What a beautiful world God in his loving kindness to his creatures has given us! What a shame that men endowed with reason and knowledge of right should mar his gifts!"

However, Confederate General Grumble Jones, who commanded a cavalry brigade under Stuart, complained about the needless review, pointing out that "no doubt the Yankees...have witnessed from their signal stations, this show in which Stuart has exposed to view his strength and aroused their curiosity. They will want to know what is going on and if I am not mistaken, will be over early in the morning to investigate."

**Grumble Jones**

Jones would be proven right, but at the time (and despite the critics), Stuart basked in the glory. Renowned Civil War historian Stephen Sears noted, "The grand review…was surely the proudest day of Jeb Stuart's thirty years. As he led a cavalcade of resplendent staff officers to the reviewing stand, trumpeters heralded his coming and women and girls strewed his path with flowers. Before all of the spectators the assembled cavalry brigade stretched a mile and a half. After Stuart and his entourage galloped past the line in review, the troopers in their turn saluted the reviewing stand in columns of squadrons. In performing a second "march past," the squadrons started off at a trot, then spurred to a gallop. Drawing sabers and breaking into the Rebel yell, the troopers rush toward the horse artillery drawn up in battery. The gunners responded defiantly, firing blank charges. Amidst this tumult of cannon fire and thundering hooves, a number of ladies swooned in their escorts' arms."

**Order of Battle at Brandy Station**

**Cavalry Corp**
**Army of the Potomac**
**Brigadier General Alfred Pleasonton**

**Pleasanton**

**Right Wing: Brigadier General John Buford**
**1st Cavalry Division.** Colonel Benjamin F. Davis
    **1st Brigade.** Colonel Benjamin F. Davis
    8th New York Cavalry. Major Edmund M. Pope
    8th Illinois Cavalry. Captain Alpheus Clark and Captain George A. Forsyth
    3rd Indiana Cavalry. Major William S. McClure
    9th New York Cavalry. Major William B. Martin
    3rd (West) Virginia. Captain Seymour B. Conger
    **2nd Brigade.** Colonel Thomas C. Devin
    6th New York Cavalry. Major William E. Beardsley
    17th Pennsylvania Cavalry. Colonel Josiah H. Kellogg
    **Reserve Brigade.** Major Charles J. Whiting
    2nd U.S. Cavalry. Captain Wesley Merritt
    5th U.S. Cavalry. Captain James E. Harrison
    6th U.S. Cavalry. Captain George C. Cram
    6th Pennsylvania Cavalry. Major Robert Morris, Jr.
    **U.S. Horse Artillery.** Captain James M. Robertson
    1st U.S. Artillery Battery. "K". Captain William M. Graham
    2nd U.S. Artillery Batteries "B," and "L". Lieutenant Albert O. Vincent
    4th U.S. Artillery Battery "E". Lieutenant Samuel S. Elder

**Buford**

**Left Wing: Brigadier General David M. Gregg**
**2nd Cavalry Division.** Colonel Alfred N.A. Duffié
    **1st Brigade.** Colonel Louis P. di Cesnola
        1st Massachusetts Cavalry. Lieutenant Colonel Greely S. Curtis
        6th Ohio Cavalry. Major William Stedman)
        1st Rhode Island Cavalry. Lieutenant Colonel John L. Thompson
    **2nd Brigade.** Colonel J. Irving Gregg
        3rd Pennsylvania Cavalry. Lieutenant Colonel Edward S. Jones
        4th Pennsylvania Cavalry. Lieutenant Colonel William E. Doster
        16th Pennsylvania Cavalry. Major William H. Fry
        2nd U.S. Arty., Batt. "M" (Lt. Alexander C.M. Pennington
    **3rd Cavalry Division.** Brigadier General David M. Gregg

**1st Brigade.** Colonel Hugh Judson Kilpatrick
2nd New York Cavalry. Lieutenant Colonel Henry E. Davies, Jr.
10th New York Cavalry. Lieutenant Colonel William Irvine and Major M. Henry Avery
1st Maine Cavalry. Colonel Calvin S. Douty
**2nd Brigade.** Colonel Percy Wyndham and Colonel John P. Taylor
1st New Jersey Cavalry. Lieutenant Colonel Virgil Brodrick, Major John H. Shelmire and Major Myron H. Beaumont
1st Pennsylvania Cavalry. Colonel John P. Taylor and Lieutenant Colonel David Gardner
1st Maryland Cavalry. Lieutenant Colonel James M. Deems
New York Light, 6th Independent Battery. Captain Joseph W. Martin
**Brigadier General David A. Russell's Select Infantry Brigade**
56th Pennsylvania Infantry. Colonel J. William Hofmann
7th Wisconsin Infantry. Colonel William Robinson
6th Maine Infantry. Colonel Hiram Burnham
119th Pennsylvania Infantry. Major Henry P. Truefitt, Jr.
5th New Hampshire Infantry & 81st Pennsylvania Infantry. Colonel Edward E. Cross
3rd U.S. Artillery Battery "C". Lieutenant William D. Fuller

**David Gregg**
**CAVALRY DIVISION**

**Army of Northern Virginia**
**Major General James Ewell Brown "Jeb" Stuart**
**Jones's Brigade.** Brigadier General William E. Jones
6th Virginia Cavalry. Major Cabell Edward Flournoy
7th Virginia Cavalry. Lieutenant Colonel Thomas C. Marshall
11th Virginia Cavalry. Colonel Lunsford L. Lomax
12th Virginia Cavalry. Colonel Asher W. Harman
35th Battalion Virginia Cavalry. Lieutenant Colonel Elijah V. White
**Rooney Lee's Brigade.** Brigadier General William H.F. "Rooney" Lee, Colonel James
Lucius Davis and Colonel John R. Chambliss, Jr.
2nd North Carolina Cavalry. Colonel Solomon William and Lieutenant Colonel William H.F.
Payne
9th Virginia Cavalry. Colonel Richard L.T. Beale
10th Virginia Cavalry. Colonel James Lucius Davis and Major Joseph Rosser
13th Virginia Cavalry. Colonel John R. Chambliss
**Hampton's Brigade.** Brigadier General Wade Hampton
Cobb's Legion. Colonel Pierce M.B. Young
1st South Carolina Cavalry. Colonel John L. Black
1st North Carolina Cavalry. Colonel Laurence S. Baker
Jeff Davis Legion. Lieutenant Colonel Joseph F. Waring
2nd South Carolina Cavalry. Colonel Matthew C. Butler and Major Thomas J. Lipscomb
**Fitz Lee's Brigade.** Colonel Thomas T. Munford
1st Virginia Cavalry. Colonel James H. Drake
2nd Virginia Cavalry. Lieutenant Colonel James W. Watts
3rd Virginia Cavalry. Colonel Thomas H. Owen
4th Virginia Cavalry. Colonel Williams C. Wickham
**Robertson's Brigade.** Brigadier General Beverly H. Robertson
4th North Carolina Cavalry. Colonel Dennis D. Ferebee
5th North Carolina Cavalry. Colonel Peter G. Evans
**Stuart's Horse Artillery.** Major Robert F. Beckham
Hart's Battery. Major James F. Hart
Breathed's Battery. Captain James Breathed
Chew's Battery. Captain Roger Preston Chew
Moorman's Battery. Captain Marcellus N. Moorman
McGregor's Battery. Captain William M. McGregor

**The Battle of Brandy Station**

Stuart obviously enjoyed "horsing around," there was serious work to be done. The following day, Lee ordered Stuart to cross the Rappahannock and raid Union forward positions, shielding the Confederate army from observation or interference as it moved north. Already anticipating this imminent offensive move, Stuart had ordered his troops back into formation around Brandy Station, but before he could move the cavalry for that raid, Stuart would endure the first of two low points in his military career: the Battle of Brandy Station, the largest cavalry battle of the Civil War.

As Grumble Jones anticipated, the Army of the Potomac couldn't help but notice the Confederate cavalry review, and Hooker accurately guessed that it was a prelude to a Confederate raid. In fact, George Meade would note in a letter to his wife days after the fighting at Brandy Station, "The day before yesterday Pleasanton, with all the cavalry and two brigades of infantry, crossed just above us, and had a very brilliant affair with the enemy's cavalry, who it appears were just ready and about starting on a grand raid, some say into Pennsylvania."

Assuming that Stuart's cavalry would be hitting Union supply lines, Hooker directed his own cavalry chief, Pleasanton, to preempt a potential Confederate raid by attacking Stuart in force to "break up Stuart's raid in its incipiency." He also ordered Pleasanton to "disperse and destroy" Stuart's force, which was obviously wildly optimistic, and to do so, Pleasanton planned a relatively complex strategy that would have one wing of cavalry under John Buford cross the Rappahannock river northeast of Brandy Station while David Gregg's wing crossed the river southeast of Brandy Station. Together, they would strike at Stuart from opposite sides, hoping to catch the Confederates by surprise and envelop them. Unfortunately for the Union, they wrongly believed that their 11,000 horsemen would greatly outnumber Stuart (when in fact Stuart had nearly 10,000 troopers), and they were unaware that Confederate forces were posted close to Beverly's Ford, the spot where Buford was to cross the river.

With that, Buford's wing set off before dawn on the 9th for Beverly's Ford, a few miles northeast of where Stuart's Confederates were gathered, and as they overwhelmed the Confederate picket line there, Grumble Jones' brigade began riding towards the sound half-awake in the dense fog. Jones' brigade collided with the lead brigade of Buford's wing, which was commanded by Col. Benjamin Davis, and Davis was mortally wounded early on during the scrum.

Heros von Borcke, a Prussian observer who eventually served as Stuart's chief of staff, described how surprised the Confederates were by this early action: "After a few hours' sleep I was awakened about day-break by the sound of several cannon-shots. In an instant I was on my legs, and stepping out of my tent I distinctly heard a brisk firing of small-arms in the direction of the river. An orderly shortly afterwards rode up, reporting that the enemy, under cover of the fog, had suddenly fallen upon our pickets, had crossed the river in strong force at several points, and pressed forward so rapidly that they had come upon Jones's brigade before the greater part of the men had had time to saddle their horses. It was fortunate that the sharpshooters of this command, seconded by a section of our horse-artillery, were enabled by a well-directed fire to impede the movements of the attacking foe, so as to give our regiments time to form, and by falling back some distance to take up a position further to the rear. It was evident, both to General Stuart and myself, that the intentions of the Federals in this movement were of a serious character, and that they were determined on making a further advance..."

**Heros von Borcke**

The cannonade that von Borcke heard almost certainly came from Stuart's Horse Artillery, which was dangerously close to the action around the Beverly's Ford Road and thus vulnerable to being captured, but even as the Confederates were scrambling to stop Buford, Stuart was thinking offensively. Von Borcke recalled in his memoirs, "The General wished to march with his whole force against the enemy, and fight them wherever he might meet them. My proposal was to place the greater part of the corps and our 24 guns on the heights, and wait there till the designs of the Yankees, who were still hidden by the woods, and their numbers, should be more clearly disclosed, and then, by offering a feint with a few of our advanced brigades, to draw them towards us. As no favourable position for their artillery would be found in the plains, our guns would play with great effect on their dense ranks when they emerged into the open before us, and for once our horsemen would have a chance of showing their superiority over the hostile cavalry by a united charge of our whole force. But Stuart's ardour was impatient of delay; and being, besides, under the impression that to allow the enemy to proceed further would let them know too much of the position of our infantry, which it was our duty to cover, he resolved to move at once against the advancing foe, and gave me orders to ride to the front and rapidly reconnoitre the state of affairs, while he would follow as quickly as the troops could be brought into action."

As the Confederates came into line against Buford, Buford wished to advance his cavalry on the Confederates' left flank to turn them, but by this time, a brigade led by Robert E. Lee's son, W.H.F. "Rooney" Lee, had positioned itself behind a stone wall and dismounted to fight. Both sides mauled each other in an effort to push each other back, but the Union cavalry also had to contend with the artillery fire that continued to sweep the Beverly's Ford Road. H.B. McClellan, who was serving as adjutant general for Stuart during the battle, recalled, "During all this time the position of the horse artillery was critical in the extreme. There was nothing between the guns and danger but Flournoy's men. Captain James F. Hart's battery had gone into camp immediately on the road. Two guns from this battery were placed in position, and opened on the enemy, while the remainder of the battalion hastened back across the field to the line subsequently held at Saint James' Church. At this juncture General W. E. Jones brought up the 7th Virginia Cavalry, in hot haste, many of his men having mounted without their coats, and some even without waiting to saddle their horses. A charge was instantly made to support Flournoy, but it was repulsed by the enemy, and in the recoil the 7th was carried back past the guns stationed on the road. These gallant cannoneers on two occasions during this memorable day proved that they were able to care for themselves. Although now exposed to the enemy, they covered their own retreat with canister, and safely retired to the line at Saint James' Church, where they found efficient support. The delay caused by the fighting of Jones' two regiments and Hart's two guns was sufficient to give safety to the other guns of the battalion and to the transportation. No loss occurred worthy of mention, except that in the hurried flight the desk of Major Beckham, commanding the artillery, was jostled from his wagon, and fell into the enemy's hands."

Von Borcke noted it was ultimately the artillery that prevented a wholesale rout: "Major Berkham had hastily placed some of his batteries in position upon an eminence which I had just passed, and was reaching a patch of wood where Jones's men were engaged in a sharp skirmish with the Federals, when in overwhelming numbers they made a sudden dash upon the most advanced regiment of that brigade, which broke in utter confusion, carrying everything with them in their flight. A scene of disgraceful stampede ensued-single horsemen galloped off the field in all directions, waggons and ambulances which had been detained to carry off camp utensils rattled over the ground, while with loud shouts of victory a dense mass of Federal horsemen broke froth from the woods. At this critical moment Berkham opened a rapid fire, throwing such a shower of canister and grape at close range upon the pursuing host, that they recoiled and retired again into the forest, thus affording an opportunity of rallying and re-forming our demoralised troops."

**Rooney Lee**

The retreat was so disorganized at this point that von Borcke remembered a desperate Confederate soldier actually hopping onto his mule in an effort to flee, but with Rooney Lee's cavalry coming in on the left of Jones and Wade Hampton III's brigade swinging into action on Jones' right, the Confederate cavalry was able to gather itself and form a three mile long line to fight Buford's wing. Von Borcke wrote, "All our brigades having now arrived from the more distant camps, our line of battle, nearly three miles in length, could be regularly formed; and along the woods which border the Rappahannock the multitudinous firing of our dismounted sharpshooters sounded like the rattle of musketry in a regular battle. We held our ground tolerably well for some time, but it soon became evident that the enemy were in far superior numbers and supported by infantry, large columns of which were reported by William Lee, who commanded on our extreme left, to be crossing the river. Towards this point I was sent by General Stuart to watch the movements of the enemy, with orders to send a report every quarter of an hour by one of the body of couriers whom I took with me."

**Hampton**

A general battle raged across the line for a few hours, with nothing much standing out to the soldiers there except for a charge made by the 6th Pennsylvania, part of Major Charles J. Whiting's reserve brigade. The charge aimed to overtake the nettlesome Confederate batteries camped near St. James Church, suffering heavy casualties but earning the grudging respect of the Confederates, some of whom called it a "brilliant and glorious" charge. Another charge was made by Union regulars, which impressed Stuart's adjutant general so much that he described the charge in his biography of the Confederate chieftain: "The latter of these charges was made over a plateau fully eight hundred yards wide, and its objective point was the artillery at the church. Never rode troopers more gallantly than did those steady Regulars, as under a fire of shell and shrapnel, and finally of canister, they dashed up to the very muzzles, then through and beyond our guns, passing between Hampton's left and Jones' right. Here they were simultaneously attacked from both flanks, and the survivors driven back."

Of course, what the Confederates did not know at the time was that there was another wing of Union cavalry coming from their southeast. In fact, Gregg's wing was supposed to strike the Confederates around the same time Buford's did in the early morning, but Gregg's lead brigade got lost on the way to Kelly's Ford, causing a substantial delay of about two hours. Given the lack of technology regarding communication, Civil War armies often found it hard to coordinate attacks by two separate wings across a vast distance, so Pleasanton's plan was already relying on having everything go right, but between Gregg's delay and the unexpected resistance in Buford's front, the Union's plan had gone off the rails almost from the start.

That said, Gregg's wing would still be working with an element of surprise, and Buford's fight near Beverly's Ford also ensured that Stuart had started pushing other units that way as reinforcements, which would presumably leave less resistance for Gregg's cavalry when they did cross the Rappahannock around 10:30 a.m.

Stuart had been savvy enough not only to leave a regiment from Hampton's brigade (Colonel M.C. Butler's 2nd South Carolina) in reserve but also ensure General Beverly H. Robertson's brigade was picketing Kelly's Ford. All told, they numbered 1,500 men, which Stuart thought was enough to cover his rear, and McClellan described these units' dispositions as Gregg's cavalry came splashing across the Rappahannock: "Before sending Hampton into action Stuart had ordered that one of his regiments be detached to guard our rear at Brandy Station. Hampton had assigned that duty to the 2d South Carolina Cavalry, commanded by Colonel M. C. Butler. This regiment had gone into camp the previous night on the road from Brandy Station to Stevensburg, about half way between the two places. Robertson had moved his brigade at early dawn to the support of his picket at Kelly's Ford, and soon reported the advance of the Federal column upon Stevensburg. Butler had hardly reached Brandy Station with his regiment when he was notified by the videttes, which he, with wise precaution, had sent toward Kelly's Ford, that the enemy was advancing in force on that road. Knowing that there was nothing to prevent that column from marching to Culpeper Court House, if so disposed, Butler, without waiting for orders, started his regiment back, in all haste, toward Stevensburg."

**Robertson**

Moreover, when Stuart himself had headed to the front around St. James Church to lead in person, he kept McClellan back at his headquarters on Fleetwood Hill, and while that would serve as the point of communications for the 2nd South Caroline and Robertson's brigade, there were almost no other forces at the Confederate headquarters other than McClellan and the couriers he relied on. As fate would have it, Gregg adroitly maneuvered most of his wing to avoid Kelly's Ford Road, which was covered by Robertson's brigade, and thus completely surprise Stuart's forces as they approached. In the meantime, he had General David A. Russell's Select Infantry Brigade skirmish with Robertson's cavalry to keep them in place as the Union cavalry went around to the south and west. Moreover, while some of Gregg's cavalry would run into Butler's 2nd South Carolina near Stevensburg, two of his brigades, led by Judson Kilpatrick and Col. Percy Wyndham, rode unimpeded right towards Fleetwood Hill south of the Confederates fighting Buford and came in view of the crest of the hill around 11:00 a.m.

**Kilpatrick**

Like Stuart, McClellan had assumed the men in reserve were adequate, so when a scout first informed him that Gregg's wing had pushed across the ford and were quickly flooding into the Confederates' rear, he couldn't believe the report. "Perhaps two hours had elapsed since Stuart had mounted for the front when an individual scout from one of Robertson's North Carolina regiments reported to me that the enemy was advancing from Kelly's Ford, in force and unopposed, upon Brandy Station, and was now directly in our rear. Not having personal acquaintance with the man, and deeming it impossible that such a movement could be made without opposition from Robertson's brigade, I ordered the scout to return and satisfy himself by a closer inspection that he had not mistaken some of our troops for the enemy. In less than five minutes the man reported that I could now see for myself. And so it was! Within cannon shot of the hill a long column of the enemy filled the road, which here skirted the woods. They were pressing steadily forward upon the railroad station, which must in a few moments be in their possession. How could they be prevented from also occupying the Fleetwood Hill, the key to the whole position? Matters looked serious!"

At this point, McClellan could merely hope to delay Gregg's troopers and make them think there was a substantial Confederate force at Fleetwood Hill, which he managed to accomplish by firing artillery near the Confederate headquarters. "Lieutenant Carter's howitzer was brought up, and boldly pushed beyond the crest of the hill; a few imperfect shells and some round shot were found in the limber chest; a slow fire was at once opened upon the marching column, and courier after courier was dispatched to General Stuart to inform him of the peril. It was all important to gain time, for should the enemy once plant his artillery on this hill it would cost many valuable lives to recover the ground, even if that could at all be accomplished. We must retain this position or suffer most seriously when enclosed between the divisions of Buford and Gregg. But the enemy was deceived by appearances. That the head of his column should have been greeted with the fire of artillery as soon as it emerged from the woods must have indicated to General Gregg the presence of a considerable force upon the hill; and the fact that his advance from Kelly's Ford had been entirely unopposed, together with his ignorance of what had transpired with Buford, must have strengthened the thought that his enemy, in force, here awaited an attack. In point of fact there was not one man upon the hill beside those belonging to Carter's howitzer and myself, for I had sent away even my last courier, with an urgent appeal for speedy help. Could General Gregg have known the true state of affairs he would, of course, have sent forward a squadron to take possession; but appearances demanded a more serious attack, and while this was being organized three rifled guns were unlimbered, and a fierce cannonade was opened on the hill."

As things were unfolding around Fleetwood Hill, McClellan urgently dispatched the news to Stuart, but like the other Confederate officers, Stuart couldn't believe the initial report. In fact, Stuart ordered the first courier to "ride back there and see what all this foolishness is about," only to have the second courier arrive with the same news just as the cannonade in the rear began. Von Borcke would describe the moment he, Stuart, and the other Confederates fighting Buford heard the fighting behind them: "All our brigades having now arrived from the more distant camps, our line of battle, nearly three miles in length, could be regularly formed; and along the woods which border the Rappahannock the multitudinous firing of our dismounted sharpshooters sounded like the rattle of musketry in a regular battle. We held our ground tolerably well for some time, but it soon became evident that the enemy were in far superior numbers and supported by infantry, large columns of which were reported by William Lee, who commanded on our extreme left, to be crossing the river. Towards this point I was sent by General Stuart to watch the movements of the enemy, with orders to send a report every quarter of an hour by one of the body of couriers whom I took with me. William Lee's brigade was placed on a ridge of hills, with its skirmishers on the river-bank and along a formidable stone fence running across an open field, over which the Federals advanced in strong numbers, but were again and again repulsed as soon as they came within range of our sharpshooters, who were well seconded by the accurate firing of one of our batteries on the heights. Buried in the deep grass, William Lee and I lay close to our guns watching the progress of the battle, when we were startled by a heavy cannonade in our rear, apparently in the direction of our headquarters at Brandy Station."

Even at this point, von Borcke still couldn't believe Union cavalry was in force in their rear until he saw it with his own eyes: "From some stragglers who galloped past me as I approached the station, I gathered, in a confused way, that the Federals were in our rear. To this report I gave little credit, but on emerging from the forest I found that they had only spoken the truth, for there a sight awaited me which made the blood run cold in my veins. The heights of Brandy and the spot where our headquarters had been were perfectly swarming with Yankees, while the men of one of our brigades were scattered wide over the plateau, chased in all directions by their enemies."

The Confederates were in such a tight position at this point that the nearest reinforcements Stuart could send south to Fleetwood Hill were regiments from Grumble Jones' brigade, which was the first to fight Buford and had been engaged most of the morning. The Confederates on Fleetwood Hill were in such dire straits by this point that the guns McClellan initially had fired at Gregg's cavalry had run out of ammunition and were retiring just as the reinforcements from Jones' brigade arrived. McClellan explained, "The nearest point from which a regiment could be sent was Jones' position, one and a half miles distant from Fleetwood. The 12th Virginia, Colonel A. W. Harman, and the 35th battalion, Lieutenant-Colonel E. V. White, were immediately withdrawn from his line and ordered to meet this new danger. But minutes expanded seemingly into hours to those anxious watchers on the hill, who feared lest, after all, help could not arrive in time. But it did come. The emergency was so pressing that Colonel Harman had no time to form his regiment in squadrons or even in platoons. He reached the top of the hill as Lieutenant Carter was retiring his gun after having fired his very last cartridge. Not fifty yards below, Colonel Percy Wyndham was advancing the 1st New Jersey Cavalry in magnificent order, in column of squadrons, with flags and guidons flying. A hard gallop had enabled only the leading files of the 12th Virginia to reach the top of the hill, the rest of the regiment stretching out behind in column of fours. It was a trying position both to the pride and the courage of this regiment to be put into action in such manner that a successful charge seemed hopeless; but with the true spirit of a forlorn hope, Colonel Harman and the few men about him dashed at the advancing Federals. Stuart reached the hill a few moments later, having ordered Hampton and Jones to retire from the position at Saint James' Church and concentrate on the Fleetwood Hill. It would seem from Hampton's report that, before he received this order, he himself perceived the danger in our rear and had commenced the necessary withdrawal, at the same time notifying Robertson, on the Kelly's Ford road, that his rear would now be exposed."

As McClellan's account indicates, Stuart had sensed the situation was so dangerous that he was compelled to withdraw Hampton and Jones from the line around St. James Church, leaving Rooney Lee's severely outnumbered brigade to deal with Buford's men. While the Union forces around Beverly's Ford couldn't know for sure, they likely presumed that the Confederates were withdrawing from their front because of the arrival of Gregg to the south. Eventually, Buford's men would take the stone wall that Rooney Lee's Confederates had used as a strongpoint and push that brigade backwards.

When people think about cavalry battles, the most popular image is of the two sides charging each other head on and fighting like medieval knights. In reality, most of the cavalry fighting in the Civil War consisted of the horsemen riding to a spot, dismounting most of the men (while keeping some to hold the horses), and having the men fight as infantry. During the Battle of Brandy Station, however, Gregg's wing caught Stuart by surprise so badly that the Confederates never had time to dismount, and the timing of the Confederates reinforcements' arrival at Fleetwood Hill meant the two sides were in such close proximity that neither could take the time to dismount. As a result, the fight for possession of Fleetwood Hill consisted almost entirely of mounted fighting, with charges and countercharges that consisted of close range pistol shooting and the use of sabers. McClellan described the scene: And now the first contest was for the possession of the Fleetwood Hill; and so stubbornly was this fought on either side, and for so long a time, that all of Jones' regiments and all of Hampton's participated in the charges and counter-charges which swept across its face. As I have already stated, the 12th regiment reached the top of the hill just in time to meet the charge of the 1st New Jersey. The 35th battalion was not far behind, but these troops were so disordered by their rapid gallop that, after the first shock, they recoiled and retired to reform. White's battalion seems to have been cut into two parts, two of his squadrons falling in with Colonel Harman on the eastern slope of the hill, while the other two retired along the crest of the ridge toward the Barbour House, in which direction they were followed by a portion of the 1st New Jersey, which now held the hill in temporary possession. Colonel Harman soon reformed his regiment, and, aided by the two squadrons of the 35th battalion, regained the hill for a short time. Colonel Harman was severely wounded in a personal encounter with the officer leading the Federal cavalry. Lieutenant-Colonel White, having reformed the two other squadrons of his battalion, swept around the west side of the hill and charged the three guns which had been advanced to its foot. The cavalry which supported these guns was driven away. Not so, however, with the gallant gunners of the 6th New York battery. They had already distinguished themselves at Chancellorsville on the 2d of May, under General Pleasonton, and on this occasion they stood by their guns with the most determined courage. Lieutenant-Colonel White says in his report."

Even hardened cavalry veterans couldn't believe the way the fighting was unfolding between Wyndham's men and Jones'. One man in the 1st North Caroline recalled, "The whole plain was covered with men and horses, charging in all directions, closed in hand to hand encounters, with banners flying, sabers glittering, and the fierce flash of firearms, amid the din, dust, and smoke of battle. Such scenes cannot last beyond a few fearful minutes. And so here." Likewise, a member of the 12th Virginia remembered, "Round and round it went; we would break their line on one side, and they would break ours on the other. Here it was pell mell, helter skelter—a yankee and there a rebel—killing, wounding, and taking prisoners." Another Virginian said, "On each side, in front, behind, everywhere on the top of the hill the Yankees closed in upon us. We fought them single-handed, by twos, fours, and by squads, just as the circumstances permitted."

Von Borcke reached the crest of Fleetwood Hill just as Wyndham's cavalry was being repulsed, and he wrote of the field, "I was not long in meeting with General Stuart, whom I found directing the operations from the highest part of the plateau. I was informed by him that the portion of Federal cavalry which had rendered our position so critical had consisted of two brigades, commanded by General Perry Windham, an Englishman in the Yankee service, who, by taking a circuitous route along an unguarded bridle-path, had succeeded in taking us in the rear, so causing all the confusion and panic which had very nearly decided the fate of the day. But just when the danger was at the highest and the stampede in full career — namely, at the very crisis I was unfortunate enough to witness — the Georgia regiment of Hampton's old brigade, under its commander, the gallant Colonel Young, and the 11th Virginia, under Colonel Lomax, had come up to the succour, and, throwing themselves with an impetuous charge on the temporary victors, had completely routed and driven them to flight, many killed and wounded, as well as prisoners, besides a battery, being left behind. General Windham himself was shot through the leg during the short melee, and had a narrow escape from capture; and several colonels and other officers were among the dead. The flight of the Federals had been so sudden and headlong that it gave rise to a number of odd incidents, among which may be recalled an accident which befell one of their buglers, who, in the blindness of his hurry, rode straight up against an old ice-house, breaking through the wooden partition, and tumbling headlong, horse and all, into the deep hole within. The horse was killed on the spot, but the rider escaped miraculously, and was hauled up with ropes amidst shouts of laughter from the by-standers at so ridiculous an adventure of battle."

Similarly, another member of Stuart's staff recalled, "What the eye saw as Stuart rapidly fell back from the river and concentrated his cavalry for the defense of Fleetwood Hill, between him and Brandy, was a great and imposing spectacle of squadrons charging in every portion of the field—men falling, cut out of the saddle with the sabre, artillery roaring, carbines cracking—a perfect hurly-burly of combat."

Much the same way Wyndham's cavalry and Jones' cavalry reached the same point on Fleetwood Hill at the same time, Judson Kilpatrick's brigade hit the southern and eastern parts of Fleetwood Hill just as Wade Hampton III's brigade arrived to reinforce the Confederate line. Once again, this resulted in charges and countercharges that resembled bedlam more than an ordinary cavalry engagement. Major Flournoy of the 6th Virginia cavalry described his unit's charge against the Union right, "I was then ordered by him (Hampton) to move quickly in the direction of Brandy Station, and while on the way I received orders from General Stuart to cut off three hundred Yankees who were near the Miller House. I moved across the railroad, and instead of three hundred, I met what prisoners reported as five regiments. I charged with my regiment, now reduced by casualties and the detachment of four of my companies, to two hundred and eight men. We drove back the whole force and had them in retreat, when we were attacked in rear and forced to fall back towards the Miller House, where the enemy opened on us with artillery. We charged and took the battery, but were unable to hold it. Having been charged by five times our number, we fell back in confusion towards the hill in front of the Miller House, where the men rallied and reformed."

Lieutenant J. Wade Wilson, who was in charge of some of the guns of the 6th New York battery, explained how the artillery helped repulse this charge: "Again, pursuant to orders from Colonel Kilpatrick, I limbered to the front and sought a position on the crest of the hill behind which the enemy was rapidly massing to force back the advance of Colonel Kilpatrick upon the house. Before reaching the crest, however, a halt was ordered by Colonel Kilpatrick, and, soon after, a retreat from that position, which was executed without panic and in admirable order. The enemy, perceiving the retreat, charged furiously up the hill and through the section fifty yards in rear of the pieces, charging desperately on the cavalry, some hundreds of yards in the advance of the pieces in retreat. The capture of the section seems to have been thought accomplished by the enemy, and the rebel line wheeled into column and pushed rapidly by the flanks, with the intent to turn the right of the 1st brigade, leaving, as they supposed, a sufficient force to secure the guns. At this time was displayed the heroism of the section, and valor of which any command and country may be justly proud. In reversing, one of the gun-limbers was nearly capsized, one wheel being in the air and the axle nearly vertical. Perceiving this, I ordered the cannoneers to dismount and restore to its position the limber. We were surrounded by a squad of rebel cavalry, firing with carbine and pistol. The order was scarcely needed, for the cannoneers had seen the peril of their gun, and, anticipating the order, had dismounted to restore it; and with revolvers in hand, they defended the gun as if determined to share its destiny and make its fate their own. The bearer of a rebel battle-flag was shot by Private Currant, who would have recovered it but for the great difficulty of approaching the color with a lame and skittish horse upon which he was at the time mounted. The flag was taken by the 1st Maine Cavalry."

As Kilpatrick saw the back and forth of the action, he exhorted the 1st Maine into action, yelling, "Men of Maine! You must save the day! Follow me!" One of the men in that unit remembered, "The whole plain was one vast field of intense, earnest action. It was a scene to be witnessed but once in a lifetime, and one well worth the risks of battle to witness." A captain in the 1st Maine described the effect of their charge: ""In one solid mass this splendid regiment circled first to the right, and then moving in a straight line at a run struck the 6th Virginia Cavalry in flank. The shock was terrific! Down went the rebels before this wild rush of maddened horses, men, biting sabres, and whistling balls." Their ferocious charge crashed into the Confederate horsemen. "The two regiments were interwoven," recalled a captain of the 1st Maine. "It was cut, thrust and fend off; numbers indulged in a personal grapple."

The 1st North Carolina, part of Hampton's brigade, also made a desperate charge to arrest the progress of Kilpatrick's cavalry. Major J.F. Hart, who commanded a Confederate battery, was at the top of Fleetwood Hill and watched the charge: "The battery I commanded moved abreast of Hampton's column in its gallop toward this new foe ; and as we came near Fleetwood Hill, its summit, as also the whole plateau east of the hill and beyond the railroad, was covered with Federal cavalry. Hampton, diverging toward his left, passed the eastern terminus of the ridge, and, crossing the railroad, struck the enemy in column just beyond it. This charge was as gallantly made and gallantly met as any the writer ever witnessed during nearly four years of active service on the outposts. Taking into estimation the number of men that crossed sabres in this single charge (being nearly a brigade on each side), it was by far the most important hand-to-hand contest between the cavalry of the two armies. As the blue and gray riders mixed in the smoke and dust of that eventful charge, minutes seemed to elapse before its effect was determined."

Just when it looked like the Confederates had won the field, Hart had to deal with another Union charge, this time made by the 1st New Jersey on the extreme left of the Union line: "Scarcely had our artillery opened on the retreating enemy from this new position than a part of the 1st New Jersey Cavalry, which formed the extreme Federal left, came thundering down the narrow ridge, striking McGregor's and Hart's unsupported batteries in the flank, and riding through between guns and caissons from right to left, but met by a determined hand to hand contest from the cannoneers with pistols, sponge-staffs, and whatever else came handy to fight with. Lieutenant-Colonel Broderick, commanding the regiment, was killed in this charge, as also the second in command, Major J. H. Shelmire, who fell from a pistol ball, while gallantly attempting to cut his way through these batteries. The charge was repulsed by the artillerists alone, not a solitary friendly trooper being within reach of us."

One of the men in Hampton's brigade explained that the give and take between the two grappling sides went on for over an hour: "Here the tide of battle alternated, brilliant charges were being made, routing the enemy and in turn being routed…and then, for an hour or more, there was a fierce struggle for the hill, which seemed to have been regarded as the key to the entire situation. This point was taken, and retaken once, and perhaps several times; each side would be in possession for a time, and plant its batteries there, when by a successful charge it would pass into the possession of the other side, and so it continued."

At this point, the Confederates had established a strong enough line on Fleetwood Hill that they could start pushing Gregg's wing back south towards Brandy Station, but to the north, there was still the matter of Rooney Lee's brigade trying to hold on against Buford's wing. In the face of overwhelming numbers, Lee's men had fallen back to establish a new line, and it soon turned into a fighting retreat of sorts that bought the Confederates time on the other side of the field. McClellan discussed this action in his memoirs: "The withdrawal of W. H. F. Lee's brigade from the open plain was, of course, in full view of the enemy, but was accomplished without provoking an attack until the new line was established, when a feeble charge in front was easily repulsed by the dismounted men. This, however, was only the beginning of the real struggle. General Buford continued to extend his right until he had entirely enveloped the left of Lee's line, and was now prepared to make an attack from the high ground just south and west of Green's house. This, if successful, would have placed Buford in rear of the left of Stuart's line.

An engagement of dismounted men — in which portions, at least, of the 2d Massachusetts and 3d Wisconsin infantry participated — was the prelude to a charge of the 6th Pennsylvania and the 2d United States Cavalry. This charge was met by the 9th Virginia, supported by the 10th and the 13th. General B. L. T. Beale, then colonel of the 9th Virginia Cavalry, in a description of this fight which he has kindly prepared for my use, claims that the 9th regiment broke the force which first attacked it, and drove it back across the stone fence in its rear. At this moment the 9th was attacked by a fresh regiment which came in on the flank, and was in turn driven back to the foot of the hill whence it had commenced the charge. Here the 9th was reinforced by the 10th and the 13th, and the tide of battle was finally turned against the Federal cavalry, which was driven back across the crest of the hill whence they had advanced. General Beale further states that having reformed his regiment after this action, he rode forward to reconnoitre before again advancing, when, to his surprise, he found the enemy moving back toward Beverly's Ford. A comparison of General Beale's statement with the narrative of Colonel Newhall indicates that this was the fight in which Adjutant Ellis, of the 6th Pennsylvania, was wounded, and in which General Wesley Merritt, then captain commanding the 2d Regulars, lost his hat in a sabre fight with a rebel officer. When the 9th Virginia first charged up the hill, General W. H. F. Lee was upon its left flank, encouraging the men of his old regiment. Just before he reached the crest of the hill he was severely wounded and was carried from the field. Colonel Sol. Williams, of the 2d North Carolina Cavalry, had begged permission, inasmuch as everything was quiet on his line, to join in this charge. He went in on the right of the 9th, was shot through the head, and instantly killed."

Ultimately, Gregg and Buford's wings were stopped, and part of the reason was that thousands of Union cavalry under Colonel Alfred N.A. Duffié couldn't make it to the field from Stevensburg to the south. Had Confederates not stood in their way, Duffié would've been able to bring up his cavalry on the Union's left and begin to flank Grumble Jones' brigade, which might very well have folded the entire Confederate cavalry in on itself between Gregg's wing and Buford's wing. Instead, the Confederates under Butler that Stuart had held back were there to block the advance.

During the Civil War, the side that held the battlefield at the end was generally acknowledged as the victor, but in this case, Pleasanton was content to claim that his "reconnaissance in force" had attained its objectives, and that they had managed to figure out not only the position of the Confederate cavalry but also some of Lee's infantry. With that, Pleasanton was happy to pull Gregg and Buford back across the Rappahannock. The Union lost an estimated 900 casualties, while the Confederates lost about 500. Von Borcke juxtaposed the scene with the grand reviews that had been held the past few days: "The loss of our opponents was very severe in dead and wounded, and a great number of officers fell, among whom was a brigadier-general, several colonels, besides many other of subordinate rank. About 400 privates and 40 officers were captured, and a battery of four guns already mentioned. The victory was a dearly-bought one on our side, and numbers of those who but a few days before had gaily attended the review, were now stretched cold and lifeless on the same ground. Among those whose death we mourned, was the gallant Colonel Hampton of the 2d South Carolina, brother of General Hampton, and Colonel Williams of the 2d North Carolina; General William Lee, Colonel Butler, and many other officers of rank, were among the wounded. Our Staff had suffered very severely: Captain White wounded, Lieutenant Goldsborough taken prisoner, and the gallant Captain Farley killed. Poor Farley! after innumerable escapes from the perils into which his brilliant gallantry led him, his fate had overtaken him at last, and he died as heroically as he had lived. While riding towards the enemy, side by side with Colonel Butler, a shell which passed clean through their horses, killed both these, shattered at the same time one of Butler's legs below the knee, and carried off one of Farley's close up to the body. When the surgeon arrived he naturally wished to attend first to the Captain as the more dangerously wounded, but this the brave young fellow positively refused, saying that Colonel Butler's life was more valuable to the country than his own, and he felt he should soon die. Two hours afterwards he was a corpse."

Historians don't even go that far; while the Confederates held the field and staved off a disaster, the Union cavalry had bloodied them, and Brandy Station is widely considered a draw that brought no strategic victory to the Confederates. Stuart obviously declared victory, but nobody in the South was fooled; it was apparent that he had been caught napping, and the results, as deadly as they were, could've been utterly disastrous.

Neg. by T. H. O. Sullivan          c. 1865  by A. Gardner
Feb. 1864

**Pictures of Union forces at Brandy Station in 1864**

## Moving North

In the days after Brandy Station, Lee began moving his army north for an invasion of Pennsylvania, looking for some sort of coup de grace that could strike a mortal blow to the North. Once again, Lee divided his forces to take different objectives, but this time they stayed within a day's marching distance of each other to avoid a repeat of the near disaster at Antietam.

Stuart's cavalry kept itself between Lee's army and Union forces by skirmishing with Union cavalry around Aldie on June 17, which represented one of the Union's most earnest attempts to push in on the Confederates. McClellan described the fighting that day:

> "The force of the enemy making this attack was the 2d cavalry division, commanded by General D. M. Gregg, and accompanied by Major-General Pleasonton. General Kilpatrick's brigade, consisting of the 2d New York, 1st Massachusetts, 6th Ohio, and 4th New York regiments, supported by the 1st Maine Cavalry, from Colonel J. I. Gregg's brigade, and by Randol's battery, appears to have done all the fighting. The two other brigades of General Gregg's division were closed up within supporting distance.
>
> The arrival of Rosser's regiment was most opportune. By an immediate sabre charge he drove back the enemy's advance upon their main body in the town of Aldie. Having relieved the pressure on the pickets, Rosser stationed his sharpshooters, under Captain R. B. Boston, on the right of the Snickersville road, where a number of haystacks afforded some protection, and held the remainder of

his small regiment ready for their support. Colonel Munford in the mean time arrived in person, and stationed Lieutenant William Walton, of the 2d Virginia Cavalry, with the reserve picket, fifteen men, behind a stone wall on the left of the Snickersville road, with orders to hold his position against any odds until the 2d and 3d regiments could come to his assistance. In the mean time, and while Colonel Wickham was stationing the 1st and 4th regiments and Breathed's battery to dispute any advance on the Middleburg road, Rosser, single-handed, had met and repulsed two charges which were made upon Captain Boston's squadron and believing that he could be maintained there with advantage, had ordered Boston to hold his position at all hazards. The result proved that this disposition was unfortunate , for during the subsequent heavy fighting Boston was so far advanced as to be beyond the reach of support, and he and his squadron were captured."

At this point the various passes in Bull Run Mountain required Stuart to divide his command in an attempt to guard them, and this led to another fight between Union and Confederate cavalry at Upperville on the 19th. McClellan summarized the results of that skirmish: "Early on the 19th Stuart's position on the Upperville turnpike was attacked by General D. M. Gregg's division, Colonel J. I. Gregg's brigade being in the advance. The attack was resisted for a long time ; but when the enemy had gained a considerable advantage on the Confederate right by a charge of dismounted men supported by two regiments of cavalry, Stuart withdrew to another line about a half a mile in his rear. This withdrawal was effected in good order, under the fire of the enemy's dismounted men and artillery, and no attempt was made to charge the retiring lines. During this movement Major Heros Yon Borcke, an officer of the Prussian army, who was serving on General Stuart's staff, received a severe wound, which disabled him from future service. General Gregg claims to have captured a large number of prisoners, but makes no specifications. Colonel J. I. Gregg reports a loss of one hundred and twenty-seven officers and men from his brigade. No attack was made on Stuart's new position on this clay, although hardly half of it was spent in this encounter."

Two days later, on the 21st, Union forces attacked Stuart near Middleburg. McClellan wrote:

"At about eight o'clock on the morning of Sunday, the 21st of June, the enemy moved out from Middleburg. Buford's division, three brigades, advanced on the road toward Union, endeavoring to turn Stuart's left flank; while Gregg's division, three brigades, supported by Vincent's infantry brigade, which alone numbered on the 19th of June an effective total of 1,545/ advanced on the Upperville pike. General D. M. Gregg states in his report that his advance was at first intended as a feint to occupy Stuart's attention in front, while Bu-ford moved upon his left flank. But Buford found Chambliss and Jones so strong that he could do no more than make a direct attack upon them. General Gregg's feint against Hampton and Robertson was, therefore, soon changed into a serious attack. Kilpatrick's brigade of cavalry and Vincent's brigade of infantry held the advance. Colonel Vincent, in his report, states with particularity the part taken by each of his four regiments up to a point west of Goose Creek, and reports a total loss of seven officers and men. Pursuing the policy already indicated, Stuart directed Hampton and Robertson not to allow themselves to become too heavily engaged, and at the same time he ordered Chambliss and Jones, to retire toward Upperville, as the artillery firing on the pike receded in that direction.

"The first position held by Stuart was about three miles west of Middleburg.

Here he delayed the enemy as long as prudence permitted, and then retired en echelon of regiments, covered by his artillery. This order of retiring was maintained throughout the entire day, and at no time was the enemy able to cause any serious disorder in his ranks. In leaving his first position a Blakely gun belonging to Hart's battery was abandoned. The axle had been broken by a shot from the enemy, and no means were at hand for its renewal. This was the first piece belonging to the horse artillery which had, up to that time, fallen into the enemy's hands, and the only one lost on that day.

"The second position held by Stuart was on the west bank of Goose Creek, and here the enemy was delayed for several hours. At this point General Gregg's cavalry and Vincent's infantry were still further reinforced by the reserve cavalry brigade from Buford's division, and from this position Stuart again withdrew, to effect a junction at Upperville with Jones and Chambliss, who were retiring slowly before Buford's advance. As the battle approached Upperville the enemy pressed with renewed visor. When within a mile of the town General Buford, believing from the appearance of the field that General Gregg was outnumbered, disengaged himself from Chambliss' front and moved rapidly to General Greg's assistance. Having the shorter line to traverse, he thus cut off Jones and Chambliss from effecting a junction with Hampton and Robertson east of Upperville."

In all, Stuart suffered about 500 casualties, but his cavalry inflicted 800 casualties and prevented the Union from determining Lee's movements. These results were exactly what the Confederates had come to expect from him, and Stuart had always proven himself expert at traditional cavalry operations such as these. However, these kinds of tasks also didn't make headlines, and Stuart's interest in public relations only made the results at Brandy Station two weeks earlier that much more bitter for him. Thus, it is widely believed that even as Stuart was stopping these thrusts adroitly, he wanted to conduct some sort of operation that would again make him the toast of the Confederacy, just as he was when he rode around McClellan's Army of the Potomac during the Peninsula Campaign in 1862 and after the Maryland campaign that culminated at Antietam.

### Plans for Stuart's Cavalry

After the skirmishing on the 21st, a decision had to be made regarding the way to utilize Stuart's cavalry as the Army of Northern Virginia entered northern Maryland and Pennsylvania. John Mosby, a notorious Confederate raider who was accompanying Stuart's cavalry at this point, suggested a plan that McClellan described. Mosby suggested "crossing the Bull Run Mountain at Glasscock's Gap, and of passing through the centre of Hooker's army in Loudon and Fairfax counties, with the purpose of crossing the Potomac at Seneca." Stuart later wrote in his official report after the battle of Gettysburg, "I submitted to the commanding general the plan of leaving a brigade or so in my present front, and passing through Hopewell or some other gap in Bull Run Mountains, attain the enemy's rear, passing between his main body and Washington, and cross into Maryland, joining our army north of the Potomac. The commanding general wrote me, authorizing this move if I deemed it practicable,-and also what instructions should be given the officer in command of the two brigades left in front of the enemy. He also notified me that one column should move via Gettysburg and the other via Carlisle, toward the Susquehanna, and directed me, after crossing, to proceed with all dispatch to join the right (Early) of the army in Pennsylvania."

According to McClellan, Lee's headquarters sent a letter to Stuart on the 23rd that detailed a route for him, and though he couldn't find a copy of it after the war, he claimed that it provided the following instructions: "The letter discussed at considerable length the plan of passing around the enemy's rear. It informed General Stuart that General Early would move upon York, Pa., and that he was desired to place his cavalry as speedily as possible with that, the advance division of Lee's right wing. The letter suggested that, as the roads leading northward from Shepherdstown and Williamsport were already encumbered by the infantry, the artillery, and the transportation of the army, the delay which would necessarily occur in passing by these would, perhaps, be greater than would ensue if General Stuart passed around the enemy's rear. The letter further informed him that, if he chose the latter route, General Early would receive instructions to look out for him and endeavor to communicate with him; and York, Pa., was designated as the point in the vicinity of which he was to expect to hear from Early, and as the possible (if not the probable) point of concentration of the army. The whole tenor of the letter gave evidence that the commanding general approved the proposed movement, and thought that it might be productive of the best results, while the responsibility of the decision was placed upon General Stuart himself."

McClellan cites Longstreet in saying that Lee had to have expected Stuart to use his discretion to determine whether to pass around the Army of the Potomac or not. Lee wrote in his report after Gettysburg, "Gen. Stuart was left to guard the passes of the mountains and observe the movements of the enemy, whom he was instructed to harass and impede as much as possible, should he attempt to cross the Potomac. In that event, Gen. Stuart was directed to move into Maryland, crossing the Potomac east or west of the Blue Ridge, as, in his judgment, should be best, and take position on the right of our column as it advanced."

Between McClellan's account and Lee's report, it's apparent that Lee at least intended for Stuart to cross the Potomac and shield the right flank of Jubal Early's division, which was on the far right of Ewell's corps. It's also clear that Lee gave Stuart considerable discretion, as was his nature when giving orders to subordinates. Granting his subordinates discretion demonstrated his trust in them, especially when he might not be on the field or in position to make a snap judgment himself. When dealing with competent subordinates like Longstreet, Stonewall Jackson, and Stuart, discretionary orders had served Lee well in the past, but there would be several times during the Pennsylvania Campaign that discretionary orders would cause major problems, beginning with Stuart's ride.

James Longstreet, leading the I Corps, would become a popular scapegoat for Gettysburg by many Confederate officials at the war, so it's somewhat fitting that he was also involved in the communications between Stuart and Lee's headquarters before June 25. Given Stuart's position serving as a screen, the Confederate cavalry communicated to Lee through Longstreet, and one of the exchanges of correspondence between Longstreet and Stuart seemed to suggest that Stuart should try to get in the rear of the Union army.

Decades after the war, Longstreet wrote his memoirs, *From Manassas to Appomattox*, and in many ways it was intended to reject allegations made by veterans like Jubal Early that he was responsible for the Battle of Gettysburg because of what happened on July 2. After the war, he had been frank in his criticism of Lee (who had died without writing his own memoirs) wherever he saw fit, and he had helped Republican administrations after the war, both of which antagonized many of the Lost Cause advocates who all but enshrined Lee as the faultless ideal of Southern values.

In his memoirs, he attributes blame for what transpired to Stuart, and he also addressed the controversy over his correspondence with Stuart:

"Connected with the cavalry raid and orders authorizing it are matters of more than usual interest. On the 22d the Confederate commander sent unsealed instructions to his cavalry chief, through Headquarters of the First Corps, to be forwarded, provided the cavalry could be spared from my front and could make the ride without disclosing our plans, expressing his preference for the ride through Hopewell Gap east of the Union army. As previously stated, I was to decide at the last moment between the two points that had been named. As my front was changed to the rear for the march north, the cavalry could be of no service there. The extent of authority with me, therefore, was to decide whether the crossing should be made at the Point of Rocks or around through Hopewell Gap east of the Union army. The crossing at Point of Rocks was not only hazardous, but more likely to indicate our plans than any move that could be made, leaving the ride through Hopewell Gap the only route for the raiding party. In my note to General Stuart enclosing General Lee's instructions was this item:

'P. S.-- think your passage of the Potomac by our rear at the present moment will, in a measure, disclose our plans. You had better not leave us, therefore, unless you can take the route in rear of the enemy.'

This has been put in italics and published as evidence that the raid was made by my orders, as well as by General Lee's. In the postscript three points are indicated:

First, the move along my rear to the crossing at Point of Rocks.

Second, my preferred march on my flank to the Shepherdstown crossing.

Third, the route indicated by General Lee.

All of which General Stuart understood as well as I did. Especially did he know that my orders were that he should ride on the right of my column, as originally designed, to the Shepherdstown crossing. In the body of my note were orders that he should report to me of affairs along the cavalry line before leaving; that he should assign General Hampton to command of the cavalry to be left with us, with orders to report at my Headquarters. These orders, emanating properly from the commander of the rear column of the army, should not have been questioned, but they were treated with contumely. He assigned General Robertson to command the cavalry that was left on the mountain, without orders to report at my headquarters; and though left there to guard passes of the Blue Ridge, he rode on a raid, so that when the cavalry was most needed it was far away from the army. The raid and the absence of the cavalry at the critical moment were severely criticised through the army and the country. If General Stuart could have claimed authority of my orders for his action, he could not have failed to do so in his official account. He offered no such excuse, but claimed to act under the orders of his chief, and reported that General Lee gave consent to his application for leave to make the march. So our plans, adopted after deep study, were suddenly given over to gratify the youthful cavalryman's wish for a nomadic ride."

That said, Lee must have or at least should have considered what kind of personality Stuart possessed when giving him the discretionary orders in late June. It was no secret that Stuart had a flair for the dramatic, and that there was a strong possibility (if not likelihood) that Stuart would exercise discretion in a way that would allow him to do something more noteworthy than something as mundane as screening the infantry march. McClellan noted this by quoting Longstreet himself: "Well may General Longstreet say: 'Authority thus given a subordinate general implies an opinion on the part of the commander that something better than the drudgery of a march along our flank might be open to him, and one of General Stuart's activity and gallantry should not be expected to fail to seek it.'"

## Stuart's Ride

Stuart's operations from June 25-July 2 would prove to be problematic even before his cavalry had embarked. One of the reasons Lee gave discretionary orders was because the battlefield was fluid, and the Confederates could not rely on the Union forces to always cooperate by staying where they wanted, so Lee wanted subordinates to make decisions without causing too much delay.

Unbeknownst to the Confederates, unexpected marches north by the Army of the Potomac would foil Stuart's proposed route immediately, and Stuart was not well served by Mosby's assertion that the Union forces were stretched thin and idle along a 25 mile front around Leesburg, Virginia. In fact, Mosby informed Stuart that the Confederate cavalry would actually be able to push through the Union line in force.

With that, Stuart decided that he would set off on the ride with three brigades of cavalry, selecting the ones led by Hampton, Fitzhugh Lee and Colonel John Chambliss. Grumble Jones and Beverly Robertson would continue to guard the nearby mountain passes with their brigades, which meant they would not be conducting any major reconnaissance or other forms of information gathering for Lee's army. McClellan tried to rationalize Stuart's decision to make these dispositions after the war: "I do not profess to give authoritatively the reasons which led General Stuart to make this disposition of his brigades, but there are some considerations which seem to lie upon the surface. Stuart was about to undertake a hazardous movement, in which he needed not only veteran troops, but officers upon whose hearty cooperation he could confidently rely. These qualities were united in the brigades and brigade commanders which he selected to accompany him. Moreover, by this division of his brigades he left in close communication with the army a force of cavalry nearly equal to that which he carried with him, for Jones' brigade was by far the largest in the division, and when joined to Robertson's two regiments, this command must have numbered more than 3,000 men, even after deducting the losses in battle since the 9th of June. This force, added to Jenkins' brigade, which constituted Ewell's advance in Pennsylvania, and which General Stuart estimated at 3,800 he was justified in considering sufficient to fulfill every duty which might be required of the cavalry by the commanding general. Another consideration doubtless had weight. I have heard General Stuart pronounce in unqualified terms that he considered General Jones 'the best outpost officer' in his command; and that his watchfulness over his pickets and his skill and energy in obtaining information were worthy of all praise. General Stuart must, therefore, have considered that he was leaving in communication with the army an officer eminently qualified for the duty of observing and reporting the enemy's movements; and that the fact that his brigade constituted, perhaps, four fifths of the force employed would cause General Robertson, who commanded the two brigades, to give full weight to his suggestions and counsels."

**Chambliss**

Stuart and the three brigades set out on the night of the 24th, and by early morning of the 25th, it was already clear that Mosby's intelligence was inaccurate because Stuart ran head first into Winfield Scott Hancock's II Corps near Haymarket. McClellan explained, "The three brigades selected to accompany Stuart rendezvoused at Salem during the earlier part of the night of the 24th, and at one o'clock on the same night marched out for Haymarket, passing through Glasscock's Gap early in the morning. As Stuart approached Haymarket it was discovered that Hancock's corps, marching northward, occupied the road upon which he expected to move. A brisk artillery fire was opened upon the marching column, and was continued until the enemy moved a force of infantry against the guns. Not wishing to disclose his force, Stuart withdrew from Hancock's vicinity after capturing some prisoners and satisfying himself concerning the movement of that corps. This information was at once started to General Lee by a courier bearing a despatch written by General Stuart himself. It is plain from General Lee's report that this messenger did not reach him; and unfortunately the despatch was not duplicated. Had it reached General Lee the movement of Hancock's corps would, of itself, have gone far to disclose to him the intentions of the enemy as to the place where a passage of the Potomac was about to be effected."

It's unclear why Lee didn't receive that message, or whether it was ever actually sent, but in any case, Lee would not have any information about the Union army's whereabouts for several more days. Moreover, once he ran into Hancock, Stuart had to choose which route to use next and thus exercise the discretion he felt Lee had afforded him. Perhaps it should come as no surprise that Stuart decided to go ahead and ride towards the rear of the Army of the Potomac, which would place him much farther east than expected, instead of crossing the Potomac at Shepherdstown, Maryland to more easily screen Ewell's corps. Again, McClellan tried to rationalize Stuart's decision, "It was now clearly impossible for Stuart to follow the route originally intended; and he was called upon to decide whether he should retrace his steps and cross the Potomac at Shepherdstown, or by making a wider detour continue his march to the rear of the Federal army. He consulted with no one concerning the decision, and no one is authorized to speak of the motives which may have presented themselves to his mind. We may, however, fairly suggest the following considerations: Stuart's orders directed him to choose the most expeditious route by which to place himself on the right of Early's advance in Pennsylvania. Early was at Waynesboro', Pa., on the 23d of June, and his movements up to that day were of course known to Stuart, who did not leave Rector's Cross Roads until late in the afternoon of the 24th. Early's march to York, Pa., was indicated to Stuart in General Lee's orders, and York was named as the place where Stuart would probably find Early. On the evening of the 25th, when Stuart drew back to Buckland out of the way of Hancock's corps, at least sixty miles of a mountainous road lay between him and Shepherdstown, the nearest ford of the Potomac west of the mountains. He could not hope to reach Shepherdstown with his artillery earlier than the evening of the 27th; and he would have been more than fortunate could he have occupied the passes of South Mountain on the 28th. He would even then have been at least thirty miles from Gettysburg, and twice that distance from York. It should not therefore be wondered at if this consideration alone decided Stuart to persist in the movement already begun, especially when there was also the hope of damaging the enemy in his rear and thus delaying his movements. Moreover he had a right to expect that the information he had forwarded concerning the movement of Hancock's corps would cause Robertson and Jones to be active on their front, and would put General Lee himself on the alert in the same direction."

Stuart himself alluded to some of the reasons he decided to take the route he did in his report after the battle: "As Hancock had the right of way on my road, I sent Fitz. Lee's brigade to Gainesville to reconnoiter, and devoted the remainder of the day to grazing our horses, the only forage procurable in the country. The best of our information represented the enemy still at Centreville, Union Mills, and Wolf Run Shoals. I sent a dispatch to General Lee concerning Hancock's movement, and moved back to Buckland, to deceive the enemy. It rained heavily that night. To carry out my original design of passing west of Centreville, would have involved so much detention, on account of the presence of the enemy, that I determined to cross Bull Run lower down, and strike through Fairfax for the Potomac the next day. The sequel shows this to have been the only practicable course. We marched through Brentsville to the vicinity of Wolf Run Shoals, and had to halt again in order to graze our horses, which hard marching without grain was fast breaking down. We met no enemy to-day (26th)."

Whatever the reasons, Stuart's decision to push east and go around the Army of the Potomac instead of move north effectively meant that he would no longer be screening Lee's army, so at this stage it was a matter of trying to harass the Union lines and perhaps create a diversion that might confuse Hooker.

During the night of June 27-28, Stuart would finally ford the Potomac River, but it would be over 50 miles away from Shepherdstown and it would cause further difficulty. McClellan described the efforts required that night: "It had been necessary to halt the command several times since the 25th to graze the horses, for the country was destitute of provisions, and Stuart had brought no vehicles with him save ambulances. Upon reaching Dranesville Hampton's brigade was sent to Rowser's Ford, and made the passage early in the night ; but the Potomac was so wide, the water so deep, and the current so strong, that the ford was reported impracticable for the artillery and ambulances. Another ford in the vicinity was examined, under circumstances of great danger, by Captain R. B. Kennon of Stuart's staff, but it was found to offer no better prospect of success, and Stuart determined to cross at Bowser's, if it were within the limits of possibility. The caissons and limber-chests were emptied on the Virginia shore, and the ammunition was carried over by the cavalrymen in their hands. The guns and caissons, although entirely submerged during nearly the whole crossing, were safely dragged through the river and up the steep and slippery bank, and by three o'clock on the morning of the 28th the rear-guard had crossed and the whole command was established upon Maryland soil. No more difficult achievement was accomplished by the cavalry during the war. The night was calm and without a moon. No prominent object marked the entrance to the ford on either side, but horse followed horse through nearly a mile of water, which often covered the saddles of the riders. Where the current was strong the line would unconsciously be borne down the river, sometimes so far as to cause danger of missing the ford, when some bold rider would advance from the opposite shore and correct the alignment. Energy, endurance, and skill were taxed to the utmost; but the crossing was effected, and so silently that the nearest neighbors were not aware of it until daylight. Possession was immediately taken of the canal, which constituted one of the lines of supply for Hooker's army; a number of boats, some containing troops, were captured, and the canal was broken. After the arduous labors of the night some rest was indispensable, especially for the artillery horses, and the sun was several hours high before the command left the Potomac for Rockville. Hampton's brigade moved in advance by way of Darnestown, and found Rockville in the possession of a small force of the enemy, which was speedily scattered."

Here, the Confederates destroyed a canal being used to supply the Union army, and this position left the Confederates nearly within sight of the Union capital, a prime spot from which they could strike supply lines. On the 28th, Stuart's cavalry captured a provisions train of 125 wagons and all of the pack animals, and this would all be taken by Stuart to Gettysburg on July 2. By then, however, the supplies would be of little consequence by that point.

In fact, the capture of these baggage trains would end up negatively impacting the Confederate campaign because the transportation of the wagons slowed Stuart down over the next several days. McClellan explained why, but he also insisted that the capture of the provisions would have been crucial if the Confederates had forced the Union to retreat from Gettysburg on July 1. In the process, he casts blame on Stonewall Jackson's replacement, Richard Ewell, for not attacking at Gettysburg on the night of July 1. Ironically, it was a decision Ewell made after being given discretionary orders by Lee. McClellan wrote, "Had General Lee gained the battle of Gettysburg, as he said he would have done if Stonewall Jackson had been present, the persistency with which Stuart held on to these wagons, and the difficulties he surmounted in transporting them safely through an enemy's country during the next three days and nights of incessant marching and fighting, would have been the cause of congratulation. But Gettysburg was lost to the Confederate arms, and not through Stuart's fault; and every circumstance which might have contributed to a different result will be judged in the light of the final catastrophe. Considered from this point of view, it must be acknowledged that the capture of this train of wagons was a misfortune. The time occupied in securing it was insignificant ; but the delay caused to the subsequent march was serious at a time when minutes counted almost as hours. Had Stuart been entirely unimpeded he would have probably passed Hanover, Pa., on the 30th, before the arrival of Kilpatrick's division, and would have been in communication with General Lee before nightfall on that day. That this would have altered the result of the campaign is a matter of grave doubt; but it would certainly have relieved the movement of the cavalry around the rear of Meade's army of the disapprobation to which some have given expression."

Once again, Stuart attempted to provide an explanation for the decisions he made on the 28th in his post-battle report: "Soon after taking possession, a long train of wagons approached from the direction of Washington, apparently but slightly guarded. As soon as our presence was known to those in charge, they attempted to turn the wagons, and at full speed to escape, but the leading brigade (W. H. F. Lee's) was sent in pursuit. The farthest wagon was within only 3 or 4 miles of Washington City, the train being about 8 miles long. Not one escaped, though many were upset and broken, so as to require their being burned. More than one hundred and twenty-five best United States model wagons and splendid teams with gay caparisons were secured and driven off. The mules and harness of the broken wagons were also secured. The capture and securing of this train had for the time scattered the leading brigade. I calculated that before the next brigade could march this distance and reach the defenses of Washington, it would be after dark; the troops there would have had time to march to position to meet attack on this road. To attack at night with cavalry, particularly unless certain of surprise, would have been extremely hazardous; to wait till morning, would have lost much time from my march to join General Lee, without the probability of compensating results. I therefore determined, after getting the wagons under way, to proceed directly north, so as to cut the Baltimore and Ohio Railroad (now becoming the enemy's main war artery) that night. I found myself now encumbered by about 400 prisoners, many of whom were officers. I paroled nearly all at Brookeville that night, and the remainder next day at Cooksville."

Thus, on the 29th, Fitz Lee's brigade tore up tracks on the Baltimore and Ohio Railroad and severed telegraph lines to make sure Washington couldn't communicate with the Army of the Potomac. That same day, other parts of Stuart's cavalry skirmished with Union forces on the way to Westminster, Maryland where they came across more supplies. Before the ride, Stuart had planned to be in southern Pennsylvania by the 28th, yet he was still in Maryland over 24 hours later than that, and here again, McClellan notes that it would've been better for the Confederates to simply destroy what they captured instead of attempting to take it all with them: "For the first time since the 24th an abundance of provisions for men and horses was obtained at Westminster; and moving the head of his column to Union Mills, on the Gettysburg road, Stuart rested for the remainder of the night. Here he ascertained that the enemy's cavalry had reached Littlestown, seven miles distant, on the same evening, and had gone into camp. At this day we can see that it would have been better had Stuart here destroyed the captured wagons. Up to this time they had caused no embarrassment, for the necessary delay in destroying the railroad and telegraph on the previous day had given ample time for the movement of the train. But now the close proximity of the enemy suggested the probability of a collision on the morrow, and the separation of the brigades by the wide interval which the train occupied was a disadvantage which might well have caused its immediate destruction. But it was not in Stuart's nature to abandon an attempt until it had been proven to be beyond his powers; and he determined to hold on to his prize until the last moment."

As if the capture of the supplies hadn't already caused enough of a delay, it may have had a material effect on the result of the fighting between Stuart's cavalry and Judson Kilpatrick's Union cavalry around Hanover, Pennsylvania on the 30th. That day, Stuart's lead brigades ran into Kilpatrick's rear, but the Confederates were unable to exploit their advantage because of the dispositions used to both guard and transport the captured supplies. Even Stuart felt compelled to admit that fact in his report: "About 10 a.m. the head of the column reached Hanover, and found a large column of cavalry passing through, going toward the gap of the mountains which I intended using. The enemy soon discovered our approach, and made a demonstration toward attacking us, which was promptly met by a gallant charge by Chambliss' leading regiment, which not only repulsed the enemy, but drove him pell-mell through the town with half his numbers, capturing his ambulances and a large number of prisoners, all of which were brought, safely through to our train, but were closely followed by the enemy s fresh troops. If my command had been well closed now, this cavalry column, which we had struck near its rear, would have been at our mercy; but, owing to the great elongation of the column by reason of the 200 wagons and hilly roads, Hampton was a long way behind, and Lee was not yet heard from on the left."

Working under the assumption that Early's division was to the northeast around York, Stuart pulled back from the fight and proceeded to plan a march that way, which would take him through Jefferson. Stuart explained, "Our wagon train was now a subject of serious embarrassment, but I thought, by making a détour to the right by Jefferson, I could save it. I therefore determined to try it, particularly as I was satisfied, from every accessible source of information, as well as from the lapse of time, that the Army of Northern Virginia must be near the Susquehanna."

McClellan also described how badly the captured supplies would slow the Confederates down on the 30th: "During the night march to Jefferson the wagons and prisoners were a serious hindrance. Nearly four hundred prisoners had accumulated since the parole at Cooksville. Many of these were loaded in the wagons; some of them acted as drivers. The mules were starving for food and water, and often became unmanageable. Not infrequently a large part of the train would halt in the road because a driver toward the front had fallen asleep and allowed his team to stop. The train guard became careless through excessive fatigue, and it required the utmost exertions of every officer on Stuart's staff to keep the train in motion. The march was continued through the entire night, turning northward at Jefferson. When Fitz Lee reached the road leading from York to Gettysburg he learned that Early had retraced his steps, and had marched westward. The best information which Stuart could obtain seemed to indicate that the Confederate army was concentrating in the vicinity of Shippensburg. After a short rest at Dover, on the morning of the 1st of July, Stuart pressed on toward Carlisle, hoping there to obtain provisions for his troops, and definite information concerning the army."

In the end, Kilpatrick's ability to block Stuart at Hanover ensured that when the battle of Gettysburg started early in the morning on the next day (July 1), Stuart would be marching his cavalry to the northeast towards York while fighting raged to the west. Stuart wrote in his report, "Reaching Dover, Pa., on the morning of July 1, I was unable to find our forces. The most I could learn was that General Early had marched his division in the direction of Shippensburg, which the best information I could get seemed to indicate as the point of concentration of our troops. After as little rest as was compatible with the exhausted condition of the command, we pushed on for Carlisle, where we hoped to find a portion of the army. I arrived before that village, by way of Dillsburg, in the afternoon. Our rations were entirely out… "

The timetable had been frustrated so greatly that Stuart now had no clue where Lee's army was and thus had to send out couriers to try to figure it out. Those couriers would be in motion while the Confederates were inadvertently bringing on a general battle with the Army of the Potomac outside of Gettysburg. McClellan explained, "From Dover he sent Major A. R. Venable, of his staff, on the trail of Early's troops, and at a later hour of the day Captain Henry Lee, of Fitz Lee's staff, was sent toward Gettysburg on a similar errand. Stuart had reached Carlisle before either of these officers could return with a report. He found the town in the possession of the enemy. When the Confederate infantry had withdrawn from it General W. F. Smith had occupied the town with two brigades of militia, supported by artillery and a small force of cavalry. General Smith was summoned to surrender, but refused. While preparing to enforce his demand Stuart received, through Major Venable and Captain Lee, the first information of the location of the Confederate army, and orders from General Lee to move at once for Gettysburg."

Stuart added, "The whereabouts of our army was still a mystery; but, during the night, I received a dispatch from General Lee (in answer to one sent by Major Venable from Dover, on Early's trail), that the army was at Gettysburg, and had been engaged on this day (July 1) with the enemy's advance. I instantly dispatched to Hampton to move 10 miles that night on the road to Gettysburg, and gave orders to the other brigades, with a view to reaching Gettysburg early the next day, and started myself that night."

Thus, the battle of Gettysburg started before Stuart had any idea where Lee's army was, let alone the fact that they were engaged in a big battle. Stuart's brigades wouldn't reach Gettysburg until late on the afternoon of July 2, and they wouldn't be able to offer much on the second day of the battle either.

Late in the afternoon on the second day of the battle, Stuart finally arrived, bringing with him the caravan of captured Union supply wagons, and he was immediately reprimanded by Lee. One account described Lee as "visibly angry" and raising his hand "as if to strike the tardy cavalry commander." One staff member of Lee's, Colonel Charles G. Marshall, apparently went so far as to recommend that Lee court-martial Stuart.

While that does not sound like Lee's style, Stuart has been heavily criticized ever since, and it has been speculated Lee took him to task harshly enough that Stuart offered his resignation. If so, Lee obviously didn't accept it, but he ultimately wrote in his post-battle report to Richmond that Stuart's absence was directly responsible for his army's unexpected confrontation with the Union army at Gettysburg:

"Gen. Stuart continued to follow the movements of the Federal Army south of the Potomac, after our own had entered Maryland, and, in his efforts to impede its progress, advanced as far eastward as Fairfax Court-House. Finding himself unable to delay the enemy materially, he crossed the river at Seneca, and marched through Westminster to Carlisle, where he arrived after Gen. Ewell had left for Gettysburg. By the route he pursued, the Federal Army was interposed between his command and our main body, preventing any communication with him until his arrival at Carlisle. The march toward Gettysburg was conducted more slowly than it would have been had the movements of the Federal Army been known...

"The leading division of Hill met the enemy in advance of Gettysburg on the morning of July 1. Driving back these troops to within a short distance of the town, he there encountered a larger force, with which two of his divisions became engaged. Ewell, coming up with two of his divisions by the Heidlersburg road, joined in the engagement. The enemy was driven through Gettysburg with heavy loss, including about 5,000 prisoners and several pieces of artillery. He retired to a high range of hills south and east of the town. The attack was not pressed that afternoon, the enemy's force being unknown, and it being considered advisable to await the arrival of the rest of our troops. Orders were sent back to hasten their march, and, in the meantime, every effort was made to ascertain the numbers and position of the enemy, and find the most favorable point of attack. It had not been intended to fight a general battle at such a distance from our base, unless attacked by the enemy, but, finding ourselves unexpectedly confronted by the Federal Army, it became a matter of difficulty to withdraw through the mountains with our large trains. At the same time, the country was unfavorable for collecting supplies while in the presence of the enemy's main body, as he was enabled to restrain our foraging parties by occupying the passes of the mountains with regular and local troops. A battle thus became, in a measure, unavoidable."

That "unavoidable" battle would ultimately be the biggest battle in the history of North America and one of the most crucial turning points of the Civil War.

## Meade Takes Command

Though he had privately confided to his wife that he desired command of the Army of the Potomac, Meade never publicly expressed his wishes to those in charge, thus avoiding the political squabbling among generals. On June 28, however, he got his wish.

Before sunrise on that morning, a messenger entered Major General George Meade's field headquarters, shook the sleeping general and said, "I'm afraid I've come to give you some trouble, General." Jumping to his feet, Meade's first thought was that he was being arrested, probably for arguing with Hooker on the battlefield. Informed that he had replaced Hooker as commander of the Army of the Potomac (Lincoln had passed over his friend, the more qualified John F. Reynolds), Meade at first protested, stating that he didn't want the job. Informed that his promotion was not a "request," Meade hitched up his sagging long underwear, ran his fingers through his thinning hair and said, "Well, I've been tried and condemned without a hearing, and I suppose I shall have to go to the execution." .

In addition to being informed by Hooker that he was in command, Meade received a telegram from general-in-chief Henry Halleck:

"General:

You will receive with this the order of the President placing you in command of the Army of the Potomac. Considering the circumstances, no one ever received a more important command; and I cannot doubt that you will fully justify the confidence which the Government has reposed in you.

You will not be hampered by any minute instructions from these headquarters. Your army is free to act as you may deem proper under the circumstances as they arise. You will, however, keep in view the important fact that the Army of the Potomac is the covering army of Washington, as well as the army of operation against the invading forces of the rebels. You will therefore manoeuvre and fight in such a manner as to cover the Capital and also Baltimore, as far as circumstances will admit. Should General Lee move upon either of these places, it is expected that you will either anticipate him or arrive with him, so as to give him battle.

All forces within the sphere of your operations will be held subject to your orders. Harper's Ferry and its garrison are under your direct orders.

You are authorized to remove from command and send from your army any officer or other person you may deem proper; and to appoint to command as you may deem expedient.

In fine, General, you are intrusted with all the power and authority which the President, the Secretary of War, or the General-in-Chief can confer on you, and you may rely on our full support.

You will keep me fully informed of all your movements and the positions of your own troops and those of the enemy, so far as known.

I shall always be ready to advise and assist you to the utmost of my ability.

Very respectfully,

Your obedient servant,

H. W. Halleck, General-in-Chief."

Meade then issued General Orders No. 67:

"By direction of the President of the United States, I hereby assume command of the Army of the Potomac.

"As a soldier, in obeying this order—an order totally unexpected and unsolicited—I have no promises or pledges to make.

"The country looks to this army to relieve it from the devastation and disgrace of a foreign invasion. Whatever fatigues and sacrifices we may be called upon to undergo, let us have in view, constantly, the magnitude of the interests involved, and let each man determine to do his duty, leaving to an all-controlling Providence the decision of the contest.

"It is with great diffidence that I relieve in the command of this army an eminent and accomplished soldier, whose name must ever appear conspicuous in the history of its achievements; but I rely upon the hearty support of my companions in arms to assist me in the discharge of the duties of the important trust which has been confided to me.

George G. Meade, Major General, commanding."

When word of Meade's promotion spread around camp, it certainly surprised many men. After all, Meade lacked charisma, did not exude confidence, and did not arouse enthusiasm among his men by his presence. In fact, considering the many times he'd been wounded (or nearly wounded), many considered him a danger to his men and to himself. Even his trusty horse "Old Baldy" had been wounded under him at Second Bull Run and again at Antietam. Ultimately, the best thing his men could say about him was that at least he had never made any ruinous mistakes.

Assuming command of the Army of the Potomac on June 28 at Prospect Hall in Frederick, Maryland, (with his second son, George, now part of his staff), Meade had his work cut out for him, though few apparently considered his position. Having to first locate his forces, he then had to review Hooker's strategy, study the most recent intelligence reports, and then determine the appropriate course of action, all the while keeping an eye fixed on Lee. Ultimately disregarding Hooker's plans to strike into the Cumberland Valley, Meade opted to march on Harrisburg, Pennsylvania to move toward the Susquehanna River, keeping his troops between Lee's army and Washington.

Upon taking command, Meade began drawing up defensive positions around northern Maryland about a dozen miles south of Gettysburg. His proposed line would be referred to as the Pipe Creek Circular, but it would never be implemented due to actions outside of Meade's control.

## July 1

With Stuart too far to the east to provide information, it is believed that one of the first notices Lee got about the Army of the Potomac's movements actually came from a spy named "Harrison", a man who apparently worked undercover for Longstreet but of whom little is known. Harrison reported that General George G. Meade was now in command of the Union Army and was at that very moment marching north to meet Lee's army. According to Longstreet, he and Lee were supposedly on the same page at the beginning of the campaign. "His plan or wishes announced, it became useless and improper to offer suggestions leading to a different course. All that I could ask was that the policy of the campaign should be one of defensive tactics; that we should work so as to force the enemy to attack us, in such good position as we might find in our own country, so well adapted to that purpose—which might assure us of a grand triumph. To this he readily assented as an important and material adjunct to his general plan." Lee later claimed he "had never made any such promise, and had never thought of doing any such thing," but in his official report after the battle, Lee also noted, "It had not been intended to fight a general battle at such a distance from our base, unless attacked by the enemy.

As a result, Lee was unaware of Meade's position when an advanced division of Hill's Corps marched toward Gettysburg on the morning of July 1. The battle began with John Buford's Union cavalry forces skirmishing against the advancing division of Heth's just outside of town. Buford intentionally fought a delaying action that was meant to allow John Reynolds' I Corps to reach Gettysburg and engage the Confederates, which eventually set the stage for a general battle.

**Buford**

The I Corps was led by Pennsylvanian General John F. Reynolds, an effective general that had been considered for command of the entire army in place of Hooker and was considered by many the best general in the army. Since Lee had invaded Pennsylvania, many believe that Reynolds was even more active and aggressive than he might have otherwise been. In any event, Reynolds was personally at the front positioning two brigades, exhorting his men, "Forward men! Forward for God's sake, and drive those fellows out of the woods."

As he was at the front positioning his men, Reynolds fell from his horse, having been hit by a bullet behind the ear that killed him almost instantly. With his death, command of the I Corps fell upon Maj. Gen. Abner Doubleday, the Civil War veteran wrongly credited for inventing baseball. Despite the death of the corps commander, the I Corps successfully managed to drive the Confederates in their sector back, highlighted by sharp fighting from the Iron Brigade, a brigade comprised of Wisconsin, Indiana, and Michigan soldiers from the "West". In an unfinished railroad cut, the 6th Wisconsin captured the 2nd Mississippi, and regimental commander Rufus Dawes reported, "The officer replied not a word, but promptly handed me his sword, and his men, who still held them, threw down their muskets. The coolness, self possession, and discipline which held back our men from pouring a general volley saved a hundred lives of the enemy, and as my mind goes back to the fearful excitement of the moment, I marvel at it."

**Reynolds**

Around noon, the battle hit a lull, in part because Confederate division commander Henry Heth was under orders to avoid a general battle in the absence of the rest of the Army of Northern Virginia. At that point, however, the Union had gotten the better of the fighting, and the Confederate army was concentrating on the area, with more soldiers in Hill's corps in the immediate vicinity and Ewell's corps marching from the north toward the town.

As the Union's I Corps held the line, General Oliver O. Howard and his XI Corps came up on the right of the I Corps, eager to replace the stain the XI Corps had suffered at Chancellorsville thanks to Stonewall Jackson. As a general battle began to form northwest of town, news was making its way back to Meade several miles away that Reynolds had been killed, and that a battle was developing.

Meade had been drawing up a proposed defensive line several miles away from Gettysburg near Emmitsburg, Maryland, but when news of the morning's fighting reached him, Meade sent II Corps commander Winfield Scott Hancock ahead to take command in the field, putting him in temporary command of the "left wing" of the army consisting of the I, II, III and XI Corps. Meade also charged Hancock with determining whether to fight the general battle near Gettysburg or to pull back to the line Meade had been drawing up. Hancock would not be the senior officer on the field (Oliver Howard outranked him), so the fact that he was ordered to take command of the field demonstrates how much Meade trusted him.

As Hancock headed toward the fighting, and while the Army of the Potomac's I and XI Corps engaged in heavy fighting, they were eventually flanked from the north by Ewell's Confederate Corps, which was returning toward Gettysburg from its previous objective. For the XI Corps, it was certainly reminiscent of their retreat at Chancellorsville, and they began a disorderly retreat through the streets of the small town. Fighting broke out in various places throughout the town, while some Union soldiers hid in and around houses for the duration of the battle. Gettysburg's citizens also fled in the chaos and fighting.

After a disorderly retreat through the town itself, the Union men began to dig in on high ground to the southeast of the town. When Hancock met up with Howard, the two briefly argued over the leadership arrangement, until Howard finally acquiesced. Hancock told the XI Corps commander, "I think this the strongest position by nature upon which to fight a battle that I ever saw." When Howard agreed, Hancock replied, "Very well, sir, I select this as the battle-field."

As the Confederates sent the Union corps retreating, Lee arrived on the field and saw the importance of the defensive positions the Union men were taking up along Cemetery Hill and Culp's Hill. Late in the afternoon, Lee sent discretionary orders to Ewell that Cemetery Hill be taken "if practicable", but ultimately Ewell chose not to attempt the assault. Lee's order has been criticized because it left too much discretion to Ewell, leaving historians to speculate on how the more aggressive Stonewall Jackson would have acted on this order if he had lived to command this wing of Lee's army, and how differently the second day of battle would have proceeded with Confederate possession of Culp's Hill or Cemetery Hill. Discretionary orders were customary for General Lee because Jackson and Longstreet, his other principal subordinate, usually reacted to them aggressively and used their initiative to act quickly and forcefully. Ewell's decision not to attack, whether justified or not, may have ultimately cost the Confederates the battle. Edwin Coddington, widely considered the historian who wrote the greatest history of the battle, concluded, "Responsibility for the failure of the Confederates to make an all-out assault on Cemetery Hill on July 1 must rest with Lee. If Ewell had been a Jackson he might have been able to regroup his forces quickly enough to attack within an hour after the Yankees had started to retreat through the town. The likelihood of success decreased rapidly after that time unless Lee were willing to risk everything."

**General Ewell**

With so many men engaged and now taking refuge on the high ground, Meade, who was an engineer like Lee, abandoned his previous plan to draw up a defensive line around Emmittsburg a few miles to the south. After a council of war, the Army of the Potomac decided to defend at Gettysburg.

Day 1 by itself would have been one of the 25 biggest battles of the Civil War, and it was a tactical Confederate victory. Union casualties were almost 9,000, and the Confederates suffered slightly more than 6,000. But the battle had just started, and thanks to the actions of Meade and Hancock, the largest battle on the North American continent would take place on the ground of their choosing.

## July 2

By the morning of July 2, Major General Meade had put in place what he thought to be the optimal battle strategy. Positioning his now massive Army of the Potomac in what would become known as the "fish hook", he'd established a line configuration that was much more compact and maneuverable than Lee's, which allowed Meade to shift his troops quickly from inactive parts of the line to those under attack without creating new points of vulnerability. Moreover, Meade's army was taking a defensive stance on the high ground anchored by Culp's Hill, Cemetery Hill, and Cemetery Ridge. Meade also personally moved the III Corps under Maj. General Daniel Sickles into position on the left of the line.

On the morning of July 2, Meade was determined to make a stand at Gettysburg, and Lee was determined to strike at him. That morning, Lee decided to make strong attacks on both Union flanks while feinting in the middle, ordering Ewell's corps to attack Culp's Hill on the Union right while Longstreet's corps would attack on the Union left. Lee hoped to seize Cemetery Hill, which would give the Confederates the high ground to harass the Union supply lines and command the road to Washington, D.C. Lee also believed that the best way to do so would be to use Longstreet's corps to launch an attack up the Emmitsburg Road, which he figured would roll up the Union's left flank, presumed to be on Cemetery Hill. Lee was mistaken, due in part to the fact Stuart and his cavalry couldn't perform reconnaissance. In fact, the Union line extended farther south than Cemetery Hill, with the II Corps positioned on Cemetery Ridge and the III Corps nearly as far south as the base of Little Round Top and Round Top. Moreover, Ewell protested that this battle plan would demoralize his men, since they'd be forced to give up the ground they had captured the day before.

As it turned out, both attacks ordered by Lee would come too late. Though there was a controversy over when Lee ordered Longstreet's attack, Longstreet's march got tangled up and caused several hours of delay. Lost Cause advocates attacking Longstreet would later claim his attack was supposed to take place as early as possible, although no official Confederate orders gave a time for the attack. Lee gave the order for the attack around 11:00 a.m., and it is known that Longstreet was reluctant about making it; he still wanted to slide around the Union flank, interpose the Confederate army between Washington D.C. and the Army of the Potomac, and force Meade to attack them. Between Longstreet's delays and the mixup in the march that forced parts of his corps to double back and make a winding march, Longstreet's men weren't ready to attack until about 4:00 p.m.

Longstreet's biographer, Jeffrey Wert, wrote, "Longstreet deserves censure for his performance on the morning of July 2. He allowed his disagreement with Lee's decision to affect his conduct. Once the commanding general determined to assail the enemy, duty required Longstreet to comply with the vigor and thoroughness that had previously characterized his generalship. The concern for detail, the regard for timely information, and the need for preparation were absent." Edwin Coddington, whose history of the Gettysburg Campaign still continues to be considered the best ever written, described Longstreet's march as "a comedy of errors such as one might expect of inexperienced commanders and raw militia, but not of Lee's ' War Horse' and his veteran troops." Coddington considered it "a dark moment in Longstreet's career as a general."

Writing about July 2, Longstreet criticized Lee, insisting once again that the right move was to move around the Union flank. "The opportunity for our right was in the air. General Halleck saw it from Washington. General Meade saw and was apprehensive of it. Even General Pendleton refers to it in favorable mention in his official report. Failing to adopt it, General Lee should have gone with us to his right. He had seen and carefully examined the left of his line, and only gave us a guide to show the way to the right, leaving the battle to be adjusted to formidable and difficult grounds without his assistance. If he had been with us, General Hood's messengers could have been referred to general Headquarters, but to delay and send messengers five miles in favor of a move that he had rejected would have been contumacious. The opportunity was with the Confederates from the assembling on Cemetery Hill. It was inviting of their preconceived plans. It was the object of and excuse for the invasion as a substitute for more direct efforts for the relief of Vicksburg. Confederate writers and talkers claim that General Meade could have escaped without making aggressive battle, but that is equivalent to confession of the inertia that failed to grasp the opportunity."

As Longstreet's men began their circuitous march, Union III Corps commander Dan Sickles took it upon himself to advance his entire corps one half mile forward to a peach orchard, poising himself to take control of higher ground. Some historians assert that Sickles had held a grudge against Meade for taking command from his friend Joseph Hooker and intentionally disregarded orders. It has also been speculated by some historians that Sickles moved forward to occupy high ground in his front due to the devastation unleashed against the III Corps at Chancellorsville once Confederates took high ground and operated their artillery on Hazel Grove. Sickles and Meade would feud over the actions on Day 2 in the years after the war, after Sickles (who lost a leg that day) took credit for the victory by disrupting Lee's attack plans. Historians have almost universally sided with Meade, pointing out that Sickles nearly had his III Corps annihilated during Longstreet's attack.

**Sickles**

Whatever the reasoning for Sickles' move, this unauthorized action completely undermined Meade's overall strategy by effectively isolating Sickles' corps from the rest of the Union line and exposing the Union left flank in the process. By the early afternoon of July 2, nothing but the fog of war was preventing the Confederates from turning and crushing Sickles' forces, then moving to outflank the entire Union Army.

With General George Meade once again in command, General Hancock and the II Corps was positioned on Cemetery Ridge, roughly in the center of the Union line. Since Lee intended to strike at both Union flanks, theoretically Hancock's men should very well not have been engaged at all on the second day of the battle. But as a result of the fact Sickles had moved his men so far out of position, it created a major gap in the Union line and brought the III Corps directly into Longstreet's path. It was 4:00 p.m. by the time Longstreet's two divisions were in position for the attack, and they were taken completely by surprise when they found the III Corps in front of them on the Emmitsburg Road. Division commander John Bell Hood lobbied Longstreet to change up the plan of attack, but at this late time in the day Longstreet refused to modify Lee's orders.

Thus, in the late afternoon, the fighting on Day 2 began in earnest, and Longstreet's assault commenced by smashing into Sickles III Corps, engaging them in a peach orchard, wheat field, and Devil's Den, an outcropping of boulders that provided the Confederates prime cover.

When it became obvious that Sickles' III Corps was in dire straits, the chaos in that sector acted like a vacuum that induced both sides to pour more men into the vicinity. Moreover, when Sickles was injured by a cannonball that nearly blew off his leg, command of the III Corps fell upon II Corps commander Hancock as well. As Meade tried to shuffle reinforcements to his left, Hancock sent in his II Corps' First Division (under Brig. General John C. Caldwell) to reinforce the III Corps in the wheat field. The fighting in the wheat field was so intense that Caldwell's division would be all but annihilated during the afternoon.

At the same time, men from Confederate General A. P. Hill's corps made their advance toward the Union center, forcing the Army of the Potomac to rally defenses and rushed unit to critical spots to patch the holes. With Hill in his front and Longstreet's attack to his left, Hancock was in the unenviable position of having to attempt to resist Confederate advances spread out over a few miles, at least until more and more reserves could be rushed over from the other side of the Union line to the army's left flank. At one point, Hancock ordered a regiment to make what was essentially a suicidal bayonet charge into the face of Hill's Confederates on Cemetery Ridge. Hancock sent the First Minnesota to charge a Confederate brigade four times its size. One of the Minnesota volunteers, one William Lochren later said, "Every man realized in an instant what the order meant -- death or wounds to us all; the sacrifice of the regiment to gain a few minutes time and save the position, and probably the battlefield -- and every man saw and accepted the necessity of the sacrifice." While extremely costly to the regiment (the Minnesotans suffered 87% casualties, the worst of any regiment at Gettysburg), this heroic sacrifice bought time to organize the defensive line and kept the battle from turning in favor of the Confederates. Hancock would write of them, "I cannot speak too highly of this regiment and its commander in its attack, as well as in its subsequent advance against the enemy, in which it lost three-fourths of the officers and men engaged."

As Longstreet's assault on the Union left continued, his line naturally got more and more entangled as well. As Longstreet's men kept moving to their right, they reached the base of Little Round Top and Round Top, two rocky hills south of Gettysburg proper, at the far left. When Meade's chief engineer, Brig. General Gouverneur Warren, spotted the sun shining off the bayonets of Longstreet's men as they moved toward the Union left, it alerted the Army of the Potomac of the need to occupy Little Round Top, high ground that commanded much of the field.

With Warren having alerted his superiors to the importance of Little Round Top, Strong Vincent's brigade moved into position, under orders from Warren to "hold this ground at any costs," As part of Strong Vincent's brigade, Chamberlain's 20th Maine was on the left of the line, and thus Chamberlain's unit represented the extreme left of the Army of the Potomac's line.

**Vincent**

In front of Vincent's brigade was General Evander Law's advancing Alabama Brigade (of Hood's Division). Law ordered 5 regiments to take Little Round Top, the 4th, 15th, and 47th Alabama, and the 4th and 5th Texas, but they had already marched more than 20 miles just to reach that point. They were now being asked to charge up high ground on a muggy, hot day.

Nevertheless, the Confederates made desperate assaults against Little Round Top, even after being repulsed by the Union defenders several times. In the middle of the fighting, after he saw Confederates trying to push around his flank, Chamberlain stretched his line until his regiment was merely a single-file line, and he then had to order his left (southernmost) half to swing back, thus forming an angle in their line in an effort to prevent a flank attack. Despite suffering heavy losses, the 20th Maine held through two subsequent charges by the 15th Alabama and other Confederate regiments for nearly 2 hours.

**Chamberlain**

Even after repulsing the Confederates several times, Chamberlain and his regiment faced a serious dilemma. With casualties mounting and ammunition running low, in desperation, Chamberlain *claimed* to have ordered his left wing to initiate an all-out, pivoting bayonet charge. With the 20th Maine charging ahead, the left wing wheeling continually to make the charging line swing like a hinge, thus creating a simultaneous frontal assault and flanking maneuver, they ultimately succeeded in not only taking the hill, but capturing 100 Confederate soldiers in the process. Chamberlain suffered two slight wounds in the battle, one when a shot ricocheted off his sword scabbard and bruised his thigh, another when his right foot was struck by a piece of shrapnel. With this success, Chamberlain was credited with preventing the Union flank from being penetrated and keeping the Confederates from pouring in behind Union lines.

Ultimately, it was the occupation and defense of Little Round Top that saved the rest of the Union line at Gettysburg. Had the Confederates commanded that high ground, it would have been able to position artillery that could have swept the Union lines along Cemetery Ridge and Cemetery Hill, which would have certainly forced the Army of the Potomac to withdraw from their lines. Chamberlain would be awarded the coveted Congressional Medal of Honor for "daring heroism and great tenacity in holding his position on the Little Round Top against repeated assaults, and carrying the advance position on the Great Round Top", and the 20th Maine's actions that day became one of the most famous attacks of the Battle of Gettysburg and the Civil War as a whole.

But did it really happen that way? Though historians have mostly given Chamberlain the credit for the order to affix bayonets and make the charge down Little Round Top, and Chamberlain received the credit from Sharaa's *The Killer Angels* and the movie *Gettysburg*, some recent researchers have claimed that Lt. Holman S. Melcher initiated the charge. According to Chamberlain however, Melcher had requested permission to make an advance to help some of his wounded men, only to be told by Chamberlain that a charge was about to be ordered anyway.

**Melcher**

While Chamberlain's men held the extreme left, the rest of Vincent's brigade struggled desperately to the right, and Vincent himself would be mortally wounded in the fighting. The Confederates had advanced as far as Devil's Den, but Warren continued to bring reinforcements to Little Round Top to hold off Confederate attempts on the high ground. For the rest of the battle, even after the Confederates were repulsed from Little Round Top, their snipers in Devil's Den made the defenders of Little Round Top miserable. Confederate sharpshooters stationed around Devil's Den mortally wounded General Stephen Weed, whose New York brigade had arrived as reinforcements, and when his friend, artilleryman Lt. Charles Hazlett leaned over to comfort Weed or hear what he was trying to say, snipers shot Hazlett dead as well.

The fighting on the Union left finally ended as night fell. George Sykes, the commander of the V Corps, later described Day 2 in his official report, "Night closed the fight. The key of the battle-field was in our possession intact. Vincent, Weed, and Hazlett, chiefs lamented throughout the corps and army, sealed with their lives the spot intrusted to their keeping, and on which so much depended.... General Weed and Colonel Vincent, officers of rare promise, gave their lives to their country."

Ewell's orders from Lee had been to launch a demonstration on the Union right flank during Longstreet's attack, which started at about 4:00 p.m. as well, and in support of the demonstration by Hill's corps in the center. For that reason, Ewell would not launch his general assault on Culp's Hill and Cemetery Hill until 7:00 p.m.

While the Army of the Potomac managed to desperately hold on the left, Ewell's attack against Culp's Hill on the other end of the field met with some success in pushing the Army of the Potomac back. However, the attack started so late in the day that nightfall made it impossible for the Confederates to capitalize on their success. Due to darkness, a Confederate brigade led by George H. Steuart was unaware that they were firmly beside the Army of the Potomac's right flank, which would have given them almost unlimited access to the Union army's rear and its supply lines and line of communication, just 600 yards away. Col. David Ireland and the 137th New York desperately fought to preserve the Union army's flank, much the same way Chamberlain and the 20th Maine had on the other side, and in the process the 137th lost a third of their men.

**Steuart**

Ewell's men would spend the night at the base of Culp's Hill and partially up the hill, in positions that had been evacuated by Union soldiers after Meade moved some of them to the left to deal with Longstreet's attack. It would fall upon the Confederates to pick up the attack the next morning.

That night, Meade held another council of war. Having been attacked on both flanks, Meade and his top officers correctly surmised that Lee would attempt an attack on the center of the line the next day. Moreover, captured Confederates and the fighting and intelligence of Day 2 let it be known that the only Confederate unit that had not yet seen action during the fighting was George Pickett's division of Longstreet's corps.

## July 3

If July 2 was Longstreet's worst day of the Civil War, July 3 was almost certainly Robert E. Lee's. After the attack on July 2, Longstreet spent the night continuing to plot potential movements around Little Round Top and Big Round Top, thinking that would again get the Confederate army around the Union's flank. Longstreet himself did not realize that a reserve corps of the Union army was poised to block that maneuver.

Longstreet did not meet with Lee on the night of July 2, so when Lee met with him the following morning he found Longstreet's men were not ready to conduct an early morning attack, which Lee had wanted to attempt just as he was on the other side of the lines against Culp's Hill. With Pickett's men not up, however, Longstreet's corps couldn't make such an attack. Lee later wrote that Longstreet's "dispositions were not completed as early as was expected."

On the morning of July 3, the Confederate attack against Culp's Hill fizzled out, but by then Lee had already planned a massive attack on the Union center, combined with having Stuart's cavalry attack the Union army's lines in the rear. A successful attack would split the Army of the Potomac at the same time its communication and supply lines were severed by Stuart, which would make it possible to capture the entire army in detail.

There was just one problem with the plan, as Longstreet told Lee that morning: no 15,000 men who ever existed could successfully execute the attack. The charge required marching across an open field for about a mile, with the Union artillery holding high ground on all sides of the incoming Confederates. Longstreet ardently opposed the attack, but, already two days into the battle, Lee explained that because the Army of the Potomac was here on the field, he must strike at it. Longstreet later wrote that he said, "General Lee, I have been a soldier all my life. It is my opinion that no fifteen thousand men ever arrayed for battle can take that position." Longstreet proposed instead that their men should slip around the Union forces and occupy the high ground, forcing Northern commanders to attack them, rather than vice versa.

**The field of Pickett's Charge, taken from the Union Line near the High Water Mark. The ridge of trees is where the Confederate Line was positioned.**

Realizing the insanity of sending 15,000 men hurtling into all the Union artillery, Lee planned to use the Confederate artillery to try to knock out the Union artillery ahead of time. Although old friend William Pendleton was the artillery chief, the artillery cannonade would be supervised by Porter Alexander, Longstreet's chief artillerist, who would have to give the go-ahead to the charging infantry because they were falling under Longstreet's command.

Longstreet was certain of failure, but Pickett and the men preparing to make the charge were confident in their commanders and themselves. As Stuart was in the process of being repulsed, just after 1:00 p.m. 150 Confederate guns began to fire from Seminary Ridge, hoping to incapacitate the Union center before launching an infantry attack. Confederate brigadier Evander Law said of the artillery bombardment, "The cannonade in the center ... presented one of the most magnificent battle-scenes witnessed during the war. Looking up the valley towards Gettysburg, the hills on either side were capped with crowns of flame and smoke, as 300 guns, about equally divided between the two ridges, vomited their iron hail upon each other."

Alexander discussed the early part of the cannonading, including some that he had not ordered:

"A little before noon there sprung up upon our left a violent cannonade which was prolonged for fully a half-hour, and has often been supposed to be a part of that ordered to precede Pickett's charge. It began between skirmishers in front of Hill's corps over the occupation of a house. Hill's artillery first took part in it, it was said, by his order. It was most unwise, as it consumed uselessly a large amount of his ammunition, the lack of which was much felt in the subsequent fighting. Not a single gun of our corps fired a shot, nor did the enemy in our front.

When the firing died out, entire quiet settled upon the field, extending even to the skirmishers in front, and also to the enemy's rear; whence behind their lines opposing us we had heard all the morning the noise of Johnson's combats.

My 75 guns had all been carefully located and made ready for an hour, while the infantry brigades were still not yet in their proper positions, and I was waiting for the signal to come from Longstreet, when it occurred to me to send for the nine howitzers under Richardson, that they might lead in the advance for a few hundred yards before coming into action. Only after the cannonade had opened did I learn that the guns had been removed and could not be found. It afterward appeared that Pendleton had withdrawn four of the guns, and that Richardson with the other five, finding himself in the line of the Federal fire during Hill's cannonade, had moved off to find cover. I made no complaint, believing that had these guns gone forward with the infantry they must have been left upon the field and perhaps have attracted a counter-stroke after the repulse of Pickett's charge.

Meanwhile, some half-hour or more before the cannonade began, I was startled by the receipt of a note from Longstreet as follows: —

'Colonel: If the artillery fire does not have the effect to drive off the enemy or greatly demoralize him, so as to make our effort pretty certain, I would prefer that you should not advise Pickett to make the charge. I shall rely a great deal upon your judgment to determine the matter and shall expect you to let Gen. Pickett know when the moment offers.'

Until that moment, though I fully recognized the strength of the enemy's position, I had not doubted that we would carry it, in my confidence that Lee was ordering it. But here was a proposition that I should decide the question. Overwhelming reasons against the assault at once seemed to stare me in the face. Gen. Wright of Anderson's division was standing with me. I showed him the letter and expressed my views. He advised me to write them to Longstreet, which I did as follows:—

'General: I will only be able to judge of the effect of our fire on the enemy by his return fire, as his infantry is little exposed to view and the smoke will obscure the field. If, as I infer from your note, there is any alternative to this attack, it should be carefully considered before opening our fire, for it will take all the artillery ammunition we have left to test this one, and if result is unfavorable we will have none left for another effort. And even if this is entirely successful, it can only be so at a very bloody cost.'

To this note, Longstreet soon replied as follows: —

'Colonel: The intention is to advance the infantry if the artillery has the desired effect of driving the enemy's off, or having other effect such as to warrant us in making the attack. When that moment arrives advise Gen. Pickett and of course advance such artillery as you can use in aiding the attack.'"

At daylight Pickett had advanced his division to a spot "into a field near a branch," a few hundred yards behind the main Confederate line on Seminary Ridge. Forming battlelines, his men advanced east a few hundred yards before being ordered to lie down and wait. Advancing again through Spangler's Woods, they were again directed to lay down—this time behind the crest on which the Confederate artillery batteries were perched. Jocking for position to form the right wing of the afternoon's assault, Pickett then had his men form two lines, with Brigadier

Generals James Kemper and Richard Garnett in the first line, right to left, and Brigadier General Lewis Armistead to the rear. As a result, Pickett's men were forced to lay down during a ferocious artillery bombardment from both sides that certainly had to unnerve his men, but Pickett continued a dangerous ride along the lines as Union shells burst all around him, shouting to his men, "Up, men, and to your posts! Don't forget today that you are from Old Virginia." One of the men in Kemper's brigade of Pickett's division recalled, "The first shot or two flew harmlessly over our heads; but soon they began to get the range, and then came--well, what General Gibbon, on the other side, called "pandemonium." First there was an explosion in the top of our friendly tree, sending a shower of limbs upon us. In a second there was another, followed by a piercing shriek, which caused Patton to spring up and run to see what was the matter. Two killed outright and three frightfully wounded, he said on his return."

As Longstreet had predicted, from the beginning the plan was an abject failure. As Stuart's cavalry met its Union counterparts near East Cavalry Field, a young cavalry officer named George Custer convinced division commander Brig. General David McMurtrie Gregg to allow his brigade to stay and fight, even while Custer's own division was stationed to the south out of the action.

The fighting at East Cavalry Field turned out to be Custer's best known action of the Civil War, and it was his brigade that bore the brunt of the casualties in repulsing Stuart's cavalry. Right as the Confederates were starting the artillery bombardment ahead of Pickett's Charge, Stuart's men met Gregg's on the field.

After Stuart's men sent Union skirmishers scurrying, Gregg ordered Custer to counterattack with the 7th Michigan Cavalry Regiment. Custer led the charge personally, exhorting his men with the rallying cry, "Come on you Wolverines!" In the ensuing melee, which featured sabers and close range shooting, Custer had his horse shot out from under him, at which point he took a bugler's horse and continued fighting. Ultimately, his men sent Stuart's cavalry retreating, forcing Stuart to order in reinforcements.

**Custer**

Stuart's reinforcements sent the 7th Michigan in retreat, but now Custer rallied the 1st Michigan regiment to charge in yet another counterattack, with the same rallying cry, ""Come on you Wolverines!" Both sides galloped toward each other and crashed head on, engaging in more fierce hand-to-hand combat. Eventually, the Union held the field and forced Stuart's men to retreat.

Custer's brigade lost over 200 men in the attack, the highest loss of any Union cavalry brigade at Gettysburg, but he had just valiantly performed one of the most successful cavalry charges of the war. Custer wasn't exactly humble about his performance, writing in his official report after the battle, "I challenge the annals of warfare to produce a more brilliant or successful charge of cavalry."

As Stuart was in the process of being repulsed, just after 1:00 p.m. 150 Confederate guns began to fire from Seminary Ridge, hoping to incapacitate the Union center before launching an infantry attack, but they mostly overshot their mark. The artillery duel could be heard from dozens of miles away, and all the smoke led to Confederate artillery constantly overshooting their targets. Realizing that the artillery was meant for them as a way of softening them up for an infantry charge, Hancock calmly rode his horse up and down the line of the II Corps, both inspiring and assuring his men with his own courage and resolve. During the massive Confederate artillery bombardment that preceded the infantry assault, Hancock was so conspicuous on horseback reviewing and encouraging his troops that one of his subordinates pleaded with him that "the corps commander ought not to risk his life that way." Hancock reportedly replied, "There are times when a corps commander's life does not count."

At some point before the charge, Pickett apparently managed to somehow hastily write a letter to his wife Sallie:

"At early dawn, darkened by the threatening rain, Armistead, Garnett, Kemper and your Soldier held a heart-to-heart powwow.

All three sent regards to you, and Old Lewis pulled a ring from his little finger and making me take it, said, "Give this little token, George, please, to her of the sunset eyes, with my love, and tell her the 'old man' says since he could not be the lucky dog he's mighty glad that you are."

Dear old Lewis—dear old "Lo," as Magruder always called him, being short for Lothario. Well, my Sally, I'll keep the ring for you, and some day I'll take it to John Tyler and have it made into a breastpin and set around with rubies and diamonds and emeralds. You will be the pearl, the other jewel. Dear old Lewis!

Just as we three separated to go our different ways after silently clasping hands, our fears and prayers voiced in the "Good luck, old man," a summons came from Old Peter, and I immediately rode to the top of the ridge where he and Marse Robert were making a reconnaissance of Meade's position. "Great God!" said Old Peter as I came up. "Look, General Lee, at the insurmountable difficulties between our line and that of the Yankees—the steep hills, the tiers of artillery, the fences, the heavy skirmish line—and then we'll have to fight our infantry against their batteries. Look at the ground we'll have to charge over, nearly a mile of that open ground there under the rain of their canister and shrapnel."

"The enemy is there, General Longstreet, and I am going to strike him," said Marse Robert in his firm, quiet, determined voice.

About 8 o'clock I rode with them along our line of prostrate infantry. They had been told to lie down to prevent attracting attention, and though they had been forbidden to cheer they voluntarily arose and lifted in reverential adoration their caps to our beloved commander as we rode slowly along. Oh, the responsibility for the lives of such men as these! Well, my darling, their fate and that of our beloved Southland will be settled ere your glorious brown eyes rest on these scraps of penciled paper—your Soldier's last letter, perhaps.

Our line of battle faces Cemetery Ridge. Our detachments have been thrown forward to support our artillery which stretches over a mile along the crests of Oak Ridge and Seminary Ridge. The men are lying in the rear, my darling, and the hot July sun pours its scorching rays almost vertically down upon them. The suffering and waiting are almost unbearable.

. . . . . . . . . . . . . . . . . . . . . . . . . . . . .

Well, my sweetheart, at one o'clock the awful silence was broken by a cannon-shot and then another, and then more than a hundred guns shook the hills from crest to base, answered by more than another hundred—the whole world a blazing volcano, the whole of heaven a thunderbolt—then darkness and absolute silence—then the grim and gruesome, low-spoken commands—then the forming of the attacking columns. My brave Virginians are to attack in front. Oh, may God in mercy help me as He never helped before!

I have ridden up to report to Old Peter. I shall give him this letter to mail to you and a package to give you if—Oh, my darling, do you feel the love of my heart, the prayer, as I write that fatal word?

Now, I go; but remember always that I love you with all my heart and soul, with every fiber of my being; that now and forever I am yours—yours, my beloved. It is almost three o'clock. My soul reaches out to yours—my prayers. I'll keep up a skookum tumtum for Virginia and for you, my darling."

Eventually, Union artillery chief Henry Hunt cleverly figured that if the Union cannons stopped firing back, the Confederates might think they successfully knocked out the Union batteries. On top of that, the Union would be preserving its ammunition for the impending charge that everyone now knew was coming. When they stopped, Lee, Alexander, and others mistakenly concluded that they'd knocked out the Union artillery.

A short time later, the Confederates were prepared to step out for the charge that bears Pickett's name, even though he commanded only about a third of the force and was officially under Longstreet's direction. Today historians typically refer to the charge as the Pickett-Pettigrew-Trimble Assault or Longstreet's Assault to be more technically correct. Since A.P. Hill was sidelined with illness, Pettigrew's and Trimble's divisions were delegated to Longstreet's authority as well. To make matters worse, Hill's sickness resulted in organizational snafus. Without Hill to assign or lead troops, some of his battle-weary soldiers of the previous two days were tapped to make the charge while fresh soldiers in his corps stayed behind.

**Pettigrew**

Porter Alexander described the drama-filled moments during which he advised Pickett to begin the charge:

"It was just 1 P. M. by my watch when the signal guns were fired and the cannonade opened. The enemy replied rather slowly at first, though soon with increasing rapidity. Having determined that Pickett should charge, I felt impatient to launch him as soon as I could see that our fire was accomplishing anything. I guessed that a half-hour would elapse between my sending him the order and his column reaching close quarters. I dared not presume on using more ammunition than one hour's firing would consume, for we were far from supplies and had already fought for two days. So I determined to send Pickett the order at the very first favorable sign and not later than after 30 minutes firing.

At the end of 20 minutes no favorable development had occurred. More guns had been added to the Federal line than at the beginning, and its whole length, about two miles, was blazing like a volcano. It seemed madness to order a column in the middle of a hot July day to undertake an advance of three-fourths of a mile over open ground against the centre of that line.

But something had to be done. I wrote the following note and despatched it to Pickett at 1.25:—

'General: If you are to advance at all, you must come at once or we will not be able to support you as we ought. But the enemy's fire has not slackened materially and there are still 18 guns firing from the cemetery.'

I had hardly sent this note when there was a decided falling off in the enemy's fire, and as I watched I saw other guns limbered up and withdrawn. We frequently withdrew from fighting Federal guns in order to save our ammunition for their infantry. The enemy had never heretofore practised such economy. After waiting a few minutes and seeing that no fresh guns replaced those withdrawn, I felt sure that the enemy was feeling the punishment, and at 1.40 I sent a note to Pickett as follows:—

'For God's sake come quick. The 18 guns have gone. Come quick or my ammunition will not let me support you properly.'

This was followed by two verbal messages to the same effect by an officer and sergeant from the nearest guns. The 18 guns had occupied the point at which our charge was to be directed. I had been incorrectly told it was the cemetery. Soon only a few scattered Federal guns were in action, and still Pickett's line had not come forward, though scarcely 300 yards behind my guns.

I afterward learned what had followed the sending of my first note. It reached Pickett in Longstreet's presence. He read it and handed it to Longstreet. Longstreet read and stood silent. Pickett said, 'General, shall I advance?' Longstreet knew that it must be done, but was unwilling to speak the words. He turned in his saddle and looked away. Pickett saluted and said, 'I am going to move forward, sir,' and galloped off.

Longstreet, leaving his staff, rode out alone and joined me on the left flank of the guns. It was doubtless 1.50 or later, but I did not look at my watch again. I had grown very impatient to see Pickett, fearing ammunition would run short, when Longstreet joined me. I explained the situation. He spoke sharply,— 'Go and stop Pickett where he is and replenish your ammunition.' I answered: 'We can't do that, sir. The train has but little. It would take an hour to distribute it, and meanwhile the enemy would improve the time.'

Longstreet seemed to stand irresolute (we were both dismounted) and then spoke slowly and with great emotion: 'I do not want to make this charge. I do not see how it can succeed. I would not make it now but that Gen. Lee has ordered it and is expecting it.'

I felt that he was inviting a word of acquiescence on my part and that if given he would again order, 'Stop Pickett where he is.' But I was too conscious of my own youth and inexperience to express any opinion not directly asked. So I remained silent while Longstreet fought his battle out alone and obeyed his orders."

Thus, about 15,000 Confederates stepped out in sight and began their charge with an orderly march starting about a mile away, no doubt an inspiring sight to Hancock and the Union men directly across from the oncoming assault. Pickett launched his attack as ordered, but within five minutes the men came to the top of a low rise where his line came into full view of Union defenses. Though Pickett was seen galloping to the left to steady his men there, and one aide is said to remember him personally ordering the division to "double-quick" at the end of the advance, his exact whereabouts during the latter stages of the assault are unknown.

As the Confederate line advanced, Union cannon on Cemetery Ridge and Little Round Top began blasting away, with Confederate soldiers continuing to march forward. One Union soldier later wrote, "We could not help hitting them with every shot . . . a dozen men might be felled by one single bursting shell." By the time Longstreet's men reached Emmitsburg Road, Union artillery switched to firing grapeshot (tin cans filled with iron and lead balls), and as the Confederate troops continued to approach the Union center, Union troops positioned behind the wall cut down the oncoming Confederates, easily decimating both flanks. And while some of the men did mange to advance to the Union line and engage in hand-to-hand combat, it was of little consequence.

After about 20 minutes, the Confederates had managed to cross the shallow valley but then hit the stone fence shielding Union soldiers (in some places, two-men deep). And although Pickett's men were finally able to reach and breach the Union line on the ridge, what followed next has been categorically described as a "blood bath." While some of the men did manage to advance to the Union line and engage in hand-to-hand combat, it was of little consequence. In the midst of the fighting, as he was conferring with one of his brigadier generals, General Hancock suddenly felt a searing pain in his thigh. He had just been severely wounded when a bullet struck the pommel of his saddle and entered his inner right thigh, along with wood splinters and a large bent nail. Helped from his horse by his aides, he removed the saddle nail himself and applied a tourniquet, colorfully swearing at his own men while demanding that they not let him bleed to death. Nevertheless, he refused to remove himself to the rear until the offensive had concluded.

One of the Virginians who marched straight into Hancock's II Corps was Pickett's brigadier Lewis A. Armistead, who famously led his brigade with his hat atop his sword, serving as a visual cue for his men. They actually breached the II Corps' line, making it about as far as any Confederate got. In the fighting, Armistead was mortally wounded and captured, dying days later. One of the men in his brigade would write about the charge after the war:

"When the advance commenced Armistead placed himself in front of the colors of the Fifty-third Regiment, and from that point watched and directed the advance until within a short distance of the enemy's line. When approximating the advance line General Kemper rode up to him and said, "General, hurry up, my men can stand no more."

He quietly turned to the officer commanding his battalion of direction and said, "Colonel, double quick." The double quick soon quickened into a run, the run into a charge, Armistead all the time in front of his line of battle, and when the desperate effort came and the final rush for the rock fence was made he drew his sword, put his hat on the end of it, called upon his men to follow, rushed over the rock fence and was shot just as he reached the enemy's guns between the two lines in the bloody angle, thus sealing with his life's blood the high water mark of the rebellion.

As Armistead was carried from the field he met Hancock as he was hurrying to the front. They recognized each other, and Hancock dismounted and grasped his hand and told him how sorry he was to see him wounded. Armistead returned his kindly expression and told him the wound was mortal and that he had on his person some things that he wish to entrust to him to be returned when opportunity presented to his people in Virginia. Hancock accepted the commission and tried to persuade Armistead to look upon the bright side, that he probably was not so seriously hurt as he feared, excused himself by saying he was compelled to hurry to the front, left Armistead, promising to see him the next day. In a short time he was wounded himself and they never met again.

This was related to me as I lay on the ground back of the battle line where hundreds of wounded were carried after the fight, by one of Hancock's staff, who rode up just about dusk and found a number of men congregated about me. When he found I was a badly wounded "Johnny Reb" Colonel he dismounted, drove everybody away that I might have fresh air, and commenced a conversation.

When he found that I was of Armistead's Brigade, he said, "Armistead, Armistead. I have just left him, he is mortally wounded," and then related the above, and said, "I will have you taken care of," etc.

Armistead lingered through the 4th and died on the 5th, leaving an example of patriotism, heroism and devotion to duty which ought to be handed down through the ages."

**Armistead**

Kemper's brigade hardly had it any easier as it moved forward, and Kemper would be seriously injured and captured at the height of the fighting. One of his men wrote about the charge after the war:

The devoted little column moved to the assault, with Garnett, and Kemper in front, and Armistead behind in close supporting distance. Soon after clearing our batteries it was found necessary to change direction to the left. While conducting the movement, which was made in perfect order under a galling flank fire from the Round Top, General Pickett, for the second time, cautioned me to be sure and keep the proper interval with General Garnett; Armistead was expected to catch up and extend the line to the left. Then we swept onward again, straight for the Golgotha of Seminary Ridge, half a mile distant, across the open plain. As we neared the Emmettsburg road, along which, behind piles of rails, the enemy's strong line of skirmishers was posted, General Kemper called to me to give attention to matters on the left, while he went to see what troops those were coming up behind us. Glancing after him, I caught a glimpse of a small body of men, compact and solid as a wedge, moving swiftly to the left oblique, as if aiming to uncover Garnett's Brigade. They were Armistead's people, and as Kemper cantered down their front on his mettlesome sorrel they greeted him with a rousing cheer, which I know made his gallant heart leap for joy. At the same moment I saw a disorderly crowd of men breaking for the rear, and Pickett, with Stuart Symington, Ned Baird, and others, vainly trying to stop the rout. And now the guns of Cushing and Abbott double-stocked by General Gibbon's express order, reinforced the terrific fire of the infantry behind the stone fence, literally riddling the orchard on the left of the now famous Cordori house, through which my regiment and some of the others passed.

Within a few steps of the stone fence, while in the act of shaking hands with General Garnett and congratulating him on being able to be with his men (he had been seriously ill a few days before), I heard some one calling me, and turning my head, saw that it was Captain Fry. He was mounted, and blood streaming from his horse's neck. Colonel Terry had sent him to stop the rush to left. The enemy in force (Stannard's Vermonters) had penetrated to our rear. He told me that Kemper had been struck down, it was feared mortally. With the help of Colonel Carrington, of the Eighteenth, and Major Bentley, of the Twenty-fourth, I hastily gathered a small band together and faced them to meet the new danger. After that everything was a wild kaleidoscopic whirl. A man near me seemed to be keeping a tally of the dead for my especial benefit. First it was Patton, then Collcote, then Phillips, and I know not how many more. Colonel Williams was knocked out of the saddle by a ball in the shoulder near the brick-house, and in falling was killed by his sword…Seeing the men as they fired, throw down their guns and pick up others from the ground, I followed suit, shooting into a flock of blue coats that were pouring down from the right, I noticed how close their flags were together. Probably they were the same people whom Hood and McLaws had handled so roughly the day before. "Used up," as General Meade said of them. Suddenly there was a hissing sound, like the hooded cobra's whisper of death, a deafening explosion, a sharp pang of pain somewhere, a momentary blank, and when I got on my feet again there were splinters of bone and lumps of flesh sticking to my clothes. Then I remembered seeing lank Tell Taliaferro, adjutant of the Twenty-fourth, jumping like a kangaroo and rubbing his crazy bone and blessing the Yankees in a way that did credit to old Jube Early's one-time law partner, and handsome Ocey White, the boy lieutenant of Company A, taking off his hat to show me where a ball had raised a whelk on his scalp and carried away one of his pretty flaxen curls, and lastly, "Old Buck" Terry, with a peculiarly sad smile on his face, standing with poor George and Val Harris and others, between the colors of the Eleventh and Twenty-fourth, near where now is the pretty monument of colonel Ward, of Massachusetts. I could not hear what he said, but he was pointing rearwards with his sword, and I knew what that meant.

As I gave one hurried glance over the field we had traversed, the thought in my mind was repeated at my side, "Oh! Colonel, why don't they support us?" It was Walker, General Kemper's orderly, unhorsed, but still unscathed and undaunted, awkward, ungainly, hard-featured, good-natured, simple-minded, stout-hearted Walker, one of the Eleventh boys, I believe; only a private doing his duty with might and main and recking no more of glory than the ox that has won the prize at a cattle show. At the storming of the Redan when Wyndham's forlorn hope tumbled into the ditch and couldn't get out, owing to the scarcity of ladders, and the few they had were too short, the men huddled together dazed and bewildered, and were mowed down like dumb beasts by the Muscovite rifles, because there were no officers left to lead them. There was a notable exception, an Irishman, scrambling up the scrap, he shouted, "Come up, boys, follow the captain." The captain fell, but Pat went on to immortality. It was not so that day at Gettysburg.

Meanwhile, Pickett's brigadier Richard Garnett, whose courage had been impugned and challenged by Stonewall Jackson unfairly in 1862, had suffered a previous leg injury and insisted on riding his horse during the charge, despite the obvious fact that riding a horse clearly indicated he was an officer. Garnett was killed during the charge, and it's unknown where he fell or where he was buried. One of the men in Garnett's brigade, C.S. Peyton of the 19th Virginia, reported on the brigade's participation in his post-battle report:

MAJOR: In compliance with instructions from division headquarters, I have the honor to report the part taken by this brigade in the late battle near Gettysburg, Pa., July 3.

Notwithstanding the long and severe marches made by the troops of this brigade, they reached the field about 9 a.m.. in high spirits and in good condition. At about 12 m. we were ordered to take position behind the crest of the hill on which the artillery, under Colonel [E. Porter] Alexander, was planted, where we lay during a most terrific cannonading, which opened at 1.30 p.m., and was kept up without intermission for one hour.

During the shelling, we lost about 20 killed and wounded. Among the killed was Lieutenant-Colonel [John T.] Ellis, of the Nineteenth Virginia, whose bravery as a soldier, and his innocence, purity, and integrity as a Christian, have not only elicited the admiration of his own command, but endeared him to all who knew him.

At 2.30 p.m., the artillery fire having to some extent abated, the order to advance was given, first by Major-General Pickett in person, and repeated by General Garnett with promptness, apparent cheerfulness, and alacrity. The brigade moved forward at quick time. The ground was open, but little broken, and from 800 to 1,000 yards from the crest whence we started to the enemy's line. The brigade moved in good order, keeping up its line almost perfectly, notwithstanding it had to climb three high post and rail fences, behind the last of which the enemy's skirmishers were first met and immediately driven in. Moving on, we soon met the advance line of the enemy, lying concealed in the grass on the slope, about 100 yards in front of his second line, which consisted of a stone wall about breast-high, running nearly parallel to and about 30 paces from the crest of the hill, which was lined with their artillery.

The first line referred to above, after offering some resistance, was completely routed, and driven in confusion back to the stone wall. Here we captured some prisoners, which were ordered to the rear without a guard. Having routed the enemy here, General Garnett ordered the brigade forward, which it promptly obeyed, loading and firing as it advanced.

Up to this time we had suffered but little from the enemy's batteries, which apparently had been much crippled previous to our advance, with the exception of one posted on the mountain, about 1 mile to our right, which enfiladed nearly our entire line with fearful effect, sometimes as many as 10 men being killed and wounded by the bursting of a single shell. From the point it had first routed the enemy, the brigade moved rapidly forward toward the stone wall, under a galling fire both from artillery and infantry, the artillery using grape and canister. We were now within about 75 paces of the wall, unsupported on the right and left, General Kemper being some 50 or 60 yards behind and to the right, and General Armistead coming up in our rear.

General Kemper's line was discovered to be lapping on ours, when, deeming it advisable to have the line extended on the right to prevent being flanked, a staff officer rode back to the general to request him to incline to the right. General Kemper not being present (perhaps wounded at the time), Captain [W. T.] Fry, of his staff, immediately began his exertions to carry out the request, but, in consequence of the eagerness of the men in pressing forward, it was impossible to have the order carried out.

Our line, much shattered, still kept up the advance until within about 20 paces of the wall, when, for a moment, it recoiled under the terrific fire that poured into our ranks both from their batteries and from their sheltered infantry. At this moment, General Kemper came up on the right and General Armistead in rear, when the three lines, joining in concert, rushed forward with unyielding determination and an apparent spirit of laudable rivalry to plant the Southern banner on the walls of the enemy. His strongest and last line was instantly gained; the Confederate battle-flag waved over his defenses, and the fighting over the wall became hand to hand, and of the most desperate character; but more than half having already fallen, our line was found too weak to rout the enemy. We hoped for a support on the left (which had started simultaneously with ourselves), out hoped in vain. Yet a small remnant remained in desperate struggle, receiving a fire in front, on the right, and on the left, many even climbing over the wall, and fighting the enemy in his own trenches until entirely surrounded; and those who were not killed or wounded were captured, with the exception of about 300 who came off slowly, but greatly scattered, the identity of every regiment being entirely lost, and every regimental commander killed or wounded.

The brigade went into action with 1,287 men and about 140 officers, as shown by the report of the previous evening, and sustained a loss, as the list of casualties will show, of 941 killed, wounded, and missing, and it is feared, from all the information received, that the majority (those reported missing) are either killed or wounded.

It is needless, perhaps, to speak of conspicuous gallantry where all behaved so well. Each and every regimental commander displayed a cool bravery and daring that not only encouraged their own commands, but won the highest admiration from all those who saw them. They led their regiments in the fight, and showed, by their conduct, that they only desired their men to follow where they were willing to lead. But of our cool, gallant, noble brigade commander it may not be out of place to speak. Never had the brigade been better handled, and never has it done better service in the field of battle. There was scarcely an officer or man in the command whose attention was not attracted by the cool and handsome bearing of General Garnett, who, totally devoid of excitement or rashness, rode immediately in rear of his advancing line, endeavoring by his personal efforts, and by the aid of his staff, to keep his line well closed and dressed. He was shot from his horse while near the center of the brigade, within about 25 paces of the stone wall. This gallant officer was too well known to need further mention.

In making the above report, I have endeavored to be as accurate as possible, but have had to rely mainly for information on others, whose position gave them better opportunity for witnessing the conduct of the entire brigade than I could have, being with, and paying my attention to, my own regiment.

**Garnett**

After the charge, there was debate (and later controversy) over where Pickett was as his brigadiers were falling at the front of their brigades. One of Pickett's staff men discussed the way communications were going from the front back to leaders like Longstreet further to the rear:

I found General Longstreet sitting on a fence alone; the fence ran in the direction we were charging. Pickett's column had passed over the hill on our side of the Emmettsburg road, and could not then be seen. I delivered the message as sent by General Pickett. General Longstreet said: "Where are the troops that were placed on your flank ?" and I answered: "Look over your shoulder and you will see them." He looked and saw the broken fragments. Just then an officer rode at half-speed, drawing up his horse in front of the General, and saying: "General Longstreet, General Lee sent me here, and said you would place me in a position to see this magnificent charge. I would not have missed it for the world." General Longstreet answered: "I would, Colonel Freemantle, the charge is over. Captain Bright, ride to General Pickett, and tell hin what you have heard me say to Colonel Freemantle." At this moment our men were near to but had not crossed the Emmettsburg road. I started and when my horse had made two leaps, General Longstreet called: "Captain Bright!" I checked my horse, and turned half around in my saddle to hear, and this was what he said: "Tell General Pickett that Wilcox's Brigade is in that peach orchard (pointing), and he can order him to his assistance."

When I reached General Pickett he was at least one hundred yards behind the division, having been detained in a position from which he could watch and care for his left flank. He at once sent Captain Baird to General Wilcox with the order for him to come in; then he sent Captain Symington with the same order, in a very few moments, and last he said: "Captain Bright, you go,' and I was about the same distance behind Symington that he was behind Baird. The fire was so dreadful at this time that I believe that General Pickett thought not more than one out of the three sent would reach

General Wilcox.

When I rode up to Wilcox he was standing with both hands raised waving and saying to me, "I know, I know." I said, "But, General, I must deliver my message." After doing this I rode out of the peach orchard, going forward where General Pickett was watching his left. Looking that way myself, I saw moving out of the enemy's line of battle, in head of column, a large force; having nothing in their front, they came around our flank as described above. Had our left not deserted us these men would have hesitated to move in head of column, confronted by a line of battle. When I reached General Pickett I found him too far down towards the Ennmettshurg road to see these flanking troops, and he asked of me the number. I remember answering 7,000, but this proved an over estimate. Some of our men had been faced to meet this new danger, and so doing somewhat broke the force of our charge on the left. Probably men of the 1st Virginia will remember this.

Charging to the left of Pickett's men, Trimble and Pettigrew were both wounded in the fighting, with Trimble losing a leg and Pettigrew suffering a minor wound to the hand. One of the generals in Pettigrew's part of the assault wrote about their participation:

In the numerous accounts of the battle of Gettysburg heretofore published, the writers have generally referred to the last effort made by the Confederate troops as "Pickett's charge," and in almost every instance have conveyed the idea that no troops but Pickett's division took an active part in that fierce and tremendous struggle. Disclaiming any intention to detract in the least from the glory won on that day by the gallant Virginia division, or its heroic commander, who had then been for more than twenty years one of my most valued friends, I may be permitted to say that some injustice has been done to the division commanded by General Pettigrew.

As colonel of the Thirteenth Alabama infantry, I was attached to Archer's brigade of Heth's division. That brigade opened the battle on the morning of July 1st, and during the fighting which immediately ensued General Heth was wounded, and the command of the division devolved upon Brigadier-General Pettigrew. General Archer was captured, and I succeeded him in command of the brigade.

During the forenoon of the 3d, while our division was resting in line behind the ridge and skirt of woods which masked us from the enemy, Generals Lee, Longstreet and A. P. Hill rode up, and, dismounting, seated themselves on the trunk of a fallen tree some fifty or sixty paces from where I sat on my horse at the right of our division. After an apparently careful examination of a map, and a consultation of some length, they remounted and rode away. Staff officers and couriers began to move briskly about, and a few minutes after General Pettigrew rode up and informed me that after a heavy cannonade we would assault the position in our front, and added: "They will of course return the fire with all the guns they have; we must shelter the men as best we can, and make them lie down." At the same time he directed me to see General Pickett at once and have an understanding as to the dress in the advance. I rode to General Pickett, whose division was formed on the right of and in line with ours. He appeared to be in excellent spirits, and, after a cordial greeting and a pleasant reference to our having been together in work of that kind at Chapultipec, expressed great confidence in the ability of our troops to drive the enemy after they had been "demoralized by our artillery." General Garnett, who commanded his left brigade, having joined us, it was agreed that he would dress on my command. I immediately returned and informed

General Pettigrew of this agreement. It was then understood that my command should be considered the centre, and that in the assault both divisions should allign themselves by it. Soon after the two divisions moved forward about a hundred paces, and the men lay down behind our line of batteries. The cannonade which followed has been often and justly described as the most terrible of the war. In it my command suffered a considerable loss. Several officers were killed and wounded, with a number of the rank and file. I received a painful wound on the right shoulder from a fragment of shell. After lying inactive under that deadly storm of hissing and exploding missiles, it seemed a relief to go forward to the desperate assault. At a signal from Pettigrew I called my command to attention. The men sprang up with cheerful alacrity, and the long line advanced. "Stormed at with shot and shell," it moved steadily on, and even when grape, canister, and musket balls began to rain upon it the gaps were quickly closed and the allignment preserved. Strong as was the position of the enemy, it seemed that such determination could not fail. I heard Garnett give a command to his men which, amid the rattle of musketry, I could not distinguish. Seeing my look or gesture of inquiry, he called our, "I am dressing on you!" A few seconds after he fell dead. A moment later- and after Captain Williams and Colonel George had been wounded by my side- a shot through the thigh prostrated me. I was so confident of victory that to some of my men who ran up to carry me off I shouted, "Go on; it will not last five minutes longer!" The men rushed forward into the smoke, which soon became so dense that I could see little of what was going on before me. But a moment later I heard General Pettigrew, behind me, calling to some of his staff to "rally them on the left." The roll of musketry was then incessant, and I believe that the Federal troops- probably blinded by the smoke- continued a rapid fire for some minutes after none but dead and wounded remained in their front. At length the firing ceased, and cheer after cheer from the enemy announced the failure of our attack. I was of course left a prisoner.

As evidence of how close was the fighting at that part of the line, I saw a Federal soldier with an ugly wound in his shoulder, which he told me he received from the spear on the end of one of my regimental colors; and I remembered having that morning observed and laughingly commented on the fact that the color-bearer of the Thirteenth Alabama had attached to his staff a formidable-looking lance head. All of the five regimental colors of my command reached the line of the enemy's works, and many of my men and officers were killed or wounded after passing over it. I believe the same was true of other brigades in General Pettigrew's command.

It is probable that Pickett's division, which up to that time had taken no part in the battle, was mainly relied upon for the final assault; but whatever may have been the first plan of attack, the division under Pettigrew went into it as part of the line of battle, and from the commencement of the advance to the closing death grapple, his right brigade was the directing one. General Pettigrew, who I know was that day in the thickest of the fire, was killed in a skirmish a few days later. No more earnest and gallant officer served in the Confederate army.

According to Longstreet, it was Pickett who finally called retreat; after about an hour, nearly 6,500 Confederates were dead or wounded, five times that of the Union, with all 13 regimental commanders in Pickett's division killed or wounded. As Pickett's men began to stream back in a broken and disorderly, Pickett's staff member recalled one of the most famous exchanges of the battle:

I informed the General that no help was to be expected from the artillery, but the enemy were closing around us, and nothing could now save his command. He had remained behind to watch and protect that left, to put in first help expected from infantry supports, then to break the troops which came around his flank with the artillery; all had failed. At this moment our left (Pickett's Division) began to crumble and soon all that was left came slowly back, 5,000 in the morning, 1,600 were put in camp that night, 3,400 killed, wounded and missing.

We moved back, and when General Pickett and I were about 300 yards from the position from which the charge had started, General Robert E. Lee, the Peerless, alone, on Traveler, rode up and said: "General Pickett, place your division in rear of this hill, and be ready to repel the advance of the enemy should they follow up their advantage." (I never heard General Lee call them the enemy before; it was always those or these people). General Pickett, with his head on his breast, said: "General Lee, I have no division now, Armistead is down, Garnett is down, and Kemper is mortally wounded."

Then General Lee said: "Come, General Pickett, this has been my fight and upon my shoulders rests the blame. The men and officers of your command have written the name of Virginia as high to-day as it has ever been written before." (Now talk about "Glory enough for one day," why this was glory enough for one hundred years.)

In the aftermath of the repulse of Pickett's Charge, General Longstreet stated, "General Lee came up as our troops were falling back and encouraged them as well as he could; begged them to reform their ranks and reorganize their forces . . . and it was then he used the expression . . . 'It was all my fault; get together, and let us do the best we can toward saving which is left to us.'" Longstreet never resisted an opportunity to distance himself from failure and direct it towards someone else, even Lee.

Today Pickett's Charge is remembered as the American version of the Charge of the Light Brigade, a heroic but completely futile march that had no chance of success. In fact, it's remembered as Pickett's Charge because Pickett's Virginians wanted to claim the glory of getting the furthest during the attack in the years after the war. The charge suffered about a 50% casualty rate while barely making a dent in the Union line before retreating in disorder back across the field. Pickett's post-battle report was apparently so bitter that Lee ordered it destroyed.

Though the charge was named Pickett's Charge by newspapers for the purpose of praising Pickett's Virginians for making the furthest progress, Pickett felt the charge had tarnished his career, and he remained upset that his name remained associated with the sharply repulsed attack. Furthermore, Pickett himself has received much criticism (both then and to this day) for surviving the battle unscathed, having established his final position well to the rear of his troops, though any charges of cowardice are strongly contradicted by his record earlier in the Civil War and in Mexico.

After the battle, Pickett wrote to Sallie offering a few details about the fateful charge. Since his official report of the battle has never been found, his letters home were his only words about the events:

"MY letter of yesterday, my darling, written before the battle, was full of hope and cheer; even though it told you of the long hours of waiting from four in the morning, when Gary's pistol rang out from the Federal lines signaling the attack upon Culp's Hill, to the solemn eight-o'clock review of my men, who rose and stood silently lifting their hats in loving reverence as Marse Robert, Old Peter and your own Soldier reviewed them—on then to the deadly stillness of the five hours following, when the men lay in the tall grass in the rear of the artillery line, the July sun pouring its scorching rays almost vertically down upon them, till one o'clock when the awful silence of the vast battlefield was broken by a cannon-shot which opened the greatest artillery duel of the world. The firing lasted two hours. When it ceased we took advantage of the blackened field and in the glowering darkness formed our attacking column just before the brow of Seminary Ridge.

I closed my letter to you a little before three o'clock and rode up to Old Peter for orders. I found him like a great lion at bay. I have never seen him so grave and troubled. For several minutes after I had saluted him he looked at me without speaking. Then in an agonized voice, the reserve all gone, he said:

"Pickett, I am being crucified at the thought of the sacrifice of life which this attack will make. I have instructed Alexander to watch the effect of our fire upon the enemy, and when it begins to tell he must take the responsibility and give you your orders, for I can't."

While he was yet speaking a note was brought to me from Alexander. After reading it I handed it to him, asking if I should obey and go forward. He looked at me for a moment, then held out his hand. Presently, clasping his other hand over mine without speaking he bowed his head upon his breast. I shall never forget the look in his face nor the clasp of his hand when I said:—"Then, General, I shall lead my Division on." I had ridden only a few paces when I remembered your letter and (forgive me) thoughtlessly scribbled in a corner of the envelope, "If Old Peter's nod means death then good-by and God bless you, little one," turned back and asked the dear old chief if he would be good enough to mail it for me. As he took your letter from me, my darling, I saw tears glistening on his cheeks and beard. The stern old war-horse, God bless him, was weeping for his men and, I know, praying too that this cup might pass from them. I obeyed the silent assent of his bowed head, an assent given against his own convictions,—given in anguish and with reluctance.

My brave boys were full of hope and confident of victory as I led them forth, forming them in column of attack, and though officers and men alike knew what was before them,—knew the odds against them,—they eagerly offered up their lives on the altar of duty, having absolute faith in their ultimate success. Over on Cemetery Ridge the Federals beheld a scene never before witnessed on this continent,—a scene which has never previously been enacted and can never take place again—an army forming in line of battle in full view, under their very eyes—charging across a space nearly a mile in length over fields of waving grain and anon of stubble and then a smooth expanse— moving with the steadiness of a dress parade, the pride and glory soon to be crushed by an overwhelming heartbreak.

. . . . . . . . . . . . . . . . . . . . . . . . . . . .

Well, it is all over now. The battle is lost, and many of us are prisoners, many are dead, many wounded, bleeding and dying. Your Soldier lives and mourns and but for you, my darling, he would rather, a million times rather, be back there with his dead, to sleep for all time in an unknown grave."

Days later, Pickett wrote yet another tense letter back to Sallie, in which his angst can be felt:

General Lee's letter has been published to the division in general orders and received with appreciative satisfaction. The soldiers, one and all, love and honor Lee, and his sympathy and praise are always very dear to them. Just after the order was published I heard one of the men, rather rough and uncouth and not, as are most of the men, to the manner born, say, as he wiped away the tears with the back of his hand, "Dag-gone him, dag-gone him, dag-gone his old soul, I'm blamed ef I wouldn't be dag-gone willin' to go right through it all and be killed again with them others to hear Marse Robert, dag-gone him, say over again as how he grieved bout'n we-all's losses and honored us for we-all's bravery! Darned ef I wouldn't." Isn't that reverential adoration, my darling, to be willing to be "killed again" for a word of praise?

It seems selfish and inhuman to speak of Love—haunted as I am with the unnecessary sacrifice of the lives of so many of my brave boys. I can't think of anything but the desolate homes in Virginia and the unknown dead in Pennsylvania. At the beginning of the fight I was so sanguine, so sure of success! Early in the morning I had been assured by Alexander that General Lee had ordered that every brigade in his command was to charge Cemetery Hill; so I had no fear of not being supported. Alexander also assured me of the support of his artillery which would move ahead of my division in the advance. He told me that he had borrowed seven twelve-pound howitzers from Pendleton, Lee's Chief of Artillery, which he had put in reserve to accompany me.

In the morning I rode with him while he, by Longstreet's orders, selected the salient angle of the wood in which my line was formed, which line was just on the left of his seventy-five guns. At about a quarter to three o'clock, when his written order to make the charge was handed to me, and dear Old Peter after reading it in sorrow and fear reluctantly bowed his head in assent, I obeyed, leading my three brigades straight on the enemy's front. You never saw anything like it. They moved across that field of death as a battalion marches forward in line of battle upon drill, each commander in front of his command leading and cheering on his men. Two lines of the enemy's infantry were driven back; two lines of guns were taken—and no support came. Pendleton, without Alexander's knowledge, had sent four of the guns which he had loaned him to some other part of the field, and the other three guns could not be found. The two brigades which were to have followed me had, poor fellows, been seriously engaged in the fights of the two previous days. Both of their commanding officers had been killed, and while they had been replaced by gallant, competent officers, these new leaders were unknown to the men.

Ah, if I had only had my other two brigades a different story would have been flashed to the world. It was too late to retreat, and to go on was death or capture. Poor old Dick Garnett did not dismount, as did the others of us, and he was killed instantly, falling from his horse. Kemper, desperately wounded, was brought from the field and subsequently, taken prisoner. Dear old Lewis Armistead, God bless him, was mortally wounded at the head of his command after planting the flag of Virginia within the enemy's lines. Seven of my colonels were killed, and one was mortally wounded. Nine of my lieutenant colonels were wounded, and three lieutenant colonels were killed. Only one field officer of my whole command, Colonel Cabell, was unhurt, and the loss of my company officers was in proportion.

I wonder, my dear, if in the light of the Great Eternity we shall any of us feel this was for the best and shall have learned to say, "Thy will be done."

No castles to-day, sweetheart. No, the bricks of happiness and the mortar of love must lie untouched in this lowering gloom. Pray, dear, for the sorrowing ones."

Pickett's Charge is the most memorable charge of July 3, but it wasn't the only fateful one made that day. As the Union cavalry repulsed Stuart, cavalry officer Hugh Judson Kilpatrick gave the order for some of his cavalry to charge north into the Confederates' right flank, Evander Law's brigade (which had opposed Chamberlain the day before). It's believed that the order was given as part of a plan by Meade to possibly follow up a repulse of Pickett's Charge with a flank attack that might lead to a rolling up of the Confederate line.

However, Kilpatrick was ordering the attack just as Pickett's infantry was starting the charge, not during its repulse, and he ordered an attack to be made piecemeal instead of one united assault.

West of Emmitsburg Road, Merrit's cavalry dismounted and began an attack on the Confederate flank, only to run into a brigade of Georgians, which easily repulsed the attack. The plan then called for Elon Farnsworth to attack, but this time Kilpatrick ordered a mounted cavalry charge. By now, with Merrit's attack having failed, the Confederate infantry was positioned behind a stone fence with wooden fence rails piled high above it to prevent horses from being able to jump into their lines. In essence, the Union cavalry would have to make a mounted charge, dismount right at the battle line, and then attempt a concerted attack. Historians have since accused Kilpatrick of shaming Farnsworth into making the suicidal chare, and Farnsworth allegedly told his superior, "General, if you order the charge I will lead it, but you must take the awful responsibility."

**Kilpatrick**

Farnsworth's charge began with a charge by the 1st West Virginia Cavalry that immediately devolved into confusion once they came under heavy fire. Eventually they dismounted near the wall, where they engaged in hand-to-hand fighting with sabers, rifles, and even rocks. The second part of the attack came from the 18th Pennsylvania, supported by companies of the 5th New York, but they were immediately repulsed.

Next, it fell upon the 400 man 1st Vermont Cavalry to charge forward, heading into a slaughter. As they rode forward, one lieutenant in an Albama regiment yelled, "Cavalry, boys, cavalry! This is no fight, only a frolic, give it to them!" All three battalions of the 1st Vermont were quickly repulsed. With that, the final attack was to be led by Farnsworth himself, which came upon the 15ᵗʰ Alabama. In the middle of the charge, Farnsworth fell dead from his horse, hit by 5 bullets. Kilpatrick's poorly designed attack resulted in Farnsworth and his men making a "Charge of the Light Brigade", and as it turned out, they would end up being the last major action of the Battle of Gettysburg.

### Controversy over Lee's Retreat

From a military perspective, Meade had made efficient use of his subordinates (particularly Generals John F. Reynolds and Winfield S. Hancock) during this three-day, course-changing battle, ultimately executing some of the most effective battleline strategies of the War. In short, Meade had successfully commanded the forces that repulsed Lee's Army and effectively won what most historians consider the battle that changed the course of the Civil War and ultimately resulted in a Confederate defeat.

While nobody questions that Meade's strategy at Gettysburg was strong, he was heavily criticized by contemporaries for not pursuing Lee's army more aggressively as it retreated. Chief-of-staff Daniel Butterfield, who would call into question Meade's command decisions and courage at Gettysburg, accused Meade of not finishing off the weakened Lee. Meade would later state that as his army's new commander, he was uncertain of his troops' capabilities and strength, especially after a battle that had just resulted in over 20,000 Union casualties. Moreover, heavy rains made pursuit almost impossible on July 4, and Lee actually invited an attack during the retreat, hoping Meade would haphazardly attack strongly fortified positions.

Though historians now mostly credit Meade with making proper decisions in the wake of the battle, Lincoln was incredibly frustrated when Lee successfully retreated south. On July 14, Lincoln drafted a letter that he ultimately put away and decided not to send to Meade, who never read it during his lifetime:

"I have just seen your despatch to Gen. Halleck, asking to be relieved of your command, because of a supposed censure of mine. I am very--very--grateful to you for the magnificent success you gave the cause of the country at Gettysburg; and I am sorry now to be the author of the slightest pain to you. But I was in such deep distress myself that I could not restrain some expression of it. I had been oppressed nearly ever since the battles at Gettysburg, by what appeared to be evidences that yourself, and Gen. Couch, and Gen. Smith, were not seeking a collision with the enemy, but were trying to get him across the river without another battle. What these evidences were, if you please, I hope to tell you at some time, when we shall both feel better. The case, summarily stated is this. You fought and beat the enemy at Gettysburg; and, of course, to say the least, his loss was as great as yours. He retreated; and you did not, as it seemed to me, pressingly pursue him; but a flood in the river detained him, till, by slow degrees, you were again upon him. You had at least twenty thousand veteran troops directly with you, and as many more raw ones within supporting distance, all in addition to those who fought with you at Gettysburg; while it was not possible that he had received a single recruit; and yet you stood and let the flood run down, bridges be built, and the enemy move away at his leisure, without attacking him. And Couch and Smith! The latter left Carlisle in time, upon all ordinary calculation, to have aided you in the last battle at Gettysburg; but he did not arrive. At the end of more than ten days, I believe twelve, under constant urging, he reached Hagerstown from Carlisle, which is not an inch over fifty-five miles, if so much. And Couch's movement was very little different.

Again, my dear general, I do not believe you appreciate the magnitude of the misfortune involved in Lee's escape. He was within your easy grasp, and to have closed upon him would, in connection with our other late successes, have ended the war. As it is, the war will be prolonged indefinitely. If you could not safely attack Lee last Monday, how can you possibly do so South of the river, when you can take with you very few more than two thirds of the force you then had in hand? It would be unreasonable to expect, and I do not expect you can now effect much. Your golden opportunity is gone, and I am distressed immeasurably because of it.

I beg you will not consider this a prosecution, or persecution of yourself As you had learned that I was dissatisfied, I have thought it best to kindly tell you why."

Still, Meade was promoted to brigadier general in the regular army and was officially awarded the Thanks of Congress, which commended Meade "... and the officers and soldiers of [the Army of the Potomac], for the skill and heroic valor which at Gettysburg repulsed, defeated, and drove back, broken and dispirited, beyond the Rappahannock, the veteran army of the rebellion."

Hancock was unquestionably one of the Union heroes at Gettysburg, but his recognition was slow in coming. In the months after the battle, the U.S. Congress thanked Meade and Howard without listing Hancock. Eventually, Major General Hancock later received the Thanks of the U. S. Congress for "gallant, meritorious, and conspicuous share in that great and decisive victory."

As usual, Hancock shared the credit with his men, writing in his post-battle report:

"To speak of the conduct of the troops would seem to be unnecessary, but still it may be justly remarked that this corps sustained its well-earned reputation on many fields, and that the boast of its gallant first commander, the late Maj. Gen. E. V. Sumner, that the Second Corps had "never given to the enemy a gun or color," holds good now as it did under the command of my predecessor, Major-General Couch. To attest to its good conduct and the perils through which it has passed, it may be stated that its losses in battle have been greater than those of any other corps in the Army of the Potomac, or probably in the service, notwithstanding it has usually been numerically weakest."

**Hancock's equestrian statue on Cemetery hill**

**Casting Blame**

From almost the moment the Civil War ended, Gettysburg has been widely viewed as one of the decisive turning points of the Civil War. As renowned Civil War historian described Gettysburg, "It might be less of a victory than Mr. Lincoln had hoped for, but it was nevertheless a victory—and, because of that, it was no longer possible for the Confederacy to win the war. The North might still lose it, to be sure, if the soldiers or the people should lose heart, but outright defeat was no longer in the cards." While some still dispute that labeling, Lee's Army of Northern Virginia was never truly able to take the strategic offensive again for the duration of the war.

Naturally, if Gettysburg marked an important turning point in the Civil War, then to the defeated South it represented one of the last true opportunities the South had to win the war. After the South had lost the war, the importance of Gettysburg as one of the "high tide" marks of the Confederacy became apparent to everyone, making the battle all the more important in the years after it had been fought. Former Confederate comrades like Longstreet and Jubal Early would go on to argue who was responsible for the loss at Gettysburg (and thus the war) in the following decades. Much of the debate was fueled by those who wanted to protect Lee's legacy, especially because Lee was dead and could not defend himself in writing anymore. However, on July 3, Lee insisted on taking full blame for what occurred at Gettysburg, telling his retreating men, "It's all my fault." Historians have mostly agreed, placing the blame for the disastrous Day 3 on Lee's shoulders.

Porter Alexander would later call it Lee's "worst day" of the war, and he further wrote: "There was one single advantage conferred by our exterior lines, and but one, in exchange for many disadvantages. They gave us the opportunity to select positions for our guns which could enfilade the opposing lines of the enemy. Enfilading fire is so effective that no troops can submit to it long. Illustrations of this fact were not wanting in the events of this day. What has been called the shank of the Federal fish-hook, extending south from the bend at Cemetery Hill toward Little Round Top, was subject to enfilade fire from the town and its flanks and suburbs. That liability should have caused special examination by our staff and artillery officers, to discover other conditions which might favor an assault. There were and are others still easily recognizable on the ground. The salient angle is acute and weak, and within about 500 yards of its west face is the sheltered position occupied by Rodes the night of July 2d, which has already been mentioned.

From nowhere else was there so short and unobstructed an approach to the Federal line, and one so free from flank fire. On the northeast, at but little greater distance, was the position whence Early's two brigades the evening before had successfully carried the east face of the same salient. Within the edge of the town between these two positions was abundant opportunity to accumulate troops and to establish guns at close ranges.

As long as Gettysburg stands and the contour of its hills remains unchanged, students of the battle-field must decide that Lee's most promising attack from first to last was upon Cemetery Hill, by concentrated artillery fire from the north and assaults from the nearest sheltered ground between the west and northeast.

That this was not realized at the time is doubtless partly due to the scarcity of trained staff and reconnoitring officers, and partly to the fact that Ewell had discontinued and withdrawn the pursuit on the afternoon of the 1st, when it was about to undertake this position. Hence the enemy's pickets were not driven closely into their lines, and the vicinity was not carefully examined. Not a single gun was established within a thousand yards, nor was a position selected which enfiladed the lines in question.

Quite by accident, during the cannonade preceding Pickett's charge, Nelson's battalion of Ewell's corps fired a few rounds from a position which did enfilade with great effect part of the 11th corps upon Cemetery Hill, but the fire ceased on being sharply replied to. Briefly the one weak spot of the enemy's line and the one advantage possessed by ours were never apprehended."

Ironically, though he had no use for post-war politics, Lee's legacy was crafted and embroiled in it. While Lee accepted the South's loss, unreconstructed rebels continued to "fight" the Civil War with the pen, aiming to influence how the war was remembered. Much of this was accomplished by the Southern Historical Society, whose stated aim was the homogenization of Southern white males. But longstanding feuds between former generals found their way into the papers, and the feuds were frequently based on regional differences. These former Confederates looked to their idealized war heroes as symbols of their suffering and struggle. Based in Richmond, the Society's ideal Southern white male embodied the "Virginian" essence of aristocracy, morality and chivalry. The Society's ideal male, of course, was Robert E. Lee. David Blight credits the Society for creating a "Lee cult" that dominates public perception to this day. Writing about this perception of Lee, Charles Osbourne described the perception as "an edifice of myth built on the foundation of truth…the image became an icon."

Still, Lee was far from perfect, despite the attempts of the Southern Historical Society to defend his war record as fault free, at the expense of some of his subordinates. Given that the Confederacy lost the war, some historians have pointed out that Lee was often too eager to engage in offensive warfare. After all, Lee scored large and smashing victories at places like Chancellorsville that deprived him of more manpower against opponents that could afford casualties more than he could. Moreover, for the engineer who used tactics to successfully defend against typical Civil War tactics, he all too often engaged in the same futile offensive tactics himself, none more costly than Pickett's Charge.

However, after the war, former Confederates would not accept criticism of Lee, and blame for the loss at Gettysburg was thus placed upon other scapegoats. Although it was not immediately apparent where the blame rested for such a devastating loss, not long after the Battle of Gettysburg two names kept surfacing: cavalry leader General "Jeb" Stuart and General James Longstreet; Stuart blamed for robbing Lee of the "eyes" he needed to know of Union movement, and Longstreet for delaying his attack on Round Top Hills the second day and acting too slowly in executing the assault on the Union left flank.

Long before Gettysburg, Longstreet was characterized by his men and commanders as "congenitally resistant to hurry himself," resistant to change of orders (even from his supreme commander, Lee), and disliked to overextend his men (once bivouacked, he allowed his men to prepare three-days' rations before breaking camp, even when they were supposed to stick to a timetable). In fact, his designation as Lee's "old reliable" appears to have been bestowed by someone who had never actually worked with him or had to rely upon him.

Similarly, Longstreet's clash with A. P. Hill, then Jackson, Hood and Toombs, were indicative of his unwillingness to accept that he was not the center of attention; not the one destined for greatness. And, of course, as the War progressed, Longstreet's propensity to find fault (and start feuds) with Lafayette McLaws (who he tried to have court-martialed), Evander Law (who he tried to have arrested), Charles Field, and ultimately, Lee himself, was highly indicative of the self-possessed illusion Longstreet was living (and fighting) under. While always quick to reprimand any subordinate who questioned his orders, he clearly hesitated to resist orders from his superiors on occasions. In his Gettysburg account, Longstreet had the impudence to blame Lee for "not changing his plans" based on Longstreet's "want of confidence in them."

After General Robert E. Lee died in October of 1870, a group of ex-Confederates led by General Jubal Early (who had led a division in Ewell's corps at Gettysburg) publicly criticized Longstreet for ignoring orders and delaying his attack on the second day of the Battle on July 2, 1863. But while many former Confederates held Longstreet accountable for not following orders, Early took it one step further, arguing that Longstreet -- not Lee -- was responsible for the Confederate defeat (deemed a "tactical disaster" by most) that by most accounts was the beginning of the end for the Confederacy.

**Early**

In his memoirs, however, Longstreet defended himself, saying that the blistering post-War attacks concerning Gettysburg were merely "payback for supporting Black suffrage", thus shifting the blame back to Lee. He wrote, "[Lee] knew that I did not believe that success was possible . . . he should have put an officer in charge who had more confidence in his plan."[3] He went on to say that Lee should have given the responsibility to Early, thus justifying his insubordination.

On the other hand, Longstreet's reputation has mostly been on the upswing in the past few decades, due in no small part to Michael Shaara's 1974 novel *The Killer Angels*, which portrayed Longstreet in a more flattering light. That novel was the basis for the 1993 film *Gettysburg*, which has also helped rehabilitate Longstreet's legacy and helped make clear to the public how instrumental he was during the war. In 1982, Thomas L. Connolly and Barbara L. Bellows published *God and General Longstreet*, which took the Lost Cause proponents like Early to task for their blatant fabrications (such as the one that Lee ordered Longstreet to attack in the early morning of Day 2 of Gettysburg), helping make clear the extent of historical revision propagated by the Lost Cause. In doing so, they cast Longstreet as a sympathetic victim of circumstances and sectional and political hostility.

It's also important to note that Lee himself never made any post-War statements to suggest that he held Longstreet responsible for the Confederacy's demise.

While it was obvious that Stuart hadn't provided information about the Army of the Potomac to Lee (or at least that none of his dispatches reached the Confederate army), McClellan would try to defend Stuart by arguing that he accomplished the objective of distracting the enemy with a diversion and delaying them: "We may dismiss at once the inconsiderate charge that Stuart disobeyed or exceeded the orders given to him by General Lee, for General Lee states that Stuart acted 'in the exercise of the discretion given to him.' Stuart had submitted his plans to his commander, in a personal interview. Those plans were approved, and he was authorized to carry

---

[3]      Gaffney, P., and D. Gaffney. *The Civil War: Exploring History One Week at a Time.* Page 442.

them out if in his opinion it seemed best to do so. The responsibility of the movement, strategically considered, rests with General Lee. Many considerations may be urged in its favor. Two objects were placed before Stuart. He was desired to gain information of the enemy's movements, and to damage and delay him on his march. Let us consider the latter object. Among the direct results of Stuart's movement we find that Meade was deprived of the services of all of his cavalry except Buford's division until noon on the 2d of July, and that Buford's division was withdrawn from Meade's left on the second day of the battle at Gettysburg to protect the depot of supplies at Westminster, leaving unguarded the flank of Sickles' corps, to which circumstance is largely attributed the success of Longstreet's attack upon that corps. A portion of French's command was also diverted eastward, to protect communication with Washington. Indeed, no one can read the despatches which passed between Meade and Halleck from the 28th of June to the 1st of July without noting the perplexity which existed in regard to Lee's movements, and the wide divergence eastward of Meade's corps, both caused by the presence of Stuart in his rear. From this cause alone the 6th corps was able to participate only in the battle of the last day. It must, therefore, be acknowledged that in one respect General Stuart's movement accomplished all that was anticipated. General Lee expected that he would be able to delay the movements of the enemy, and produce confusion and uncertainty in regard to the movements of his own army. This Stuart accomplished, and it does not appear that he could have secured these results by any other mode of operations; for had he decided to cross the Potomac at Shepherdstown he must have remained near Rector's Cross Roads until the morning of the 26th, when the northward movement of Hooker's army would have been developed to him. He could have crossed at Shepherdstown on the 27th, but he could not have done more than occupy the gaps of South Mountain with a portion of his command on the 28th, even if unopposed. These movements could hardly have been concealed from the signal stations of the enemy, and would have been met by corresponding movements of the enemy's cavalry; for on the 28th Buford's division was at Middletown and Kilpatrick's at Frederick, ready to force a passage through the mountains and fall upon Lee's trains. A concentration of these divisions upon any one of the gaps would have enabled them to accomplish this result, and with nothing to attract attention on the other side of Meade's army there can be but little doubt that some plan of this nature would have been adopted. But on the 28th Halleck was urging Meade to send cavalry in pursuit of the raiders, and Gregg's and Kilpatrick's divisions were diverted from Meade's left to protect his right and rear, while Buford was left to bear alone a two hours' conflict with the Confederate infantry at Gettysburg. The result shows that no better plan could have been adopted to secure Lee's right flank from annoyance."

Of course, given the way the battle of Gettysburg unfolded, the diversions and distractions didn't prevent the Army of the Potomac from winning the battle, and it was the lack of reconnaissance that had Lee's army unwittingly march right into Union defenders outside of Gettysburg without realizing where the Army of the Potomac was. Heth, whose division began the battle by unwittingly marching into Buford's cavalry, later asserted, "The failure to crush the Federal army in Pennsylvania in 1863, in the opinion of almost all of the officers of the Army of Northern Virginia, can be expressed in five words—the absence of the cavalry."

In the end, even McClellan had to concede, "This movement of Stuart in the rear of the Federal army has been the subject of much discussion, and the prevalent opinion among writers, both Federal and Confederate, is that it was an error in strategy." After the war, Stuart's subordinate, General Thomas L. Rosser, was even blunter: "On this campaign, [Stuart] undoubtedly [made] the fatal blunder which lost us the battle of Gettysburg."

That said, it's only fair to point out that to a great extent, the Confederates' search for scapegoats occurred because they were so used to being successful that a defeat had to be explained by a Southern failure, not a Northern success. In casting about for Southern deficiencies, it is often overlooked that Meade and his top subordinates fought a remarkably efficient battle. Meade created an extremely sturdy defensive line anchored on high ground, he held the interior lines by having his army spread out over a smaller area, and he used that ability to shuffle troops from the right to the left on July 2. Moreover, Meade was able to rely on his corps commanders, especially Hancock, to properly use their discretion. Before the battle, Lee reportedly said that Meade "would commit no blunders on my front and if I make one ... will make haste to take advantage of it." If he said it, he was definitely right.

Perhaps none other than George Pickett himself put it best. When asked (certainly ad nauseam) why Pickett's Charge had failed, Pickett is said to have tersely replied, "I've always thought the Yankees had something to do with it."

### Grant Comes East

Failing to secure the capture of any major northern cities, or the recognition of Great Britain or France, or the complete destruction of any northern armies, the Confederacy's last chance to survive the Civil War was the election of 1864. Democrats had been pushing an anti-war stance or at least a stance calling for a negotiated peace for years, so the South hoped that if a Democrat defeated President Lincoln, or if anti-war Democrats could retake the Congress, the North might negotiate peace with the South. In the election of 1862, anti-war Democrats made some gains in Congress and won the governorship of the State of New York. Confederates were therefore hopeful that trend would continue to the election of 1864.

Although the Army of the Potomac had been victorious at Gettysburg, Lincoln was still upset at what he perceived to be General George Meade's failure to trap Robert E. Lee's Army of Northern Virginia in Pennsylvania. When Lee retreated from Pennsylvania without much fight from the Army of the Potomac, Lincoln was again discouraged, believing Meade had a chance to end the war if he had been bolder. Though historians dispute that, and the Confederates actually invited attack during their retreat, Lincoln was constantly looking for more aggressive fighters to lead his men.

Lincoln's appreciation for aggressive fighters had made him a defender of Ulysses S. Grant as far back as 1862. In April 1862, Grant's army had won the biggest battle in the history of North America to date at Shiloh, with nearly 24,000 combined casualties among the Union and Confederate forces. Usually the winner of a major battle is hailed as a hero, but Grant was hardly a winner at Shiloh. The Battle of Shiloh took place before costlier battles at places like Antietam and Gettysburg, so the extent of the casualties at Shiloh shocked the nation. Moreover, at Shiloh the casualties were viewed as needless; Grant was pilloried for allowing the Confederates to take his forces by surprise, as well as the failure to build defensive earthworks and fortifications, which nearly resulted in a rout of his army. Speculation again arose that Grant had a drinking problem, and some even assumed he was drunk during the battle. Though the Union won, it was largely viewed that their success owed to the heroics of General William Tecumseh Sherman in rallying the men and Don Carlos Buell arriving with his army, and General Buell was happy to receive the credit at Grant's expense.

**Grant**

As a result of the Battle of Shiloh, General Halleck demoted Grant to second-in-command of all armies in his department, an utterly powerless position. And when word of what many considered a "colossal blunder" reached Washington, several congressmen insisted that Lincoln replace Grant in the field. Lincoln famously defended Grant, telling critics, "I can't spare this man. He fights."

Lincoln may have defended Grant, but he found precious few supporters, and the negative attention bothered Grant so much that it is widely believed he turned to alcohol again. While historians still debate that, what is known is that he considered resigning his commission, only to be dissuaded from doing so by General Sherman. While Grant was at the low point of his career, Sherman's career had been resurrected, and he was promoted to major-general the following month. With rumors that Grant was falling off the wagon with alcohol, Sherman tried to reassure Grant not to quit the war, telling him "some happy accident might restore you to favor and your true place." Sherman's appreciation of Grant's faith in his abilities cemented his loyalty and established a friendship between the two that would last a lifetime. In later years Sherman would say, "General Grant is a great general! He stood by me when I was crazy, and I stood by him when he was drunk; and now, sir, we stand by each other always."

Although Grant stayed in the army, it's unclear what position he would have held if Lincoln had not called Halleck to Washington to serve as general-in-chief in July 1862. At the same time, Halleck was given that position in large measure due to Grant's successes in the department under Halleck's command. Thankfully for the Union, Halleck's departure meant that Grant was reinstated as commander.

Lincoln's steadfastness ensured that Grant's victories out West continued to pile up, and after Vicksburg and Chattanooga, Grant had effectively ensured Union control of the states of Kentucky and Tennessee, as well as the entire Mississippi River. Thus, at the beginning of 1864, Lincoln put him in charge of all federal armies, a position that required Grant to come east.

Grant had already succeeded in achieving two of President Lincoln's three primary directives for a Union victory: the opening of the Mississippi Valley Basin, and the domination of the corridor from Nashville to Atlanta. If he could now seize Richmond, he would achieve the third.

Before beginning the Overland Campaign against Lee's army, Grant, Sherman and Lincoln devised a new strategy that would eventually implement total war tactics. Grant aimed to use the Army of the Potomac to attack Lee and/or take Richmond. Meanwhile, General Sherman, now in command of the Department of the West, would attempt to take Atlanta and strike through Georgia. In essence, having already cut the Confederacy in half with Vicksburg campaign, he now intended to bisect the eastern half.

On top of all that, Grant and Sherman were now intent on fully depriving the Confederacy of the ability to keep fighting. Sherman put this policy in effect during his March to the Sea by confiscating civilian resources and literally taking the fight to the Southern people. For Grant, it meant a war of attrition that would steadily bleed Lee's Army of Northern Virginia. To take full advantage of the North's manpower, in 1864 the Union also ended prisoner exchanges to ensure that the Confederate armies could not be bolstered by paroled prisoners.

By 1864, things were looking so bleak for the South that the Confederate war strategy was simply to ensure Lincoln lost reelection that November, with the hope that a new Democratic president would end the war and recognize the South's independence. With that, and given the shortage in manpower, Lee's strategic objective was to continue defending Richmond, while hoping that Grant would commit some blunder that would allow him a chance to seize an opportunity.

**Lee**

With that, the stage was set for the two most successful generals of the Civil War to finally face each other. Confederate Brigadier-General John B. Gordon, whose brigade would play a crucial role at the Battle of the Wilderness, aptly summarized the situation entering May 1864: "Grant had come from his campaigns in the Southwest with the laurels of Fort Donelson, Shiloh, Vicksburg, and Missionary Ridge on his brow. Lee stood before him with a record as military executioner unrivalled by that of any warrior of modern times. He had, at astoundingly short intervals and with unvarying regularity, decapitated or caused the official 'taking off' of the five previously selected commanders-in-chief of the great army which confronted him…This advance by General Grant inaugurated the seventh act in the 'On to Richmond' drama played by the armies of the Union."

### Entering the Wilderness

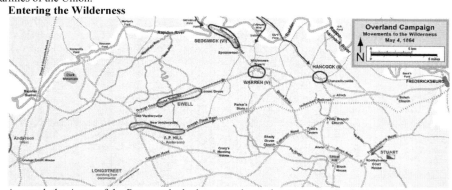

As usual, the Army of the Potomac had a large numbers advantage over Lee's Army of Northern Virginia, with Grant bringing an estimated 100,000 into the Wilderness to face Lee's 60,000. Although George Meade was nominally in command of the Union army, the fact that Grant marched with the army essentially meant that he would be making the overall decisions.

The Army of the Potomac was organized into three infantry corps, John Sedgwick's VI Corps, Winfield Scott Hancock's II Corps, and Gouverneur Warren's V Corps, along with a cavalry corps led by Phil Sheridan, who Grant brought east with him. Sedgwick was considered one of the most competent and aggressive corps commanders in the Union, and Hancock's heroics during the last two days of the Battle of Gettysburg more than demonstrated his ability to lead a corps. Warren had been a staff officer who alertly manned Little Round Top on the second day at Gettysburg, but he was relatively new to commanding a corps, and it would show. Ambrose Burnside's IX Corps was an independent command in the vicinity, but it would not fight in the Wilderness.

**Phil Sheridan**

**George Meade**

**Winfield Scott Hancock**

The Army of Northern Virginia started the Overland Campaign with the same structure as it had after losing Stonewall Jackson at Chancellorsville in May 1863. Lee's army was also divided into three corps commanded by James Longstreet, A.P. Hill and Richard S. Ewell. Longstreet was perhaps the best corps commander on either side during the Civil War, but Hill and Ewell struggled leading their corps at Gettysburg after having distinguished themselves in charge of smaller commands earlier in the war. The Confederate cavalry was led by their flamboyant but skilled cavalier, JEB Stuart, who was nearly as competent as he was vainglorious.

**Longstreet**

**A.P. Hill**

**JEB Stuart**

While the Union's advantage in manpower colored Grant's attritional strategy, on a tactical level it would not help the Army of the Potomac in the Wilderness because of the terrain. Grant explained why in his memoirs:

"The country over which the army had to operate, from the Rapidan to the crossing of the James River, is rather flat, and is cut by numerous streams which make their way to the Chesapeake Bay. The crossings of these streams by the army were generally made not far above tide-water, and where they formed a considerable obstacle to the rapid advance of troops even when the enemy did not appear in opposition. The country roads were narrow and poor. Most of the country is covered with a dense forest, in places, like the Wilderness and along the Chickahominy, almost impenetrable even for infantry except along the roads. All bridges were naturally destroyed before the National troops came to them."

Moreover, the Confederate soldiers' faith in their own abilities and General Lee ensured that they were constantly up to the challenge when facing the bigger Army of the Potomac. Gordon described the mood in camp that spring, "The reports of General Lee's scouts were scarcely necessary to our appreciation of the fact that the odds against us were constantly and rapidly increasing: for from the highland which bordered the southern banks of the Rapidan one could almost estimate the numbers that were being added to Grant's ranks by the growth of the city of tents spreading out in full view below. The Confederates were profoundly impressed by the situation, but they rejected as utterly unworthy of a Christian soldiery the doctrine that Providence was on the side of the heaviest guns and most numerous battalions."

When Grant began marching the army on May 4, he actually hoped to avoid a general battle against Lee in the Wilderness, given that the heavy forestry and thick underbrush would make infantry coordination impossible and artillery practically unusable. To avoid fighting on this ground, Grant needed to move the army southeast as quickly as he could, and he hoped to reach Spotsylvania Court House before fighting Lee.

As it turned out, Grant would fight Lee at Spotsylvania Court House, but it would be the second pitched battle of the campaign. The sheer size of the army made it difficult to move everything, especially its supplies. Grant's army was marching with just 10 days of rations, so a lot of live cattle had to be brought along to be butchered along the way, not to mention the thousands of wagons and ambulances as well. By some counts the rear of the marching army would've extended over 60 miles if marching down a single road. Grant wrote about all the work and necessities that went into provisioning his large army:

"There never was a corps better organized than was the quartermaster's corps with the Army of the Potomac in 1864. With a wagon-train that would have extended from the Rapidan to Richmond, stretched along in single file and separated as the teams necessarily would be when moving, we could still carry only three days' forage and about ten to twelve days' rations, besides a supply of ammunition. To overcome all difficulties, the chief quartermaster, General Rufus Ingalls, had marked on each wagon the corps badge with the division color and the number of the brigade. At a glance, the particular brigade to which any wagon belonged could be told. The wagons were also marked to note the contents: if ammunition, whether for artillery or infantry; if forage, whether grain or hay; if rations, whether, bread, pork, beans, rice, sugar, coffee or whatever it might be. Empty wagons were never allowed to follow the army or stay in camp. As soon as a wagon was empty it would return to the base of supply for a load of precisely the same article that had been taken from it. Empty trains were obliged to leave the road free for loaded ones. Arriving near the army they would be parked in fields nearest to the brigades they belonged to. Issues, except of ammunition, were made at night in all cases. By this system the hauling of forage for the supply train was almost wholly dispensed with."

To alleviate the logistical issues, Grant intended to have his three corps march separately on two different roads toward their objective, as he explained in his memoirs:

"The 5th corps, General Warren commanding, was in advance on the right, and marched directly for Germania Ford, preceded by one division of cavalry, under General J. H. Wilson. General Sedgwick followed Warren with the 6th corps. Germania Ford was nine or ten miles below the right of Lee's line. Hancock, with the 2d corps, moved by another road, farther east, directly upon Ely's Ford, six miles below Germania, preceded by Gregg's division of cavalry, and followed by the artillery. Torbert's division of cavalry was left north of the Rapidan, for the time, to picket the river and prevent the enemy from crossing and getting into our rear. The cavalry seized the two crossings before daylight, drove the enemy's pickets guarding them away, and by six o'clock A.M. had the pontoons laid ready for the crossing of the infantry and artillery. This was undoubtedly a surprise to Lee. The fact that the movement was unopposed proves this.

Burnside, with the 9th corps, was left back at Warrenton, guarding the railroad from Bull Run forward to preserve control of it in case our crossing the Rapidan should be long delayed. He was instructed, however, to advance at once on receiving notice that the army had crossed; and a dispatch was sent to him a little after one P.M. giving the information that our crossing had been successful.

The country was heavily wooded at all the points of crossing, particularly on the south side of the river. The battle-field from the crossing of the Rapidan until the final movement from the Wilderness toward Spottsylvania was of the same character. There were some clearings and small farms within what might be termed the battle-field; but generally the country was covered with a dense forest. The roads were narrow and bad. All the conditions were favorable for defensive operations."

Lee hadn't opposed the crossings because he had dispersed his army to prepare for several avenues of attack that Grant might choose. In fact, he anticipated that Grant would cross exactly how he did, using the Germanna and Ely Fords across the Rapidan River, but he hadn't concentrated his army until he knew for sure. As a result, Ewell's corps and Hill's corps were within marching distance of the Wilderness, but Longstreet was about 20 miles southwest near Gordonsville.

Grant's march intended to turn Lee's right flank, but once Lee realized which way Grant was marching on May 4, he began swiftly moving to meet the Union army in the Wilderness, since it was ideal for defense and negated the artillery advantage enjoyed by the Army of the Potomac. And as a result of the manner in which Grant's army was marching down separate roads, Lee was being given a chance to strike the Union's right flank instead of vice-versa. Ewell's corps and Hill's corps were close enough to fight in the Wilderness, but it would take a day for Longstreet's corps to come up.

Lee's intentions were assisted by the nature of the terrain, which allowed his two corps to march almost entirely undetected, as well as the Union's misuse of their cavalry. While cavalry was typically used to screen the infantry's advance and to conduct reconnaissance, Sheridan's cavalry was east of the army responding to a report that JEB Stuart's cavalry was near Fredericksburg, presumably with the intention of harassing the Union army's rear. The only problem was that the report was completely inaccurate; Stuart was actually southeast near Spotsylvania, where his cavalry would be in a position to ride north and intercept Warren's advancing V Corps.

As the armies' movements progressed on May 4, Grant and Meade had no clue that Lee's army was in close proximity, so they ultimately decided to camp near Chancellorsville, giving their gigantic wagon trains a chance to stay close. It had only taken a day for everything to fall Lee's way. Two of his corps were in position to intercept the Army of the Potomac from the west as it was marching south, and one of the Union army's three corps was marching on a separate road and wouldn't be able to immediately come to the other two corps' assistance in the event of a surprise attack.

**May 5**

**The armies' dispositions on the morning of May 5**

Although Grant did not realize that Lee's army was closing in on his, he did have the wherewithal to face his army west when it wasn't marching south, aware that if an attack did come, it would come from that direction. Indeed, it wouldn't take long for the armies to run into each other on May 5.

As Warren's column started marching south around dawn on the 5th, it ran into Ewell's corps heading east on the Orange Turnpike toward him around 6:00 a.m. Shortly after that, Union cavalry reported Confederate infantry (Hill's Corps) marching in force east down the Orange Plank Road. In response, Grant immediately scrambled to form a battle line on both of Warren's flanks while preparing to attack whatever force was in his front, but with Hancock's II Corps too far away, Grant had to order up one of the divisions in Sedgwick's corps to advance and join Warren's left flank while the rest of the VI Corps formed on Warren's right flank:

"My orders were given through General Meade for an early advance on the morning of the 5th. Warren was to move to Parker's store, and Wilson's cavalry—then at Parker's store—to move on to Craig's meeting-house. Sedgwick followed Warren, closing in on his right. The Army of the Potomac was facing to the west, though our advance was made to the south, except when facing the enemy. Hancock was to move south-westward to join on the left of Warren, his left to reach to Shady Grove Church.

At six o'clock, before reaching Parker's store, Warren discovered the enemy. He sent word back to this effect, and was ordered to halt and prepare to meet and attack him. Wright, with his division of Sedgwick's corps, was ordered, by any road he could find, to join on to Warren's right, and Getty with his division, also of Sedgwick's corps, was ordered to move rapidly by Warren's rear and get on his left. This was the speediest way to reinforce Warren who was confronting the enemy on both the Orange plank and turnpike roads."

Grant's aide, Theodore Lyman, would later describe just how difficult the Wilderness was to maneuver around near the Orange Plank Road: "The very worst of it is parallel with Orange plank and upper part of the Brock road. Here it is mostly a low, continuous, thick growth of small saplings, fifteen to thirty feet high and seldom larger than one's arm. The half-grown leaves added to the natural obscurity, and there were many places where a line of troops could with difficulty be seen at fifty yards. This was the terrain on which we were called to manoeuvre a great army."

**Photo of the region around the Wilderness and Spotsylvania**

As Grant's orders were put into motion and Warren started to prepare a battle line, Ewell's corps started going about digging in, building earthworks and fortifications to the west near Saunders Field, a small clearing in the dense woods near the Turnpike. Though Lee obviously wanted to block Grant's march and ensnare him in the Wilderness, he also didn't want to give battle himself until he could get Longstreet up. When Longstreet received orders to march, it was nearly 1:00 p.m. and his corps would have to march nearly 30 miles. Luckily for the Confederates, Hancock's II Corps would also not be in position to link up with Getty's division on Warren's left until the middle of the afternoon at the earliest.

Grant and Meade initially believed that Ewell's corps was not an entire corps but merely an advance guard, an assumption that was dispelled when Warren's men approached Saunders Field only to find the Confederates' defensive line extended past his right flank. Warren suggested to Meade that his assault on the Confederate line not take place until Sedgwick's VI Corps joined his right, but delays in their march eventually induced the frustrated Meade into ordering an attack at 1:00 p.m. regardless of Sedgwick's positioning.

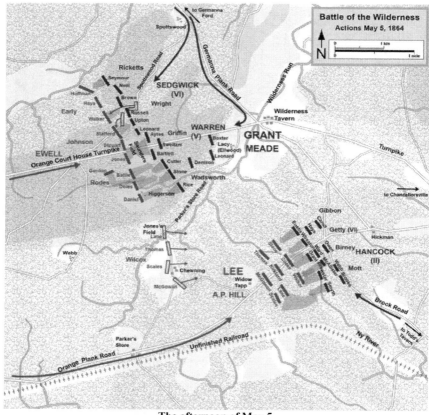

**The afternoon of May 5**

It didn't take long for Warren's men to suffer for the decision. Although the clearing actually allowed for a cohesive line to form and advance, the outflanked Union soldiers experienced devastating enfilades from Confederate soldiers on their right, compelling Romeyn Ayres's brigade to halt its forward movement even as the brigades to their left kept moving forward. In fact, Joseph Bartlett's brigade managed to pierce the Confederate line by overrunning a Confederate brigade led by John M. Jones, who was killed during the fight. Unfortunately, this breakthrough could not be exploited due to the fact that the inability of Ayres to move his brigade forward opened up Bartlett's right flank to the same kind of enfilade that pinned down Ayres in the first place.

As the general fight continued, Lyman described what it was like behind the lines, as general officers from the various Union corps were trying to get their commands to their respective positions.

I found General Getty at the plank road (a spot I shall remember for some years) and gave him instructions. He told me the whole of Hill's Corps was in his front and the skirmishers only 300 yards from us. For all I could see they might have been in Florida, but the occasional wounded men who limped by, and the sorry spectacle of two or three dead, wrapped in their blankets, showed that some fighting had already taken place. I got back and reported a little before one o'clock, and had scarcely got there when B-r-r-r-r wrang went the musketry, in front of Griffin and of Wright, which for the next hour and a half was continuous — not by volley, for that is impossible in such woods; but a continuous crackle, now swelling and now abating, and interspersed with occasional cannon. Very soon the ambulances began to go forward for their mournful freight. A little before two, I was sent with an order to a cavalry regiment, close by. The pike was a sad spectacle indeed; it was really obstructed with trains of ambulances and with the wounded on foot; all had the same question, over and over again; 'How far to the 5th Corps' hospital?'"

Although Bartlett's advance was repulsed by the shooting on his right flank, the Iron Brigade continued advancing on the left. Although this was one of the hardest and most famous brigades of the entire war, it had been so badly devastated at Gettysburg that the brigade needed to be refilled with raw recruits, to the extent that the character of the Iron Brigade in 1864 was no longer what it was in 1862 and 1863. But for a time, it didn't seem like that would matter, because the Iron Brigade made a steady advance that sent a Confederate brigade under Cullen Battle into a disorderly retreat.

The Confederates were fortunate enough to have John B. Gordon's brigade behind the line. Indicative of the confusion that both sides were experiencing in the early fighting, Gordon's brigade found itself in position to reinforce the line simply because it had marched in the direction where the gunfire sounded heaviest. Gordon recalled the scene as his men were coming up to provide reinforcements:

"Alternate confidence and apprehension were awakened as the shouts of one army or the other reached our ears. So distinct in character were these shouts that they were easily discernible. At one point the weird Confederate 'yell' told us plainly that Ewell's men were advancing. At another the huzzas, in mighty concert, of the Union troops warned us that they had repelled the Confederate charge; and as these ominous huzzas grew in volume we know that Grant's lines were moving forward. Just as the head of my column came within range of the whizzing Miniés, the Confederate yells grew fainter, and at last ceased; and the Union shout rose above the din of battle. I was already prepared by this infallible admonition for the sight of Ewell's shattered forces retreating in disorder. The oft-repeated but spasmodic efforts of first one army and then the other to break through the opposing ranks had at last been ended by the sudden rush of Grant's compact veterans from the dense covert in such numbers that Ewell's attenuated lines were driven in confusion to the rear. These retreating divisions, like broken and receding waves, rolled back against the head of my column while we were still rapidly advancing along the narrow road. The repulse had been so sudden and the confusion so great that practically no resistance was now being made to the Union advance; and the elated Federals were so near me that little time was left to bring my men from column into line in order to resist the movement or repel it by countercharge."

**Gordon**

As his men were coming up, Gordon ran into Ewell himself, who told Gordon that the fate of the day rested on his men's shoulders. With that, Gordon ordered his men forward, producing what he called the "strangest" scene he saw during the Civil War:

. " At this moment of dire extremity I saw General Ewell, who was still a superb horseman, notwithstanding the loss of his leg, riding in furious gallop toward me, his thoroughbred charger bounding like a deer through the dense underbrush…'General Gordon, the fate of the day depends on you, sir,' he said. 'These men will save it, sir,' I replied, more with the purpose of arousing the enthusiasm of my men than with any well-defined idea as to how we were to save it. Quickly wheeling a single regiment into line, I ordered it forward in a countercharge, while I hurried the other troops into position. The sheer audacity and dash of that regimental charge checked, as I had hoped it would, the Union advance for a few moments, giving me the essential time to throw the other troops across the Union front. Swiftly riding to the centre of my line, I gave in person the order: 'Forward!' With a deafening yell which must have been heard miles away, that glorious brigade rushed upon the hitherto advancing enemy, and by the shock of their furious onset shattered into fragments all that portion of the compact Union line which confronted my troops.

At that moment was presented one of the strangest conditions ever witnessed upon a battle-field. My command covered only a small portion of the long lines in blue, and not a single regiment of those stalwart Federals yielded except those which had been struck by the Southern advance. On both sides of the swath cut by this sweep of the Confederate scythe, the steady veterans of Grant were unshaken and still poured their incessant volleys into the retreating Confederate ranks. My command had cut its way through the Union centre, and at that moment it was in the remarkably strange position of being on identically the same general line with the enemy, the Confederates facing in one direction, the Federals in the other. Looking down that line from Grant's right toward his left, there would first have been seen a long stretch of blue uniforms, then a short stretch of gray, then another still longer of blue, in one continuous line. The situation was both unique and alarming…

As soon as my troops had broken through the Union ranks, I directed my staff to halt the command; and before the Union veterans could recover from the shock, my regiments were moving at double-quick from the centre into file right and left, thus placing them in two parallel lines, back to back, in a position at a right angle to the one held a moment before. This quickly executed manoeuvre placed one half of my command squarely upon the right flank of one portion of the enemy's unbroken line, and the other half facing in exactly the opposite direction, squarely upon the left flank of the enemy's line."

Gordon's counterattack had saved the Confederate line in that spot, but the Confederate line to his right was also being attacked by Union brigades led by Roy Stone and James C. Rice. As those attacks were being repulsed, Warren tried to bring up artillery to help the advance, only to have the Confederates surge forward and initiate hand-to-hand fighting for control of the two guns in the field. In the melee, Saunders Field caught fire, consigning some of the unfortunate injured men lying on the field to literally watch flames creep up to them before burning them to death. One of the soldiers, Private Frank Wilkeson, later recalled, "I saw many wounded soldiers in the Wilderness who hung on to their rifles, and whose intention was clearly stamped on their pallid faces. I saw one man, both of whose legs were broken, lying on the ground with his cocked rifle by his side and his ramrod in his hand, and his eyes set on the front. I knew he meant to kill himself in case of fire—knew it is surely as though I could read his thoughts."

Warren's assault had failed to exploit any of its breakthroughs, but just as his V Corps was ending its fighting, Sedgwick's VI Corps came up on their right around 3:00 p.m. and started attacking Ewell's left. Sedgwick made the attack up the Spottswood Road, but Ewell's line forced him to try to align a battle line well into the Wilderness off the road as well. For the next hour, Sedgwick's corps tried to dislodge Ewell's line, but the inability to keep a line moving forward with any semblance of coordination doomed the attempts of Union and Confederates alike to attack and counterattack. After just an hour, Sedgwick's attack began to peter out.

About a mile to the southeast, A.P. Hill's corps was confronting Getty's division, which had come up on Warren's left to hold the crossroad where the east-west Orange Plank Road intersected the north-south Brock Road. It was essential for the Union to hold that intersection to make sure that Hancock could rejoin the other two corps by marching northwest up the Brock Road toward the now pitched battle. Getty was assisted in holding the spot with some a brigade of cavalry, keeping Hill's soldiers a few hundred yards to the west while Hancock's men began to trickle up.

Some of Hancock's men came up around 4:00 p.m., and with their arrival in mind, Getty's division was ordered to attack Hill. Lyman described the scene on the Union left that afternoon:

At 3.15 I was sent with an order to General Getty to attack at once, and to explain to him that Hancock would join also. He is a cool man, is Getty, quite a wonder; as I saw then and after. 'Go to General Eustis and General Wheaton,' he said to his aides, 'and tell them to prepare to advance at once.' And so we were getting into it! And everybody had been ordered up, including Burnside, who had crossed that very morning at Germanna Ford. General Grant had his station with us (or we with him); there he took his seat on the grass, and smoked his briarwood pipe, looking sleepy and stern and indifferent. His face, however, may wear a most pleasing smile, and I believe he is a thoroughly amiable man. That he believes in his star and takes a bright view of things is evident. At 4.15 P. M. General Meade ordered me to take some orderlies, go to General Hancock (whose musketry we could now hear on the left) and send him back reports, staying there till dark. Delightful! At the crossing of the dotted cross-road with the plank sat Hancock, on his fine horse — the preux chevalier of this campaign — a glorious soldier, indeed! The musketry was crashing in the woods in our front, and stray balls — too many to be pleasant — were coming about. It's all very well for novels, but I don't like such places and go there only when ordered. 'Report to General Meade,' said Hancock, 'that it is very hard to bring up troops in this wood, and that only a part of my Corps is up, but I will do as well as I can.' Up rides an officer: 'Sir! General Getty is hard pressed and nearly out of ammunition!' 'Tell him to hold on and General Gibbon will be up to help him.' Another officer: 'General Mott's division has broken, sir, and is coming back.' 'Tell him to stop them, sir!!' roared Hancock in a voice of a trumpet. As he spoke, a crowd of troops came from the woods and fell back into the Brock road. Hancock dashed among them. 'Halt here! halt here! Form behind this rifle-pit. Major Mitchell, go to Gibbon and tell him to come up on the double-quick!' It was a welcome sight to see Carroll's brigade coming along that Brock road, he riding at their head as calm as a May morning. 'Left face — prime — forward,' and the line disappeared in the woods to waken the musketry with double violence. Carroll was brought back wounded. Up came Hays's brigade, disappeared in the woods, and, in a few minutes, General Hays was carried past me, covered with blood, shot through the head.

As Lyman's account indicates, the fighting was back-and-forth, with both Hill's corps and Hancock's corps entangled in underbrush and forest near a small stream called the Ny River. Lee had made his headquarters at the Widow Tapp's house in a small clearing just behind Hill's defensive line, and at one point some Union soldiers came streaming out of the woods and into the clearing, coming into eyesight of Lee while he was discussing the fighting with Hill and JEB Stuart. Thankfully for the three Confederate officers, the Union soldiers were just as confused as they were, and when they realized there were Confederates in their front they turned right back around and reentered the forest.

When the fighting ended that night, both lines had maintained their respective positions, and the soldiers on both sides immediately started digging in and preparing strong defensive fortifications. There was still a gap separating the two armies from completely forming one line, something Grant would attempt to remedy the next day by bringing up Burnside's IX Corps and something that Lee could do nothing about other than to gamble that the confusing Wilderness would protect Hill's left flank and Ewell's right flank.

"After the close of the battle of the 5th of May my orders were given for the following morning. We knew Longstreet with 12,000 men was on his way to join Hill's right, near the Brock Road, and might arrive during the night. I was anxious that the rebels should not take the initiative in the morning, and therefore ordered Hancock to make an assault at 4.30 o'clock. Meade asked to have the hour changed to six. Deferring to his wishes as far as I was willing, the order was modified and five was fixed as the hour to move.

Hancock had now fully one-half of the Army of the Potomac. Wadsworth with his division, which had arrived the night before, lay in a line perpendicular to that held by Hill, and to the right of Hancock. He was directed to move at the same time, and to attack Hill's left.

Burnside, who was coming up with two divisions, was directed to get in between Warren and Wadsworth, and attack as soon as he could get in position to do so. Sedgwick and Warren were to make attacks in their front, to detain as many of the enemy as they could and to take advantage of any attempt to reinforce Hill from that quarter. Burnside was ordered if he should succeed in breaking the enemy's centre, to swing around to the left and envelop the right of Lee's army. Hancock was informed of all the movements ordered."

Despite being outnumbered and not gaining any ground, Lee had kept Grant's army in the Wilderness, and he could count on Longstreet arriving at some point to fight tomorrow. Lee reported back to Richmond:

"The enemy crossed the Rapidan yesterday at Ely's and Germanna Fords. Two corps of this army moved to oppose him: Ewell's, by the old turnpike, and Hill's, by the plank road. They arrived this morning in close proximity to the enemy's line of march. A strong attack was made upon Ewell, who repulsed it, capturing many prisoners and four pieces of artillery. The enemy subsequently concentrated upon General Hill, who, with Heth's and Wilcox's divisions, successfully resisted repeated and desperate assaults. A large force of cavalry and artillery on our right flank was driven back by Rosser's brigade. By the blessing of God we maintained our position against every effort until night, when the contest closed."

Gordon summed up Confederate sentiments on the night of May 5:

"Both sides labored all night in the dark and dense woodland, throwing up such breastworks as were possible--a most timely preparation for the next day's conflicts. My own command was ordered during the night to the extreme left of Lee's lines, under the apprehension that Grant's right overlapped and endangered our left flank.

Thus ended the 5th of May, which had witnessed the first desperate encounter between Grant and Lee. The fighting had not involved the whole of either army, but it was fierce and bloody. It would be unjust to claim that either of the famous leaders had achieved a signal victory. Both sides had left their dead scattered through the bullet-riddled underbrush. The Confederates drew comfort from the fact that in the shifting fortunes of the day theirs was the last advance, that the battle had ended near where it had begun, and that the Union advance had been successfully repulsed."

## May 6

At the beginning of May 6, Grant was hoping that his advantage in manpower would make it possible for Burnside's IX Corps to interpose itself between Hill and Ewell, making it possible to cut Lee's army in half and destroy them. But he wasn't the only one intending to make an attack; the characteristically aggressive Lee had decided to keep Hill's outnumbered men in position and even use them to attack Hancock's corps, operating under the assumption that Longstreet's corps would be up in the morning and could sustain the momentum of the advance.

Naturally, things would not go according to plan for either Grant or Lee. Due to miscommunications, or due to the understanding that they would be used to attack the following morning, multiple divisions in Hill's corps decided not to dig in and build defensive fortifications on the night of May 5. While that may have been understandable and normal in 1862, experience had taught both sides by 1864 that the first thing to do once they had an established line was to start digging in and building earthworks that would protect them during an attack. By the end of the war, the Civil War had become a forerunner to the trench warfare of

World War I, and if an army was given 24 hours to entrench, their position became practically unassailable. Grant described the process in his memoirs:

"[I]n every change of position or halt for the night, whether confronting the enemy or not, the moment arms were stacked the men intrenched themselves. For this purpose they would build up piles of logs or rails if they could be found in their front, and dig a ditch, throwing the dirt forward on the timber. Thus the digging they did counted in making a depression to stand in, and increased the elevation in front of them. It was wonderful how quickly they could in this way construct defences of considerable strength. When a halt was made with the view of assaulting the enemy, or in his presence, these would be strengthened or their positions changed under the direction of engineer officers."

Moreover, Lee had expected that Longstreet's men would be up at dawn, allowing him to slide Hill's corps to the left and eventually link up with Ewell, which would have put Hill in the gap that Grant intended to push Burnside's IX Corps through. However, the nature of the night marching, the nature of the roads, and the nature of the terrain all delayed Longstreet's marching during the early morning hours of May 6. Longstreet expressed some of the causes of the inevitable delays:

"About eleven o'clock in the night the guide reported from General Lee to conduct my command through the wood across to the Plank road, and at one o'clock the march was resumed. The road was overgrown by the bushes, except the side-tracks made by the draft animals and the ruts of wheels which marked occasional lines in its course. After a time the wood became less dense, and the unused road was more difficult to follow, and presently the guide found that there was no road under him; but no time was lost, as, by ordering the lines of the divisions doubled, they were ready when the trail was found, and the march continued in double line. At daylight we entered the Plank road, and filed down towards the field of strife of the afternoon of the 5th and daylight of the 6th."

Longstreet's men would be advancing down the Orange Plank Road toward Hill's corps and the Union line by the break of dawn, but by then Hancock's attack, which began at Grant's appointed time of 5:00 a.m., was already starting to steadily drive Hill's corps back. Even several decades later, Longstreet's frustration with Hill's corps was evident when explaining what happened in his memoirs:

"R. H. Anderson's division of the Third Corps, marching on the Plank road, had rested at Verdierville during the night, and was called to the front in the morning. The divisions of Heth and Wilcox rested during the night of the 5th where the battle of that day ceased, but did not prepare ammunition nor strengthen their lines for defence, because informed that they were to be relieved from the front. Both the division commanders claim that they were to be relieved, and that they were ordered not to intrench or replenish supplies. So it seems that they were all night within hearing of the voices of Hancock's men, not even reorganizing their lines so as to offer a front of battle! General Heth has stated that he proposed to arrange for battle, but was ordered to give his men rest. While Hancock was sending men to his advanced line during the night and intrenching there and on his second line, the Confederates were all night idle."

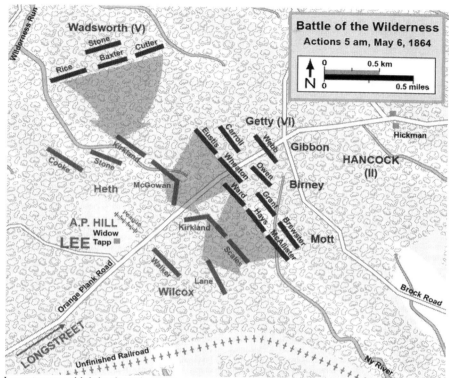

**Battle of the Wilderness**

Actions 5 am, May 6, 1864

Longstreet wouldn't be the only one frustrated. One of the reasons Meade had lobbied Grant to push back the time for Hancock's assault was concern that Burnside wouldn't be in position yet. While that convinced Grant to push back the attack to 5:00, that still wasn't enough time for Burnside's IX Corps to be in position, something that at least a few of his comrades anticipated. Lyman was ordered to ride over to Hancock and keep Meade and Grant informed of the attack's results, and he later recalled the morning attack:

"It was after five when I mounted, and already the spattering fire showed that the skirmishers were pushing out; as I rode down the crossroad, two or three crashing volleys rang through the woods, and then the whole front was alive with musketry. I found General Hancock at the crossing of the plank: he was wreathed with smiles. 'We are driving them, sir; tell General Meade we are driving them most beautifully. Birney has gone in and he is just cleaning them out be-au-ti-fully!' This was quite apparent from the distance of the receding firing and the absence of those infernal minie balls. 'I am ordered to tell you, sir, that only one division of General Burnside is up, but that he will go in as soon as he can be put in position.' Hancock's face changed. 'I knew it!' he said vehemently. 'Just what I expected. If he could attack now, we would smash A. P. Hill all to pieces!' And very true were his words. Meantime, some hundreds of prisoners were brought in; all from Hill's troops. Presently, however, the firing seemed to wake again with renewed fury; and in a little while a soldier came up to me and said: 'I was ordered to report that this prisoner here belongs to Longstreet's Corps.' 'Do you belong to Longstreet?' I hastened to ask. 'Ya-as, sir,' said grey-back, and was marched to the rear. It was too true!

Writing in his memoirs, Grant later expressed the belief that it was the Wilderness, not Longstreet, that would prove Hancock's undoing:

"I believed then, and see no reason to change that opinion now, that if the country had been such that Hancock and his command could have seen the confusion and panic in the lines of the enemy, it would have been taken advantage of so effectually that Lee would not have made another stand outside of his Richmond defences.

Gibbon commanded Hancock's left, and was ordered to attack, but was not able to accomplish much.

On the morning of the 6th Sheridan was sent to connect with Hancock's left and attack the enemy's cavalry who were trying to get on our left and rear. He met them at the intersection of the Furnace and Brock roads and at Todd's Tavern, and defeated them at both places. Later he was attacked, and again the enemy was repulsed.

Hancock heard the firing between Sheridan and Stuart, and thinking the enemy coming by that road, still further reinforced his position guarding the entrance to the Brock Road. Another incident happened during the day to further induce Hancock to weaken his attacking column. Word reached him that troops were seen moving towards him from the direction of Todd's Tavern, and Brooke's brigade was detached to meet this new enemy; but the troops approaching proved to be several hundred convalescents coming from Chancellorsville, by the road Hancock had advanced upon, to join their respective commands. At 6.50 o'clock A.M., Burnside, who had passed Wilderness Tavern at six o'clock, was ordered to send a division to the support of Hancock, but to continue with the remainder of his command in the execution of his previous order. The difficulty of making a way through the dense forests prevented Burnside from getting up in time to be of any service on the forenoon of the sixth."

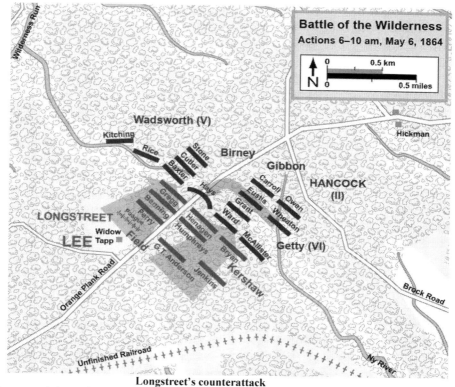

**Longstreet's counterattack**

Longstreet's late arrival meant Lee could not slide Hill's corps to the left, but it meant that his corps was in just the right place to blunt Hancock's assault and launch a fierce counterattack itself. As Longstreet's column came marching up, Lee was so excited that he began riding at the head of the column, acting as though he intended to lead the counterattack himself. Writing about the episode decades later, Longstreet quipped that if Lee was going to lead the charge, he'd like to move farther behind the lines to safety:

"Hancock advanced and struck the divisions before sunrise, just as my command reported to General Lee. My line was formed on the right and left of the Plank road, Kershaw on the right, Field on the left. As the line deployed, the divisions of Heth and Wilcox came back upon us in disorder, more and more confused as their steps hurried under Hancock's musketry. As my ranks formed the men broke files to give free passage for their comrades to the rear. The advancing fire was getting brisk, but not a shot was fired in return by my troops until the divisions were ready. Three of Field's brigades, the Texas, Alabama, and Benning's Georgia, were formed in line on the left of the road, and three of Kershaw's on the right. General Lee, appalled at the condition of affairs, thought to lead the Texas brigade alone into desperate charge, before my lines were well formed. The ordeal was trying, but the steady troops, seeing him off his balance, refused to follow, begged him to retire, and presently Colonel Venable, of his staff, reported to me General Lee's efforts to lead the brigade, and suggested that I should try to call him from it. I asked that he would say, with my compliments, that his line would be recovered in an hour if he would permit me to handle the troops, but if my services were not needed, I would like to ride to some place of safety, as it was not quite comfortable where we were."

Of course, Lee would not end up leading the charge, and he wouldn't need to. Longstreet has often been criticized for being reluctant to move, and slow when he did, but once he put his corps into action, he was one of the best generals the Civil War had. As one Confederate soldier put it, "Like a fine lady at a party, Longstreet was often late in his arrival at the ball. But he always made a sensation and that of delight, when he got in, with the grand old First Corps sweeping behind him as his train."

Longstreet's counterattack also had the advantage of coming at a time when the Union charge had progressed a mile and inevitably resulted in soldiers getting intermingled with other commands and unit cohesion becoming relatively impossible. The Wilderness also hid Longstreet's impending attack until his men were within just a few hundred yards, but it also caused Longstreet some difficulty as well. Longstreet explained, "As full lines of battle could not be handled through the thick wood, I ordered the advance of the six brigades by heavy skirmish lines, to be followed by stronger supporting lines. Hancock's lines, thinned by their push through the wood, and somewhat by the fire of the disordered divisions, weaker than my line of fresh and more lively skirmishers, were checked by our first steady, rolling fire, and after a brisk fusillade were pushed back to their intrenched line, when the fight became steady and very firm, occasionally swinging parts of my line back and compelling the reserves to move forward and recover it."

While the counterattack blunted Hancock's momentum and also kept some of the men from Burnside's IX Corps occupied, Longstreet had heard about an unfinished railroad bed south of the Plank Road that his troops might be able to travel through and come up on Hancock's left flank by surprise. When the four brigades traveled through the railroad cut and hit Hancock's left flank at 11:00, it completely rolled up Hancock's battle line. Hancock would later claim that his line was rolled up "like a wet blanket", but Longstreet's men were still advancing as Hancock's men retreated. Longstreet wrote:

"As soon as the troops struck Hancock his line began to break, first slowly, then rapidly. Somehow, as they retreated, a fire was accidentally started in the dry leaves, and began to spread as the Confederates advanced. Mahone's brigade approached the burning leaves and part of it broke off a little to get around, but the Twelfth Virginia was not obstructed by the blaze and moved directly on. At the Plank road Colonel Sorrel rode back to join us. All of the enemy's battle on the right of the Plank road was broken up, and General Field was fighting severely with his three brigades on the left against Wadsworth and Stevenson, pushing them a little.

General Smith then came and reported a way across the Brock road that would turn Hancock's extreme left. He was asked to conduct the flanking brigades and handle them as the ranking officer. He was a splendid tactician as well as skilful engineer, and gallant withal. He started, and, not to lose time or distance, moved by inversion, Wofford's left leading, Wofford's favorite manoeuvre. As Wofford's left stepped out, the other troops moved down the Plank road, Jenkins's brigade by the road, Kershaw's division alongside. I rode at the head of the column, Jenkins, Kershaw, and the staff with me. After discussing the dispositions of their troops for reopening battle, Jenkins rode closer to offer congratulations, saying, 'I am happy; I have felt despair of the cause for some months, but am relieved, and feel assured that we will put the enemy back across the Rapidan before night." Little did he or I think these sanguine words were the last he would utter.'"

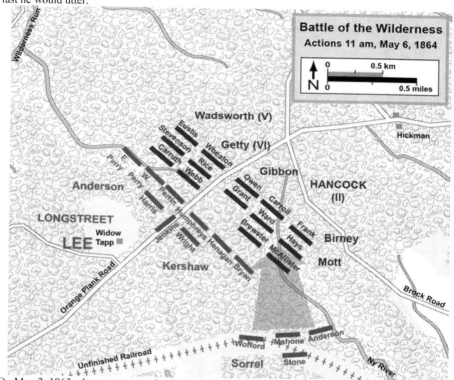

On May 2, 1863, almost a year to the day that the battle was raging in the Wilderness, Stonewall Jackson had been mortally wounded by his own men while leading a successful flank attack after being mistaken for advancing Union soldiers. On May 6, 1864, less than 5 miles to the west, Longstreet nearly suffered the same fate.

"As the Twelfth Regiment marched back to find its place on the other side of the Plank road, it was mistaken, in the wood, for an advance of the enemy, and fire was opened on it from the other regiments of the brigade. The men threw themselves to the ground to let the fire pass. Just then our party of officers was up and rode under the fire. General Jenkins had not finished the expressions of joyful congratulations which I have quoted when he fell mortally wounded.

Captain Doby and the orderly, Bowen, of Kershaw's staff, were killed. General

Kershaw turned to quiet the troops, when Jenkins's brigade with levelled guns were in the act of returning the fire of the supposed enemy concealed in the wood, but as Kershaw's clear voice called out 'F-r-i-e-n-d-s!' the arms were recovered, without a shot in return, and the men threw themselves down upon their faces.

At the moment that Jenkins fell I received a severe shock from a minie ball passing through my throat and right shoulder. The blow lifted me from the saddle, and my right arm dropped to my side, but I settled back to my seat, and started to ride on, when in a minute the flow of blood admonished me that my work for the day was done. As I turned to ride back, members of the staff, seeing me about to fall, dismounted and lifted me to the ground."

Longstreet's day was done, and so was his involvement in the Overland Campaign as a whole. He would have to spend the next 5 months convalescing and wouldn't return to Lee's army until October, several months into the siege of Petersburg. To say his loss at this juncture would be an understatement, something acknowledged by both sides. Grant claimed, "His loss was a severe one to Lee, and compensated in a great measure for the mishap, or misapprehensions, which had fallen to our lot during the day." The leader of the artillery in Longstreet's corps, Porter Alexander, went even further, arguing, "I have always believed that, but for Longstreet's fall, the panic which was fairly underway in Hancock's Corps would have been extended and have resulted in Grant's being forced to retreat back across the Rapidan."

The delays and confusion brought about by Longstreet's injury hampered the effectiveness of his counterattack. Richard Anderson succeeded him, but he was unfamiliar with the entire corps' dispositions and needed to try to confer with the grievously wounded Longstreet to get the information after the corps commander had been shot through the throat. Lee would also be forced to take a more active role on his right, personally directing the line.

How much of a difference Longstreet's loss made continues to be debated, but there's no question that Hancock's defensive line ultimately held because of the defensive fortifications his men had constructed the night before. Although the Confederates were able to get into their rifle pits, the II Corps eventually repulsed them, forcing Lee to take time to reform his lines and prepare another attack for later in the afternoon.

Grant later wrote in his memoirs, "After Longstreet's removal from the field Lee took command of his right in person. He was not able, however, to rally his men to attack Hancock's position, and withdrew from our front for the purpose of reforming. Hancock sent a brigade to clear his front of all remnants that might be left of Longstreet's or Hill's commands. This brigade having been formed at right angles to the intrenchments held by Hancock's command, swept down the whole length of them from left to right. A brigade of the enemy was encountered in this move; but it broke and disappeared without a contest...Firing was continued after this, but with less fury. Burnside had not yet been able to get up to render any assistance. But it was now only about nine in the morning, and he was getting into position on Hancock's right."

When Burnside arrived, Anderson had to swing part of Longstreet's corps to face that new threat, until the corps had practically formed at a right angle. Burnside's arrival and Hancock's defensive fortifications ensured that the Army of the Potomac's left would remain secure throughout the day.

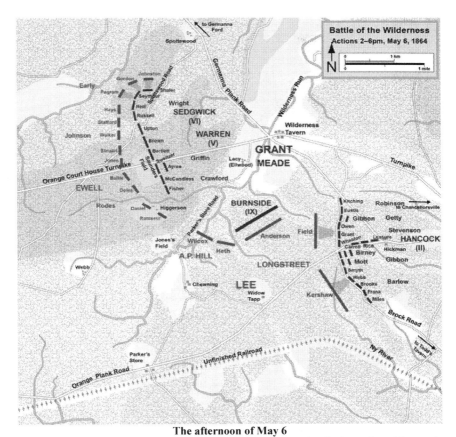

**The afternoon of May 6**

Grant's left flank had come close to disaster as a result of a surprise flank attack, and it turned out that his right would suffer nearly the same fate later in the day. While the fighting was going on south of them, John Gordon's scouts on the extreme left of the Confederate line reported the potential of turning Sedgwick's right flank. Gordon verified the situation for himself, and later wrote of his great surprise:

"THE night of the 5th of May was far spent when my command reached its destination on the extreme Confederate left. The men were directed to sleep on their arms during the remaining hours of darkness. Scouts were at once sent to the front to feel their way through the thickets and ascertain, if possible, where the extreme right of Grant's line rested. At early dawn these trusted men reported that they had found it: that it rested in the woods only a short distance in our front, that it was wholly unprotected, and that the Confederate lines stretched a considerable distance beyond the Union right, overlapping it. I was so impressed with the importance of this report and with the necessity of verifying its accuracy that I sent others to make the examination, with additional instructions to proceed to the rear of Grant's right and ascertain if the exposed flank were supported by troops held in reserve behind it. The former report was not only confirmed as to the exposed position of that flank, but the astounding information was brought that there was not a supporting force within several miles of it.

Much of this scouting had been done in the late hours of the night and before sunrise on the morning of the 6th. Meantime, as this information came my brain was throbbing with the tremendous possibilities to which such a situation invited us, provided the conditions were really as reported. Mounting my horse in the early morning and guided by some of these explorers, I rode into the unoccupied woodland to see for myself. It is enough to say that I found the reports correct in every particular. Riding back toward my line, I was guided by the scouts to the point near which they had located the right of the Union army. Dismounting and creeping slowly and cautiously through the dense woods, we were soon in ear-shot of an unsuppressed and merry clatter of voices. A few feet nearer, and through a narrow vista, I was shown the end of General Grant's temporary breastworks. There was no line guarding this flank. As far as my eye could reach, the Union soldiers were seated on the margin of the rifle-pits, taking their breakfast. Small fires were burning over which they were boiling their coffee, while their guns leaned against the works in their immediate front.

No more time was consumed in scouting. The revelations had amazed me and filled me with confident anticipations of unprecedented victory. It was evident that General Grant had decided to make his heaviest assaults upon the Confederate right, and for this purpose had ordered his reserves to that flank. By some inconceivable oversight on the part of his subordinates, his own right flank had been left in the extremely exposed condition in which my scouts had found it. Undoubtedly the officer who located that battle line for General Grant or for General Sedgwick was under the impression that there were no Confederates in front of that portion of it; and this was probably true at the time the location was made. That fact, however, did not justify the officer in leaving his flank (which is the most vulnerable part of an army) thus unguarded for a whole night after the battle…

During the night, while the over-confident Union officer and his men slept in fancied security, my men stole silently through the thickets and planted a hostile line not only in his immediate front, but overlapping it by more than the full length of my command. All intelligent military critics will certainly agree that such an opportunity as was here presented for the overthrow of a great army has rarely occurred in the conduct of a war."

Once he was certain of the Union line's situation, Gordon began forming the plan that he thought could destroy the entire Army of the Potomac:

"As later developments proved, one brigade on the flank was all that was needed for the inauguration of the plan and the demonstration upon its possibilities. The details of the plan were as follows: While the unsuspecting Federals were drinking their coffee, my troops were to move quickly and quietly behind the screen of thick underbrush and form squarely on Sedgwick's strangely exposed flank, reaching a point far beyond that flank and lapping around his rear, so as to capture his routed men as they broke to the rear. While my command rushed from this ambush a simultaneous demonstration was to be made along his front. As each of Sedgwick's brigades gave way in confusion, the corresponding Confederate brigade, whose front was thus cleared on the general line, was to swing into the column of attack on the flank, thus swelling at each step of our advance the numbers, power, and momentum of the Confederate forces as they swept down the line of works and extended another brigade's length to the unprotected Union rear. As each of the Union brigades, divisions, and corps were struck by such an absolutely resistless charge upon the flank and rear, they must fly or be captured. The effective force of Grant's army would be thus constantly diminished, and in the same proportion the column of attack would be steadily augmented."

Despite the fact Gordon had determined the state of Sedgwick's flank in the early morning hours of May 6, the flank attack did not start until the late afternoon. As Gordon anticipated, the flank attack was decisive from the very beginning:

"The Georgia brigade (Gordon's) was directed to make the assault, and the North Carolina brigade (Johnson's) was ordered to move farther to the Union rear and to keep as nearly as possible in touch with the attacking force and to gather up Sedgwick's men as they broke to the rear. As the sun went down these troops were ordered forward. In less than ten minutes they struck the Union flank and with thrilling yells rushed upon it and along the Union works, shattering regiments and brigades, and throwing them into wildest confusion and panic. There was practically no resistance. There could be none. The Georgians, commanded by that intrepid leader, Clement A. Evans, were on the flank, and the North Carolinians, led by a brilliant young officer, Robert Johnson, were sweeping around to the rear, without a shot in their front. There was nothing for the brave Federals to do but to fly. There was no time given them to file out from their works and form a new line of resistance. This was attempted again and again; but in every instance the swiftly moving Confederates were upon them, pouring a consuming fire into their half-formed ranks and shivering one command after another in quick succession. The gallant Union leaders, Generals Seymour and Shaler, rode among their panic-stricken troops in the heroic endeavor to form them into a new line. Their brave efforts were worse than unavailing, for both of these superb officers, with large numbers of their brigades, were quickly gathered as prisoners of war in the Confederate net; and nearly the whole of Sedgwick's corps was disorganized.

It will be seen that my troops were compelled to halt at last, not by the enemy's resistance, but solely by the darkness and the cross-fire from Confederates. Had daylight lasted one half-hour longer, there would not have been left an organized company in Sedgwick's corps. Even as it was, all accounts agree that his whole command was shaken. As I rode abreast of the Georgians, who were moving swiftly and with slight resistance, the last scene which met my eye as the curtain of night shut off the view was the crumbling of the Union lines as they bravely but vainly endeavored to file out of their works and form a new line under the furious onset and withering fire of the Confederates."

Gordon's flank attack on Sedgwick also led to one of Grant's most famous quotes of the war, as remembered by Union general Horace Porter. Porter recalled the scene at headquarters when Sedgwick's line began to unravel:

"It was now about sundown; the storm of battle which had raged with unabated fury from early dawn had been succeeded by a calm . . . . . Just then the stillness was broken by heavy volleys of musketry on our extreme right, which told that Sedgwick had been assaulted and was actually engaged with the enemy. The attack against which the general-in-chief during the day had ordered every precaution to be taken had now been made . . . . . Generals Grant and Meade, accompanied by me and one or two other staff officers, walked rapidly over to Meade's tent, and found that the reports still coming in were bringing news of increasing disaster. It was soon reported that General Shaler and part of his brigade had been captured; then that General Seymour and several hundred of his men had fallen into the hands of the enemy; afterward that our right had been turned, and Ferrero's division cut off and forced back upon the Rapidan . . . . . Aides came galloping in from the right, laboring under intense excitement, talking wildly and giving the most exaggerated reports of the engagement. Some declared that a large force had broken and scattered Sedgwick's entire corps. Others insisted that the enemy had turned our right completely and captured the wagon-train. . . . A general officer came in from his command at this juncture and said to the general-in-chief, speaking rapidly and laboring under considerable excitement:'General Grant, this is a crisis that cannot be looked upon too seriously; I know Lee's methods well by past experience; he will throw his whole army between us and the Rapidan and cut us off completely from our communications.'

The general rose to his feet, took his cigar out of his mouth, turned to the officer, and replied, with a degree of animation which he seldom manifested: 'Oh, I am heartily tired of hearing about what Lee is going to do. Some of you always seem to think he is suddenly going to turn a double somersault, and land in our rear and on both of our flanks at the same time. Go back to your command, and try to think what we are going to do ourselves, instead of what Lee is going to do.' The officer retired rather crestfallen, and without saying a word in reply. This recalls a very pertinent criticism regarding his chief once made in my presence by General Sherman. He said: 'Grant always seemed pretty certain to win when he went into a fight with anything like equal numbers. I believe the chief reason why he was more successful than others was that while they were thinking so much about what the enemy was going to do, Grant was thinking all the time about what he was going to do himself.'"

Ultimately, Gordon's flank attack was conducted too late in the day to achieve the result he had hoped for. It would have been difficult enough in the Wilderness to conduct such an attack during the day, but with night falling and reinforcements brought up, Gordon's flank attack ultimately lost its momentum.

While Gordon obviously gave a rosy projection of what his flank attack could have achieved, the real historical question is why there was a delay of nearly 9 hours before the attack started. Gordon later blamed Ewell and his division commander, Jubal Early:

"When the plan for assault was fully matured, it was presented, with all its tremendous possibilities and with the full information which had been acquired by scouts and by my own personal and exhaustive examination. With all the earnestness that comes from deep conviction, the prompt adoption and vigorous execution of the plan were asked and urged. General Early at once opposed it. He said that Burnside's corps was immediately behind Sedgwick's right to protect it from any such flank attack; that if I should attempt such movement, Burnside would assail my flank and rout or capture all my men. He was so firmly fixed in his belief that Burnside's corps was where he declared it to be that he was not perceptibly affected by the repeated reports of scouts, nor my own statement that I myself had ridden for miles in rear of Sedgwick's right, and that neither Burnside's corps nor any other troops were there.

General Ewell, whose province it was to decide the controversy, hesitated. He was naturally reluctant to take issue with my superior officer in a matter about which he could have no personal knowledge, because of the fact that his headquarters as corps-commander were located at considerable distance from this immediate locality. In view of General Early's protest, he was unwilling to order the attack or to grant me permission to make it, even upon my proposing to assume all responsibility of disaster, should any occur."

Early explained why he was hesitant to support making the flank attack in his own memoirs, and why the attack was made when it was:

"In the meantime General Gordon had sent out a scouting party on foot, which discovered what was supposed to be the enemy's right flank resting in the woods, in front of my division; and, during my absence while posting Johnston's brigade, he reported the fact to General Ewell, and suggested the propriety of attacking this flank of the enemy with his brigade, which was not engaged. On my return, the subject was mentioned to me by General Ewell, and I stated to him the danger and risk of making the attack under the circumstances, as a column was threatening our left flank and Burnside's corps was in rear of the enemy's flank, on which the attack was suggested. General Ewell concurred with me in this opinion, and the impolicy of the attempt at that time was obvious, as we had no reserves, and, if it failed, and the enemy showed any enterprise, a serious disaster would befall, not only our corps, but General Lee's whole army. In the afternoon, when the column threatening our left had been withdrawn, and it had been ascertained that Burnside had gone to Grant's left, on account of the heavy fighting on that flank, at my suggestion, General Ewell ordered the movement which Gordon had proposed…

Gordon succeeded in throwing the enemy's right flank into great confusion, capturing two brigadier generals (Seymour and Shaler), and several hundred prisoners, all of the 6th corps, under Sedgwick. The advance of Pegram's brigade, and the demonstration of Johnston's brigade in the rear, where it encountered a part of the enemy's force and captured some prisoners, contributed materially to the result. It was fortunate, however, that darkness came to close this affair, as the enemy, if he had been able to discover the disorder on our side, might have brought up fresh troops and availed himself of our condition. As it was, doubtless, the lateness of the hour caused him to be surprised, and the approaching darkness increased the confusion in his ranks, as he could not see the strength of the attacking force, and probably imagined it to be much more formidable than it really was. All of the brigades engaged in the attack were drawn back, and formed on a new line in front of the old one, and obliquely to it."

While Early may have been accurate in the belief that Burnside was behind Sedgwick early in the morning of May 6, it's also true that Burnside had been given orders to march further south and post himself on Sedgwick's left and Hancock's right. For his part, Grant pointed to the fact that he was sending reinforcements in his memoirs and also cited Early's memoirs, writing, "The defence, however, was vigorous; and night coming on, the enemy was thrown into as much confusion as our troops, engaged, were. Early says in his Memoirs that if we had discovered the confusion in his lines we might have brought fresh troops to his great discomfort. Many officers, who had not been attacked by Early, continued coming to my headquarters even after Sedgwick had rectified his lines a little farther to the rear, with news of the disaster, fully impressed with the idea that the enemy was pushing on and would soon be upon me."

Regardless, Gordon's attack brought an end to the fighting. On May 7, with the two armies in the same lines staring each other down, Grant issued marching orders to his army, beginning the process of delicately pulling out of his defensive lines in the face of Lee's army. The two days had produced nearly 30,000 casualties, with over 17,000 Union soldiers killed, wounded or captured and over 11,000 Confederates suffering the same fate.

## The Campaign Continues

The battle was over, but who had won it? Grant would later call the Battle of the Wilderness a Union victory, writing, "Our victory consisted in having successfully crossed a formidable stream, almost in the face of an enemy, and in getting the army together as a unit. We gained an advantage on the morning of the 6th, which, if it had been followed up, must have proven very decisive. In the evening the enemy gained an advantage; but was speedily repulsed. As we stood at the close, the two armies were relatively in about the same condition to meet each other as when the river divided them. But the fact of having safely crossed was a victory."

Naturally, Lee saw it from a different perspective, telling Richmond at the end of May 6, " Early this morning as the divisions of General Hill, engaged yesterday, were being relieved, the enemy advanced and created some confusion. The ground lost was recovered as soon as the fresh troops got into position and the enemy driven back to his original line. Afterward we turned the left of his front line and drove it from the field, leaving a large number of dead and wounded in our hands, among them General Wadsworth. A subsequent attack forced the enemy into his intrenched lines on the Brock road, extending from Wilderness Tavern, on the right, to Trigg's Mill. Every advance on his part, thanks to a merciful God, has been repulsed. Our loss in killed is not large, but we have many wounded; most of them slightly, artillery being little used on either side. I grieve to announce that Lieutenant-General Longstreet was severely wounded and General Jenkins killed. General Pegram was badly wounded yesterday. General Stafford, it is hoped, will recover."

Both sides claimed victory, but who was right? In a sense, they were both right and wrong. For the third straight year, Lee's army had successfully defended an advance toward Richmond by the Army of the Potomac and inflicted more casualties upon them. Moreover, it would be Grant who disengaged from the battle and left the field to Lee. But while these suggest the Confederates had won a tactical victory, the Battle of the Wilderness would not be a strategic victory because it would not end Grant's campaign.

Although Grant had suffered more casualties, he and Lee had both lost about 17% of their armies. This worked in Grant's favor not only because his army remained much larger than Lee's but also because he could replenish his manpower much more easily. While the casualties would astound and mortify the American public, it was all part of Grant's plan to grind down the Army of Northern Virginia until it could put up no resistance. This was evident to Lee, who became increasingly more desperate to score some kind of dramatic victory that would destroy the Army of the Potomac later in the Overland Campaign.

Ultimately, if there's any legacy to come out of the Battle of the Wilderness, or any way in which it was a turning point, it was enshrined in Grant's official orders on May 7.

"Make all preparations during the day for a night march to take position at Spottsylvania C. H. with one army corps, at Todd's Tavern with one, and another near the intersection of the Piney Branch and Spottsylvania road with the road from Alsop's to Old Court House. If this move is made the trains should be thrown forward early in the morning to the Ny River.

I think it would be advisable in making the change to leave Hancock where he is until

Warren passes him. He could then follow and become the right of the new line. Burnside will move to Piney Branch Church. Sedgwick can move along the pike to Chancellorsville and on to his destination. Burnside will move on the plank road to the intersection of it with the Orange and Fredericksburg plank road, then follow Sedgwick to his place of destination.

All vehicles should be got out of hearing of the enemy before the troops move, and then move off quietly.

It is more than probable that the enemy concentrate for a heavy attack on Hancock this afternoon. In case they do we must be prepared to resist them, and follow up any success we may gain, with our whole force. Such a result would necessarily modify these instructions."

Unlike McClellan, Burnside and Hooker before him, Grant's orders directed the Army of the Potomac to continue heading south. The Battle of the Wilderness had only been a beginning, not an ending. As Grant would famously telegraph Washington, D.C. a few days later, "I propose to fight it out on this line, if it takes all summer."

If the Battle of the Wilderness had been a Confederate victory, that was an opinion lost on Grant's men when they learned the new marching orders. Grant himself would recount one such scene as he put his army into motion on May 7:

"Soon after dark Warren withdrew from the front of the enemy, and was soon followed by Sedgwick. Warren's march carried him immediately behind the works where Hancock's command lay on the Brock Road. With my staff and a small escort of cavalry I preceded the troops. Meade with his staff accompanied me. The greatest enthusiasm was manifested by Hancock's men as we passed by. No doubt it was inspired by the fact that the movement was south. It indicated to them that they had passed through the 'beginning of the end' in the battle just fought. The cheering was so lusty that the enemy must have taken it for a night attack. At all events it drew from him a furious fusillade of artillery and musketry, plainly heard but not felt by us."

With that, Grant began marching his army toward Spotsylvania Court House, the area he had hoped to reach before fighting Lee in a pitched battle. Things hadn't gone according to plan in the Wilderness, but Grant and Lee would have their battle at Spotsylvania soon enough.

### Racing to Spotsylvania

When Grant ordered Meade on the night of May 7 to have the Army of the Potomac march to Spotsylvania Court House, he did so for several reasons. In addition to disengaging from Lee at the Wilderness and bring him out into the open, Grant hoped that swift marching might get his army inbetween Lee and Richmond, which would make the Confederates even more desperate. But there was also another reason, as Grant noted in his memoirs:

"On the afternoon of the 7th I received news from Washington announcing that Sherman had probably attacked Johnston that day, and that Butler had reached City Point safely and taken it by surprise on the 5th. I had given orders for a movement by the left flank, fearing that Lee might move rapidly to Richmond to crush Butler before I could get there.

My object in moving to Spottsylvania was two-fold: first, I did not want Lee to get back to Richmond in time to attempt to crush Butler before I could get there; second, I wanted to get between his army and Richmond if possible; and, if not, to draw him into the open field. But Lee, by accident, beat us to Spottsylvania. Our wagon trains had been ordered easterly of the roads the troops were to march upon before the movement commenced. Lee interpreted this as a semi-retreat of the Army of the Potomac to Fredericksburg, and so informed his government. Accordingly he ordered Longstreet's corps—now commanded by Anderson—to move in the morning (the 8th) to Spottsylvania. But the woods being still on fire, Anderson could not go into bivouac, and marched directly on to his destination that night. By this accident Lee got possession of Spottsylvania. It is impossible to say now what would have been the result if Lee's orders had been obeyed as given; but it is certain that we would have been in Spottsylvania, and between him and his capital. My belief is that there would have been a race between the two armies to see which could reach Richmond first, and the Army of the Potomac would have had the shorter line. Thus, twice since crossing the Rapidan we came near closing the campaign, so far as battles were concerned, from the Rapidan to the James River or Richmond. The first failure was caused by our not following up the success gained over Hill's corps on the morning of the 6th, as before described: the second, when fires caused by that battle drove Anderson to make a march during the night of the 7th-8th which he was ordered to commence on the morning of the 8th. But accident often decides the fate of battle."

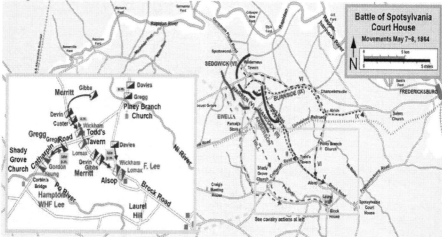

Grant's route to Spotsylvania Court House had been opened by Phil Sheridan's cavalry in the days before, due to the fact that Grant had initially intended to march there before engaging in battle. Sheridan's cavalry had been holding important spots, including crossings of the Ny and Po Rivers, in anticipation of that movement, but when Hancock's left was turned by Longstreet's corps on May 6, the cavalry had been hurried back north. As a result, when Grant issued the orders to march toward Spotsylvania on May 7, it was once again incumbent on the Union cavalry to ride to those spots and hold them for the infantry advance. Sheridan explained in his memoirs:

"On the 7th of May, under directions from headquarters, Army of the Potomac, the trains were put in motion to go into park at Piney Branch Church, in anticipation of the movement that was about to be made for the possession of Spotsylvania Court House. I felt confident that the order to move the trains there had been given without a full understanding of the situation, for Piney Branch Church was now held by the enemy, a condition which had resulted from the order withdrawing the cavalry on account of the supposed disaster to Hancock's left the day before; but I thought the best way to remedy matters was to hold the trains in the vicinity of Aldrich's till the ground on which it was intended to park them should be regained.

This led to the battle of Todd's Tavern, a spirited fight for the possession of the crossroads at that point, participated in by the enemy's cavalry and Gregg's division, and two brigades of Torbert's division, the latter commanded by Merritt, as Torbert became very ill on the 6th, and had to be sent to the rear. To gain the objective point — the crossroads — I directed Gregg to assail the enemy on the Catharpen road with Irvin Gregg's brigade and drive him over Corbin's bridge, while Merritt attacked him with the Reserve brigade on the Spottsylvania road in conjunction with Davies's brigade of Gregg's division, which was to be put in on the Piney Branch Church road, and unite with Merritt's left. Davies's and Irvin Gregg's brigades on my right and left flanks met with some resistance, yet not enough to deter them from executing their orders. In front of Merritt the enemy held on more stubbornly, however, and there ensued an exceedingly severe and, at times, fluctuating fight. Finally the Confederates gave way, and we pursued them almost to Spottsylvania Court House; but deeming it prudent to recall the pursuers about dark, I encamped Gregg's and Merritt's divisions in the open fields to the east of Todd's Tavern."

As previously noted by Grant in his memoirs, the Confederates were not idle on May 7. The movements of the Union Army's logistics train had suggested to him that Grant was either moving east toward Fredericksburg or south toward Spotsylvania. Either way, Lee needed to hold the crossroads at Spotsylvania, so he gave orders to Richard Anderson's corps to occupy Spotsylvania Court House on May 8. Luckily for the Confederates, however, the desperate fighting of the 6th by that corps had sparked fires in the area of the fighting, and the putrid smells of the burning and death compelled Anderson and his soldiers to go ahead and march to Spotsylvania that night, rather than try to bivouac near the burning and dying. By 10:00 p.m., Anderson's corps was on the march toward Spotsylvania.

The same fires that had compelled the Confederates to march that night were also causing logistical problems for the Army of the Potomac's movement. In addition to the inevitable traffic jams on the roads, the Union's unfamiliarity with the area caused fits and starts, as Grant mentioned in his memoirs:

"Meade and I rode in advance. We had passed but a little way beyond our left when the road forked. We looked to see, if we could, which road Sheridan had taken with his cavalry during the day. It seemed to be the right-hand one, and accordingly we took it. We had not gone far, however, when Colonel C. B. Comstock, of my staff, with the instinct of the engineer, suspecting that we were on a road that would lead us into the lines of the enemy, if he, too, should be moving, dashed by at a rapid gallop and all alone. In a few minutes he returned and reported that Lee was moving, and that the road we were on would bring us into his lines in a short distance. We returned to the forks of the road, left a man to indicate the right road to the head of Warren's column when it should come up, and continued our journey to Todd's Tavern, where we arrived after midnight."

While the infantry struggled to get underway in the right direction, the poor relationship between Meade and Sheridan played an important role on the night of the 7th. After Sheridan's cavalry had taken up their posts to hold the necessary ground for the infantry, Meade lost his temper when he and Grant arrived near Todd's Tavern and found Sheridan's cavalry troopers sleeping near their posts. At that point, Meade ordered part of Sheridan's cavalry to help clear the road for the infantry's march, which incensed Sheridan. Sheridan later claimed that this decision prevented his cavalry from blocking the Confederates at Spotsylvania, writing:

"Had Gregg and Merritt been permitted to proceed as they were originally instructed, it is doubtful whether the battles fought at Spottsylvania would have occurred, for these two divisions would have encountered the enemy at the Po River, and so delayed his march as to enable our infantry to reach Spottsylvania first, and thus force Lee to take up a line behind the Po. I had directed Wilson to move from the left by 'the Gate' through Spottsylvania to Snell's bridge, while Gregg and Merritt were to advance to the same point by Shady Grove and the Block House. There was nothing to prevent at least a partial success of these operations; that is to say, the concentration of the three divisions in front of Snell's bridge, even if we could not actually have gained it. But both that important point and the bridge on the Block House road were utterly ignored, and Lee's approach to Spottsylvania left entirely unobstructed, while three divisions of cavalry remained practically ineffective by reason of disjointed and irregular instructions.

On the morning of the 8th, when I found that such orders had been given, I made some strong remonstrances against the course that had been pursued, but it was then too late to carry out the combinations I had projected the night before, so I proceeded to join Merritt on the Spottsylvania road. On reaching Merritt I found General Warren making complaint that the cavalry were obstructing his column, so I drew Merritt off the road, and the leading division of the Fifth Corps pushed up to the front. It got into line about 11 o'clock, and advanced to take the village, but it did not go very far before it struck Anderson's corps, and was hurled back with heavy loss. This ended all endeavor to take Spottsylvania that day."

As Sheridan's account indicates, Anderson's corps eventually forced the advanced elements of his cavalry to fall back up the road. At the same time, it's unclear whether Sheridan's two divisions of cavalry could have held off an entire Confederate corps of infantry long enough for Warren's V Corps to beat Anderson's corps to the spot. For his part, Grant later insisted it would have been likely, writing, "Wilson, who was ordered to seize the town, did so, with his division of cavalry; but he could not hold it against the Confederate corps which had not been detained at the crossing of the Po, as it would have been but for the unfortunate change in Merritt's orders. Had he been permitted to execute the orders Sheridan gave him, he would have been guarding with two brigades of cavalry the bridge over the Po River which Anderson had to cross, and must have detained him long enough to enable Warren to reinforce Wilson and hold the town."

If Grant was going to occupy Spotsylvania, he now needed to dislodge Anderson's corps or destroy it on May 8 before the rest of the Confederate army joined him.

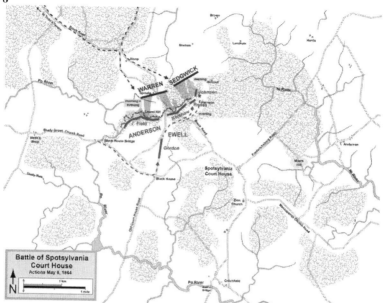

As soon as the sun came up on May 8, the Union cavalry busied itself trying to break through the Confederate defenses on Brock Road just north of Spotsylvania. If Sheridan's cavalry could dislodge the Confederates there, it would prevent the rest of the Confederate army from being able to march northeast toward Spotsylvania along the Old Court House Road, which would have required Lee's army to fall back several miles south to the next natural defensive line along the Po River. While Wesley Merritt's division skirmished with Fitzhugh Lee's Confederate cavalry on the Brock Road, Anderson's corps and Warren's corps marched toward the action, both intending to hold Brock Road for their respective armies.

While Fitzhugh Lee's cavalry fought a delaying action around the Alsop farm, two brigades from Anderson's corps marched north to arrive at Laurel Hill, just south of the farm. As those men pulled into position on the ridge of Laurel Hill, they spotted men from Warren's V Corps just 100 yards away.

Warren was operating under the assumption that the men he saw on Laurel Hill were just Confederate cavalry, unaware that an entire corps of Confederate infantry was in the vicinity. While Warren's men prepared for that assault, Joseph Kershaw's division of Anderson's corps was clearing away a brigade of Union cavalry south of Laurel Hill, ensuring that the rear was safe and then allowing the rest of Anderson's corps to march up to the impromptu line at Laurel Hill. Perhaps due to his incorrect belief that he was only dealing with a small number of Confederate cavalry, Warren's initial attacks consisted of piecemeal maneuvers by separate divisions. Grant discussed the morning fighting in his memoirs, as well as a candid appraisal of Warren, whose strengths as an engineer led to frequent criticism that he was too slow and cautious as an infantry corps commander:

"Anderson soon intrenched himself—if indeed the intrenchments were not already made—immediately across Warren's front. Warren was not aware of his presence, but probably supposed it was the cavalry which Merritt had engaged earlier in the day. He assaulted at once, but was repulsed. He soon organized his men, as they were not pursued by the enemy, and made a second attack, this time with his whole corps. This time he succeeded in gaining a position immediately in the enemy's front, where he intrenched. His right and left divisions—the former Crawford's, the latter Wadsworth's, now commanded by Cutler—drove the enemy back some distance.

At this time my headquarters had been advanced to Piney Branch Church. I was anxious to crush Anderson before Lee could get a force to his support. To this end Sedgwick who was at Piney Branch Church, was ordered to Warren's support. Hancock, who was at Todd's Tavern, was notified of Warren's engagement, and was directed to be in readiness to come up. Burnside, who was with the wagon trains at Aldrich's on our extreme left, received the same instructions. Sedgwick was slow in getting up for some reason—probably unavoidable, because he was never at fault when serious work was to be done—so that it was near night before the combined forces were ready to attack. Even then all of Sedgwick's command did not get into the engagement. Warren led the last assault, one division at a time, and of course it failed.

Warren's difficulty was twofold: when he received an order to do anything, it would at once occur to his mind how all the balance of the army should be engaged so as properly to co-operate with him. His ideas were generally good, but he would forget that the person giving him orders had thought of others at the time he had of him. In like manner, when he did get ready to execute an order, after giving most intelligent instructions to division commanders, he would go in with one division, holding the others in reserve until he could superintend their movements in person also, forgetting that division commanders could execute an order without his presence. His difficulty was constitutional and beyond his control. He was an officer of superior ability, quick perceptions, and personal courage to accomplish anything that could be done with a small command."

**Gouverneur Warren**

While Warren was miscalculating the force in his front, the confusion of the marches and the armies' relative dispositions led to an encounter further north at the intersection of Brock Road and Catharpin Road, where a division of Jubal Early's corps encountered Winfield Scott Hancock's II Corps protecting the rear of the Union army. The aggressive Early tested Barlow's division of Hancock's corps but ultimately chose not to test the rearguard. Grant took this as evidence that Lee was unaware of Grant's intentions and movements, and that Anderson's arrival at Spotsylvania had thus been by chance, not due to Lee's skill: "Lee had ordered Hill's corps—now commanded by Early—to move by the very road we had marched upon. This shows that even early in the morning of the 8th Lee had not yet become acquainted with my move, but still thought that the Army of the Potomac had gone to Fredericksburg. Indeed, he informed the authorities at Richmond he had possession of Spotsylvania and was on my flank. Anderson was in possession of Spottsylvania, through no foresight of Lee, however. Early only found that he had been following us when he ran against Hancock at Todd's Tavern. His coming detained Hancock from the battle-field of Spottsylvania for that day; but he, in like manner, kept Early back and forced him to move by another route."

As a result of Warren's inability to push Anderson's men at Laurel Hill, men from Ewell's corps were able to slide into the line to the right of Anderson before John Sedgwick's VI Corps was in position on Warren's left. The two Union corps attempted a coordinated assault on the night of May 8, with Warren finally willing to put in all his men, but by then they were surprised to find Ewell's men in position and the assault was quickly and sharply repulsed.

May 8 had not been a good day for the Union. Delays in their marches and countermanded cavalry orders had let Anderson occupy the crossroads at Spotsylvania in force, Warren's inability to initially beat back two brigades on Laurel Hill allowed those defenders to allow two whole corps to take up positions there, and Sedgwick's inability to get up quickly enough prevented the Union from launching a decisive assault that night. Grant wrote about what he may have been able to do differently that day in his memoirs, both noting that he was still not familiar enough with the army's corps commanders and weighing the risks and rewards:

"Had I ordered the movement for the night of the 7th by my left flank, it would have put Hancock in the lead. It would also have given us an hour or earlier start. It took all that time for Warren to get the head of his column to the left of Hancock after he had got his troops out of their line confronting the enemy. This hour, and Hancock's capacity to use his whole force when necessary, would, no doubt, have enabled him to crush Anderson before he could be reinforced. But the movement made was tactical. It kept the troops in mass against a possible assault by the enemy. Our left occupied its intrenchments while the two corps to the right passed. If an attack had been made by the enemy he would have found the 2d corps in position, fortified, and, practically, the 5th and 6th corps in position as reserves, until his entire front was passed. By a left flank movement the army would have been scattered while still passing the front of the enemy, and before the extreme right had got by it would have been very much exposed. Then, too, I had not yet learned the special qualifications of the different corps commanders. At that time my judgment was that Warren was the man I would suggest to succeed Meade should anything happen to that gallant soldier to take him from the field. As I have before said, Warren was a gallant soldier, an able man; and he was beside thoroughly imbued with the solemnity and importance of the duty he had to perform."

Meanwhile, Meade was in his notorious "snapping turtle" mode, with his short temper long gone by the end of the day. He was irate at Warren's caution, Sedgwick's slowness, and Sheridan's command of the cavalry, over which they had serious philosophical differences of opinion. Meade preferred having his cavalry perform traditional duties like screening army movements and reconnaissance, but Sheridan was a soldier who had previously commanded infantry and spoiled for a fight. Sheridan explained the roots of the friction between the two of them in his memoirs:

"Before and at the review I took in this situation, and determined to remedy it if possible; so in due time I sought an interview with General Meade and informed him that, as the effectiveness of my command rested mainly on the strength of its horses, I thought the duty it was then performing was both burdensome and wasteful. I also gave him my idea as to what the cavalry should do, the main purport of which was that it ought to be kept concentrated to fight the enemy's cavalry. Heretofore, the commander of the Cavalry Corps had been, virtually, but an adjunct at army headquarters — a sort of chief of cavalry-and my proposition seemed to stagger General Meade not a little. I knew that it would be difficult to overcome the recognized custom of using the cavalry for the protection of trains and the establishment of cordons around the infantry corps, and so far subordinating its operations to the movements of the main army that in name only was it a corps at all, but still I thought it my duty to try.

At first General Meade would hardly listen to my proposition, for he was filled with the prejudices that, from the beginning of the war, had pervaded the army regarding the importance and usefulness of cavalry, General Scott then predicting that the contest would be settled by artillery, and thereafter refusing the services of regiment after regiment of mounted troops. General Meade deemed cavalry fit for little more than guard and picket duty, and wanted to know what would protect the transportation trains and artillery reserve, cover the front of moving infantry columns, and secure his flanks from intrusion, if my policy were pursued. I told him that if he would let me use the cavalry as I contemplated, he need have little solicitude in these respects, for, with a mass of ten thousand mounted men, it was my belief that I could make [194] it so lively for the enemy's cavalry that, so far as attacks from it were concerned, the flanks and rear of the Army of the Potomac would require little or no defense, and claimed, further, that moving columns of infantry should take care of their own fronts. I also told him that it was my object to defeat the enemy's cavalry in a general combat, if possible, and by such a result establish a feeling of confidence in my own troops that would enable us after a while to march where we pleased, for the purpose of breaking General Lee's communications and destroying the resources from which his army was supplied.

The idea as here outlined was contrary to Meade's convictions, for though at different times since he commanded the Army of the Potomac considerable bodies of the cavalry had been massed for some special occasion, yet he had never agreed to the plan as a permanency, and could not be bent to it now. He gave little encouragement, therefore, to what I proposed, yet the conversation was immediately beneficial in one way, for when I laid before him the true condition of the cavalry, he promptly relieved it from much of the arduous and harassing picket service it was performing, thus giving me about two weeks in which to nurse the horses before the campaign opened.

The interview also disclosed the fact that the cavalry commander should be, according to General Meade's views, at his headquarters practically as one of his staff, through whom he would give detailed directions as, in his judgment, occasion required. Meade's ideas and mine being so widely divergent, disagreements arose between us later during the battles of the Wilderness, which lack of concord ended in some concessions on his part after the movement toward Spottsylvania Court House began, and although I doubt that his convictions were ever wholly changed, yet from that date on, in the organization of the Army of the Potomac, the cavalry corps became more of a compact body, with the same privileges and responsibilities that attached to the other corps-conditions that never actually existed before."

On the night of May 8, Meade and Sheridan continued arguing over the use of cavalry, when Sheridan suggested that his cavalry be massed and allowed to find and engage JEB Stuart's cavalry in mass. While Meade was against it, Grant held his former Western subordinate in higher regard and acceded to Sheridan's request, stating, "Well, he generally knows what he is talking about. Let him start right out and do it." As a result, Sheridan's entire force of 10,000 cavalry left the Army of the Potomac and would end up missing the most important fighting of the battle on May 12. Although they fought Stuart's cavalry at the Battle of Yellow Tavern on May 11 and mortally wounded the iconic Confederate cavalry chieftain in the process, most modern historians have since sided with Meade's side of the argument, with Overland Campaign historian Gordon Rhea going so far as to write, "In the larger picture, Sheridan's raid proved to be a costly mistake. Chasing Stuart was another side show for the campaign, which would be decided by what the armies did at Spotsylvania. By abandoning the main theater of conflict to pursue his whimsical raid south, Sheridan deprived Grant of an important resource. His victory at Yellow Tavern offered scant solace to the blue-clad soldiers hunkering in trenches above the courthouse town. Sheridan's absence hurt Grant at Spotsylvania in much the same way that Stuart's absence from Gettysburg had handicapped Lee."

## Digging In

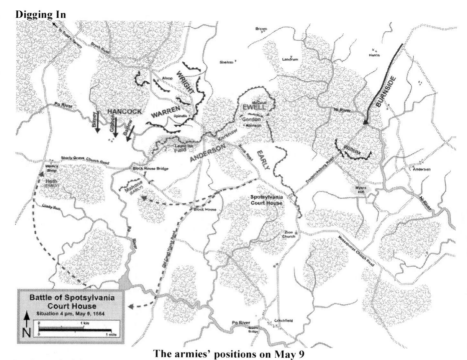

**The armies' positions on May 9**

By the end of the war, the Civil War had become a forerunner to the trench warfare of World War I, and if an army was given 24 hours to entrench, their position became practically unassailable. Grant described the process in his memoirs:

"[I]n every change of position or halt for the night, whether confronting the enemy or not, the moment arms were stacked the men intrenched themselves. For this purpose they would build up piles of logs or rails if they could be found in their front, and dig a ditch, throwing the dirt forward on the timber. Thus the digging they did counted in making a depression to stand in, and increased the elevation in front of them. It was wonderful how quickly they could in this way construct defences of considerable strength. When a halt was made with the view of assaulting the enemy, or in his presence, these would be strengthened or their positions changed under the direction of engineer officers."

Thus, the Army of the Potomac's inability to clear Brock Road on May 8 allowed the Confederates to begin the process of digging in, a crucial advantage. By the end of the Civil War, some generals who fought in it had come to believe that a well-entrenched defensive line could only be taken if there were 4 times as many attackers as defenders. John Gordon, who led a brigade in Early's corps, discussed the nature of the line as the Confederates dug in on the night of May 8:

"As the heads of the columns collided, the armies quickly spread into zigzag formation as each brigade, division, or corps struck its counterpart in the opposing lines. These haphazard collisions, however, rapidly developed a more orderly alignment and systematic battle, which culminated in that unparalleled struggle for the possession of a short line of Lee's breastworks. I say unparalleled, because the character of the fighting, its duration, and the individual heroism exhibited have no precedent, so far as my knowledge extends, in our Civil War, or in any other war.

During these preliminary and somewhat random engagements, General Lee, in order to secure the most advantageous locality offered by the peculiar topography of the country, had placed his battle line so that it should conform in large measure to the undulations of the field. Along the brow of these slopes earthworks were speedily constructed. On one portion of the line, which embraced what was afterward known as the 'Bloody Angle,' there was a long stretch of breastworks forming almost a complete semicircle. Its most advanced or outer salient was the point against which Hancock made his famous charge.

My command had been withdrawn from position in the regular line, and a role was assigned me which no officer could covet if he had the least conception of the responsibilities involved. I was ordered to take position in rear of that salient, and as nearly equidistant as practicable from every point of the wide and threatened semicircle, to watch every part of it, to move quickly, without waiting for orders, to the support of any point that might be assaulted, and to restore, if possible, any breach that might be made. We were reserves to no one command, but to all commands occupying that entire stretch of works. It will be seen that, with no possibility of knowing when or where General Grant would make his next effort to penetrate our lines, the task to be performed by my troops was not an easy one, and that the tension upon the brain and nerves of one upon whom rested the responsibility was not light nor conducive to sleep."

As the Confederates dug in, they were well aware that a salient was being created in the line at the Mule Shoe, which jutted out nearly a mile in front of the rest of their defensive line. Civil War armies always tried to avoid creating a salient in the line because it allowed the salient to be attacked in multiple directions. In this case, despite the fact the Mule Shoe was a salient, the Confederates dug in there to hold onto the nearest high ground in the area, hoping to prevent Union soldiers from occupying it and disrupting the rest of their line.

At the same time, the Army of the Potomac began digging in and erecting earthworks along their own lines, just as aware of their importance. With that, the two armies hunkered down into the kind of trench warfare that would've seemed foreign to the soldiers and generals in 1861. With sharpshooters among the lines, which were about half a mile away from each other, soldiers were afraid to even show their heads above their trenches for fear of being sniped.

While this process was going on during the morning of May 9, Union VI Corps commander John Sedgwick was placing his artillery and directing the men in his line when scattered shots from snipers started coming in from several hundred yards away. The soldiers in his corps had been harassed by the sharpshooters all morning, and one bullet had already knocked one of Sedgwick's brigadier-generals off his horse. Nevertheless, Sedgwick projected calm as he went about his business, even acting amused when some of his staff joined the soldiers in taking cover. Sedgwick mocked them, "What? Men dodging this way for single bullets? What will you do when they open fire along the whole line? I am ashamed of you. They couldn't hit an elephant at this distance." After one bullet whizzed by, one of his soldiers told Sedgwick that he had already nearly had his own head taken off by an artillery shell, to which Sedgwick reassured him and told him to stay in his position. His men would note that Sedgwick kept repeating, "I'm ashamed of you, dodging that way. They couldn't hit an elephant at this distance."

**Sedgwick**

Just then, another shot whizzed through the air, the unmistakable sound of a bullet fired by a .451 caliber Whitworth rifle. But this one found a mark, as noted by one of the soldiers in the vicinity, Lieutenant Colonel Martin McMahon, who wrote, "For the third time the same shrill whistle, closing with a dull, heavy stroke." Far from being unable to hit an elephant, a Confederate sharpshooter had just hit Sedgwick right in the face, killing him almost instantly. McMahon would later note that as he tried to catch Sedgwick from falling, blood spurted out just below his left eye, and that Sedgwick died so quickly that he still had a smile on his face.

Sedgwick was the highest ranking Union officer to die during the war (though James McPherson died while commanding an army during Sherman's Atlanta campaign that same year). When news reached Grant's headquarters, Grant was so shocked that he repeatedly asked, "Is he really dead?" Grant later wrote, "His loss was a severe one to the Army of the Potomac and to the Nation. General H. G. Wright succeeded him in the command of his corps." According to Grant's aide, Horace Porter, the grief-stricken Grant was telling those around him, "His loss to this army is greater than the loss of a whole division of troops."

Meanwhile, Burnside's IX Corps, which had been late to show up at the Battle of the Wilderness, marched southwest along the Fredericksburg Road and came up on the far left of the Union line, leaving a gap between his men and Wright's VI Corps. When Burnside's corps were confronted by cavalry led by Fitzhugh Lee, the cautious Burnside stopped moving forward and began digging in. That skirmish induced Grant into thinking that Lee might be trying to turn his left flank, when Lee had no such plan. As a result, Grant prepared Hancock's II Corps to make an attack on the Confederates' left flank, figuring that would be the weaker part of their line, while Lee was actually shifting some of Early's corps along his left in the hopes of attacking Hancock's flank.

Grant had no idea that Burnside's corps was poised to strike Lee's right flank and had only been opposed by cavalry, and he would not realize it until after the war, much to his consternation.

**May 10**

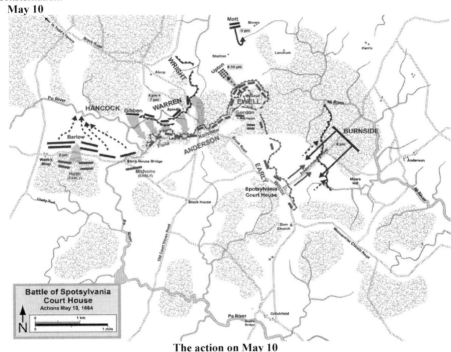

**The action on May 10**

On several occasions throughout the Overland Campaign, Grant ordered general attacks out of a sense that he could break Lee's army, and he had conceived of such an attack for May 10:

"Accordingly in the morning, orders were issued for an attack in the afternoon on the centre by Warren's and Wright's corps, Hancock to command all the attacking force. Two of his divisions were brought to the north side of the Po. Gibbon was placed to the right of Warren, and Birney in his rear as a reserve. Barlow's division was left south of the stream, and Mott of the same corps was still to the left of Wright's corps. Burnside was ordered to reconnoitre his front in force, and, if an opportunity presented, to attack with vigor."

Grant's plan actually started to go haywire on the evening of May 9, when the Confederates noticed some of Hancock's II Corps shifting their position that night. This allowed Lee to counter the perceived threat by trying to outflank Hancock's corps with Early's corps, which led the Union high command to mistakenly assume that Early's men were being shifted to the

Confederates' right flank. By the morning of May 10, Grant realized his mistake, but when he pulled back most of Hancock's corps behind the Po River, he left Francis Barlow's division on the other side to keep manning the earthworks there, which all but invited a Confederate attack.

Sure enough, that attack came at 2:00 p.m., with Henry Heth's division of Early's corps and William Mahone's division in support on the right. Early noted in his memoirs:

"Our line was then north of the Po, with its left, Fields' division of Longstreet's corps, resting on that stream, just above the crossing of the Shady Grove road. The whole of the enemy's force was also north of the Po, prior to this movement of his. Mahone's division was sent to occupy the banks of the Po on Fields' left, while with Heth's division and a battalion of artillery I moved to the rear, crossing the Po on the Louisa Court-House road, and then following that road until we reached one coming in from Waite's Shop on the Shady Grove road. After moving about a mile on this road, we met Hampton gradually falling back before the enemy, who had pushed out a column of infantry considerably to the rear of our line. This column was in turn forced back to the posi tion on Shady Grove road which was occupied by what was reported to be Hancock's corps. Following up and crossing a small stream just below a mill pond, we succeeded in reaching Waite's Shop, from whence an attack was made on the enemy, and the entire force, which had crossed the Po, was driven back with a loss of one piece of artillery, which fell into our hands, and a considerable number in killed and wounded. This relieved us from a very threatening danger, as the position the enemy had attained would have enabled him to completely enfilade Fields' position and get possession of the line of our communications to the rear, within a very short distance of which he was, when met by the force which drove him back. In this affair Heth's division behaved very handsomely, all of the brigades (Cook's, Davis', Kirkland's and Walker's) being engaged in the attack. General H. H. Walker had the misfortune to receive a severe wound in the foot, which rendered amputation necessary, but otherwise our loss was slight. As soon as the road was cleared, Mahone's division crossed the Po, but it was not practicable to pursue the affair further, as the north bank of the stream at this point was covered by a heavily entrenched line, with a number of batteries, and night was approaching."

While Hancock was trying to extricate Barlow's division, it left Warren in command of the general attack that Grant intended to make on the center. Warren was eager to make the assault, still smarting from perceived criticism over his timidity the previous two days, but in so doing he ended up ordering an attack that was uncoordinated with Hancock's men on the right or Wright's men on the left. Despite having tried to reconnoiter in force twice and being pushed back both times, Warren recommended making an assault on the Confederate center, and his uncoordinated attack was quickly repulsed at 4:00 p.m.

As Warren began reforming his lines, this time to make a coordinated attack, one of the divisions in Wright's VI Corps did not realize that the general attack at 5:00 p.m. had been delayed. Gershom Mott, whose division had performed poorly at the Wilderness, had even less luck when it made an uncoordinated attack at that hour.

When Early's two divisions had shifted to the left to attack Hancock, it left Cadmus Wilcox's division on the right flank, where it opposed Burnside's entire corps. Luckily for the Confederates, Grant had thought that the Confederates had been shifting more soldiers to their right instead of their left, leaving the Union high command with no idea that Burnside so heavily outnumbered the enemy in his front. Since Burnside was only ordered to reconnoiter in force, he stopped advancing down the road almost as soon as he came into contact with Wilcox's division, and at that point Grant started to worry about the gap between Wright's corps and Burnside's corps. Had Grant kept Sheridan's cavalry with him, such a reconnaissance might have already been done by the cavalry, and he would have had a better idea of what was in Burnside's front. But since he had allowed Sheridan to leave the army with no cavalry, later that night he pulled Burnside back to close the gap with Wright's corps, losing a chance to overwhelm Lee's right flank. It was something he greatly regretted after the war, writing, "Burnside on the left had got up to within a few hundred yards of Spottsylvania Court House, completely turning Lee's right. He was not aware of the importance of the advantage he had gained, and I, being with the troops where the heavy fighting was, did not know of it at the time. He had gained his position with but little fighting, and almost without loss. Burnside's position now separated him widely from Wright's corps, the corps nearest to him. At night he was ordered to join on to this. This brought him back about a mile, and lost to us an important advantage. I attach no blame to Burnside for this, but I do to myself for not having had a staff officer with him to report to me his position."

There had been fighting by all of the Union corps along each sector of the lines, but the most famous assault on the 10th was made by 12 regiments under the command of 24 year old Colonel Emory Upton, consisting of mixed elements of Wright's corps. This "storming party" was sent out at 6:00 p.m. with the intention of quickly rushing into the Confederate trenches and creating at least a minor breakthrough in the Confederate lines that could then be further breached by reinforcements. By using an unusual battle formation and not pausing to stop and fire, Upton's small attack force gained a surprising success, at least at first. Grant explained:

"Wright also reconnoitred his front and gained a considerably advanced position from the one he started from. He then organized a storming party, consisting of twelve regiments, and assigned Colonel Emory Upton, of the 121st New York Volunteers, to the command of it. About four o'clock in the afternoon the assault was ordered, Warren's and Wright's corps, with Mott's division of Hancock's corps, to move simultaneously. The movement was prompt, and in a few minutes the fiercest of struggles began. The battle-field was so densely covered with forest that but little could be seen, by any one person, as to the progress made. Meade and I occupied the best position we could get, in rear of Warren.

Warren was repulsed with heavy loss, General J. C. Rice being among the killed. He was not followed, however, by the enemy, and was thereby enabled to reorganize his command as soon as covered from the guns of the enemy. To the left our success was decided, but the advantage was lost by the feeble action of Mott. Upton with his assaulting party pushed forward and crossed the enemy's intrenchments. Turning to the right and left he captured several guns and some hundreds of prisoners. Mott was ordered to his assistance but failed utterly. So much time was lost in trying to get up the troops which were in the right position to reinforce, that I ordered Upton to withdraw; but the officers and men of his command were so averse to giving up the advantage they had gained that I withdrew the order. To relieve them, I ordered a renewal of the assault. By this time Hancock, who had gone with Birney's division to relieve Barlow, had returned, bringing the division with him. His corps was now joined with Warren's and Wright's in this last assault. It was gallantly made, many men getting up to, and over, the works of the enemy; but they were not able to hold them. At night they were withdrawn. Upton brought his prisoners with him, but the guns he had captured he was obliged to abandon. Upton had gained an important advantage, but a lack in others of the spirit and dash possessed by him lost it to us. Before leaving Washington I had been authorized to promote officers on the field for special acts of gallantry. By this authority I conferred the rank of brigadier-general upon Upton on the spot, and this act was confirmed by the President. Upton had been badly wounded in this fight."

**Upton**

Had Upton's successful assault been made in a coordinated fashion along with Mott's previous attack at 5:00 p.m. or Warren's attack at 4:00 p.m., it's possible that there would have been a much bigger breakthrough that wouldn't have allowed Lee to flush Upton's attack party out with reinforcements. But as it was, Upton's success in reaching the western side of the Mule Shoe salient had established both the model for attacking the line and the point at which the Confederate line should be attacked.

**May 11**

Every attack made by the Army of the Potomac on May 10 had been repulsed, and the lines had barely moved since the end of fighting on May 8, but Grant had reason for optimism. On May 11, he began plans to conduct another attack in the innovative style Upton had used, but with Hancock's entire II Corps instead of just 5,000 men. He also continued to believe that Lee's army was on the verge of being broken, partly the result of overestimating how many casualties he had inflicted on the Army of Northern Virginia and underestimating the Confederates. That day, he telegraphed Washington:

"We have now ended the 6th day of very hard fighting. The result up to this time is much in our favor. But our losses have been heavy as well as those of the enemy. We have lost to this time eleven general officers killed, wounded and missing, and probably twenty thousand men. I think the loss of the enemy must be greater—we having taken over four thousand prisoners in battle, whilst he has taken from us but few except a few stragglers. I am now sending back to Belle Plain all my wagons for a fresh supply of provisions and ammunition, and propose to fight it out on this line if it takes all summer.

The arrival of reinforcements here will be very encouraging to the men, and I hope they will be sent as fast as possible, and in as great numbers. My object in having them sent to Belle Plain was to use them as an escort to our supply trains. If it is more convenient to send them out by train to march from the railroad to Belle Plain or Fredericksburg, send them so.

I am satisfied the enemy are very shaky, and are only kept up to the mark by the greatest exertions on the part of their officers, and by keeping them intrenched in every position they take.

Up to this time there is no indication of any portion of Lee's army being detached for the defence of Richmond.

U. S. GRANT,
Lieut.-General."

After a couple of days in which Grant's incorrect assumptions had cost him chances for success, Lee made a terrible mistake on May 11 while reacting to movements by the Union army. Grant's plan for Hancock's assault required pulling his men out of the line and assembling them about a mile north of the Mule Shoe. By having Hancock attack the north face of the Mule Shoe while Wright advanced on the west face and Burnside advanced on the east face, the salient in the Confederate line would be as exposed as possible. Hancock's men would be advancing over open ground, while the part in the line they pulled out of was woody, which would keep Lee from fully understanding the movements and prevent the Confederates from launching a potentially devastating attack in the gap while Warren shifted to the left to replace Hancock's men.

Even worse, the movements of Hancock's corps and intelligence reports that Lee received convinced him that Grant was actually starting to retreat. Thinking this was the case, Lee intended to try to attack Grant's army while it was most vulnerable on the move, and since that would require improving the Army of Northern Virginia's mobility, he started withdrawing his artillery from around the salient for the purpose of having it prepared to advance more quickly. His nephew Fitzhugh Lee explained, "On the 11th he thought Grant was preparing for another move, and that night ordered most of the cannon out of the salient so as to be ready for a counter move, all of which a deserter from [Allegheny] Johnson's line reported, and which may account for the assault which, though favored by a climatic condition, was courageously executed."

Though Fitzhugh Lee credited that Confederate deserter for the assault, it was apparent that Grant already had it in mind. As Hancock's men began moving to their staging ground at the Brown farm, thunderstorms provided a torrential downpour, making it that much harder to truly understand the purpose of the movement. That was of little comfort to Allegheny Johnson and his division, who were defending the salient in the line and watching Hancock's men marching north in their front even while their artillery was being withdrawn. Johnson pleaded with corps commander Richard Ewell to bring the guns back to his line, but by the time Ewell accepted the request and the orders reached the artillery units, it was 3:30 a.m. on the morning of May 12. Hancock's assault was scheduled to come crashing right into Allegheny Johnson's division just half an hour later.

**Allegheny Johnson**

### The Bloody Angle

"I fancy this war has furnished no parallel to the desperation shown here by both parties. It must be called, I suppose, the taking of the Salient." – Theodore Lyman, George Meade's aide-de-camp

The ugly weather conditions had slowed Hancock's men to the extent that they reached the Brown farm around midnight, and then had to spend most of the next 4 hours forming their battle lines. The attack was delayed half an hour, back to 4:30 a.m., and Grant ordered Burnside to attack the east face of the Mule Shoe at the same time in force.

As if Grant's attack hadn't already been aided by Lee pulling the artillery away from the salient, there was a dense fog over the battlefield when Hancock's men stepped off to begin their assault. Hancock's men would not have come into view until they were within 300 yards of the Confederate lines, and now they would be obscured by mist.

At 4:30 a.m. that morning, nobody could have believed what the salient would look like 24 hours later. Gettysburg hero Rufus Dawes, Colonel of the 6th Wisconsin in the Iron brigade, described the final approach to the salient and the nature of the entrenchments:

"We stood perhaps one hundred feet from the enemy's line, and so long as we maintained a continual fire they remained hidden in their entrenchments. But if an attempt to advance was made, an order would be given and they would all rise up together and fire a volley upon us. They had constructed their works by digging an entrenchment about four feet deep, in which at intervals there were traverses to protect the flanks. This had the effect of making a row of cellars without drainage, and in them was several inches of mud and water. To protect their heads, they had placed in front logs which were laid upon blocks, and it was intended to put their muskets through the chinks under the head logs, but in the darkness this became impracticable and the head log proved a serious obstruction to their firing."

Battle of Spotsylvania
Court House
Actions May 12, 1864

Hancock's corps, nearly 15,000 strong, quickly overwhelmed the salient and almost immediately destroyed the initial defenders comprised of William Witcher's brigade. As Hancock's men entered the Confederate trenches, Barlow's division fanned out to their left and flanked George Steuart's brigade facing Burnside's men on the eastern face of the Mule Shoe, capturing both Steuart and Allegheny Johnson. Meanwhile, David Birney's division advanced along the western part of the Mule Shoe until confronting the old Stonewall Brigade, once commanded by the legendary Stonewall Jackson but now commanded by James Walker.

Within half an hour, Hancock's corps had breached the Confederates' main line, capturing nearly 4,000 men and 20 guns, including their horses and ammunition. As the men kept advancing, Hancock had the captured Confederate guns turned around and began firing them down the Confederate lines, providing a devastating enfilade. Around this time, news of the initial success was making its way back to Grant's headquarters, and Theodore Lyman described the scene:

"At a little after five o'clock, General Williams approached from the telegraph tent; a smile was on his face: Hancock had carried the first line! Thirty minutes after, another despatch: he had taken the main line with guns, prisoners and two generals! Great rejoicings now burst forth. Some of Grant's Staff were absurdly confident and were sure Lee was entirely beaten. My own experiences taught me a little more scepticism. Hancock presently sent to ask for a vigorous attack on his right, to cover and support his right flank. General Wright was accordingly ordered to attack with a part of the 6th

Corps. As I stood there waiting, I heard someone say, 'Sir, this is General Johnson.' I turned round and there was the captured Major-General, walking slowly up. He was a strongly built man of a stern and rather bad face, and was dressed in a double-breasted blue-grey coat, high riding boots and a very bad felt hat. He was most horribly mortified at being taken, and kept coughing to hide his emotion. Generals Meade and Grant shook hands with him, and good General Williams bore him off to breakfast. His demeanor was dignified and proper. Not so a little creature, General Steuart, who insulted everybody who came near him, and was rewarded by being sent on foot to Fredericksburg, where there was plenty of mud and one stream up to his waist."

Horace Porter also recounted a rather tense exchange between Steuart and Hancock: "General George H. Steuart was also captured, but was not sent in to general headquarters on account of a scene which had been brought about by an unseemly exhibition of temper on his part. Hancock had known him in the old army, and in his usual frank way went up to him, greeted him kindly, and offered his hand. Steuart drew back, rejected the offer, and said rather haughtily, 'Under the present circumstances, I must decline to take your hand.' Hancock, who was somewhat nettled by this remark, replied, 'Under any other circumstances, general, I should not have offered it.'"

Burnside's men had attacked in concert with Hancock's and had greatly assisted in destroying the Confederate line on the eastern face of the Mule Shoe, but in the process his men had lost contact with the faster advancing II Corps. When Burnside informed Grant that his men had lost contact with Hancock's men, Grant responded, "Push the enemy with all your might; that's the way to connect."

Now, with a breach in the Confederate line nearly half a mile wide, both sides began quickly reacting by ordering more men to the fighting. For Grant, this meant that Wright's corps would support Hancock on the right, but because Grant had only planned for Wright to remain in a defensive posture during the initial assault, it required time for Wright's men to prepare for a similar kind of advance.

Meanwhile, Lee was so desperate that as he was ordering up reinforcements from John Gordon's division, he rode to the front of their marching column as though he was going to lead the charge himself. Fitzhugh Lee recalled the scene, writing, "On this occasion the general rode to the head of the column forming for the charge, took off his hat, and pointed to the captured line; but General John B. Gordon proposed to lead his own men, and no one in the army could do it better, for he was in dash and daring inferior to none. 'These are Virginians and Georgians who have never failed,' said Gordon. 'Go to the rear, General Lee.' And appealing to his men, he cried: 'Is it necessary for General Lee to lead this charge?' 'No, no,' they exclaimed; 'we will drive them back if General Lee will go to the rear.'

Gordon was unquestionably one of the toughest soldiers in the South. He had led a desperate flank attack at the Battle of the Wilderness on May 6, and he had been wounded several times at Antietam. But not even Gordon was ready for his division's initial contact with Hancock's corps:

"So rapidly and silently had the enemy moved inside of our works-- indeed, so much longer time had he been on the inside than the reports indicated--that before we had moved one half the distance to the salient the head of my column butted squarely against Hancock's line of battle. The men who had been placed in our front to give warning were against that battle line before they knew it. They were shot down or made prisoners. The sudden and unexpected blaze from Hancock's rifles made the dark woodland strangely lurid. General Johnson, who rode immediately at my side, was shot from his horse, severely but not, as I supposed, fatally wounded in the head. His brigade was thrown inevitably into great confusion, but did not break to the rear. As quickly as possible, I had the next ranking officer in that brigade notified of General Johnson's fall and directed him at once to assume command. He proved equal to the emergency. With great coolness and courage he promptly executed my orders. The Federals were still advancing, and every movement of the North Carolina brigade had to be made under heavy fire. The officer in charge was directed to hastily withdraw his brigade a short distance, to change front so as to face Hancock's lines, and to deploy his whole force in close order as skirmishers, so as to stretch, if possible, across the entire front of Hancock. This done, he was ordered to charge with his line of skirmishers the solid battle lines before him. His looks indicated some amazement at the purpose to make an attack which appeared so utterly hopeless, and which would have been the very essence of rashness but for the extremity of the situation. He was, however, full of the fire of battle and too good a soldier not to yield prompt and cheerful obedience. That order was given in the hope and belief that in the fog and mists which concealed our numbers the sheer audacity of the movement would confuse and check the Union advance long enough for me to change front and form line of battle with the other brigades. The result was not disappointing except in the fact that Johnson's brigade, even when so deployed, was still too short to reach across Hancock's entire front. This fact was soon developed: not by sight, but by the direction from which the Union bullets began to come."

As Gordon's account indicated, the fog and damp conditions made musket volleys and firing far more ineffective than they otherwise would have usually been. Moreover, the nature of the Confederate lines, which were composed of trenches that were upwards of 4 feet deep in some positions, made it all but impossible for Hancock's corps to reform their battle lines once they had stormed the Confederates' positions. With men getting mixed up in the chaos, it became impossible for officers to control their commands, and the fighting around the breached salient began to devolve into hand-to-hand fighting.

As Hancock was proudly boasting, "I have used up Johnson and am going into Early", Gordon's division came countercharging into the breach and checked Hancock's progress with a series of desperate attacks. As they began to push back Hancock's now-exhausted attackers on the eastern portion of the Mule Shoe, division commander Robert Rodes was reestablishing the Confederate line on the western part of the Mule Shoe.

The Confederates had just desperately stopped Hancock's momentum, but the worst was yet to come. By the time the Confederates had fought off Hancock, Wright's entire corps was ready to press forward around 6:30 a.m., and Grant had also ordered Warren's corps to attack the Confederates on their left and pin them down. By now, the steady rain that was still coming down had combined with the mud and the blood of the fighting soldiers to produce a nauseating stream in the trenches near the salient that one soldier recalled being half-way up to his knees. It was only about to get worse.

Around 6:30 a.m., Wright's corps had been assembled in a similar manner to Upton's assault, and they rushed forward into the salient even while some of Hancock's men were streaming to the rear. G. Norton Galloway, a member of the 95th Pennsylvania in Wright's corps, described the scene:

"Under cover of the smoke-laden rain the enemy was pushing large bodies of troops forward, determined at all hazards to regain the lost ground. Could we hold on until the remainder of our brigade should come to our assistance? Regardless of the heavy volleys of the enemy that were thinning our ranks, we stuck to the position and returned the fire until the 5th Maine and the 121st New York of our brigade came to our support, while the 96th Pennsylvania went in on our right ; thus reenforced, we redoubled our exertions. The smoke, which was dense at first, was intensified by each discharge of artillery to such an extent that the accuracy of our aim became very uncertain, but nevertheless we kept up the fire in the supposed direction of the enemy. Meanwhile they were crawling forward under cover of the smoke, until, reaching a certain point, and raising their usual yell, they charged gallantly up to the very muzzles of our pieces and reoccupied the Angle.

Upon reaching the breastwork, the Confederates for a few moments had the advantage of us, and made good use of their rifles. Our men went down by the score; all the artillery horses were down ; the gallant Upton was the only mounted officer in sight. Hat in hand, he bravely cheered his men, and begged them to 'hold this point.' All of his staff had been either killed, wounded, or dismounted.

At this moment, and while the open ground in rear of the Confederate works was choked with troops, a section of Battery C, 5th United States Artillery, under Lieutenant Richard Metcalf, was brought into action and increased the carnage by opening at short range with double charges of canister. This staggered the apparently exultant enemy. In the maze of the moment these guns were run up by hand close to the famous Angle, and fired again and again, and they were only abandoned when all the drivers and cannoneers had fallen. The battle was now at white heat.

The rain continued to fall, and clouds of smoke hung over the scene. Like leeches we stuck to the work, determined by our fire to keep the enemy from rising up. Captain John D. Fish, of Upton's staff, who had until this time performed valuable service in conveying ammunition to the gunners, fell, pierced by a bullet. This brave officer seemed to court death as he rode back and forth between the caissons and cannoneers with stands of canister under his 'gum' coat. 'Give it to them , boys! I'll bring you the canister,' said he; and as he turned to cheer the gunners, he fell from his horse, mortally wounded. In a few moments the two brass pieces of the 5th Artillery, cut and hacked by the bullets of both antagonists, lay unworked with their muzzles projecting over the enemy's works, and their wheels half sunk in the mud. Between the lines and near at hand lay the horses of these guns, completely riddled. The dead and wounded were torn to pieces by the canister as it swept the ground where they had fallen."

**Earthworks near the Bloody Angle**

With Wright's VI Corps crashing into the line, the Confederates were forced to quickly bring in more reinforcements, beginning with William Mahone's division. Mahone had been near the extreme left the previous day while Heth's division was attacking the Union's right flank, and now he was forced to quickly countermarch two of his brigades from the extreme left to the Mule Shoe. By 9:30 a.m., all of the VI Corps had been committed and were desperately fighting to hold on as more Confederates streamed to the breach.

Grant had hoped to avoid allowing massive reinforcements by having Warren's corps pin down the Confederate left. Given that Mahone was able to march his entire division from that sector to the Mule Shoe, it was apparent that Warren's assault was a failure. Warren's men had been ordered to attack near Laurel Hill multiple times the past few days, and the failures of the previous days had demoralized them. Despite the fact that Warren's entire corps was opposed by just one division of Anderson's corps, their attack completely stalled in under an hour. When Warren had to tell Meade that he could not advance, the short-tempered Meade exploded and ordered him to attack "at once at all hazards with your whole force, if necessary." Once again, Warren's men made a half-hearted advance that was quickly bogged down, and by now Grant was so frustrated that he authorized Meade to relieve Warren of command. Although Warren technically avoided being relieved, one of his divisions was placed under Wright's command and another was placed under Hancock's, leaving him with only one division. For the one division still nominally under Warren's command, Meade had his chief of staff, General Humphreys, attached to Warren's division and the authority to give it orders in his name. Grant would ruefully note in his memoirs, "If the 5th corps, or rather if Warren, had been as prompt as Wright was with the 6th corps, better results might have been obtained."

As Lee kept pulling men from his left to reinforce the Mule Shoe, a stalemate developed in which neither side could fully dislodge the other. For Lee, this meant that Union artillery positions made his current defensive line precarious, while Grant was still holding out hope of achieving a decisive breakthrough that would cut Lee's army in two, separating Ewell and Early from Anderson. As a result, both commanders kept ordering more and more men forward into the salient.

By the mid-afternoon, the Union and Confederate soldiers had been fighting at the salient for over 10 hours. Galloway discussed the nature of the fighting at the Bloody Angle during this time:

"The great difficulty was in the narrow limits of the Angle, around which we were fighting, which precluded the possibility of getting more than a limited number into action at once. At one time our ranks were crowded in some parts four deep by reenforcements. Major Henry P. Truefitt, commanding the 119th Pennsylvania, was killed, and Captain Charles P. Warner, who succeeded him, was shot dead. Later in the day Major William Ellis, of the 49th New York, who had excited our admiration, was shot through the arm and body with a ramrod during one of the several attempts to get the men to cross the works and drive off the enemy. Our losses were frightful. What remained of many different regiments that had come to our support had concentrated at this point and planted their tattered colors upon a slight rise of ground close to the Angle, where they staid during the latter part of the day.

To keep up the supply of ammunition pack mules were brought into use, each animal carrying three thousand rounds. The boxes were dropped close behind the troops engaged, where they were quickly opened by the officers or file-closers, who served the ammunition to the men. The writer fired four hundred rounds of ammunition, and many others as many or more. In this manner a continuous and rapid fire was maintained, to which for a while the enemy replied with vigor.

Finding that we were not to be driven back, the Confederates began to use more discretion, exposing themselves but little, using the loop-holes in their works to fire through, and at times placing the muzzles of their rifles on the top logs, seizing the trigger and small of the stock, and elevating the breech with one hand sufficiently to reach us."

However, while more and more men packed into the tight lines, Lee was busy creating a new defensive line south of the Mule Shoe that would prevent him from having to defend a salient. All throughout the afternoon Confederate engineers began shuffling men south of the fighting and digging in, so that there would be a new set of entrenchments for the Confederates to use once the new line was established.

By the time the Confederates were ready to dislodge Wright's corps, the men from Hancock's corps had been reformed and ordered back to the salient, keeping the fight going throughout the night. It was not until 4:00 a.m. on the 13th, nearly 24 hours after Hancock's assault began, that the Confederates at the salient began to pull back to the newly formed trenches a few hundred yards south. Nearly 9,000 Union soldiers had been killed or wounded, while 5,000 Confederates had been killed or wounded and 3,000-4,000 had been captured.

When dawn broke on the 13th, the Bloody Angle produced a sight unlike anything the battle hardened soldiers had seen before. Theodore Lyman recounted injured men being pulled out from under multiple corpses, and seeing one corpse that looked like it had been shot 80 times. Dawes, who had fought at Antietam and Gettysburg, was so horrified by the Bloody Angle that he ordered his men to pull out so they wouldn't have to sleep near the spot, writing, "In the morning the rebel works presented an awful spectacle. The cellars were crowded with dead and wounded, lying in some cases upon each other and in several inches of mud and water. I saw the body of a rebel soldier sitting in the corner of one of these cellars in a position of apparent ease, with the head entirely gone, and the flesh burned from the bones of the neck and shoulders. This was doubtless caused by the explosion of a shell from some small Cohorn mortars within our lines."

Grants aide, Horace Porter, was astounded by what he saw: "The appalling sight presented was harrowing in the extreme. Our own killed were scattered over a large space near the "angle," while in front of the captured breastworks the enemy's dead, vastly more numerous than our own, were piled upon each other in some places four layers deep, exhibiting every ghastly phase of mutilation. Below the mass of fast-decaying corpses, the convulsive twitching of limbs and the writhing of bodies showed that there were wounded men still alive and struggling to extricate themselves from the horrid entombment. Every relief possible was afforded, but in too many cases it came too late. The place was well named the 'Bloody Angle.'"

Galloway noted one morbid way that the Union soldiers still holding the salient went about burying the dead: "Hundreds of Confederates, dead or dying, lay piled over one another in those pits. The fallen lay three or four feet deep in some places, and, with but few exceptions, they were shot in and about the head. Arms, accouterments, ammunition, cannon, shot and shell, and broken foliage were strewn about. With much labor a detail of Union soldiers buried the dead by simply turning the captured breastworks upon them. Thus had these unfortunate victims unwittingly dug their own graves. The trenches were nearly full of muddy water. It was the most horrible sight I had ever witnessed."

Grant was more circumspect, writing, "Lee massed heavily from his left flank on the broken point of his line. Five times during the day he assaulted furiously, but without dislodging our troops from their new position. His losses must have been fearful. Sometimes the belligerents would be separated by but a few feet. In one place a tree, eighteen inches in diameter, was cut entirely down by musket balls. All the trees between the lines were very much cut to pieces by artillery and musketry. It was three o'clock next morning before the fighting ceased. Some of our troops had then been twenty hours under fire. In this engagement we did not lose a single organization, not even a company. The enemy lost one division with its commander, one brigade and one regiment, with heavy losses elsewhere. Our losses were heavy, but, as stated, no whole company was captured. At night Lee took a position in rear of his former one, and by the following morning he was strongly intrenched in it."

### Lee Lives to Fight Another Day

"The enemy are obstinate, and seem to have found the last ditch." – Ulysses S. Grant, May 12 telegraph to Washington.

**Movements on May 13-14**

Lee's army had barely escaped disaster on the 12th, leaving Grant anxious to continue offensive operations, but he was also well aware that an attack against the newly entrenched line would be suicidal. Thus, he began the delicate process of marching the men on his right flank to come up on the left flank of the army, requiring them to countermarch and then head south and southeast. From May 13-14, he accomplished this by having the VI Corps and the remaining men of the V Corps move behind Hancock's men and march to the left of Burnside's IX Corps. The steady rains, which had now continued for nearly 4 days, slowed the progress and bogged them down. In response to these movements, Lee shifted Anderson's corps from his left to his right to counter them.

On May 16, Grant telegraphed Washington to explain that the rain had all but halted his campaign: "We have had five days almost constant rain without any prospect yet of it clearing up. The roads have now become so impassable that ambulances with wounded men can no longer run between here and Fredericksburg. All offensive operations necessarily cease until we can have twenty-four hours of dry weather. The army is in the best of spirits, and feel the greatest confidence of ultimate success."

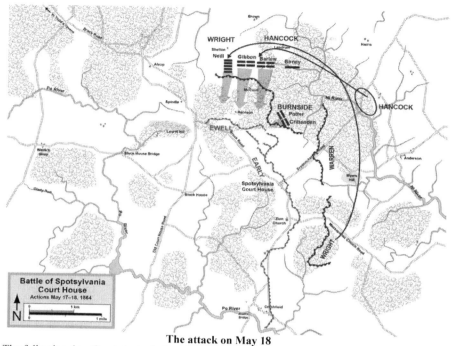

## The attack on May 18

The following day, Grant devised plans for another assault, hoping to catch the Confederates by surprise. Since Grant had been marching men from his right to his left, he hoped and guessed that Lee was countering that by building up that flank to meet the new threat, so he decided to try to attack Lee's left flank with Hancock's men and Burnside's men, near the Mule Shoe. The problem with the plan was that Lee was still fearful that an assault might come at any time, so the Confederates were alert. Moreover, Ewell's men had been in the same defensive lines for several days, which had allowed them to dig in so effectively that their line was all but impregnable. When Hancock's corps led this attack, the felled trees (abates) bogged them down and made them sitting ducks for Confederate artillery, which had not been withdrawn this time. The Union attack was repulsed without Ewell's infantry having to fire a single musket.

With that, Grant had finally been convinced of the hopelessness of striking a decisive blow at Spotsylvania Court House, noting in his memoirs, "I immediately gave orders for a movement by the left flank, on towards Richmond, to commence on the night of the 19th. I also asked Halleck to secure the cooperation of the navy in changing our base of supplies from Fredericksburg to Port Royal, on the Rappahannock."

On May 19, as Grant was getting ready to march south by pulling his right flank out of the lines, Lee ordered Ewell's corps to conduct a reconnaissance in force that would probe the Union's right flank. This was the kind of reconnaissance that would have been assigned to JEB Stuart's cavalry in previous years, but Stuart's badly outnumbered cavalry had their hands full with Sheridan, and the famous cavalier had been mortally wounded in a skirmish at the Battle of Yellow Tavern on May 11. As a result, two of Ewell's divisions pushed forward until they came across some of Hancock's corps at Harris Farm, a skirmish that lasted most of the 19th. By the time Lee withdrew Ewell's men, they had suffered 900 casualties. Meanwhile, Grant was disappointed by Warren yet again, writing, "Warren had been ordered to get on Ewell's flank and in his rear, to cut him off from his intrenchments. But his efforts were so feeble that under the cover of night Ewell got back with only the loss of a few hundred prisoners, besides his killed and wounded. The army being engaged until after dark, I rescinded the order for the march by our left flank that night."

After Harris Farm, the last major fighting of the Battle of Spotsylvania Court House was finished. From May 8-21, the two armies had inflicted nearly 32,000 casualties on each other. Grant had lost over 18,000 killed, captured or wounded, meaning he had lost over 35,000 since entering the Wilderness less than three weeks earlier. Meanwhile, Lee had lost another 13,000 soldiers, over 20% of his entire army. It was the deadliest battle of the Overland Campaign and one of the 5 bloodiest battles of the entire Civil War.

At Spotsylvania, just like at the Battle of the Wilderness, Lee's army had skillfully defended against Grant's attacks and had inflicted more casualties than they suffered. But once again, the Confederates had suffered a larger % of casualties within their army and failed to stop Grant's campaign. The Army of the Potomac and Army of Northern Virginia would continue to move south, destined to meet again along the North Anna River.

**Moving to the North Anna, May 21-22**

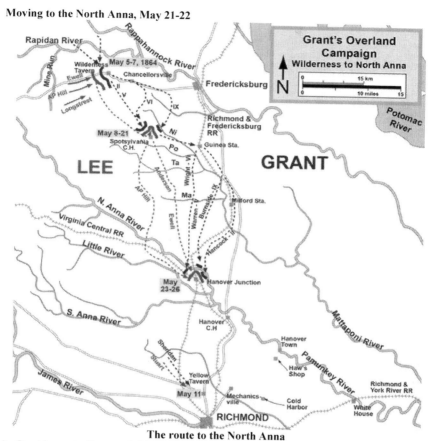

**The route to the North Anna**

As Grant began to disentangle his army from the lines at Spotsylvania and march by his left flank, he hoped to use some of his men to pin down Lee's army while marching others to the North Anna River and the railroad line at Hanover Junction about 25 miles away. If he could accomplish that by beating Lee's army to those spots, he would have captured one of Lee's most natural supply lines (the railroad) while depriving the Army of Northern Virginia from using the North Anna River as a defensive line. At the same time, Grant knew that the Confederates had the interior lines, meaning their march from Spotsylvania to the North Anna River would be considerably shorter. With that in mind, Grant figured that the aggressive Lee might try to strike at his separated corps while they were on the march, as he noted in his memoirs:

"We were now to operate in a different country from any we had before seen in Virginia. The roads were wide and good, and the country well cultivated. No men were seen except those bearing arms, even the black man having been sent away. The country, however, was new to us, and we had neither guides nor maps to tell us where the roads were, or where they led to. Engineer and staff officers were put to the dangerous duty of supplying the place of both maps and guides. By reconnoitering they were enabled to locate the roads in the vicinity of each army corps. Our course was south, and we took all roads leading in that direction which would not separate the army too widely.

Hancock who had the lead had marched easterly to Guiney's Station, on the Fredericksburg Railroad, thence southerly to Bowling Green and Milford. He was at Milford by the night of the 21st. Here he met a detachment of Pickett's division coming from Richmond to reinforce Lee. They were speedily driven away, and several hundred captured. Warren followed on the morning of the 21st, and reached Guiney's Station that night without molestation. Burnside and Wright were retained at Spottsylvania to keep up the appearance of an intended assault, and to hold Lee, if possible, while Hancock and Warren should get start enough to interpose between him and Richmond.

Lee had now a superb opportunity to take the initiative either by attacking Wright and Burnside alone, or by following by the Telegraph Road and striking Hancock's and Warren's corps, or even Hancock's alone, before reinforcements could come up. But he did not avail himself of either opportunity. He seemed really to be misled as to my designs; but moved by his interior line—the Telegraph Road—to make sure of keeping between his capital and the Army of the Potomac. He never again had such an opportunity of dealing a heavy blow."

While Grant would later write that he believed Lee missed an opportunity, Lee's own subordinates thought his maneuvering toward North Anna was nothing short of an ingenious prophecy. John Gordon, who led a Confederate brigade during the campaign, praised Lee, "Lee divined Grant's movement to Spottsylvania almost at the very instant the movement was taking shape in Grant's brain, so on each succeeding field he read the mind of the Union commander, and developed his own plans accordingly. There was no mental telepathy in all this. Lee's native and tutored genius enabled him to place himself in Grant's position, to reason out his antagonist's mental processes, to trace with accuracy the lines of his marches, and to mark on the map the points of future conflict which were to become the blood-lettered mile-posts marking Grant's compulsory halts and turnings in his zigzag route to Richmond."

In truth, it's no surprise that Lee chose the course he ultimately did: the North Anna was the next obvious defensive line for Lee's army. Situated less than 30 miles north of Richmond, the river would be hard to cross for the Union Army if the Army of Northern Virginia was on the southern bank of it. Theodore Lyman, one of Meade's staffers, described the river in his writings after the war: "The North Anna is a pretty stream, running between high banks, so steep that they form almost a ravine, and, for the most part, heavily wooded with oak and tulip trees, very luxuriant. It is perhaps 125 feet wide and runs with a tolerably swift and deep stream, in most places over one's head. The approaches are by steep roads cut down the banks…"

Moreover, as the armies moved south, Grant's supply lines and communication lines inevitably got longer while Lee's became shorter, an important advantage for the Confederates. And while Lee would have had an opportunity to attack Hancock's II Corps with his entire army, such a move also would have allowed the rest of Grant's army to fall on his own, one of the reasons Grant felt safe sending Hancock's corps ahead while two of his other corps remained near Spotsylvania.

Grant ceded the use of the Telegraph Road to Lee's army, ensuring a shorter route to the North

Anna, but that would also require Lee's army to cross the Ni, Po, and Matta rivers, small streams that would nonetheless slow down his movement. Grant would have a longer route by marching his corps east of that road, but he could avoid having to cross the three rivers because they all merged downstream into the Mattaponi River to the southeast, meaning Grant would only have to make one river crossing. However, this also meant that Grant's army would have a longer march to the North Anna, as pointed out by Confederate artillery chief Porter Alexander in his memoirs: "To make the effort, Hancock had been sent by a route about nine miles longer than the most direct from Grant's left to Hanover Junction, which was only 25 miles, and three miles shorter than Lee's shortest. Having the additional advantage of the initiative, it was doubtless an error on Grant's part to undertake it."

When Hancock's men and some Union cavalry ran into Confederates from George Pickett's division near Milford Station, it was because Pickett's division was marching to reinforce Lee's army. While Hancock correctly guessed this was the case, the fact that his corps was isolated on May 21 made him understandably cautious after he had repulsed Pickett's men. After all, Grant was using his corps as bait in an attempt to draw Lee out into an open battle without the advantage of defensive fortifications, and Pickett's presence might have meant Lee's army was in the area.

In reality, most of Lee's army was still around Spotsylvania when Hancock stopped around Milford Station early on May 21. Still unaware of Grant's strategy, Lee was reluctant to move his army out of its powerfully fortified defensive lines. He took just one of his corps, Ewell's corps, and extended his line to the right by having them move south along Telegraph Road, while also ordering a small force under General John C. Breckinridge to move to Hanover Junction until the Army of Northern Virginia could join him, shrewdly figuring even a token force could provide him needed time to reach the next natural defensive line if necessary.

Although Lee had not intended to go after Hancock and was still not ready to abandon Spotsylvania's lines, his maneuvering of Ewell's corps effectively ensured Grant's army could not use the Telegraph Road, which would have been the quickest route to link Hancock's isolated corps back up with the rest of the army. As a result, when Ewell blocked that avenue, it unnerved Grant enough to order Meade to move the army to Hancock's assistance. This would require some of the army's corps to follow the same route Hancock's corps had used, essentially meaning the Army of the Potomac would be moving backward before moving southeast.

Once it was apparent that it was safe to do so, Lee began pulling his army out of their defensive lines at Spotsylvania on the night of May 21 and began marching them south toward the North Anna River. As it turned out, Ewell's corps and Anderson's corps were in some places less than a mile west of Warren's V Corps as they made their night march south toward the river. Had the Union cavalry been in a position in advance of the Union army, Warren's corps may have delayed two of Lee's corps or at least inflicted some damage on them while they were in marching formation, but cavalry commander Phil Sheridan was a career infantry officer and an aggressive one. Earlier in the campaign he had used his entire cavalry force for raids and to attack JEB Stuart's cavalry, instead of performing the traditional reconnaissance and screening duties. As a result, the Union cavalry were away on a raid that night, leading one Northern officer to gripe, "Never was the want of cavalry more painfully felt."

Once again, bad luck, the fog of war, and poor performances had prevented Grant's army from winning a race to his desired objective point. Grant was already starting to lose his patience with Warren, who performed poorly on multiple days at Spotsylvania, and his approval of Sheridan's raids had deprived him of necessary reconnaissance on multiple occasions. Furthermore, Lee managed to successfully thwart him at seemingly every turn, stopping him in the Wilderness, beating him to Spotsylvania, and then beating him to the North Anna.

As the first soldiers from Lee's army began to reach the North Anna on the morning of May 22, much of the Army of the Potomac was still over 20 miles away. Hancock was still at Milford Station, while Burnside's IX Corps and Wright's VI Corps were even further north at Guinea Station. In the early morning hours on May 22, Grant issued the orders that would set the armies on a collision course at the North Anna:

"Direct corps commanders to hold their troops in readiness to march at five A.M. tomorrow. At that hour each command will send out cavalry and infantry on all roads to their front leading south, and ascertain, if possible, where the enemy is. If beyond the South Anna, the 5th and 6th corps will march to the forks of the road, where one branch leads to Beaver Dam Station, the other to Jericho Bridge, then south by roads reaching the Anna, as near to and east of Hawkins Creek as they can be found.

The 2d corps will move to Chesterfield Ford. The 9th corps will be directed to move at the same time to Jericho Bridge. The map only shows two roads for the four corps to march upon, but, no doubt, by the use of plantation roads, and pressing in guides, others can be found, to give one for each corps."

Thus, the Union army began pushing south on different roads and would ultimately be trying to make crossings of the North Anna River in two places: the crossing around Jericho Mills and the crossing at the Chesterfield Bridge. Unfortunately for Grant, Lee's men were just reaching that vicinity at about the same time he was drawing up those orders and massing around Hanover Junction, winning yet another race in the Overland Campaign.

## May 23

Although Grant's Army of the Potomac was nearly 70,000 strong and Lee's Army of Northern Virginia was about 55,000 strong, Lee was thinking aggressively as the two armies reached the North Anna. With each successive battle and move south, Lee was running out of time to destroy Grant's army before being pinned down around Richmond. Moreover, Grant would be able to draw more reinforcements than Lee, who had successfully defended against Grant in two critical but costly battles. Grant may not have been defeating Lee tactically, but he was steadily grinding Lee's army down to the point that Lee would soon lack the firepower to deliver the kind of decisive blow he would need to truly reverse the South's fortunes. The sizes of the two armies would never again be as close to equal as they were around the North Anna.

It seems Lee had taken all of this into account as he reached the North Anna, and several of Lee's men would note that he was rarely more animated during the Civil War than he was during the Battle of North Anna. Lee's thinking and mood were readily explained by a letter he wrote to his wife on the 23rd: "General Grant, having apparently become tired of forcing his passage through, began on the night of the 20th to move around our right toward Bowling Green, placing the Mattapony River between us. Fearing he might unite with Sheridan and make a sudden and rapid move upon Richmond, I determined to march to this point so as to be in striking distance of Richmond, and be able to intercept him. The army is now south of the North Anna. We have the advantage of being nearer our supplies and less liable to have our communication trains, etc., cut by his cavalry, and he is getting farther from his base. Still, I begrudge every step he takes toward Richmond."

The Union army had moved south throughout the 22nd, and in the early morning hours of the 23rd, the corps linked back up with each other around Mount Carmel Church, just a few miles north of the North Anna River. Grant intended for Warren and Wright to cross around Jericho

Mills while Hancock would march across the Chesterfield Bridge. Burnside's corps would try to cross at Ox Ford between the two other crossings, and Grant hoped by making these separate crossings the entire army could get across the North Anna and maintain a solid battle line on the southern bank of the river.

Naturally, the corps got tangled up around Mount Carmel Church due to their unfamiliarity with the region, delaying Warren and Hancock a few hours respectively from reaching their separate crossing points. However, even as they approached the North Anna later that day, they found almost no Confederate defenders in their front. As Lee's letter to his wife suggested, Lee believed Grant had grown tired of trying to force his way through the Confederate army to reach Richmond and would now start avoiding the kind of pitched battle that had been fought in the Wilderness and Spotsylvania. Thus, Lee had not dug in because he thought Grant would make a diversion around the North Anna while swinging his army to outflank the Confederates' position to the right.

As a result, when Warren and Hancock moved south toward the two intended crossing points, they found that Lee was barely defending the crossing points at all. The Chesterfield Bridge was defended by just one brigade of South Carolinians led by Col. John W. Henagan, which had constructed a small dirt redoubt on the northern bank of the river, and there was even less organized resistance in Warren's front around Jericho Mills.

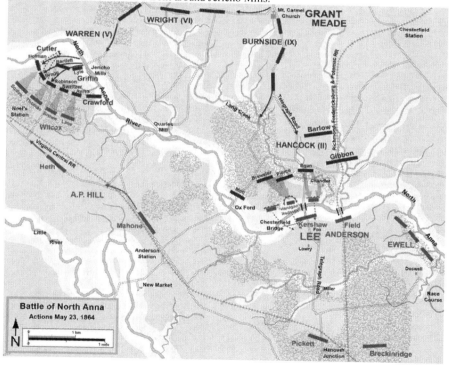

Around 5:00 p.m., one of the divisions from Warren's corps started fording across the North Anna and secured their beachhead on the southern bank while pontoon bridges were constructed to allow the rest of the divisions to march across the river. By the time Warren's corps made it across the North Anna, he had heard reports that Lee's army was in force nearby, so he drew up his corps in one battle line.

**A pontoon bridge around Jericho Mills**

The intelligence reports were correct. Just as Warren's men were forming a line, Confederates from A.P. Hill's corps were sent forward to engage the Union soldiers. However, Hill was operating under his commander's mistaken belief that Grant was merely using diversionary tactics along the North Anna while the bulk of the Army of the Potomac moved along Lee's right flank, and Hill's corps was on Lee's left. Thinking it was just a few brigades instead of an entire corps, Hill only sent one division under Cadmus Wilcox and some artillery from William Pegram. As a result, 6,000 Confederates were marching straight into 15,000 Federals.

Luckily for Hill, his timing was nearly perfect. As Porter Alexander later explained in his memoirs, "Warren had formed line of battle in very favorable position, He was able to cover his front with the edge of a wood concealing his actual line. His left rested on the river, which made a large concave bend in his rear and again drew near his right, with open ground upon that flank commanded by the artillery. But the rare opportunity of an isolated corps unintrenched was here offered, and Hill hastened to attack it." Wilcox's division came smashing into Warren's line while it was still forming, with Charles Griffin's division and Lysander Cutler's division both being hit on the right of the Union line. Although the line broke and Cutler's division fled back toward the banks of the North Anna, the Confederates couldn't follow it up without being shelled by Union artillery still on the other side of the river. When the 83rd Pennsylvania regiment flanked the Confederate brigade led by Edward Thomas, it undid the Confederates' line and sent them scurrying in retreat.

Since the Confederates would run out of daylight before another division from Hill's corps could reinforce them, Wilcox called off the attack, having suffered nearly 750 casualties with nothing to show for it. The crossing point had been secured for the Army of the Potomac.

Meanwhile, Hancock's corps was having a more difficult time dealing with Henagan's redoubt. As Birney's division marched along the Telegraph Road toward the bridge, they fanned out and attacked the redoubt with two brigades straddling the east and west side of the road. At the same time, the artillery on both sides opened up on each other. Lee was still feeling well enough to observe the fighting from behind the lines at Parson Thomas Fox's house, only to be nearly hit by a cannonball that was stopped by a door frame a few feet away from him. Unfazed, Lee thanked Fox for his hospitality and rode away from the house. Porter Alexander was also directing his artillery from the house and was nearly showered by bricks after Union artillery hit the chimney and destroyed it.

**The interior of Henagan's redoubt**

The infantry fighting was just as spirited. As the Union soldiers struggled to storm the redoubt, they resorted to actually piercing the dirt at the base of the redoubt with their bayonets and creating impromptu ladders that the soldiers behind them could then climb atop to get into Henagan's redoubt. Eventually Henagan had to pull his men back across the Chesterfield Bridge, but their failure to destroy the bridge by setting fire to it was prevented by Hancock's men, leaving the Union in control of a second crossing point.

**The Chesterfield Bridge**

As night fell on the 23rd, Warren's entire corps was across the North Anna, Wright's corps was in support of Warren on the other side of the river, and Hancock kept his corps on the northern side of the Chesterfield Bridge. Most importantly, Burnside had arrived so late in the day that he decided not to try to cross his corps across the Ox Ford and thus stopped on the north side of it that night. Having secured two crossing points, Grant was threatening to get past the North Anna without the Confederates being able to offer a strong defense, eliminating one more defensive line on the way to Richmond.

By now, Lee realized that Grant had intended to force a passage through his army after all and was willing to fight a pitched battle along the North Anna, but by then Grant already had part of his army across the river and control of several crossings. Lee seemed to be in a predicament, but he figured a masterful way out of it on the night of the 23rd. Together with his chief engineer, Lee devised one of the most clever defensive lines of the war: an inverted V shaped line that would rest the tip of the inverted V on bluffs near the North Anna overlooking Ox Ford. Given the commanding nature of the bluffs, the salient in the line could not be attacked like the Mule Shoe salient at Spotsylvania had been, and Burnside's failure to cross Ox Ford made it possible for the Confederates to dig in the line there. Meanwhile, the left and right flanks on the ends of the inverted V both rested on the Virginia Central Railroad.

The most obvious advantage offered by this defensive line was that it afforded the Confederates the use of interior lines. With a shorter line than Grant's army, Lee could move men from one flank to the other much more quickly, even by railroad if need be. The natural positions, including bluffs at the center of the line, also offered strong defensive advantages.

While Lee certainly appreciated all the advantages it would offer as a defensive line, Lee realized that the most important aspect of the inverted V line was that Grant had to divide his army to cross the river and attack him, leaving the North Anna in their back. For example, if

Grant pushed his corps forward at Jericho Mills and the Chesterfield Bridge, Lee could quickly shift more men to one of his flanks to outman and attack one of the Union wings before it could be helped by the other wing, which would have to recross to the north side of the North Anna, march awhile, and then cross the North Anna again to reach the other Union corps. With a river in their back, if Lee's army overwhelmed one of the Union wings, it would be in danger of being destroyed before it could get back across the river or before it could be reinforced.

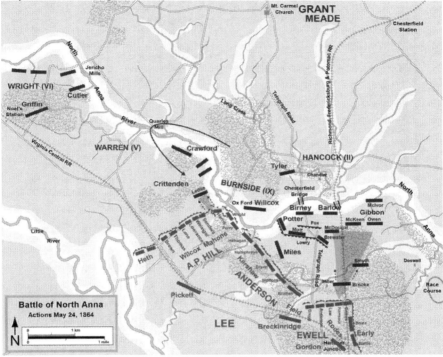

**Lee's inverted V line**

Once Lee drew up the plan, the Confederates went about digging and manning the line throughout the night of the 23rd, made possible by the fact Burnside had not secured the southern side of Ox Ford. When Lee had successfully managed to establish the new line, all that was left to do was wait and hope Grant would try to cross the two wings of his army separately as it seemed he was planning to do earlier in the day. Aware that the inverted V line offered him perhaps his best chance yet to deliver a huge blow to the Army of the Potomac, Lee explained to one of the physicians treating him, "If I can get one more pull at him, I will defeat him."

**May 24**

"We must strike them a blow. We must never let them pass us again. We must strike them a blow." – Robert E. Lee

When Lee finished his work on the night of May 23, he certainly hoped that May 24 would be one of the decisive days of the war, so one can only imagine his frustration when he began suffering dysentery early that morning. One of his men described the bedridden commander being "cross as an old bear," and A.P. Hill received an unusually stern rebuke from Lee for only attacking Warren with one division the previous day: "General Hill, why did you let those people cross here? Why didn't you throw your whole force on them and drive them back as Jackson would have done?" The reference to Stonewall Jackson, who was not only a Southern demigod but also a man Hill had feuded with back in 1862, had to have been a particularly biting criticism for Hill to take, but he was also well aware that Lee was acting uncharacteristically due to the dysentery and did not snap back at Lee.

Meanwhile, Grant was about to proceed just as Lee had hoped. Having found almost no resistance along the North Anna the previous day, Grant triumphantly informed Washington that morning, "The enemy have fallen back from North Anna." Of course, Grant could not have been more wrong. By 8:00 a.m., Hancock's corps had crossed the Chesterfield Bridge, and Grant gave his subordinates marching orders that would result in linking up the entire army on the southern bank of the North Anna. As he explained in his memoirs:

"Before the exact position of the whole of Lee's line was accurately known, I directed Hancock and Warren each to send a brigade to Ox Ford by the south side of the river. They found the enemy too strong to justify a serious attack. A third ford was found between Ox Ford and Jericho. Burnside was directed to cross a division over this ford, and to send one division to Hancock. Crittenden was crossed by this newly-discovered ford, and formed up the river to connect with Crawford's left. Potter joined Hancock by way of the wooden bridge. Crittenden had a severe engagement with some of Hill's corps on his crossing the river, and lost heavily."

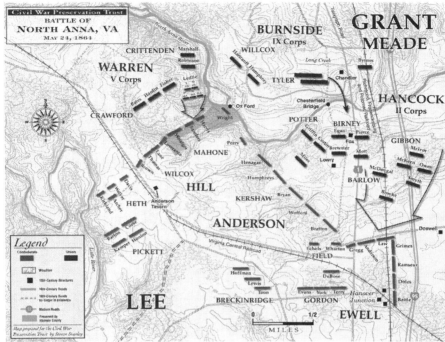

BATTLE OF
NORTH ANNA, VA
MAY 24, 1864

Initially, Grant thought the Confederates near Ox Ford were part of a rearguard covering Lee's retreating army. One of Burnside's divisions led by Thomas Crittenden was thus ordered to cross at Quarles Mills to the west and then march back toward the southern bank of Ox Ford, under the assumption that this would allow him to flank the Confederate defenders on the left. Instead, the orders were unwittingly sending Crittenden right into the heart of the Confederate line manned by William Mahone's division of Hill's corps.

Making matters worse, the lead brigade of Crittenden's division was being led by James H. Ledlie, who was notorious for drinking while in the field and happened to have quite a bit of liquid courage on the morning of the 24th. As Ledlie's brigade crossed at the head of Crittenden's division and worked its way back toward Ox Ford, Ledlie ordered his brigade headlong into the Confederate line, despite seeing breastworks at the top of the bluff, an obvious indication that this was not a rearguard. Incredibly, Ledlie ordered just one of the regiments in his brigade, the 35th Massachusetts, to advance, and he exhorted his men by riding along the heights and shouting, "Come on, Yank!". Meanwhile, one of his aides rode alongside Ledlie with his hat twirling around the tip of his sword, and as if to suggest an attack would be futile, a Confederate sharpshooter shot a hole right through the hat as the two men rode around.

Not surprisingly, the 35th Massachusetts' attack on an entire Confederate division bogged down almost immediately, but even when his initial attack was repulsed, Ledlie sought reinforcements from Crittenden, who was understandably stunned to learn that an attack had been made in the first place without the rest of the division across the river yet. By the time staffers from Crittenden returned to Ledlie, they found him totally inebriated, and as the Confederates moved artillery batteries into place on the bluffs, he still ordered his men forward. The brigade made a suicidal charge toward the bluffs and was badly repulsed, with men having to take cover in a ditch at the base of the bluffs. One soldier ruefully noted, "Nothing whatever was accomplished, except a needless slaughter, the humiliation of the defeat of the men, and the complete loss of all confidence in the brigade commander who was wholly responsible."

Incredibly, Ledlie would be promoted to command of a division after the battle because Crittenden cited Ledlie's brigade for behaving gallantly during the fight, unaware of just what kind of condition Ledlie himself was in. As a result, Ledlie would play a crucial role in the debacle at the Battle of the Crater a few months later during Grant's siege of Petersburg.

While Ledlie's brigade was making its foolish attack, a thunderstorm hit the area, and it was during the rain that Hancock's corps advanced only to find Confederate fortifications manned by Evander Law's brigade from Ewell's corps. In addition to unnerving Theodore Lyman, who was near the flammable ammunition trains, the thunderstorm brought the fighting between the Confederates and Federals to a stop for fear that the conditions would ruin the gunpowder and make their muskets worthless. When David Birney's division and John Gibbon's division both tried to advance toward the Confederates and still could not dislodge them, Hancock began to suspect that Lee's army was actually there in force and not retreating at all.

Just as Lee had hoped, Grant had split his army against Lee's line on the southern side of the North Anna, with a majority of his army available to attack Hancock in the east while Wright and Warren were miles away to the west and Burnside was north of the river. As one Union staffer noted, Lee "now had one of those opportunities that occur but rarely in war, but which, in the grasp of a master, make or mar the fortunes of armies and decide the result of campaigns." Grant also recognized the precarious position he had put himself in, noting in his memoirs:

"Lee now had his entire army south of the North Anna. Our lines covered his front, with the six miles separating the two wings guarded by but a single division. To get from one wing to the other the river would have to be crossed twice. Lee could reinforce any part of his line from all points of it in a very short march; or could concentrate the whole of it wherever he might choose to assault. We were, for the time, practically two armies besieging."

However, the Confederates would not end up counterattacking or taking advantage of their interior lines on the 24th to attack Hancock's corps near the Chesterfield Bridge or the men near Ox Ford and Jericho Mills. That night, Lee would report to Richmond, "The enemy has been making feeble attacks upon our lines to-day, probably with a view of ascertaining our position. They were easily repulsed. General Mahone drove three regiments across the river, capturing a stand of colors and some prisoners, among them 1 aide-de-camp of General Ledlie."

If Grant had fallen into Lee's trap as he had hoped, why did a counterpunch never come from the Army of Northern Virginia? The answer is still unclear, but there's no doubt that Lee's illness played a crucial role. With Lee bedridden throughout the day, he could not ascertain things for himself, relying on reports from the rear. Making matters worse, A.P. Hill, who had a history of illnesses that had made him miss the climactic third day of the Battle of Gettysburg, was still suffering from illness and had already performed poorly the day before (at least in Lee's eyes). And on the very same day that Lee and Hill were incapacitated, Richard Ewell turned over command of his corps due to exhaustion, ending his participation in the Overland Campaign. With Longstreet having been wounded in the Wilderness and cavalry chief JEB Stuart killed two weeks earlier, none of the original corps commanders were available for operations on May 24. As Lee's nephew Fitzhugh Lee would point out in a biography of his uncle, "the whole army was in good condition; but its commanding general was ill, and so was one of his corps commanders, while another had been disabled by wounds. Lee's sickness made it 'manifest he was the head and front, the very life and soul of his army.'"

With that said, some military historians have claimed that the general consensus that the Confederates missed a crucial opportunity on the 24th is wrong. Mark Grimsley points out that the inverted V line did not seem to suggest a plan for offensive operations and that quotes about Lee wanting to attack at the North Anna may have been misremembered or simply falsified, writing, "no surviving contemporaneous correspondence alludes to such an operation, and the troop movements made on the night of May 23 and on May 24 were limited and defensive in nature." As Grant notes in his memoirs, "Lee had been reinforced, and was being reinforced, largely. About this time the very troops whose coming I had predicted, had arrived or were coming in. Pickett with a full division from Richmond was up; Hoke from North Carolina had come with a brigade; and Breckinridge was there: in all probably not less than fifteen thousand men. But he did not attempt to drive us from the field."

By the early evening, it had become painfully clear to the Army of the Potomac that the Army of Northern Virginia was indeed in their front and had created a solid defensive line that Hancock considered to be as strong as their defensive line at Spotsylvania. Grant now realized that it was his army in peril, and he switched the nature of his own army's operations by having them dig in and establish their own defensive line while engineers feverishly worked to construct pontoon bridges that would allow them to cross the river faster and facilitate the linking up of his separate wings. His staffer Horace Porter would later recount Grant saying, "It now looks as if Lee's position were such that it would not be prudent to fight a battle in the narrow space between these two rivers, and I shall withdraw our army from its present position, and make another flank march to the left."

A Union news journalist would later report the "game of war seldom presents a more effectual checkmate than was here given by Lee", but Grant had actually avoided a potential disaster on the 24th. Still, Grant was not yet out of the woods; he would have to figure out a way to delicately extricate both wings of his army in the face of Lee's line.

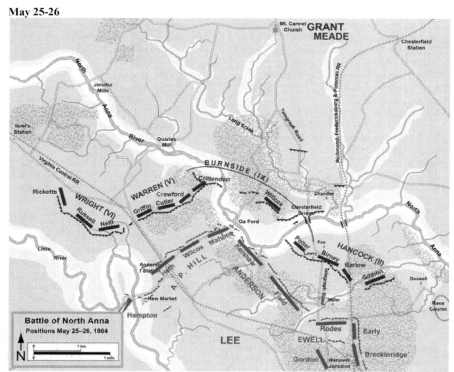

By the morning of the 25th, the two armies were staring across each other in well-entrenched defensive lines, reminiscent of what had happened at Spotsylvania. One Union soldier recalled, "To raise a head above the works involved a great personal risk, and as nothing was to be gained by exposure, most of the men wisely took advantage of their cover." At the same time, the two armies' lines were so close that one Meade staffer compared it to "two schoolboys trying to stare each other out of countenance."

With Grant's army along his entire line, the only maneuvering Lee could do via marching was to move south toward Richmond, something he clearly did not want to do. While this meant Grant had the initiative to make the next move, Grant was also naturally worried that the second he put one of his wings in motion to recross the North Anna, Lee could bring the brunt of his army down upon the one wing that retreated or the other wing that remained entrenched and isolated across the river.

The first movements of the day involved Wright and Warren probing Hill's line on the Confederate left, only to quickly learn (or verify) that the Confederate line was extremely strong there. Instead of testing the Confederates, that wing of Grant's army contented itself with tearing up several miles of railroad tracks along the Virginia Central Railroad, one of the key supply lines to Richmond. Grant also received intelligence that was clearly wishful thinking, as he recounted in his memoirs:

"On the same day news was received that Lee was falling back on Richmond. This proved not to be true. But we could do nothing where we were unless Lee would assume the offensive. I determined, therefore, to draw out of our present position and make one more effort to get between him and Richmond. I had no expectation now, however, of succeeding in this; but I did expect to hold him far enough west to enable me to reach the James River high up. Sheridan was now again with the Army of the Potomac."

On the evening of the 25th, Grant met with his principal subordinates to discuss which way to move. Knowing that Lee constantly anticipated the Army of the Potomac to move by his right flank, some of his generals suggested throwing the Confederates a changeup by moving to the west against his left flank. However, that would've required maneuvering the Army of the Potomac across several rivers, including the North Anna, Little River and South Anna, while also moving further away from Union supply lines along the Chesapeake Bay. Grant explained the problems with his current line and a movement west in his dispatch to Washington:

"To make a direct attack from either wing would cause a slaughter of our men that even success would not justify. To turn the enemy by his right, between the two Annas is impossible on account of the swamp upon which his right rests. To turn him by the left leaves Little River, New Found River and South Anna River, all of them streams presenting considerable obstacles to the movement of our army, to be crossed. I have determined therefore to turn the enemy's right by crossing at or near Hanover Town. This crosses all three streams at once, and leaves us still where we can draw supplies."

As Grant's dispatch intimated, moving to the east would only require crossing the Pamunkey River, and the Union could more easily establish supply lines via that river and the Richmond & York River Railroad, which ran to the east. Moreover, Grant could reinforce his army with men from the command of Benjamin Butler, which would once again give him a massive advantage in manpower:

"On the 26th I informed the government at Washington of the position of the two armies; of the reinforcements the enemy had received; of the move I proposed to make; and directed that our base of supplies should be shifted to White House, on the Pamunkey. The wagon train and guards moved directly from Port Royal to White House. Supplies moved around by water, guarded by the navy. Orders had previously been sent, through Halleck, for Butler to send Smith's corps to White House. This order was repeated on the 25th, with directions that they should be landed on the north side of the Pamunkey, and marched until they joined the Army of the Potomac."

The reinforcements were a critical aspect of Grant's strategy because he had reached the conclusion that Lee's army was reaching its breaking point, due to the fact that Lee had not tried to press an advantage on the 24th. Of course, Grant had no idea how badly illness had ravaged the Confederate high command during that crucial day, but his lack of knowledge led him to the mistaken conclusion that he was on the verge of breaking Lee's back. On the 25th, he fired off a dispatch to Washington triumphantly asserting, "Lee's army is really whipped. The prisoners we now take show it, and the actions of his Army show it unmistakably. A battle with them outside of intrenchments cannot be had. Our men feel that they have gained the morale over the enemy, and attack him with confidence. I may be mistaken but I feel that our success over Lee's army is already assured."

While Grant was engaging in overly optimistic wishful thinking, there was still the matter of getting his army out of its tight spot. Grant hoped to accomplish this by tricking Lee into thinking he was moving west, which he would attempt by sending one of Sheridan's cavalry divisions west. This would hopefully induce Lee into thinking the cavalry was moving to screen the infantry and perform reconnaissance in front. Meanwhile, the corps of Hancock, Warren and Wright would carefully recross the river on the night of the 26th and begin the movement east. This would theoretically allow Grant's army the chance to steal a march on Lee, safely get to the Pamunkey River, and maybe even interpose itself between the Army of Northern Virginia and Richmond.

Throughout May 26, the rain made both armies miserable as they continued to huddle in trenches that were now filling up with mud and water. During the afternoon, James Wilson's cavalry division began its diversionary tactics by conspicuously crossing Jericho Mills and moving west. To add to the subterfuge, one of the cavalrymen noted that the division set fire to "fences, boards, and everything inflammable within our reach…to give the appearance of a vast force, just building its bivouac fires." One division of infantry began a circuitous march that added to Lee's belief that the movement was west instead of east, and he sent a message to Richmond stating, "From present indications the enemy seems to contemplate a movement on our left flank."

On the night of the 26th, both wings of Grant's army began their stealthy withdrawal. Grant staffer Horace Porter explained:

"As soon as it was dark the other divisions of Wright's corps had begun the recrossing of the river. This corps followed the route which had been taken by Russell's division, while Warren took a road a little farther to the north. Burnside and Hancock next withdrew, and so cautiously that their movements entirely escaped detection by the enemy. All the corps left strong guards in their fronts, which were withdrawn at the last moment. The pontoon-bridges were taken up after crossing the river, and cavalry was sent to the several fords to hold them after they had been abandoned by the infantry, and to destroy any facilities for crossing which had been neglected."

To help mask the army's withdrawal, the Union bands were ordered to play, leaving the impression that they were still in the same lines. A soldier explained, "Such bands as there were had been vigorously playing patriotic music, always soliciting responses from the rebs with Dixie, My Maryland, or other favorites of theirs." When the last of Hancock's men recrossed the North Anna, the Chesterfield Bridge was set ablaze and destroyed. Grant had safely withdrawn his army, and Lee's army would not discover the withdrawal of the Union army until the morning of the 27th. Once Lee realized early that morning that the Union army had escaped his trap and moved east, he began marching his army southeast, planning once again to block Grant's path to Richmond.

Compared to the other major actions of the Overland Campaign, the Battle of North Anna is a misnomer, since the two sides only lost about a combined 5,000 casualties, 2500 or so on each side. If anything, the battle was most notable for Lee's cunning defensive line and the great what-if that was presented when the Confederates were unable to strike out at Grant on the 24th. As with the Wilderness and Spotsylvania, Grant had failed to tactically win the battle, but he had also not been prevented from continuing his advance toward Richmond. Lee, on the other hand, had to bitterly accept the fact that illness may have deprived him of his best chance to destroy Grant. By the time the two armies engaged in the next major pitched battle at Cold Harbor, reinforcements had bolstered Grant's army back up to nearly 100,000 men, nearly 40,000 more men than he had on hand at the North Anna.

As the Battle of North Anna technically came to a close, the inconclusive results of the fighting and the general mood of the Union army was summed up by an anecdote recalled by Horace Porter as the Army of the Potomac marched east:

"On the march the general-in-chief, as he rode by, was vociferously cheered, as usual, by the troops. Every movement directed by him inspired the men with new confidence in his ability and his watchfulness over their interests; and not only the officers, but the rank and file, understood fully that he had saved them on the North Anna from the slaughter which would probably have occurred if they had been thrown against Lee's formidable intrenchments, and had had to fight a battle with their backs to a river; that he had skilfully withdrawn them without the loss of a man or a wagon, and that they were again making an advance movement."

## Heading Toward Cold Harbor

"The enemy knew the importance of Cold Harbor to us, and seemed determined that we should not hold it." – Ulysses S. Grant

On the 28th, the two armies began the movements that would lead them toward Cold Harbor. Having decided to push east and cross the Pamunkey River, Grant's new supply line at White House all but necessitated that he had to concentrate his army near Hanover Town, which was just 20 miles northeast of Richmond. From there, the advance toward Richmond would bring the Army of the Potomac toward Cold Harbor, as Grant aide Horace Porter explained in his memoirs, *Campaigning with Grant*:

"Three main roads lead from Hanovertown to Richmond. The most northerly is called the Hanovertown or Shady Grove road; the second route, the Mechanicsville road; the third and most southerly, which runs through Old Cold Harbor, New Cold Harbor, and Gaines's Mill, is known as the Cold Harbor road. Old Cold Harbor, half-way between Hanovertown and Richmond, consisted merely of a few scattered houses; but its strategic position was important for reasons which will hereafter appear. New Cold Harbor was little more than the intersection of crossroads about a mile and a half west of Old Cold Harbor. It was at first supposed that Cold Harbor was a corruption of the phrase Cool Arbor, and the shade-trees in the vicinity seemed to suggest such a name; but it was ascertained afterward that the name Cold Harbor was correct, that it had been taken from the places frequently found along the highways of England, and means 'shelter without fire.'"

As he had so many times before, Lee moved to keep his army between Grant and Richmond by marching southeast to Atlee's Station, a stop on the Virginia Central Railroad less than 10 miles north of the Confederate capital itself. This spot gave Lee the chance to position his army behind the Totopotomoy Creek, using the water as an obstacle and countering any effort by Grant to move against Richmond or the Virginia Central Railroad. However, this position also left Lee little breathing room outside of his capital; his army was now positioned near the same ground that the two armies had fought over during the Seven Days Battles of Mechanicsville and Gaines's Mill in June 1862, when the Army of the Potomac had gotten so close to Richmond that they could see its church steeples.

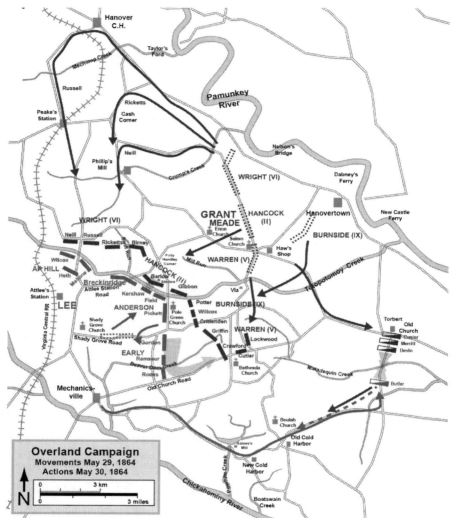

As the armies were in motion on the 28th, their respective cavalries squared off around Haw's Shop, fighting a dismounted cavalry battle that pitted David Gregg's division of cavalry against Wade Hampton III. Though the battle was long and inconclusive, by locating Gregg's cavalry there, it suggested to Lee the general vicinity and direction Grant's army was marching toward. It also prevented Grant's cavalry from pushing on toward Mechanicsville, as he had ordered, which forced Grant to use his infantry to conduct a reconnaissance in force to try to determine the location of Lee's lines the following day. However, the action on May 29 still left Grant largely in the dark, as he noted in his memoirs:

"On the 29th a reconnoissance was made in force, to find the position of Lee. Wright's corps pushed to Hanover Court House. Hancock's corps pushed toward Totopotomoy Creek; Warren's corps to the left on the Shady Grove Church Road, while Burnside was held in reserve. Our advance was pushed forward three miles on the left with but little fighting. There was now an appearance of a movement past our left flank, and Sheridan was sent to meet it."

The inconclusive results of that day's reconnaissance only told Grant that Lee's army was above the Chickahominy River, which he almost certainly had to have presumed, and he wouldn't truly learn Lee's dispositions on the southern bank of the Totopotomoy until May 30. That's because Lee's aggressive fighting spirit was up, and he ordered Jubal Early (who had succeeded to command of Richard Ewell's corps after Ewell relinquished command due to exhaustion) to attack Warren's V Corps near Bethesda Church as it was moving on the left of the Union line. Confederate I Corps artillery chief Porter Alexander explained Lee's thinking on the 30th:

"In many of the Federal accounts, it is assumed that Lee's attitude at this period was strictly the defensive. Perhaps it should have been, but all who were near him recognized that never in the war was he so ready to attack upon the slightest opportunity. An instance occurred on May 30, of which I was a spectator. A half-mile in front of our line we could see Bethesda Church, an important junction point, well within the enemy's territory, and sure to be included within his lines, rapidly being extended to his left. Down a long, straight road, we had seen their cavalry all the morning, and, about noon, a brigade of infantry appeared. Immediately, Lee ordered Early to send a brigade to attack it. Early selected Pegram's brigade, commanded by Gen. Edward Willis, a brilliant young officer, just promoted from the 12th Ga., who had been a cadet at West Point at the beginning of the war. He had been a personal friend and I saw his brigade start on its errand with apprehension of disaster, for it was evident that a hornets' nest would be stirred up. The Federal brigade was quickly routed and pursued, but the pursuers soon encountered a division with its artillery and were repulsed with severe loss."

A Union soldier recalled the attack, "The slaughter was so sickening that Major Hartshorne leaped to his feet and called upon his assailants to surrender. Some hundreds did so. Rebels or no rebels, their behavior and bearing during the charge had won the admiration of their captors, who did not hesitate to express it." One of the Confederates who survived the attack later wrote, "Our line melted away as if by magic. Every brigade, staff and field officer was cut down, (mostly killed outright) in an incredibly short time."

The short but vicious fighting, known as the Battle of Bethesda Church, resulted in nearly 2,000 casualties among the two sides, men Lee could ill afford to lose. It also made clear to Grant that Lee's army was in force near the Totopotomoy Creek, and the U.S. War Department correspondent Charles Dana, who was attached to the army, relayed back to Washington, "There was no doubt that Lee's whole army ... was close at hand and strongly entrenched again. Grant ... declared emphatically he would not run his head against heavy works."

Grant's bigger concern, however, was his inkling that Lee's army was further to the right and thus threatened his army's left flank. For that reason, he ordered Sheridan to move his cavalry to the crossroads at Cold Harbor and "to hold the place at all hazards, until reinforcements could be sent". Ironically, the reason Lee ultimately did send some of his infantry that way was because he had gotten word Grant was receiving reinforcements from Baldy Smith's XVIII Corps, which had left Benjamin Butler's campaign and sailed up the Pamunkey to join Grant. Lee knew that if Smith landed at White House, the main supply base for the Union army, he could link up with Grant's left by taking the road to Old Cold Harbor, which would have then flanked his own right. A small cavalry skirmish near Old Church on the 30th suggested to Lee that Grant was indeed moving infantry toward Cold Harbor.

10,000 of Smith's men would indeed link up with Grant's army on June 1, but by then Lee had received his own reinforcements, a division of 7,000 men under the command of Robert Hoke, which he had rushed toward Old Cold Harbor. As a result, Hoke's division was being placed on a collision course with Sheridan, and the concerns of both commanders, due to the fog of war and their lack of knowledge of the other's intentions, would lead them to a major battle at Cold Harbor.

### Fighting over the Crossroads, May 31

After the events of the 30th, Grant issued orders to Meade that would reinforce Sheridan's cavalry near Cold Harbor. Tensions had been running high due to the unusual command structure of the Army of the Potomac, and during the time spent around Cold Harbor, Grant had decided to delegate the tactical movements and fighting of the army to Meade, who was still nominally the commander of the Army of the Potomac. Feeling more empowered, Meade acted with vigor upon Grant's orders, but it would also make him more aggressive during the next several days. On the 31st, Grant ordered Meade:

"General Smith will debark his force at the White House tonight and start up the south bank of the Pamunkey at an early hour, probably at 3 A.M. in the morning. It is not improbable that the enemy, being aware of Smith's movement, will be feeling to get on our left flank for the purpose of cutting him off, or by a dash to crush him and get back before we are aware of it. Sheridan ought to be notified to watch the enemy's movements well out towards Cold Harbor, and also on the Mechanicsville road. Wright should be got well massed on Hancock's right, so that, if it becomes necessary, he can take the place of the latter readily whilst troops are being thrown east of the Totopotomoy if necessary.

I want Sheridan to send a cavalry force of at least half a brigade, if not a whole brigade, at 5 A.M. in the morning, to communicate with Smith and to return with him. I will send orders for Smith by the messenger you send to Sheridan with his orders."

Grant was ordering two of his infantry corps to arrive at Cold Harbor on June 1, but he was doing so at a time when he was unaware that Lee had Hoke's division, his reinforcements, ready to push in on Sheridan's cavalry at the crossroads of Old Cold Harbor on the afternoon of the 31st. And as Hoke's division made their way toward Cold Harbor, they were coming up in support Fitzhugh Lee's Confederate cavalry near the Cold Harbor crossroads. This ensured a fight between the Confederates and Sheridan's cavalry troopers in the vicinity, which Sheridan described in his memoirs:

"The morning of the 31st I visited Torbert to arrange for his further advance, intending thus to anticipate an expected attack from Fitzhugh Lee, who was being reinforced by infantry. I met Torbert at Custer's headquarters, and found that the two had already been talking over a scheme to capture Cold Harbor, and when their plan was laid before me it appeared so plainly feasible that I fully endorsed it, at once giving directions for its immediate execution, and ordering Gregg to come forward to Torbert's support with such troops as he could spare from the duty with which he had been charged.

Torbert moved out promptly, Merritt's brigade first, followed by Custer's, on the direct road to Cold Harbor, while Devin's brigade was detached, and marched by a left-hand road that would bring him in on the right and rear of the enemy's line, which was posted in front of the crossroads. Devin was unable to carry his part of the programme farther than to reach the front of the Confederate right, and as Merritt came into position to the right of the Old Church road Torbert was obliged to place a part of Custer's brigade on Merritt's left so as to connect with Devin. The whole division was now in line, confronted by Fitzhugh Lee's cavalry, supported by Clingman's brigade from Hoke's division of infantry; and from the Confederate breastworks, hastily constructed out of logs, rails, and earth, a heavy fire was already being poured upon us that it seemed impossible to withstand. None of Gregg's division had yet arrived, and so stubborn was the enemy's resistance that I began to doubt our ability to carry the place before reinforcements came up, but just then Merritt reported that he could turn the enemy's left, and being directed to execute his proposition, he carried it to a most successful issue with the First and Second regular cavalry. Just as these two regiments passed around the enemy's left and attacked his rear, the remainder of the division assailed him in front. This maneouvre of Merritt's stampeded the Confederates, and the defenses falling into our hands easily, we pushed ahead on the Bottom's bridge road three-fourths of a mile beyond Cold Harbor.

Cold Harbor was now mine, but I was about nine miles away from our nearest infantry, and had been able to bring up only Davies's brigade of cavalry, which arrived after the fight. My isolated position therefore made me a little uneasy."

As more of Hoke's division came up, the pressure on Sheridan's cavalry was quickly becoming unbearable, and in the late afternoon he was compelled to pull back to Old Church. Unfortunately for the Union, just as Sheridan did so, he received orders to hold his ground at all cost, as Grant still needed to secure the crossroads to get Baldy Smith's men to his army. Sheridan recalled, "In view of this state of affairs, I notified General Meade that I had taken Cold Harbor, but could not with safety to my command hold it, and forthwith gave directions to withdraw during the night. The last of my troops had scarcely pulled out, however, when I received a despatch from Meade directing me to hold Cold Harbor at every hazard. "

Luckily for Sheridan and the Union army, the desperate fighting had induced Hoke's division to start digging in further west of the crossroads at Old Cold Harbor, which allowed Sheridan's cavalry to take back its previous position from earlier in the day without a fight. Ironically, Sheridan's troopers were able to use the Confederates' own temporary breastworks as their own: "We now found that the temporary breastworks of rails and logs which the Confederates had built were of incalculable benefit to us in furnishing material with which to establish a line of defense, they being made available by simply reversing them at some points, or at others wholly reconstructing them to suit the circumstances of the ground." More importantly, this also secured the vital crossroads that would allow Grant to get Smith's corps and Wright's corps onto the left of his line, if they could make it in time.

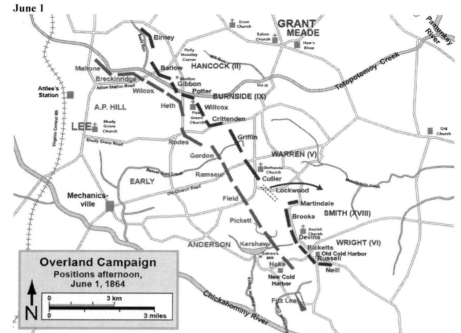

**Overland Campaign**
Positions afternoon,
June 1, 1864

N

0 ____ 3 km

0 ____ 3 miles

Coincidentally, both Lee and Grant intended to take the offensive near Cold Harbor on June 1. That morning, Lee only knew that some of Sheridan's cavalry was at Old Cold Harbor, while he had at least Hoke's division and Fitzhugh Lee's cavalry entrenched nearby. Meanwhile, Grant hoped that Baldy Smith's corps and Wright's corps would arrive at Old Cold Harbor and immediately overwhelm Lee's token resistance, thus pushing in Lee's right flank.

Unfortunately for Grant, events had conspired against the Union army in the early morning hours of June 1. It had been raining heavily the week before while the armies were near North Anna, and the poor quality of the roads badly slowed Wright's VI Corps as it marched during the night to relieve Sheridan at Cold Harbor. Even worse, Baldy Smith's men received mistaken orders from Grant's staff to move to New Castle Ferry instead of Cold Harbor, sending them several miles in the wrong direction. As a result, both infantry corps would be forced to make all night marches of at least 15 miles, and they would be exhausted when they finally made it to their spot.

Grant was also poorly served by the lethargic performance of Warren's V Corps, a problem that he had to deal with on numerous occasions throughout the Overland Campaign. He noted in his memoirs:

"Before the removal of Wright's corps from our right, after dark on the 31st, the two lines, Federal and Confederate, were so close together at that point that either side could detect directly any movement made by the other. Finding at daylight that Wright had left his front, Lee evidently divined that he had gone to our left. At all events, soon after light on the 1st of June Anderson, who commanded the corps on Lee's left, was seen moving along Warren's front. Warren was ordered to attack him vigorously in flank, while Wright was directed to move out and get on his front. Warren fired his artillery at the enemy; but lost so much time in making ready that the enemy got by, and at three o'clock he reported the enemy was strongly intrenched in his front, and besides his lines were so long that he had no mass of troops to move with. He seemed to have forgotten that lines in rear of an army hold themselves while their defenders are fighting in their front. Wright reconnoitred some distance to his front: but the enemy finding Old Cold Harbor already taken had halted and fortified some distance west."

Warren's inability to prevent Anderson's movement allowed Anderson to come up on Lee's right before Wright and Smith were fully in position on Lee's left. This gave Lee his own opportunity, because, as Porter Alexander pointed out, "it was only at 4 P. M. of the 1st that [Smith] joined at Cold Harbor the 6th corps, the head of which had reached the ground about 10 A. M. after a fatiguing all-night march. It is plain, then, that here a rare opportunity had been offered the Confederates."

Unfortunately for Lee, his subordinates seemed to be confused as to the plan. Lee had intended for Anderson's corps and Hoke's division to make a concerted advance on Old Cold Harbor that morning, which at the time only had Sheridan and Wright's worn out men to defend, but Hoke was under the impression that he was supposed to wait until after Anderson's assault.

**Hoke**

With Anderson and Hoke operating under different assumptions, Anderson's attack against Sheridan's cavalry was a fiasco. Porter Alexander described what happened:

"With Hoke's large division on its right flank, [Anderson's] corps should have been able to quickly clear the way of three brigades of cavalry. It would have had then the opportunity to meet the 6th corps scattered along the road for many miles and in an exhausted condition. Unfortunately, Hoke's brigade had not been put under Anderson's command, so neither felt full responsibility. It only formed in line, but did not attack the cavalry breastworks, reporting them as too strong. Kershaw made an attack about 6 A. M., but only put into it two brigades. The enemy, with their magazine carbines behind intrenchments, repulsed two assaults with severe loss, and then the turning enterprise was abandoned. Lee was not upon the ground in the early hours of the day, and Longstreet was absent, wounded. No effort worthy the name was used to carry out Lee's plan of attack, nor were the favorable conditions appreciated, although they might have been, as only cavalry was found in our front. Hoke's division should have been used to turn their flank and get among their dismounts.

While Kershaw made his attack, the remainder of the long column halted in the road, expecting the march to be presently resumed. But when the delay was prolonged, and a few random bullets from the front began to reach the line, without any general instructions, the men here and there began to dig dirt with their bayonets and pile it with their tin cups to get a little cover. Others followed suit, and gradually the whole column was at work intrenching the line along which they had halted. Gradually it became known that the enemy were accumulating in our front, and then, as the country was generally flat, orders were given to close up the column and adopt its line as the line of battle, distributing our guns upon it at suitable points. Our intrenchments were scarcely more than a good beginning, a line of knee-deep trench with the earth thrown in front. It was entirely without abattis or obstruction in front, except at a point on our picket line where a small entanglement had been left by our cavalry. Meanwhile, Grant, under the mistaken idea that Lee was afraid to fight in the open, was urging an early attack before Lee had time to fortify. But it was 1 P. M. before the whole of the 6th corps was up, and it was 6 P. M. before Smith's command was in position."

As a result of the communications snafu, an entire Confederate corps, as well as a division, were prevented from taking Old Cold Harbor by dismounted cavalry troopers. This allowed the lead elements of Wright's corps to arrive around 9:00 a.m. that morning, after which Sheridan's hard-pressed cavalry retired from the front. Though Wright's soldiers began improving the defensive fortifications held by Sheridan's cavalry, they were also completely fatigued by the marching and hardly in fighting shape.

Lee's plans had gone totally awry by the morning of the 1st, but the comedy of errors was just beginning. Grant had intended for Wright and Smith to make an attack as soon as they had gotten in position, but the delays ultimately added to the time they spent marching and left them completely exhausted by the time they had actually reached Cold Harbor. Moreover, as Porter Alexander's account had noted, the Confederates had begun digging their own defensive fortifications in an impromptu fashion as Anderson's attack was fizzling out that morning. Sending tired soldiers headlong into well-entrenched positions would be nothing short of suicidal, and prisoners captured by Sheridan during the fighting that morning made clear that at least 3 Confederate brigades were in front of the Union position.

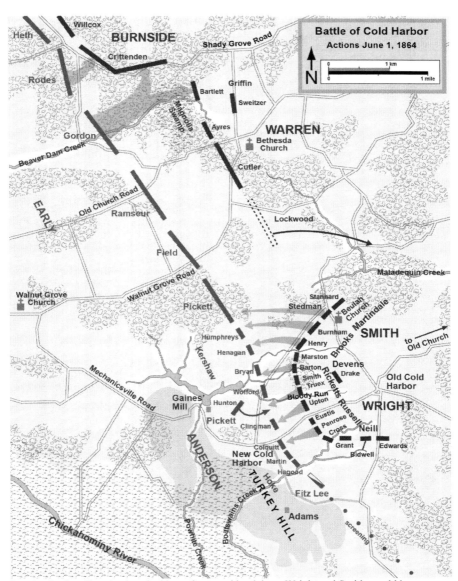

Despite the fact Grant's plans had been frustrated by delays, Wright and Smith would be ordered to go forward with an assault in the early evening of June 1 anyway, stunning many of the men in that sector. The Union soldiers had to cross open ground for several hundred yards before reaching the Confederate positions, which were in a lightly wooded area. One Union soldier described the fighting as they reached the enemy lines as "a sheet of flame, sudden as lightning, red as blood, and so near that it seemed to singe the men's faces." With regiments getting confused in the woods, at one point some of the Union soldiers found a gap in the Confederate line due to the lack of coordination between Anderson's corps and Hoke's division, and they began to push through, allowing the Union attackers to take the Confederates' rifle-pits and capture several hundred Confederates. However, an inevitable counterattack pushed the Federals back and made clear that it would be hard to dislodge Lee's right flank.

While it's almost certain the Union attack would have failed anyway, miscommunications between Warren and one of his division commanders resulted in a failure to support the Union attack. Meade had ordered Warren, "Generals Wright and Smith will attack this evening. It is very desirable you should join this attack, unless in your judgment it is impracticable." Thus, at 6:00 p.m., Warren ordered one of his divisions under Henry Lockwood to march out of the line and support the attack, but the lack of reconnaissance led Lockwood in the wrong direction and to the rear, where the division was completely useless. Inexplicably, Warren protested ignorance to Meade, telling him, ""In some unaccountable way, he took his whole division, without my knowing it, away from the left of the line of battle, and turned up the dark 2 miles in my rear, and I have not yet got him back. All this time the firing should have guided him at least. He is too incompetent, and too high rank leaves us no subordinate place for him. I earnestly beg that he may at once be relieved of duty with this army." Thus, a corps commander that had proven unfit for his own command several times in the past month had one of his own division commanders cashiered.

**Warren**

The failures of the day weighed so heavily on Meade that he lost his notorious temper. The commander, who was often compared to a snapping turtle, flew off the handle at just about anyone within earshot on the night of the 1st, as recounted by his staffer Theodore Lyman:

"General Meade was in one of his irascible fits to-night, which are always founded in good reason though they spread themselves over a good deal of ground that is not always in the limits of the question. First he blamed Warren for pushing out without orders; then he said each corps ought to act for itself and not always be leaning on him. Then he called Wright slow (a very true proposition as a general one). In the midst of these night-thoughts, comes here from General Smith bright, active, self-sufficient Engineer-Lieutenant Farquhar, who reports that his superior had arrived, fought, etc., etc., but that he had brought little ammunition, no transportation and that 'he considered his position precarious.' 'Then, why in Hell did he come at all for?' roared the exasperated Meade, with an oath that was rare with him."

At the same time, Lee was still desperate to wrest control of Old Cold Harbor from Grant, and his army made a series of futile attacks all along the line that night. Grant said of the attacks, "The enemy charged Warren three separate times with vigor, but were repulsed each time with loss. There was no officer more capable, nor one more prompt in acting, than Warren when the enemy forced him to it. There was also an attack upon Hancock's and Burnside's corps at the same time; but it was feeble and probably only intended to relieve Anderson who was being pressed by Wright and Smith. During the night the enemy made frequent attacks with the view of dispossessing us of the important position we had gained, but without effecting their object."

In the end, both armies had failed to dislodge the other from around Cold Harbor, and both had suffered nearly 2,000 casualties. While Grant could afford that kind of attrition, especially after all the reinforcements left him with nearly 100,000 men, Lee's army, which was only about half that size, could not.

**June 2**

On the night of June 1, Grant intended to take the offensive the following morning by swinging Hancock's II Corps from the right of the line to the left, as he had done with Wright the night before. Once again, it would fall to Warren and Burnside to pin down Lee's left flank so that he could not send reinforcements toward Cold Harbor as he had with Anderson's corps the day before. At the same time, when Meade told Baldy Smith of the plan to resume the offensive in the morning, Smith protested that the plan was "simply preposterous".

Naturally, Grant's plan for a morning offensive was frustrated by the fact that Hancock ran into some of the same problems Wright did, as Grant recalled in his memoirs:

"Hancock was moved from his place in line during the night and ordered to the left of Wright. I expected to take the offensive on the morning of the 2d, but the night was so dark, the heat and dust so excessive and the roads so intricate and hard to keep, that the head of column only reached Old Cold Harbor at six o'clock, but was in position at 7.30 A.M. Preparations were made for an attack in the afternoon, but did not take place until the next morning. Warren's corps was moved to the left to connect with Smith: Hancock's corps was got into position to the left of Wright's, and Burnside was moved to Bethesda Church in reserve. While Warren and Burnside were making these changes the enemy came out several times and attacked them, capturing several hundred prisoners. The attacks were repulsed, but not followed up as they should have been. I was so annoyed at this that I directed Meade to instruct his corps commanders that they should seize all such opportunities when they occurred, and not wait for orders, all of our manoeuvres being made for the very purpose of getting the enemy out of his cover."

Meade and Grant had become so frustrated by events and the performances of their subordinates that both of them had apparently decided to take the counterintuitive step of offering them more leeway and delegating more responsibility to them. Baldy Smith's understandable reluctance to make a frontal assault on well-entrenched Confederate defenders had only angered Meade, while Grant seemed to be suffering under the impression that delays could be avoided if the corps commanders were given their own discretion. As Lee's experiences from the previous day could have told him, allowing subordinates to exercise discretion often resulted in uncoordinated attacks and miscommunication between them. Charles Wainwright, one of the officers in Sheridan's cavalry, would note in his diary days later that the decision to delegate the authority for the attack to each corps commander was incomprehensible, writing, "there was a still more absurd order issued, for each command to attack without reference to its neighbors, as they saw fit; an order which looked as if the commander, whoever he is, had either lost his head entirely, or wanted to shift the responsibility off his own shoulders."

Since Grant's plan for a morning attack had been delayed twice and eventually put off until June 3, Lee was able to move more men to his right near Cold Harbor, and he also had an entire day to build defensive fortifications. The result was, as one man put it, the "most ingenious defensive configuration the war had yet witnessed." The Civil War soldiers of 1864 had become masters of building trenches and earthworks, but they rarely had an entire day to do so. Lee's men erected barricades of dirt and logs, abatis consisting of tree branches that would break up an attacking line, and even stakes in the ground that allowed Confederate artillery to measure distances and properly aim their batteries. One journalist in the area later reported that the fortifications were "intricate, zig-zagged lines within lines, lines protecting flanks of lines, lines built to enfilade an opposing line, ... a maze and labyrinth of works within works."

One problem with Grant and Meade's orders to make a frontal assault on June 3 is that they did not personally reconnoiter the ground. Moreover, the Union corps that were slated to make the assault could not make a strong enough reconnaissance in force to determine the exact nature of the Confederate line. Nevertheless, those who had the slightest bit of experience in the Overland Campaign knew full well that the Confederates had likely utilized the day to construct the kind of fortifications that would make the position impregnable. Baldy Smith, who had been reluctant when told of the plan to make an attack on the morning of June 2, was beside himself when he learned that his superiors still planned to go ahead with an attack on the morning of June 3. Smith later wrote that he was "aghast at the reception of such an order, which proved conclusively the utter absence of any military plan", and he confided to his staff that the attack was "simply an order to slaughter my best troops." Hancock's adjutant would later write that they had no time to 'make an adequate reconnaissance of the enemy's line" and that the order to make the assault "was, beyond question, the most unfortunate decision made during that bloody campaign."

**Baldy Smith**

The Battle of Cold Harbor is remembered almost solely for the attack that would go forward on the morning of June 3, and one of the most memorable anecdotes of the entire war came from Grant aide Horace Porter, who related the following story in his memoirs:

"In passing along on foot among the troops at the extreme front that evening while transmitting some of the final orders, I observed an incident which afforded a practical illustration of the deliberate and desperate courage of the men. As I came near one of the regiments which was making preparations for the next morning's assault, I noticed that many of the soldiers had taken off their coats, and seemed to be engaged in sewing up rents in them. This exhibition of tailoring seemed rather peculiar at such a moment, but upon closer examination it was found that the men were calmly writing their names and home addresses on slips of paper, and pinning them on the backs of their coats, so that their dead bodies might be recognized upon the field, and their fate made known to their families at home. They were veterans who knew well from terrible experience the danger which awaited them, but their minds were occupied not with thoughts of shirking their duty, but with preparation for the desperate work of the coming morning. Such courage is more than heroic — it is sublime."

Porter's anecdote has become one of the great legends of Cold Harbor, but no other source has ever substantiated the story, even though others would later include Porter's story in their own memoirs. As a result, the story remains popular today, even though it is likely apocryphal. Regardless, there's no question that many of the Union soldiers in the line echoed the concerns of Baldy Smith and others that the scheduled assault for June 3 was suicidal, which begs the question of why Grant ordered it.

Whether Grant believed the assault would be a success is unclear, but for nearly two weeks he had believed that Lee's army was on the ropes. In fact, he had assured Washington that Lee's army was "whipped" at the North Anna, and if Grant could succeed at Cold Harbor, it might be the straw that broke the camel's back. If the assault worked, it might either destroy Lee's army as an effective fighting force or force Lee to make a hasty and disorderly retreat south of the Chickahominy at least and possibly into Richmond itself. Grant didn't describe his thinking ahead of the attack in his memoirs, but Horace Porter was probably close to accurate when he summed up the situation in his own memoirs:

"A serious problem now presented itself to General Grant's mind — whether to attempt to crush Lee's army on the north side of the James, with the prospect in case of success of driving him into Richmond, capturing the city perhaps without a siege, and putting the Confederate government to flight; or to move the Union army south of the James without giving battle, and transfer the field of operations to the vicinity of Petersburg. It was a nice question of judgment. After discussing the matter thoroughly with his principal officers, and weighing all the chances, he decided to attack Lee's army in its present position. He had succeeded in breaking the enemy's line at Chattanooga, Spottsylvania, and other places under circumstances which were not more favorable, and the results to be obtained now would be so great in case of success that it seemed wise to make the attempt.

The general considered the question not only from a military standpoint, but he took a still broader view of the situation. The expenses of the war had reached nearly four million dollars a day. Many of the people in the North were becoming discouraged at the prolongation of the contest. If the army were transferred south of the James without fighting a battle on the north side, people would be impatient at the prospect of an apparently indefinite continuation of operations; and as the sickly season of summer was approaching, the deaths from disease among the troops meanwhile would be greater than any possible loss encountered in the contemplated attack. The loss from sickness on the part of the enemy would naturally be less, as his troops were acclimated and ours were not. Besides, there were constant rumors that if the war continued much longer European powers would recognize the Confederacy, and perhaps give it material assistance; but this consideration influenced Grant much less than the others. Delays are usually dangerous, and there was at present too much at stake to admit of further loss of time in ending the war, if it could be avoided."

Whatever the reason, the appearance of daylight on June 3 would bring one of the most fateful assaults of the entire Civil War.

**June 3**

"I have always regretted that the last assault at Cold Harbor was ever made." – Ulysses S. Grant

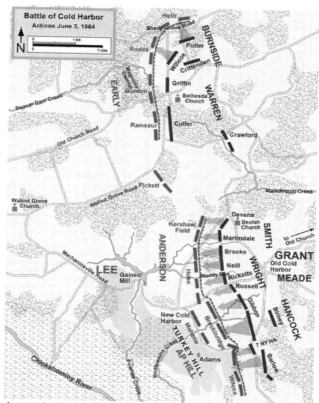

During the early morning hours of June 3, every corps in the Army of the Potomac began forming a uniform battle line, but the only thing they had in common was an order to attack at 4:30 a.m. Though they were all linked together, Burnside and Warren were to try to pin down Lee's left flank while Hancock, Smith, and Wright all attacked around Cold Harbor.

Not surprisingly, the uncoordinated nature of the Union's orders, the lack of reconnaissance, and the Confederate earthworks all served to make the general assault a complete mess. Within minutes of the signal gun sounding off, unit cohesion all but vanished as the Union soldiers moved forward into wooded areas that also included swamps nobody knew were there. Of course, the Union soldiers also had to deal with Confederate artillery sweeping the field and the infantry posted along sunken roads, trenches, and other fortifications. Not surprisingly, one Union soldier in Hancock's corps later noted, "We felt it was murder, not war, or at best a very serious mistake had been made."

On the Union right, Warren and Burnside, overly cautious corps commanders to begin with, made only a half-hearted advance before being quickly bogged down. Warren's cautious nature seemed to be affected by the fact he was having trouble coming to grips with the carnage of the entire campaign, saying that morning, "For thirty days now, it has been one funeral procession, past me; and it is too much! Today I saw a man burying a comrade, and, within half an hour, he himself was brought in and buried beside him. The men need some rest." To the right of Warren, Burnside's men stopped after pushing aside Confederate skirmishers in front of the line due to the mistaken belief that they had actually overrun the Confederates' first line of fortifications, taking time out to regroup for an afternoon attack.

Wright's corps had been used up in the attack on June 1 and made such a feeble attack that many of the men in Hoke's division and Anderson's corps were not even aware that a major Union assault was underway. Even Union general Emory Upton, who had led an innovative attack against the heavily entrenched Confederate line that pierced the Mule Shoe at Spotsylvania, stopped his division from advancing too far, deeming it "impracticable."

Smith's complaint that the order would slaughter his best troops proved all too prophetic. As Smith's corps pushed forward, they found themselves moving forward into two ravines that made them sitting ducks for the Confederates in their front. One of the Union officers explained, "The men bent down as they pushed forward, as if trying, as they were, to breast a tempest, and the files of men went down like rows of blocks or bricks pushed over by striking against one another." Adding to the misery, Warren's conservative movements had not pinned down Lee's left line, and the Confederate artillery in front of the V Corps simply swung to their right and took aim at Smith's men. One Confederate noted the artillery did "deadly, bloody work."

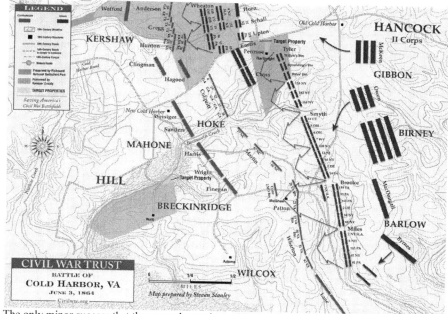

The only minor success that the general assault would provide the Union came from Hancock's corps. Although Gibbon's division got bogged down in a swamp, Barlow's division on the very end of the Union line provided a temporary breakthrough. Hancock described the results of his corps' attack in his post-battle report:

"The attack was to be made by Barlow's and Gibbon's divisions, supported by Birney. Barlow formed in two deployed lines, the brigades of Miles and Brooke in the front line and the other two brigades, Byrnes and MacDougall, in the second line. Gibbon formed his division in two lines. The first deployed, consisting of Tyler's and Smyth's brigades; the second line of McKeen's and Owen's brigades in close column of regiments. Barlow advanced at the time indicated and found the enemy strongly posted in a sunken road in front of his works, from which they were driven after a severe struggle and followed into their works under a very heavy artillery and musketry fire. Two hundred or 300 prisoners, 1 color, and 3 pieces of artillery fell into our hands. The guns were turned upon the enemy, forcing them to retreat in confusion from that portion of the line. But this partial success of Barlow was speedily turned into a reverse by the failure of the second line to get up to the prompt support of the first, which was forced out of the captured works by the re-enforced enemy, and an enfilading artillery fire brought to bear on it. The troops of the first line showed a persistency rarely seen, and, taking advantage of a slight crest, held a position within from 30 to 75 yards of the enemy's line, covering themselves in an astonishingly short time by rifle-pits.

The gallant commander of the Fourth Brigade, of Barlow's division, Colonel (now Brevet Major-General) Brooke was severely wounded in this assault. He fell at the moment when his troops entered the enemy's works. On the right Gibbon had been even less success-full, and had met with heavy losses. His attack was a little delayed, he reports, by the failure of General Owen to have his troops formed, but the delay was brief. Gibbon's line was unfortunately cut in two by a marsh, which widened as the line neared the enemy's works. The country over which he advanced was cut up by ravines. The line moved gallantly forward, however, until close to the enemy's works, but was not able to advance farther under the destructive fire. General Tyler was wounded and taken from the field, and the lamented McKeen, after pushing his command as far as his example could urge it, was killed. The gallant Haskell succeeded to the command, but was carried from the field mortally wounded, while making renewed efforts to carry the enemy's works. On the left, and separated from his brigade by the swamp described above, Colonel McMahon with a part of his regiment, the One hundred and sixty-fourth New York, reached the enemy's works, planting with his own hand his regimental colors on the parapet, where he fell covered with wounds and expired in the enemy's hands, losing his colors with honor. A portion of Smyth's brigade also reached the enemy's works, but failed to effect a lodgment owing, General Gibbon states, to the fact that General Owen did not bring his brigade promptly to the support, as he had been directed, but deploying it on Smyth's left when he first became engaged. A portion of Gibbon's troops held ground so close to the enemy that they could only be reached by means of covered ways. Thus ended the assault at Cold Harbor. The major-general commanding was anxious that I should renew the attempt, if practicable, but I did not consider it wise to make another assault, if the matter was left to my judgment."

Hancock had been so concerned about the seeming futility of the order that he never bothered ordering his reserve division, Birney's, to support Barlow. Those who were fortunate enough to survive were pinned down and did the only thing they could do: start digging trenches for themselves and taking cover, sometimes behind the corpses of their comrades. Ironically (and absurdly), the formation of an impromptu defensive line by survivors digging in for their lives would be championed as some sort of success by their superiors. At the same time, those who were injured had to deal with being stuck in the hot summer sun between the two lines, adding to their suffering.

It's unclear just how many casualties the Union suffered in the general assault on the morning of June 3. While some have described it as being 6,000 casualties in 30 minutes, it's more likely that they suffered about 3,000 over a longer time. Either way, the attack on June 3 was the most lopsided and futile attack in the East since the attack on Marye's Heights during the Battle of Fredericksburg on December 13, 1862.

Despite the disastrous nature of the attack, the Union high command was uncertain of the progress, and, incredibly, Grant and Meade were considering a further attack at 7:00 a.m. This was a byproduct of the fact that the topography and environment made it unclear how the morning assault was going. Meade staffer Theodore Lyman explained, "There has been no fight of which I have seen so little as this. The woods were so placed that the sound, even, of the musketry was much kept away, and the fighting, though near us, was completely shut from view. All the warfare for us was an occasional roundshot, or shell, that would come about us from the Rebel batteries. In the direction of the 18th Corps the crash of the musketry was very loud, but elsewhere, scarcely to be noticed." Meanwhile, the Confederates were having the exact opposite experience; Porter Alexander wrote of the fighting, "the roar of the battle, while it lasted, probably exceeded even that of the combats in the Wilderness, which Humphreys described as often approaching the sublime. It broke forth, mingled with vast cheering, in the stillness of early dawn, but it was no surprise. For over an hour the men in the trenches had been alert at hearing in front muffled commands and smothered movements."

Moreover, the bizarre and foolish nature of the way Grant and Meade had delegated responsibility for the assault contributed to the confusion. As each corps reported their results to Meade or complained that the inaction of one corps allowed the Confederates to provide enfilading fire on another corps, he simply sent copies to the other corps commanders instead of taking charge of the situation. Furthermore, when Meade, who had not bothered to do reconnaissance, exhorted his corps commanders to keep being aggressive and push forward, it only angered them, and they kept insisting the assault was futile.

Around 7:00 a.m., after most of the Union assault had fizzled out, Meade wrote to Grant, "I should be glad to have your views as to the continuance of these attacks, if unsuccessful." To that, Grant responded, 'The moment it becomes certain that an assault cannot succeed, suspend the offensive, but when one does succeed push it vigorously, and if necessary pile in troops at the successful point from wherever they can be taken." Meade had been chafing at the fact he felt powerless with Grant attached to his army, but after he had been given tactical control at Cold Harbor, he seemed to invite Grant to take back control at this critical juncture. Indeed, Grant responded by moving his own headquarters to Meade's headquarters, taking back tactical control in full.

At 12:30, Grant issued an order suspending the assault but keeping open the option of renewing it later in the afternoon:

"The opinion of corps commanders not being sanguine of success in case an assault is ordered, you may direct a suspension of farther advance for the present. Hold our most advanced positions and strengthen them. Whilst on the defensive our line may be contracted from the right if practicable.

Reconnoissances should be made in front of every corps and advances made to advantageous positions by regular approaches. To aid the expedition under General Hunter it is necessary that we should detain all the army now with Lee until the former gets well on his way to Lynchburg. To do this effectually it will be better to keep the enemy out of the intrenchments of Richmond than to have them go back there.

Wright and Hancock should be ready to assault in case the enemy should break through General Smith's lines, and all should be ready to resist an assault."

When these orders went around to the individual corps commanders and their men, it finally became too much for many to bear. Baldy Smith responded with insubordination, explicitly vowing not to move forward, and the correctness of his position would seemingly be verified by the fact that he was not officially sanctioned for refusing to obey orders. The common soldier also happened to agree with Baldy Smith; as one Union soldier noted, "The army to a man refused to obey the order, presumably from General Grant, to renew the assault. I heard the order given, and I saw it disobeyed."

While Grant was considering another attack, some Southern officials unfamiliar with trench warfare and unaware of the situation were concerned that Lee's line might be broken. That morning, the Confederate postmaster general and a delegation of civilians from Richmond came to Lee's headquarters and asked him, "General, if the enemy breaks your line, what reserve have you?" Lee, who had been under heavy stress for nearly a month straight, snapped back in an unusually stern fashion, "Not a regiment, and that has been my condition ever since the fighting commenced on the Rappahannock. If I shorten my lines to provide a reserve, he will turn me; if I weaken my lines to provide a reserve, he will break them." Grant may have failed to destroy Lee's army, but the Confederate commander was all too aware that his army was being ground down with each battle while his opponent kept reinforcing itself.

Once his subordinates and his soldiers made clear that there would be no more assaults on June 3, Grant was circumspect, and some would say downright untruthful, in reporting the assault and its results to Washington. Grant wrote back to Washington that afternoon, "Our loss was not severe, nor do I suppose the enemy to have lost heavily." His post-battle report was also circumspect, but at least it was also a bit more accurate: "On the 3d of June we again assaulted the enemy's works in the hope of driving him from his position. In this attempt our loss was heavy, while that of the enemy, I have reason to believe, was comparatively light. It was the only general attack made from the Rapidan to the James which did not inflict upon the enemy losses to compensate for our own losses. I would not be understood as saying that all previous attacks resulted in victories to our arms, or accomplished as much as I had hoped from them, but they inflicted upon the enemy severe losses, which tended in the end to the complete overthrow of the rebellion."

However, Grant was much more candid about the results with his staff that night, telling them, "I regret this assault more than any one I have ever ordered. I regarded it as a stern necessity, and believed it would bring compensating results; but, as it has proved, no advantages have been gained sufficient to justify the heavy losses suffered." Grant also explicitly expressed his regret for the attack after the war, writing in his memoirs:

"I have always regretted that the last assault at Cold Harbor was ever made. I might say the same thing of the assault of the 22d of May, 1863, at Vicksburg. At Cold Harbor no advantage whatever was gained to compensate for the heavy loss we sustained. Indeed, the advantages other than those of relative losses, were on the Confederate side. Before that, the Army of Northern Virginia seemed to have acquired a wholesome regard for the courage, endurance, and soldierly qualities generally of the Army of the Potomac. They no longer wanted to fight them "one Confederate to five Yanks." Indeed, they seemed to have given up any idea of gaining any advantage of their antagonist in the open field. They had come to much prefer breastworks in their front to the Army of the Potomac. This charge seemed to revive their hopes temporarily…"

Civil War historian Robert N. Thompson may have summed it up best when describing the results of the Battle of Cold Harbor: "The tragedy of Cold Harbor was that it was avoidable. Its leadership failed, and failed miserably. Cold Harbor was a horrible example of what happens when command cohesion breaks down under the weight of an unworkable system, when the stress of battle overcomes professionalism and when otherwise good officers forget the basics of command and their responsibilities as commanders. In the end, their men, average soldiers, paid the ultimate and terrible price."

**The Aftermath of Cold Harbor and the Overland Campaign**

"This remarkable assault deserves more attention than the brief statement in which Grant disposes of it. Its isolation on the pages of history as the most extraordinary blunder in military annals will alone make it famous." – Fitzhugh Lee

The main fighting at Cold Harbor ended with the morning assault on June 3, but there were still some momentous decisions to make. The first, and one of the most tragic, was the failure not to call a truce to collect the wounded and bury the dead shortly after the decision not to renew the attack. Grant noted in his memoirs, "During the night the enemy quitted our right front, abandoning some of their wounded, and without burying their dead. These we were able to care for. But there were many dead and wounded men between the lines of the contending forces, which were now close together, who could not be cared for without a cessation of hostilities." However, historians have speculated that Grant simply did not want to ask Lee for a truce because it would be an acknowledgement that he had lost the fight.

For his part, Grant blamed Lee for the impasse. According to Grant, when he sent a communication to Lee on June 5 suggesting that there be a cessation of hostilities, "Lee replied that he feared such an arrangement would lead to misunderstanding, and proposed that in future, when either party wished to remove their dead and wounded, a flag of truce be sent."

As a result of the decisions, or lack of them, between Lee and Grant, the injured were needlessly left on the field without assistance for several days. A cessation of hostilities would not go into effect until June 7. As a result, some injured and dying Union soldiers were stuck in no man's land for several days. Some of them were able to keep diary entries that mentioned their plight, and one man who knew he was dying dated his last diary entry and managed to write, "I died."

**The dead at Cold Harbor were still being buried in April 1865**

By the time the fighting at Cold Harbor was over, Grant had suffered about 13,000-15,000 casualties, and Lee had lost 2,500-5,000 in his army. Cold Harbor was the last major pitched battle of the Overland Campaign, and Grant had suffered more casualties during the campaign than Lee had in his entire army at the start of May. Understandably, the American public was shocked by the carnage, and to this day Grant has been accused of being a butcher, but attrition had become a vital war aim for the North, and Confederate generals were all too aware from it. Writing about Grant's reputation after the war, Horace Porter noted:

"Grant could have effectually stopped the carnage at any time by withholding from battle. He could have avoided all bloodshed by remaining north of the Rapidan, intrenching, and not moving against his enemy: but he was not placed in command of the armies for that purpose. It had been demonstrated by more than three years of campaigning that peace could be secured only by whipping and destroying the enemy. No one was more desirous of peace; no one was possessed of a heart more sensitive to every form of human suffering than the commander: but he realized that paper bullets are not effective in warfare; he knew better than to attempt to hew rocks with a razor; and he felt that in campaigning the hardest blows bring the quickest relief."

Most importantly, Grant and his army were largely undeterred from their main objective by temporary setbacks. Refusing to attack Lee in frontal assaults, and aware that Lee dared not venture out to counterattack, Grant had to determine the next major movement of his army. He explained his ultimate decision in his memoirs:

"Lee's position was now so near Richmond, and the intervening swamps of the Chickahominy so great an obstacle to the movement of troops in the face of an enemy, that I determined to make my next left flank move carry the Army of the Potomac south of the James River. Preparations for this were promptly commenced. The move was a hazardous one to make: the Chickahominy River, with its marshy and heavily timbered approaches, had to be crossed; all the bridges over it east of Lee were destroyed; the enemy had a shorter line and better roads to travel on to confront me in crossing; more than fifty miles intervened between me and Butler, by the roads I should have to travel, with both the James and the Chickahominy unbridged to cross; and last, the Army of the Potomac had to be got out of a position but a few hundred yards from the enemy at the widest place. Lee, if he did not choose to follow me, might, with his shorter distance to travel and his bridges over the Chickahominy and the James, move rapidly on Butler and crush him before the army with me could come to his relief. Then too he might spare troops enough to send against Hunter who was approaching Lynchburg, living upon the country he passed through, and without ammunition further than what he carried with him."

Switching the operations south of the James meant that the Army of the Potomac would no longer be between Lee's army and Washington, which unnerved the Lincoln Administration. Nevertheless, when it was suggested to Grant that he move along Lee's left instead of crossing the James, thereby keeping himself between Lee and the Union capital, he rejected the idea, explaining to his staff, "We can defend Washington best by keeping Lee so occupied that he cannot detach enough troops to capture it. If the safety of the city should really become imperiled, we have water communication, and can transport a sufficient number of troops to Washington at anytime to hold it against attack. This movement proposed by Halleck would separate the Army of the Potomac by a still greater distance from Butler's army, while it would leave us a long vulnerable line of communication, and require a large part of our effective force to properly guard it. I shall prepare at once to move across the James River, and in the mean time destroy to a still greater extent the railroads north of Richmond."

### The First Battle of Petersburg

Even before Grant's army moved away from Cold Harbor, the First Battle of Petersburg was fought on June 9 between part of Benjamin Butler's Union Army of the James and a ragtag Confederate force led by former Virginia governor Henry Wise. Butler's failure during the Bermuda Hundred campaign south of Grant and Lee had allowed Confederate reinforcements to come to Lee before Cold Harbor, and Grant had become so frustrated with Butler's lack of progress that he had Baldy Smith's corps leave the Army of the James and join the Army of the Potomac before the fighting at Cold Harbor. Naturally, Butler found other scapegoats for his failure to make progress in his Bermuda Hundred campaign, writing in his memoirs:

"I at length learned that General Grant would now certainly come and join me at City Point, and that he was waiting for events to determine whether he would call to his assistance the Eighteenth Corps.10 Having also learned that there was in Petersburg a possible aggregation, including reserves, militia, and convalescents, of some two thousand men, of which not more than two thirds would be substantially effective, I organized an expedition of eleven thousand men under General Smith, and put them in column at Bermuda Hundred to attack Petersburg on the 29th of May. They were ready to march the very next morning, but on the evening of the 28th the transportation to take them away arrived with positive orders that they should at once go to Grant.

Much as I desired the capture of Petersburg, which was as certain as any future event could be, I felt it my duty, knowing in what straits General Grant believed himself to be, to give, although reluctantly, the order for their embarkation.

The Eighteenth Corps, as then reorganized, contained some sixteen thousand effective men, and their removal left me actually at Bermuda,--reckoning the cavalry, a part of whom were armed only with pistols, and possible convalescents in the hospitals,--less than eight thousand effective troops,..

I should have felt little alarm for the safety of Bermuda had my fortifications been completed in Gillmore's front. Although twice as much time had been wasted as was necessary to complete them, General Weitzel, my chief engineer, reported to me that not half the work which I supposed had been completed, had been done.

Still the capture of Petersburg lay near my heart. It will be seen that the removal of Smith's corps on the 29th of May, when they were ready to march to capture Petersburg, had frustrated that capture for the second time, as the false reports from Washington had done the first time. I caused the most accurate reports possible of the strength of my forces to be made to me, and I also caused the most accurate investigations to be made into the question whether some portions of the enemy's troops had not been withdrawn from Petersburg after the removal of Smith's corps had become known to the rebels, upon the supposition on their part that I would afterwards undertake no offensive operations."

**Butler**

Butler's self-serving account aside, he would still have his chance in early June, and he sought to vindicate himself by crossing the Appomattox with his men and capturing Petersburg. Relying on the fact that the Confederates thought he would evacuate from Bermuda Hundred, Butler planned to have some of his men hold the line while crossing others south of the Appomattox River on the night of June 8 to capture Petersburg by surprise. He tasked a division led by General Edward Hinks, but General Quincy Gillmore, commander of the X Corps, had other plans. Butler recalled:

"When the condition of things at Petersburg was disclosed to [Gillmore], and when he learned that I proposed to send General Hinks in command of the expedition, he became very strongly impressed with the great probability of its success, and insisted that he ought to command it, being senior officer. He volunteered to go, and claimed it as his right and as a matter of courtesy, and I was fool enough to yield to him. I did not then think him a coward, although Grant declined to employ him because he had shown 'timidity.'"

Another reason behind the change in plans, as Butler noted, was that Hinks' division had a number of black soldiers, and they still weren't trusted by most of the general officers in the Army of the James. Thus, the amended plan called for about 4,500 Union soldiers, consisting mostly of men from Gillmore's corps, to cross the Appomattox and attack the eastern side of Petersburg's defensive lines, while about 1,000 cavalry would ride further south and attack the southeastern side of the lines. With Hinks and Gillmore marching in three columns and the cavalry representing a fourth, Butler's plan relied on at least one of the columns breaching the Confederate line, which would then allow them to roll up the Confederates' defensive line and get into their rear, all but breaking the defenses of Petersburg.

While Butler would later overestimate the size of the force he sent at about 6,500 men and 2,000 cavalry in his memoirs, there was no question that the force he was sending to Petersburg would greatly outnumber its defenders. P.G.T. Beauregard, the Confederate hero at Fort Sumter and First Bull Run, had fallen out of favor due to poor relations with President Jefferson Davis, and in the middle of the war he had been relegated to defending the coast line of the Confederacy. As Grant moved south against Lee, Beauregard had to defend against Butler's surprise Bermuda Hundred Campaign. Having convinced General Braxton Bragg (who after the disastrous defeat at Chattanooga in 1863 had been removed from command and became Jefferson Davis' military adviser) not to transfer units of his small force north of Richmond, coupled with Butler's own relative incompetence, Beauregard was successful in bottling up that Union army, effectively nullifying its threat to Petersburg and Lee's supply line. In the aftermath of this highly-effective strategy, Lee offered Beauregard command of the right wing of the Army of Northern Virginia, due to Longstreet's near fatal injury at the Battle of the Wilderness, but Beauregard refused to leave his department without orders from the War Department.

As a result of these actions, Beauregard, who had been shuffled out of high command in both the East and West, found himself responsible for the defense of Richmond and Petersburg while Lee faced Grant. It was an ironic twist of fate, given that Beauregard was only in that position precisely because Davis had attempted to marginalize him and remove him away from important responsibilities.

**Beauregard**

Beauregard was already heavily outnumbered at Bermuda Hundred, and at Petersburg he only had a makeshift force of no more than 2,500 that was literally comprised of old men, young boys, and wounded veterans convalescing nearby. However, the Confederate defenders had the benefits of using Petersburg's previously constructed fortifications. The defensive fortifications east of the city were known as the Dimmock Line; Confederate engineers had dug an imposing set of trenches and breastworks that stretched nearly 10 miles east of the city and rested on the Appomattox River, making it an imposing defensive line. On June 9, however, it would be critically undermanned; instead of having men standing shoulder to shoulder, there would be gaps of several feet between each defender.

**Picture of part of the Dimmock Line**

Unfortunately for Butler's plans, the attempt to march at night caused considerable delays and frustration, something Grant knew all too much about during the Overland Campaign. Gillmore's columns got lost in the darkness, and at one point he sent a message back to Butler that incensed the commander:

"The first telegram I received after the expedition started was a complaint and grumble from Gillmore, in which he said: "My command has just crossed the river; some of it has been delayed by losing the road. I have no doubt that the enemy are fully apprised of my movement by the noise of the bridge. It is not muffled at all, and the crossing of the cavalry can be heard for miles."

But why was not the bridge muffled, General Gillmore? You had the command of the expedition in all its parts, and it was your duty to see it properly conducted; why didn't you muffle the bridge? Was it the duty of the commanding general to lug straw and other materials with which pontoon bridges are usually muffled? Further, I have never supposed that the tramp of horses on a bridge could be heard seven miles. And why were your troops not instructed in the road across their own camps so that there should not have been delay in getting there?

From the hour of getting that despatch, heartsick I doubted the result of the expedition."

Eventually, the Union infantry had reached the Confederate picket line in front of the Dimmock Line shortly after daylight on June 9, but the light also made the Dimmock Line visible to Gillmore and Hinks. Gillmore had earned his stripes in siege warfare at the battle of Fort Pulaski, when he reduced a stone fort with siege artillery, and his engineering background upon seeing the Dimmock Line unnerved him more than it might have others. While Gillmore dithered, Hinks didn't dare use the men from his division to attack the Dimmock Line without the support of Gillmore's men.

**Gillmore**

As the hours started to pass, Hinks and Gillmore talked each other into making an attack, but only once the cavalry arrived to their left. The cavalry, led by August Kautz, were delayed in arriving, but when they reached Petersburg around noon they began to attack the line. But even as Kautz started actively fighting, including probing the Confederate line and then dismounting his cavalry to attack as infantry, Gillmore and Hinks did not attack with their men, leaving Kautz to fight the Confederate defenders alone. Kautz began to drive in the inexperienced "Home Guard" of old men, young boys, and wounded warriors, capturing artillery and taking dozens of prisoners, but the delays and the inactivity by Gillmore and Hinks allowed Beauregard to draw reinforcements from nearby Richmond and bring them to the defense. Eventually, Kautz felt compelled to pull back, having seen or heard nothing from Gillmore. Butler explained:

"Kautz had charged up the Jerusalem plank road, driven the force opposing him away, captured a piece of artillery and forty prisoners, and ridden into the town as far up as Jordan's, and then, not hearing anything from Gillmore, although he was within the sound of musketry, he came leisurely back, and without being interfered with.

Gillmore reported to me on his return that the expedition had not succeeded, and that he had not heard of Kautz.

I had the sorrowful pleasure of answering that I had heard of Kautz, as Kautz had been into Petersburg and waited for him as long as he could, and had reported to my headquarters, and brought in his prisoners.

General Kautz reports that he passed the entire line of the intrenchments, being opposed only by a small body of infantry and artillery which did him no damage, and hearing nothing from Gillmore, and not hearing his guns, he burned the camp of the enemy, destroyed their stores and ammunition, and came quietly home."

Butler had an angry and bitingly sarcastic take on Gillmore's actions during the First Battle of Petersburg:

"Kautz went on to the Jerusalem Road, and at ten o'clock Gillmore had approached within 'twenty minutes march' of the intrenchments at the point where he was to make the attack. Then he halted his troops and went to a 'secesh' lady's house to get his dinner. While there, as he afterwards averred, he was informed by her that Petersburg was full of troops. He also halted Hinks' division so far off as not to be in supporting distance of him, he says, but only the same distance from the enemy's lines. Both columns rested there and went no further. The position of affairs will explain itself to one looking at the very accurate map showing their relative positions.

Gillmore got his dinner, picked his teeth, waited until half past 3 o'clock on a still fair day, with a three quarter moon at night, and then turned about and marched home, encountering the same opposition that he met in marching out, leaving Kautz and his cavalry to take care of themselves."

Butler was so disgusted by Gillmore's "wholly inexcusable and cowardly" conduct that he ordered the corps commander relieved of his command and arrested, to which Gillmore responded with a request for a court of inquiry. Grant ultimately defused the situation by pulling Gillmore away from the operations on that front, and a court of inquiry was never convened to decide the matter.

### Crossing the James

While Butler's attempt to capture Petersburg had gone awry on June 9, Grant was putting the finishing touches on his own plan. Grant planned to start his army's movement across the James River on June 12, touching off the final movements of the Overland Campaign and ultimately beginning the siege of Petersburg. Although he had steadily continued his advance closer and closer to Richmond, Cold Harbor and the Overland Campaign damaged the Union war effort in the interim. Morale suffered among the public, and, as the South was banking on, Lincoln grew so unpopular that his reelection was in doubt. But Grant obviously had to worry about his own army and objectives, and a movement south of the James River would require stealth, which could only be had if the Confederate cavalry were kept away from his army. To accomplish this, Grant had ordered the Union's cavalry, led by Little Phil Sheridan, to keep the Confederate cavalry at bay, and Sheridan explained the orders he and his men received a few days earlier:

"In view of these difficulties it became necessary to draw off the bulk of the enemy's cavalry while the movement to the James was in process of execution, and General Meade determined to do this by requiring me to proceed with two divisions as far as Charlottesville to destroy the railroad bridge over the Rivanna River near that town, the railroad itself from the Rivanna to Gordonsville, and, if practicable, from Gordonsville back toward Hanover Junction also...

The diversion of the enemy's cavalry from the south side of the Chickahominy was its main purpose, for in the presence of such a force as Lee's contracted lines would now permit him to concentrate behind the Chickahominy, the difficulties of crossing that stream would be largely increased if he also had at hand a strong body of horse, to gain the time necessary for him to oppose the movement at the different crossings with masses of his infantry."

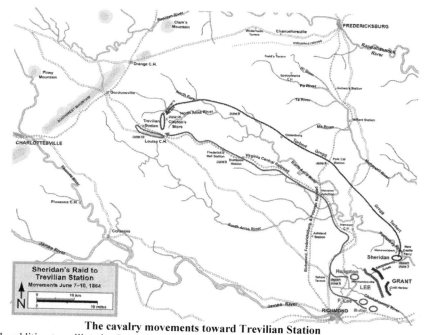

### The cavalry movements toward Trevilian Station

In addition to pulling the Confederate cavalry away from the battle field, Grant also wanted Sheridan's cavalry to move northwest because an independent Union command under David Hunter had just defeated a small Confederate army in the Shenandoah Valley, and Grant wished for Hunter to link up with Sheridan near Charlottesville, which would allow that force to descend on Lee from a different front and add pressure on the Army of Northern Virginia. By June, Sheridan's cavalry was so worn out that the two divisions he took on the raid could only muster 6,000 effectives, and even though the raid was supposed to last 5 days, the men only took three days of rations to make sure they traveled light and weren't bogged down by supply wagons.

The Confederate cavalry were compelled to follow, aware that Sheridan could cut the Virginia Central railroad if he was unopposed, and the two sides fought at the Battle of Trevilian Station from June 11-12, the bloodiest cavalry fight of the war. With nearly 1,000 casualties on each side, Sheridan's cavalry were forced to fall back and rejoin Grant's army without completing their objectives of destroying the railroad or linking up with Hunter. Nevertheless, Sheridan claimed victory, writing in his memoirs, "The result was constant success and the almost total annihilation of the rebel cavalry. We marched when and where we pleased; were always the attacking party, and always successful."

**Sheridan**

Modern historians have strongly disputed the notion that Sheridan won anything at Trevilian Station, but it had the strategic benefit of keeping the Confederate cavalry away from the Army of the Potomac as Grant set his army in motion on the night of June 12. Meanwhile, after the First Battle of Petersburg on June 9, Beauregard began warning Lee and Richmond that Grant's objective would be Petersburg, not Richmond, but his prophetic predictions fell on deaf ears.

On the night of the 12th, Grant had Gouverneur Warren's V Corps cross the Chickahominy and guard the roads leading from Richmond, hoping that corps could screen the rest of his army's movements if Lee tried to probe the line. Lee continued to think Grant's objective was Richmond, so he merely had part of his army posted in Warren's front without trying to attack. This allowed Grant to move several of his other corps behind Warren and toward the James River during the 13th and 14th:

"No attempt was made by the enemy to impede our march, however, but Warren and Wilson reported the enemy strongly fortified in their front. By the evening of the 13th Hancock's corps was at Charles City Court House on the James River. Burnside's and Wright's corps were on the Chickahominy, and crossed during the night, Warren's corps and the cavalry still covering the army. The material for a pontoon bridge was already at hand and the work of laying it was commenced immediately, under the superintendence of Brigadier-General Benham, commanding the engineer brigade. On the evening of the 14th the crossing commenced, Hancock in advance, using both the bridge and boats...

The advance of the Army of the Potomac reached the James on the 14th of June. Preparations were at once commenced for laying the pontoon bridges and crossing the river. As already stated, I had previously ordered General Butler to have two vessels loaded with stone and carried up the river to a point above that occupied by our gunboats, where the channel was narrow, and sunk there so as to obstruct the passage and prevent Confederate gunboats from coming down the river. Butler had had these boats filled and put in position, but had not had them sunk before my arrival. I ordered this done, and also directed that he should turn over all material and boats not then in use in the river to be used in ferrying the troops across."

By the end of the 14th, Grant had managed to move most of his army south and east toward the James River while Lee remained in a defensive line behind the Chickahominy near Cold Harbor. Grant had lost the race to every objective point during the Overland Campaign against Lee, including Spotsylvania Court House and the North Anna, but now he had managed to steal more than an entire day's march on Lee, and Lee still had no idea what his plan was. In fact, as Beauregard was sounding the alarms about the need to reinforce his defenses around Petersburg, Lee was making plans to reinforce his own army by bringing some of Beauregard's men north.

**June 15**

"I believed then, and still believe, that Petersburg could have been easily captured at that time." – Ulysses S. Grant

It was impressive enough that Grant managed to get some of his army across the James River without Lee's knowledge, but the accomplishment was all the more amazing considering that crossing the James was an engineering feat in and of itself. To do so, Grant's army required the help of Butler's army and supplies near City Point, which would become Grant's headquarters during the siege. Meade's staffer, Theodore Lyman, would later note in his memoirs that civil engineers would have typically been given several months to plan a bridge across a river the size of the James, and possibly a year to construct the bridge. Butler described the difficulties in creating the pontoon bridge that spanned the river:

"I examined the pontoon train as it went up the river to ascertain the provisions for anchoring the bridge. The tidal current opposite the fort where the bridge was to be built, was very strong both ways. The engineer officer had nothing to hold the boats but ordinary grapnels of a few pounds in weight, and inch warps, about sixty feet long, to each boat. I saw that those, the moment the boats were pressed down, with the current running, would not hold, and that the bridge would give way, and the troops, and especially the artillery crossing it, would be lost.

Here was a dilemma and what to do I did not know. But remembering there were quiet a number of large sized sutler schooners anchored at City Point, I turned my boat to Bermuda Hundred, called for the provost guard, and seized as many schooners as were necessary. I had them tugged down and anchored stem and stern across the river in two rows, leaving and interval between them wide enough for the bridge, and also leaving an opening for a draw that the bridge would give way, and the troops, and especially the in the bridge to allow vessels to pass up and down when it was not occupied. All of them had strong chains and heavy anchors by which they were securely fastened so as not to swing with the tide. The sterns of the vessels were to be placed on opposite sides of the bridge facing each other. That is, all the vessels on the upper side of the bridge were anchored with their sterns down river. All below the bridge were anchored with their sterns up river. Then by fastening the warps of the pontoons, head and stern, to the schooners the bridge could be laid and held with safety. The bridge train men worked under my personal direction until late at night, and in the morning the bridge was ready for passage. The engineer had provided himself with no material with which to cover the planks, and they would have been worn out before one third of the troops with their supplies and wagons could have crossed; but, fortunately, I had six saw-mills sawing out planks from the timber of the vicinity for use in building hospitals, and from these mills we were enabled to renew those planks three times, as was necessary, before the bridge ceased to be used. But they would not have so lasted had not great pains been taken to cover the roadway over the bridge as thickly as possible with hay and straw. This was imperative, because when the wheels of a heavy gun rested upon one portion of a pontoon it would be sunk down, and that would turn up the edge of the plank nearest the gun, and it would be almost inevitably splintered and ground off. I received the personal thanks of General Grant for my endeavors in putting the bridge in order with so little delay."

Everyone who saw the size of the bridge and the men and wagons traveling across it were in awe, as Grant's aide Horace Porter noted in his memoirs:

"As the general-in-chief stood upon the bluff on the north bank of the river on the morning of June 15, watching with unusual interest the busy scene spread out before him, it presented a sight which had never been equaled even in his extended experience in all the varied phases of warfare. His cigar had been thrown aside, his hands were clasped behind him, and he seemed lost in the contemplation of the spectacle. The great bridge was the scene of a continuous movement of infantry columns, batteries of artillery, and wagon-trains. The approaches to the river on both banks were covered with masses of troops moving briskly to their positions or waiting patiently their turn to cross. At the two improvised ferries steamboats were gliding back and forth with the regularity of weavers' shuttles. A fleet of transports covered the surface of the water below the bridge, and gunboats floated lazily upon the stream, guarding the river above. Drums were beating the march, bands were playing stirring quicksteps, the distant booming of cannon on Warren's front showed that he and the enemy were still exchanging compliments; and mingled with these sounds were the cheers of the sailors, the shouting of the troops, the rumbling of wheels, and the shrieks of steam-whistles. The bright sun, shining through a clear sky upon the scene, cast its sheen upon the water, was reflected from the burnished gun-barrels and glittering cannon, and brought out with increased brilliancy the gay colors of the waving banners. The calmly flowing river reflected the blue of the heavens, and mirrored on its surface the beauties of nature that bordered it. The rich grain was standing high in the surrounding fields. The harvest was almost ripe, but the harvesters had fled. The arts of civilization had recoiled before the science of destruction; and in looking from the growing crops to the marching columns, the gentle smile of peace contrasted strangely with the savage frown of war. It was a matchless pageant that could not fail to inspire all beholders with the grandeur of achievement and the majesty of military power. The man whose genius had conceived and whose skill had executed this masterly movement stood watching the spectacle in profound silence."

By stealing a march on Lee and getting Baldy Smith's corps across the James by the 15th, Grant was in position to throw a Union corps of about 16,000 soldiers against the Confederate defenses in Petersburg. Beauregard's men had managed to defend Petersburg on June 9 against about 6,000 Union soldiers, but that was almost certainly due to the inaction of Hinks and Gillmore. As before, Beauregard still had to keep more than half of his available forces in front of Butler's Army of the James at Bermuda Hundred, leaving about 2,500 to defend Petersburg.

Given the staggering numbers advantage that the Union had, Grant can be forgiven for being somewhat bitter in his memoirs about the fact that the siege of Petersburg would end up lasting 9 months. A lot would go wrong for the Union during the next three days, but it was a mistake in the first place that Grant chose Baldy Smith and some of Butler's men to try capturing Petersburg. Smith had lost some of his best men at Cold Harbor, and he was so outraged by the futile charge on June 3 that he explicitly threatened to disobey orders if his men were ordered to charge again. Even more inconceivably, when Grant ordered Butler to reinforce Smith's depleted corps with some men from the Army of the James, some of the reinforcements included black soldiers from Hinks' division, despite the fact Hinks had been part of the disastrous First Battle of Petersburg less than a week earlier.

In his tome about the history of the Confederacy, Jefferson Davis played down Grant's accomplishments during the Overland Campaign and the route by which he had crossed the James, writing:

"On June 14th and 15th the crossing of Grant's army was completed. It will be remembered that he had crossed the Rapidan on May 3d. It had therefore taken him more than a month to reach the south side of the James. In his campaign he had sacrificed a hecatomb of men, a vast amount of artillery, small arms, munitions of war, and supplies, to reach a position to which McClellan had already demonstrated there was an easy and inexpensive route. It is true that the Confederate army had suffered severely, and though the loss was comparatively small to that of its opponents, it could not be repaired, as his might be, from the larger population and his facility for recruiting in Europe. To those who can approve the policy of attrition without reference to the number of lives it might cost, this may seem justifiable, but it can hardly be regarded as generalship, or be offered to military students as an example worthy of imitation."

That was a statement that could only have been made with the benefit of hindsight, and even then it was an assessment that amply demonstrated why Jefferson Davis was not a general. McClellan's Peninsula Campaign of 1862 likely would have been bottled up at Yorktown if it had faced the entirety of Lee's Army of Northern Virginia in 1864, and on the morning of June 15, Grant actually had a good chance of capturing Petersburg and Richmond without much of a fight, as he noted in his memoirs:

"The distance which Smith had to move to reach the enemy's lines was about six miles, and the Confederate advance line of works was but two miles outside of Petersburg. Smith was to move under cover of night, up close to the enemy's works, and assault as soon as he could after daylight. I believed then, and still believe, that Petersburg could have been easily captured at that time. It only had about 2,500 men in the defences besides some irregular troops, consisting of citizens and employees in the city who took up arms in case of emergency."

From the very beginning, things started going wrong on June 15. Smith's men began crossing the Appomattox at dawn, but the vessels that were used to cross the creek either lacked or ignored directions when it came to dropping off each division, forcing the Union soldiers to reorganize their line. Adding to that delay, Kautz's cavalry found Confederate defenders northeast of the Petersburg defensive lines, and it took time for Baldy Smith's men to dislodge them.

As if those delays weren't enough, by the time Smith had worked up his nerve to try to attack

Petersburg's defensive line, he discovered that his artillery could not be brought up to bombard the lines until early evening. This change in plans was not communicated to Kautz, who had the misfortune of swinging his cavalry to the south and attacking the southeastern part of the defensive line without support from Smith's infantry. The Union cavalry officer must have thought he was suffering déjà vu, as this was the second time in less than a week that his men tried to attack in concert with infantry, only to find that the infantry had never advanced on their right

Despite the uncoordinated attacks, Smith's men had conducted a reconnaissance in force during the afternoon, and by about 7:00 p.m., Smith ordered his men into skirmish lines and prepared an advance. In a bit of hard fighting, Smith's soldiers drove the undermanned Confederate defenders out of their defensive lines, capturing several hundred Confederates and several artillery pieces.

With the Confederate defenders, many of whom weren't regular soldiers, in complete disarray, it has long been believed that Smith could have captured Petersburg that night. Beauregard himself claimed Petersburg "at that hour was clearly at the mercy of the Federal commander, who had all but captured it." However, Smith halted his advance after driving the defenders from the initial defensive line, one of the most controversial decisions of the war. It would also be the last decision Smith would make as a combat commander in the Civil War.

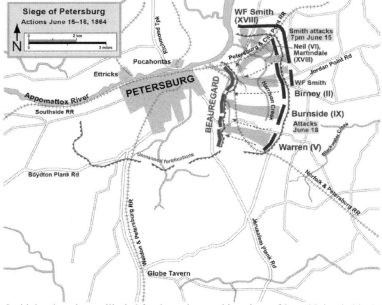

Baldy Smith has long been pilloried for the actions and inactions of June 15, but in his defense there seemed to have been serious miscommunications regarding whether he would be receiving support from Hancock's corps on the afternoon of the 15th. A comedy of errors and mixed messages would result in Hancock's men not reaching the outskirts of Petersburg until early evening, and the II Corps commander himself not having a clue precisely what his orders were. According to Grant, he ordered Hancock's men to receive rations as quickly as possible before heading toward Petersburg and to advance until being apprised of the situation by Baldy Smith. He explained in his memoirs:

I informed General Butler that Hancock's corps would cross the river and move to Petersburg to support Smith in case the latter was successful, and that I could reinforce there more rapidly than Lee could reinforce from his position.

I returned down the river to where the troops of the Army of the Potomac now were, communicated to General Meade, in writing, the directions I had given to General Butler and directed him (Meade) to cross Hancock's corps over under cover of night, and push them forward in the morning to Petersburg; halting them, however, at a designated point until they could hear from Smith. I also informed General Meade that I had ordered rations from Bermuda Hundred for Hancock's corps, and desired him to issue them speedily, and to lose no more time than was absolutely necessary. The rations did not reach him, however, and Hancock, while he got all his corps over during the night, remained until half-past ten in the hope of receiving them. He then moved without them, and on the road received a note from General W. F. Smith, asking him to come on. This seems to be the first information that General Hancock had received of the fact that he was to go to Petersburg, or that anything particular was expected of him. Otherwise he would have been there by four o'clock in the afternoon."

For some reason, Hancock did not get the orders, but Smith received the message from Grant's aides in the middle of the afternoon that Hancock's men were marching toward him. Meanwhile, Butler criticized Grant for ordering him to issue rations to Hancock's corps:

"I had advised very strongly that the Second Corps, commanded by General Hancock, which was leading, and Burnside's corps, which was following, both arriving at the river on the 14th, should be hurried with the utmost celerity to occupy the intrenchments around Petersburg. I was sorry, however, to receive an order to send Hancock sixty thousand rations at Windmill Point, which was quite out of the direction for the purpose of a rapid march on Petersburg. Hancock had rations enough to last him three days, and I received an order to send the rations to City Point and thence up the Appomattox to be landed within four or five miles of the rear of Hancock's corps.

I did not share Grant's apprehensions that Lee had undertaken to outmarch him via Richmond to Petersburg. I supposed that Lee would have seen the rear of Grant's forces while they were being passed over the river, always the most dangerous movement for a withdrawing army, and if Lee had marched for the purpose of getting ahead of him he would have been far ahead, for the delays in getting across the river were to me at the time unexplainable.

I knew also that up to that time no troops could have passed through Richmond or below to Petersburg. My lookouts commanded that matter by their eyes and ears day and night. If so much of the defences of Petersburg could be taken as would enable our force to reach the bridges at Swift Creek so as to get that creek and the Appomattox between us and Lee, then by holding that line of communication and demonstrating toward Richmond so as to cut the Danville road thoroughly and the canal, Lee would be immediately forced South and Richmond would be ours. After consultation I directed General Smith to make his attack upon the upper batteries of the line around Petersburg, although I had learned that the fortifications were stronger there,--that is, they were more pronounced works than those lower works over which Kautz had trotted on the 9th of June. This Smith did."

Due to the miscommunications and the delay in ordering rations, Hancock's men did not reach Smith's until night was setting, and the usually aggressive Hancock merely asked Smith what should be done with his men, despite the fact he outranked Smith. As a result, Smith, who had been overly cautious, simply ordered Hancock's men to relieve his men in the trenches and defensive line that they had taken from the Confederates. Smith later wrote in his official report, "We had thus broken through the strong line of rebel works, but heavy darkness was upon us, and as I heard some hours before that Lee's army was rapidly crossing at Drury's Bluff, I deemed it was wiser to hold what we had than by attempting to reach the bridges to lose what we had gained, and have the troops meet with a disaster. I knew also that some portion of the Army of the Potomac was coming to aid us, and therefore the troops were placed so as to occupy the commanding positions and wait for daylight. The Second Corps began to come in after midnight and relieved my extended lines, and our gallant men rested after a toilsome day."

According to Butler, Grant was laboring under the impression that Lee's army might take the railroad to Petersburg and arrive with rapid reinforcements, which was something Grant seemed to deny in his own memoirs when writing that he told Butler he could reinforce Smith before Lee could reinforce Petersburg. Regardless of Grant's opinion, what is clear is that Smith seemed to believe Lee might be reinforcing Petersburg, which was the primary reason he didn't advance on Petersburg the night of the 15th. Butler savagely criticized him for that decision:

"Smith had with him some eighteen thousand effective men. There were in Petersburg, as I have said, but twenty-two hundred, or one man to every four and one half feet of intrenchments around that city. Of all that Smith had been so thoroughly informed that he knew it. He knew the situation of that part of the fortifications of Petersburg, because up to the time of his attack there had been no substantial change in them for months. My proposition to him was, as to Gillmore, to go in by an attack and "rush," and I represented to him strongly that Gillmore on his expedition had only rushed at his dinner.

Now I think Smith was an efficient soldier in many respects,--although it would seem that I have every cause to dislike the man in every relation of life. But he had one inevitable regular army failing — the vice Assistant Secretary Dana wrote to the War Department Wright and Warren were accused of: 'interminable reconnoissances' -- waiting and waiting, not going at a thing when he was told, but looking all around to see if he could not do something else than what he was told to do, or do it in a different way from what he was told.

Fearing lest he might believe, as an excuse for reconnoitring, that Lee's troops had gone into Petersburg or could get there before him, I telegraphed him that since he marched, not a body of troops had passed through Richmond on the Petersburg road, the only way they could get to Petersburg. This information I also gave to Grant."

However it happened, Grant would blame the failure to get the proper orders to Hancock as the reason Petersburg wasn't taken on the 15th, writing in his memoirs:

"If General Hancock's orders of the 15th had been communicated to him, that officer, with his usual promptness, would undoubtedly have been upon the ground around Petersburg as early as four o'clock in the afternoon of the 15th. The days were long and it would have given him considerable time before night. I do not think there is any doubt that Petersburg itself could have been carried without much loss; or, at least, if protected by inner detached works, that a line could have been established very much in rear of the one then occupied by the enemy. This would have given us control of both the Weldon and South Side railroads. This would also have saved an immense amount of hard fighting which had to be done from the 15th to the 18th, and would have given us greatly the advantage in the long siege which ensued."

The Union command wasn't the only one suffering from delays and confusion on the 15th. As Beauregard's meager defenders were pushed out of the lines surrounding Petersburg, he frantically sought reinforcements from Lee and communicated his predicament to Richmond. After the war, when the back and forth messages were publicly published, one historian noted, "Nothing illustrates better the fundamental weakness of the Confederate command system than the weary series of telegrams exchanged in May and early June between Davis, Bragg, Beauregard, and Lee. Beauregard evaded his responsibility for determining what help he could give Lee; Davis and Bragg shirked their responsibility to decide when he refused. The strangest feature of the whole affair was that, in the face of Lee's repeated requests, nobody in the high command thought to order Beauregard to join Lee."

Baldy Smith may have inexcusably failed to take Petersburg when he heavily outnumbered Beauregard's defenders on the 15th, but the Union would have another chance the following day.

**June 16**

With no hope of receiving substantial reinforcements from Lee's Army of Northern Virginia, Beauregard opened June 16 only able to rely on the men he had in Petersburg, Richmond, and the Bermuda Hundred, which consisted of about 14,000 men. Between Hancock and Smith's corps near Petersburg, most of Butler's army near Bermuda Hundred, and the Army of the Potomac near the James River, Beauregard had about 50,000 Union soldiers in his vicinity.

During the morning, Beauregard concentrated his men in a defensive line closer to Petersburg, while Hancock and Smith waited for Burnside's IX Corps to come up. Grant also had Meade order Warren's corps to hurry forward to Petersburg. Grant was at the front with Burnside's corps and ordered a reconnaissance in force, but by now they could see Confederate reinforcements streaming into the line, without knowing for certain how many Confederates there were or whether they were from Lee's army. However, at the same time, Grant figured that Lee's army might move against Butler's army near Bermuda Hundred, so after ordering that reconnaissance in force, he headed back to City Point and away from Petersburg.

As if enough hadn't already gone wrong, the serious wound that Hancock had suffered during Pickett's Charge on Day 3 at Gettysburg, which had kept him out of command for several weeks after the battle, reopened, forcing Hancock to relinquish command of his corps. Grant ordered Meade himself to take Hancock's place temporarily, adding yet another bizarre and unforeseeable delay in an attack plan. Meade needed to travel the James River on a steamer and then ride to the front to take command in person, which meant the attack on June 16 would not come until the late afternoon.

Finally, just before 6:00 p.m., a concerted Union attack with Burnside's corps, Hancock's corps, and Smith's corps pushed forward against the severely outnumbered Confederates. By now, however, the Confederates had the advantage of strong entrenchments and artillery, allowing them to put up a strong fight. Porter recalled seeing Meade as the attack was ongoing:

"It was discovered before [6:00 p.m.] that the enemy was advancing upon Butler's front, and General Grant directed me to ride at full speed to Meade and tell him that this made it still more important that his attack should be a vigorous one, and that the enemy might be found weaker there on account of troops having been collected at

Bermuda Hundred. I found Meade standing near the edge of a piece of woods, surrounded by some of his staff, and actively engaged in superintending the attack, which was then in progress. His usual nervous energy was displayed in the intensity of his manner and the rapid and animated style of his conversation. He assured me that no additional orders could be given which could add to the vigor of the attack. He was acting with great earnestness, and doing his utmost to carry out the instructions which he had received. He had arrived at the front about two o'clock, and his plans had been as well matured as possible for the movement. Three redans, as well as a line of earthworks connecting them, were captured. The enemy felt the loss keenly, and made several desperate attempts during the night to recover the ground, but in this he did not succeed."

The Confederates were being pushed back, but they fought enough of a delayed defense by constructing impromptu breastworks as they fell back that they were able to keep the Union soldiers from fully breaking their line on the 16th. Meade would claim the men were simply too tired to keep advancing, writing to Grant:

"Advantage was taken of the fine moonlight to press the enemy all night. A rough return would make our loss two thousand killed and wounded. I regret to say that many officers are among the numbers. Our men are tired and the attack could not be made with the vigor and force which characterized our fighting in the Wilderness. If they had not been, I think they might have been more successful.

The men were tired and weary of assaulting works, of being led to assault intrenchments; not tired and weary in the sense of physical fatigue. Most of them had rested quietly during the night of the 15th, and the day of the 16th before they were led to the attack without having any distance to march."

On the 16th, the only reinforcements Beauregard had received came in the form of Robert Hoke's division, which had been sent to Lee less than 3 weeks earlier as reinforcements ahead of the Battle of Cold Harbor. The depleted nature of Hoke's division from the fighting in Cold Harbor ensured that Beauregard was still badly outnumbered, and as he would quickly learn on the 17th, no reinforcements from Lee were forthcoming anytime soon.

### June 17

In the last two days, Beauregard had been the beneficiary of a scrappy defense and good luck, but he still anticipated that he could lose Petersburg at any time, and he was unquestionably beside himself when he received a series of dispatches from Lee beginning around noon on the 17th. Despite the fact that almost all of Grant's army was south of the James River, and several corps had attacked his defensive line on the 16th, Beauregard received a communication from Lee around noon that read, "Until I can get more definite information of Grant's movements, I do not think it prudent to draw more troops to this side of the river." Later that afternoon, Beauregard received another message from Lee stating, "Have no information of Grant's crossing the James River, but upon your report have ordered troops up to Chaffin's Bluff."

For whatever reason, Lee had refused to believe Beauregard's reports over the previous couple of days, and Beauregard would write after the war, "The Army of Northern Virginia was yet far distant, and I had failed to convince its distinguished commander of the fact that I was then fighting Grant's whole army with less than eleven thousand men." In fact, Lee would not believe that Grant had crossed the river until his cavalry verified it late on the 17th, and he would not be sending any men from the Army of Northern Virginia until the early morning hours of the 18th. Once again, Beauregard was all on his own.

This time, Beauregard would be saved by the Army of the Potomac's seeming inability to coordinate a massive assault. The first attack came from just two brigades of the IX Corps, which was able to surprise the Confederate defenders and capture nearly 600 men, but their lack of numbers prevented them from achieving a true breakthrough. Eventually, Confederate artillery compelled them to fall back. Hours later, a single brigade from Burnside's IX Corps moved forward in the early afternoon, only to march directly into enfilading fire.

An attack was made in the evening by a division of troops led by General James Ledlie, who had led men while drunk into a disastrous assault at the Battle of North Anna. Despite that debacle, Ledlie had actually been promoted for the bravery of his men, many of whom had been ignorantly and drunkenly ordered to their deaths for no gain. On the 17th, Ledlie was drunk yet again, and his assault was quickly repulsed. Once again, Ledlie would escape censure, a travesty that would have tragic consequences for many Union soldiers during the Battle of the Crater.

It's unclear why the Army of the Potomac acted so cautiously on the 17th, but the reason might be found in a letter Meade wrote to his wife that night, in which he wrote, "We find the enemy, as usual, in a very strong position, defended by earthworks, and it looks very much as if we will have to go through a siege of Petersburg before entering on the siege of Richmond." The Union officers may not have known how many men were in their front, or whether Lee had sent reinforcements to Petersburg, but they had spent all of May learning at battles like Spotsylvania and Cold Harbor just how costly frontal assaults on well-entrenched positions could be. That cautious nature had been on display by Baldy Smith from the very beginning on the 15th, and it was probably no coincidence that Smith's men suffered badly at Cold Harbor, to the extent that the incensed corps commander explicitly told his superiors he would disobey orders to make another assault at Cold Harbor if they came. As Meade's words suggest, the soldiers and generals in the Army of the Potomac had become so accustomed to the Confederates establishing nearly impregnable defensive lines that the mere sight of Confederate soldiers behind elaborate defensive fortifications was enough to spook them.

## June 18

While his men were fighting on the 17th, Beauregard had been busily constructing a new defensive line in the rear of his men's current line, so that they could keep falling back if necessary. Once the fighting had ended, he pulled them back to that new line. As he was doing so, he received yet another dispatch from Lee that must have shocked him: "Am not yet satisfied as to General Grant's movements, but upon your representations will move at once on Petersburg."

To Beauregard's great relief, Lee was finally convinced during the night of the 17th that Grant's army was south of the James River, and around 3:00 a.m. on the 18th he sent two divisions to Petersburg as reinforcements. Even still, while this bolstered Beauregard's defenses to about 20,000 strong, the arrival of Warren's V Corps in front of Petersburg meant Grant had over 60,000 men with which to try to capture the city on the 18th.

On the 18th, Grant pitched multiple corps into the fight, but once again the attacks were uncoordinated. The first attack came from Hancock and Smith's corps, and they were shocked to find that the line they had fought so hard to take had been abandoned by the Confederates, with the dead still in the trenches. Before they could advance much further, however, the reinforced Confederates in their new defensive line repulsed them and kept them from overrunning the new line.

After that failed attack, it was Burnside and Warren's corps on the left of the Union line that attacked together. They came up while Hancock's men were still in the previous Confederate defensive line, but they soon came under murderous fire as well. One of the IX Corps divisions, commanded by Orlando Willcox, was so decimated that it could only field 1,000 effectives after the fighting, which would have been the size of a single regiment in 1862. It was no easier for Warren's men. Leading the First Division of the V Corps, Colonel Joshua Chamberlain's men rushed toward a strongly-defended Confederate position colloquially known as, "Fort Hell." While initially defending the position from a crest above the ground fighting, Chamberlain received orders to lead his men in a frontal charge, with orders to form two columns and "not to stop and fire" since this would slow their advance and expose them longer. The hero of Little Round Top at Gettysburg was ordered to "carry the defenses with their bayonets."

With his horse shot out from under him in the first minutes, Chamberlain led the charge as directed on foot, with the defense quickly becoming bitter and the casualties heavy. When his color-bearer was shot dead at his side, Chamberlain picked up and hoisted the standard, holding the flag in one hand, his saber in the other. Realizing that his men could not hear his order to "oblique to the left," he waved his saber and flag into the air to gain their attention, essentially making a target of himself. At that moment, a bullet slammed into his right hip, ripped through his body, and exited through the other hip. Steadying himself with his sword, he continued to direct his men before collapsing to the ground unconscious from loss of blood.

Taken back behind the lines, the profusely-bleeding Colonel Chamberlain was given up for dead by the field surgeons, who were all certain his wound was mortal. After being notified by Warren, General Grant promoted him to brigadier general on the spot, the only battlefield promotion of that rank during the Civil War, stating, "He has been recommended for promotion for gallant and efficient conduct on previous occasion and yesterday led his brigade against the enemy under most destructive fire. He expresses the wish that he may receive the recognition of his services by promotion before he dies for the gratification of his family and friends." As it turned out, Chamberlain would actually survive the wound and be on hand for Lee's surrender at Appomattox.

As it became clear to Meade that his army was not going to break through, he told his subordinates, "Sorry to hear you cannot carry the works. Get the best line you can and be prepared to hold it. I suppose you cannot make any more attacks, and I feel satisfied all has been done that can be done." Meade would order one more night attack on the 18th, but it relied on an infantry unit that consisted of artillery men who had been converted into infantry and were completely green. One of these "infantry" regiments, the 1st Maine Heavy Artillery, lost over 600 men alone in this final attack, nearly two-thirds of the regiment and the highest number of casualties lost in one battle by a regiment in the entire war. After that, it was evident that Beauregard's defenses were going to hold the city. That night, he reported to Grant, "It is a source of great regret that I am not able to report more success."

Shortly before noon on the 18th, Lee had finally arrived in Petersburg and met with Beauregard, who couldn't have been happier to see him. Lee's nephew, cavalry officer Fitzhugh Lee, noted after the war:

"It was very difficult for Lee to ascertain on the north side of the James what troops Grant was crossing to its southern side, because his crossing was masked by the presence of troops interposed between the point of crossing and Lee's position; and he had to be most careful lest, in his anxiety to save Petersburg, he would lose Richmond. He could not afford to take the risk of denuding the Richmond lines until it had been demonstrated beyond doubt that the real battle was to be delivered at Petersburg. The admirably selected new line of Beauregard was strengthened, and maintained until the end of the war."

## Beginning the Siege of Petersburg

The failure to destroy Beauregard's defense on June 18 all but assured that there would be a siege of Petersburg. Grant had lost nearly 12,000 casualties over the past three days, while Beauregard had lost only about 4,000. Horace Porter rationalized the Union's failure to capture Petersburg in mid-June, while also explaining how the senior officers of the Army of the Potomac reacted in the immediate aftermath:

"It was apparent in the recent engagements that the men had not attacked with the same vigor that they had displayed in the Wilderness campaign; but this was owing more to the change in their physical than in their moral condition. They had moved incessantly both day and night, and had been engaged in skirmishing or in giving battle from the 4th of May to the 18th of June. They had seen their veteran comrades fall on every side, and their places filled by inexperienced recruits, and many of the officers in whom they had unshaken confidence had been killed or wounded. Officers had been in the saddle day and night, securing snatches of sleep for a few hours at a time as best they could. Sleeping on horseback had become an art, and experienced riders had learned to brace themselves in their saddles, rest their hands on the pommel, and catch many a cat-nap while riding. These snatches of sleep were of short duration and accomplished under many difficulties, but often proved more refreshing than might be supposed.

There was considerable suffering from sickness in many of the camps. It may be said that the enemy had suffered equally from the same causes that impaired the efficiency of our men, but there was a vast difference between the conditions of the two armies. The enemy had been engaged principally in defending strong intrenchments and in making short marches; he was accustomed to the Southern climate, and was buoyed up with the feeling that he was defending his home and fireside.

A controversy had arisen as to the cause of Hancock's not reaching Petersburg earlier on the 15th. Hancock conceived the idea that the circumstances might be construed as a reproach upon him, and he asked for an official investigation; but General Grant had no intention of reflecting either upon him or Meade. He assured them that, in his judgment, no investigation was necessary. He recommended them both for promotion to the grade of major-general in the regular army, and each was appointed to that rank."

After failing to take Petersburg over the course of those four days in mid-June, Grant began making preparations to dig his men in, as he noted in his memoirs:

"I now ordered the troops to be put under cover and allowed some of the rest which they had so long needed. They remained quiet, except that there was more or less firing every day, until the 22d, when General Meade ordered an advance towards the Weldon Railroad. We were very anxious to get to that road, and even round to the South Side Railroad if possible.

Meade moved Hancock's corps, now commanded by Birney, to the left, with a view to at least force the enemy to stay within the limits of his own line. General Wright, with the 6th corps, was ordered by a road farther south, to march directly for the Weldon road. The enemy passed in between these two corps and attacked vigorously, and with very serious results to the National troops, who were then withdrawn from their advanced position.

The Army of the Potomac was given the investment of Petersburg, while the Army of the James held Bermuda Hundred and all the ground we possessed north of the James River. The 9th corps, Burnside's, was placed upon the right at Petersburg; the 5th, Warren's, next; the 2d, Birney's, next; then the 6th, Wright's, broken off to the left and south. Thus began the siege of Petersburg."

Once Grant had decided that the only way to capture Petersburg was to lay siege to it, the nature of operations and the objectives changed. Instead of assaults on the Confederate line in an attempt to capture the city, Grant now sought to make his own army unassailable and cut all the supply lines to Petersburg, which would starve Lee's army out of their own impregnable lines. Fitz Lee described how quickly Grant's men made their own defensive lines, writing, "In an incredibly short time high, impregnable, bastioned works began to erect their crests. It was designed to make the Union defensive lines so formidable as to be unassailable. A system of redans chained together by powerful parapets, whose approaches were to be obstructed by abatis, were constructed. Behind these gigantic earthworks a small force could safely remain, and thus the "loyal legions" could be drawn out at any time for other work."

To starve Petersburg into submission, Grant had to cut Confederate access to the three railroads that ran into and out of the city. By the end of the Second Battle of Petersburg, the Union lines controlled the Petersburg & City Point railroad, which was made all the more crucial by the fact that City Point would be Grant's headquarters during the siege, meaning resources could be quickly transported from the major supply base to the lines. The Union line also cut off the Norfolk & Petersburg Railroad southeast of Petersburg. However, the Confederates could still rely on the Southside Railroad, which ran west out of Petersburg to Lynchburg, and the Weldon & Petersburg Railroad, which ran south out of Petersburg to Weldon, North Carolina. Since Wilmington, North Carolina was the last major Confederate port still active in the summer of 1864, it was almost necessary for Lee to keep Grant's line away from that railroad. Otherwise, the Confederates would be forced to stop the supplies many miles away from Petersburg and transfer them by wagons along roads in a roundabout way that would avoid the Union forces.

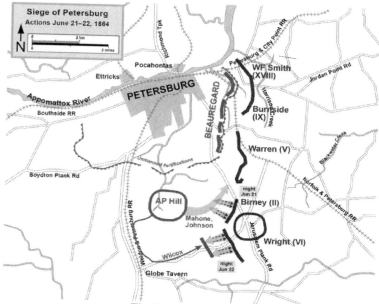

**The lines on June 21-22**

    Grant could use Sheridan's cavalry to ride around and break up the South's railroads in certain places, but that was usually a temporary problem that could be fixed in a matter of a few weeks. Thus, in addition to sending out cavalry to raid the Weldon & Petersburg Railroad, Grant tried to move Hancock's II Corps (still temporarily commanded by David Birney) and Horatio Wright's VI Corps southwest to extend the siege line to the railroad or at least closer to it, after which he could man the trenches with men from Butler's Army of the James.

    Like the previous attacks from days earlier, the fighting, which became known as the Battle of Jerusalem Plank, was a debacle for the Union. Grant intended for the two army corps to cross the Jerusalem Plank Road and then push northwest, keeping close to the Confederates' defensive line, but after crossing the road the II Corps ran into impassable terrain, including swamps. As they kept pushing through June 21-22, a gap opened between the two advancing corps. The II Corps began skirmishing with Confederate cavalry, but as they pivoted to march northwest, the men from the VI Corps stopped and began digging in as soon as they ran into Cadmus Wilcox's division from A.P. Hill's corps, which had become the modus operandi over the last two months. With one corps digging in while the other kept pushing northwest, a gap was exposed in front of William Mahone, one of the best division commanders in either army. Furthermore, Mahone's antebellum experience as a railroad engineer made him intimately familiar with the terrain around the Weldon railroad, and he knew he could take advantage of a ravine on the field that would allow his attacking Confederates to march close up to the II Corps and surprise it.

**"Little Billy" Mahone**

When Mahone's attack came on the afternoon of June 22, one Confederate soldier explained, "The attack was to the Union troops more than a surprise. It was an astonishment." One of Mahone's artillerists explained:

"With a wild yell which rang out shrill and fierce through the gloomy pines, Mahone's men burst upon the flank—a pealing volley, which roared along the whole front—a stream of wasting fire, under which the adverse left fell as one man—and the bronzed veterans swept forward, shriveling up Barlow's division as lightning shrivels the dead leaves of autumn."

As it slammed into the left flank and rear of the II Corps, Francis Barlow's division disintegrated, and John Gibbon's division, which had spent time digging in, found their earthworks worthless against Confederates coming from their flank and behind them. The II Corps was sent in flight back to the previous line of earthworks they had constructed the previous night on the 21st.

The next day, the Union soldiers attempted to push back toward their objective, and as the II Corps started moving forward, Wright and the VI Corps remained overly cautious with Wilcox's division in their front. Lyman, who Meade left with Wright that afternoon, marveled at the inaction by the VI Corps, writing:

"I rode about with General Wright, who visited his line, which was not straight or facing properly. That's a chronic trouble in lines in the woods. Indeed there are several chronic troubles. The divisions have lost connection; they cannot cover the ground designated, their wing is in the air, their skirmish line has lost its direction, etc., etc. Then General Meade gets mad with the delay. The commanders say they do as well as they can, etc. Well, Ricketts ran one way and Russell another; and then the 2d Corps-- how did that run? and were the skirmishers so placed as to face ours? and what would General Birney do about it? How long was the line? could it advance in a given direction, and, if so, how? All of which is natural with a good many thousand men in position in a dense wood, which nobody knows much about. All this while the men went to sleep or made coffee; profoundly indifferent to the perplexities of their generals; that was what generals were paid for. When General Wright had looked a great deal at his line, and a great deal more at his pocket compass, he rode forth on the left to look at the pickets, who were taking life easy like other privates. They had put up sun-shades with shelter-tents and branches, and were taking the heat coolly…"

Meanwhile, as Wright dithered, some of the men from Lewis Grant's brigade, part of his corps, actually reached part of the Weldon railroad and went about tearing up some of the railroad. Lyman explained:

"About this time a Vermont captain (bless his soul!) went and actually did something saucy and audacious. With eighty sharpshooters he pushed out boldly, drove in a lot of cavalry, and went a mile and a quarter to the railroad, which he held, and came back in person to report, bringing a piece of the telegraph wire. . . . Some time in the morning, I don't exactly know when, the signal officers reported a large force, say two divisions, marching out from the town, along the railroad…"

Wright and Birney discussed an advance with each other, but the time was wasting, and soon enough Lewis Grant's men came under attack by a much larger number of Confederates. Y now Meade was losing his temper with Wright, and the irascible commander insisted that Wright try to push forward to relieve Grant's men near the railroad. Wright continued to resist orders to advance, worried that Wilcox would hammer his men the same way Mahone ravaged the II Corps the previous day. Finally, an exasperated Meade ripped into Wright that night, telling him, "Your delay has been fatal."

The VI Corps and II Corps utterly failed to take control of the Weldon railroad, but they had extended Grant's siege line further west, which had the benefit of also forcing Lee to extend his defensive line further to the right. This would begin Grant's gradual process of slowly but surely extending his line west and forcing Lee to extend his line, knowing all along that the Union would always have the manpower advantage. Theoretically, it was just a matter of time before Lee's defenders would be stretched to the breaking point.

While the VI Corps and II Corps failed, Meade had also sent about 3500 cavalry under James Wilson and August Katz to tear up railroad to the west of Petersburg, in conjunction with the army's attempt to extend their lines to the west and cover the open railroads. The raid was a complete fiasco, as Fitz Lee's cavalry constantly harassed the Union cavalry, ensuring that they did little damage to the railroads. And on June 29, the Union cavalry anticipated meeting up with the Army of the Potomac near Reams Station, only to find it held by Confederate infantry. The Union cavalry had to burn their wagons and destroy their artillery before fleeing north and melting back into the Army of the Potomac's lines around July 1. Though Wilson tried to call their raid a strategic success, the raid had actually been an almost total failure. The railroad track that the cavalry tore up was quickly repaired, and the Confederate supply lines were still intact.

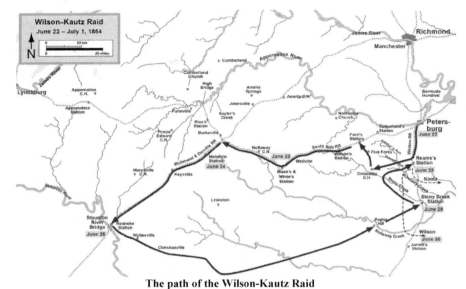

**The path of the Wilson-Kautz Raid**

### Planning the Mine

By the end of June, the Army of the Potomac had failed to deliver a knockout blow, and the Confederates were able to keep the remaining railroads open. During the last week of the month, the two sides settled into a routine that was trying on the soldiers in the trenches on each side. Confederate artillery chief Porter Alexander explained:

> "[A] daily entry in my note-book was 'severe sharpshooting and artillery practice without intermission day or night.' Our whole time was spent in improving our lines and getting our batteries protected and with good communications. Never until in this campaign had the enemy used mortar fire in the field, but now Abbot's reserve artillery regiment of 1700 men brought into use 60 mortars ranging from 24-Pr. Coehorns to 10-inch Sea-coast, which caused us great annoyance, as we had to keep our trenches fully manned and had no protection against the dropping shells. Fortunately, I had ordered some mortars constructed in Richmond about two weeks before, and they began to arrive on June 24, and were at once brought into use. They were only 12-pounders, but were light and convenient, and at close ranges enabled us to hold our own, with less loss than might have been expected. The cannoneers in the batteries, and the infantry in the lines who were exposed to this mortar fire, managed to build little bomb-proofs, and a labyrinth of deep and narrow trenches in rear of the lines."

**A Union siege mortar**
Given the ability of the sides to protect themselves from artillery, the siege promised to go on indefinitely. But Grant and Lee were well aware that the status quo favored the Union. Left with little initiative, a position he always hated, Lee attempted to shake things up by detaching Jubal Early's 10,000 strong corps from the siege lines and sending him north to threaten Washington. This tried and true tactic had always scared the Lincoln Administration just enough to overreact by bringing too many reinforcements to Washington, which at the time was the most heavily fortified city in the world.

Grant discussed the different units he sent to protect Washington, and they were not an insignificant number:

> "General Lew Wallace, with headquarters at Baltimore, commanded the department in which the Shenandoah lay. His surplus of troops with which to move against the enemy was small in number. Most of these were raw and, consequently, very much inferior to our veterans and to the veterans which Early had with him; but the situation of Washington was precarious, and Wallace moved with commendable promptitude to meet the enemy at the Monocacy. He could hardly have expected to defeat him badly, but he hoped to cripple and delay him until Washington could be put into a state of preparation for his reception. I had previously ordered General Meade to send a division to Baltimore for the purpose of adding to the defences of Washington, and he had sent Ricketts's division of the 6th corps (Wright's), which arrived in Baltimore on the 8th of July. Finding that

Wallace had gone to the front with his command, Ricketts immediately took the cars and followed him to the Monocacy with his entire division. They met the enemy and, as might have been expected, were defeated; but they succeeded in stopping him for the day on which the battle took place. The next morning Early started on his march to the capital of the Nation, arriving before it on the 11th.

Learning of the gravity of the situation I had directed General Meade to also order Wright with the rest of his corps directly to Washington for the relief of that place, and the latter reached there the very day that Early arrived before it. The 19th corps, which had been stationed in Louisiana, having been ordered up to reinforce the armies about Richmond, had about this time arrived at Fortress Monroe, on their way to join us. I diverted them from that point to Washington, which place they reached, almost simultaneously with Wright, on the 11th. The 19th corps was commanded by Major-General Emory."

Early's men ultimately reached the outskirts of Washington D.C., and in one battle around Fort Stevens from July 11-12, President Lincoln became the only sitting president to come under enemy fire in American history. Ultimately, Lincoln's presence is the only reason the fighting around Washington D.C. is remembered, as Early clearly didn't have enough men to conduct anything other than a diversion. Early's men would remain away from Petersburg and fight Phil Sheridan, among others, in the Valley Campaigns of 1864.

**Jubal Early**

Even while Grant was sending men to block Early around Washington, he had focused his attention on a new project, which would ultimately bring about the most famous battle of the Petersburg Campaign. Grant's aide, Horace Porter, explained how men from Burnside's corps came up with a plan for breaking the stalemate in late June:

After the assaults on the 17th and 18th of June, Burnside's corps established a line of earthworks within one hundred yards of those of the enemy. In rear of his advanced position was a deep hollow. In front the ground rose gradually until it reached an elevation on which the Confederate line was established. Colonel Pleasants, commanding the 48th Pennsylvania Regiment, composed largely of miners, conceived the idea of starting a gallery from a point in the hollow which was concealed from the enemy's view, pushing it forward to a position under his earthworks, and there preparing a mine large enough to blow up the parapets and make a sufficiently wide opening for assaulting columns to rush through. Before the end of June he communicated the project to Burnside, who talked the matter over with General Meade. It was then submitted to General Grant for his action. This point of the line was in some respects unfavorable for an assault; but it was not thought well to check the zeal of the officer who had proposed the scheme, and so an authorization was given for the undertaking to continue.

**Pleasants**

In his memoirs, Porter Alexander wrote that he correctly anticipated the plan by Burnside's men, but nobody else in Lee's army believed him:

"On June 30, I became convinced that the enemy were preparing to mine our position at the Elliott Salient. At that point, incessant fire was kept up by their sharpshooters, while a few hundred yards to the right and left the fire had been gradually allowed to diminish and men might show themselves without being fired at. That indicated that some operation was going on, and for several days I had expected to see zigzag approaches started on the surface of the ground. When several days had passed and nothing appeared, I became satisfied that their activity was underground. On my way home, I was that day wounded by a sharpshooter and received a furlough of six weeks to visit my home in Ga. On my way to the cars next day, I was driven by Lee's headquarters, where I reported my belief about the mine. There happened to be present Mr. Lawley, the English correspondent of the London times, who was much interested and asked how far it would be necessary to tunnel to get under our works. I answered about 500 feet. He stated that the longest military tunnel or gallery which had ever been run was at the siege of Delhi, and that it did not exceed 400 feet. That it was found impossible to ventilate for any greater distance. I replied that in the Federal army were many Pa. coal miners who could be relied on to ventilate mines any distance that might be necessary, and it would not do to rely upon military precedents. It proved that my suspicion was correct.

It was June 30 when I guessed it. The gallery had been commenced on June 27."

The Confederates might not have believed the Union would try it, but it's no surprise that Grant favored such an attempt. He had besieged Vicksburg for several months the year before, and even though it was ultimately successful, it had been trying on his soldiers. According to rumors, it had also been trying on Grant, who was accused of turning to the bottle and being drunk at times during the siege.

Interestingly, and perhaps with the benefit of hindsight, Grant wrote in his memoirs that he initially approved of the mining plan "as a means of keeping the men occupied." Pleasants and the Pennsylvania boys took the task very seriously, however. They dug with hands and tools, removing the dirt with cracker boxes, while using wood and timber to support the roof and shaft itself. Wood was so scarce that the men even ripped apart a bridge nearby to use it.

As the men dug forward, they also dug upwards, which would help keep the entire tunnel dry. The Confederates hadn't believed it was possible to dig a mine 500 feet because the workers would run out of air and asphyxiate. To avoid that problem, the miners also built a ventilation shaft and used a fire to force the bad air up into the ventilation shaft. This also ensured that the mine sucked in pure oxygen, which the miners ran through a wooden duct the entire length of the mine. This process made sure that the miners didn't have to build ventilation shafts as they neared the Confederate line, which would have been noticed by the Confederates.

Just ensuring the miners could breathe was difficult enough, but it would be an understatement to say the conditions in the mine itself were uncomfortable. The entrance into the mine was only 3 feet wide and less than 5 feet high, forcing soldiers to squeeze into it. It then ran over 500 feet before the miners dug sideways in both directions, creating a T shape. The digging in both directions extended about 75 feet, and there were 8 different chambers within those 75 feet. Each chamber would hold 40 kegs of gunpowder, a total of 1,000 pounds of gunpowder in each. Pleasants had managed to have the mine end right at Elliot's Salient, where a Confederate battery was perched above.

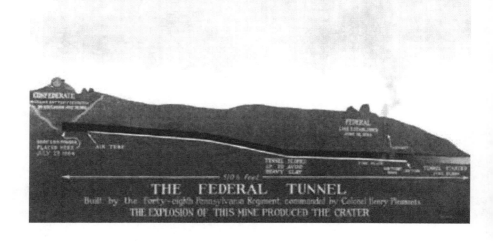

## Diagram of the mine

## A sketch of Pleasants directing the men in the mine

Along with Porter Alexander's warnings, rumors had reached Lee that the Union was attempting to mine their position in mid-July. Alexander discussed the Confederate attempts to countermine:

"Lee, on receipt of my message on July 1, ordered our engineers to start countermines at the Elliott Salient. Two shafts were sunk about 10 feet and listening galleries were run out from each. Unfortunately, the shafts were located on the right and left flanks of the battery, and the enemy's gallery passed at a depth of 20 feet under the apex, and was so silently built that our miners never knew of their proximity. Had they detected it, they would have hastened to explode what is called a camouflet, an undercharged or 'smothered mine,' which does not disturb the surface, but caves in adjacent galleries.

By July 10, our miners had done enough work, had it been done at the apex of the salient, to have heard the enemy, who would have been directly beneath them. Work was not only kept up, however, on the flanks, but at two other positions farther to the left, known as Colquitt's and Gracie's salients, countermines were also begun; at Colquitt's on the 10th and at Gracie's on the 19th. All four of our mines were constantly pushed until the 30th, when the explosion occurred, the total length of our galleries being then about 375 feet. Of the two galleries on each side of the mine, one, which was unoccupied, was destroyed by the explosion. In the other, the miners were at work, but, though much shaken up, the galleries were not crushed and the miners climbed out and escaped."

Nevertheless, on July 26, Burnside reported to Meade that the mine had seemingly not been discovered by the Confederates:

"It is altogether probable that the enemy are cognizant of the fact that we are mining, because it has been mentioned in their newspapers and they have been heard to work on what are supposed to be shafts in close proximity to our galleries, but the rain of night before last no doubt filled their shafts and much retarded their work. We have heard no sounds of work in them either yesterday or to-day, and nothing is heard by us in the mine but the usual sounds of work on the surface above. This morning we had some apprehension that the left lateral gallery was in danger of caving in from the weight of the batteries above it and the shock of their firing, but all possible precautions have been taken to strengthen it and we hope to preserve in intact. The placing of the charges in the mine will not involve the necessity of making a noise. It is therefore probable that we will escape discovery if the mine is to be used within two or three days. It is nevertheless highly important, in my opinion, that the mine should be exploded at the earliest possible moment consistent with the general interests of the campaign. I state to you the facts as nearly as I can, and in the absence of any knowledge as to the meditated movements of the army I must leave you to judge the proper time to make use of the mine. But it may not be improper for me to say that the advantages reaped from the work would be but small if it were exploded without any co-operative movement. My plan would be to explode the mine just before daylight in the morning or about 5 o'clock in the afternoon mass the two brigades of the colored division in rear of my line in column of divisions, double column closed in mass, the head of each brigade resting on the front, and as soon as the explosion has taken place move them forward with instructions for the division to take half distance, and as soon as the leading regiments of the two brigades pass through the gap in the enemy's line, the leading regiment of the right brigade to come into line perpendicular to the enemy's line by the right companies, on the right into line wheel, the left companies on the right into line, and proceed at once down the line of the enemy's works as rapidly as possible, the leading regiment of the left brigade to execute the reverse movement to the left, moving up the enemy's line. The remainders of the two columns to move directly toward the crest in front as rapidly as possible, diverging in such a way as to enable them to deploy into columns of regiments, the right column making as nearly as may be for Cemetery Hill. These columns to be followed by the other divisions of this corps as soon as they can be thrown in. This would involve the necessity of relieving these divisions by other troops before the movement, and of holding columns of other troops in readiness to take out place on the crest in case we gain it and sweep down it. It would be advisable, in my opinion, if we succeed in gaining the crest, to throw the colored division right into the town. There is a necessity for the cooperation, at least in the way of artillery, of the troops on my right and left. Of the extent of this you will necessarily be the judge. I think our chances of success in a plan of this kind are more than even."

Grant's aide Horace Porter described the finished mine and Grant's plans for its use:

"There was a main gallery, 511 feet long and 41 feet square, and two lateral galleries. The terminus was under the enemy's parapet, and at a depth of about 23 feet below the surface of the ground. These preparations were completed July 23, and the mine was soon after charged with eight thousand pounds of powder, and made ready for use. A movement preliminary to its explosion was begun on July 26, that required the exercise of much ingenuity and good generalship, and which the general-in-chief had planned with great care. It involved making a feint against Richmond, which should be conducted with such a show of serious intention that it would induce Lee to throw a large portion of his command to the north side of the James, and leave the works at Petersburg so depleted that the movement on Burnside's front would have in its favor many chances of success."

Horace Porter was making reference to the action that would be known as the First Battle of Deep Bottom, which he labeled a feint. But according to Grant's memoirs (and again perhaps in hindsight), the commanding general didn't like the terrain for making an attack after detonating the mine:

"[Burnside's] position was very favorable for carrying on this work, but not so favorable for the operations to follow its completion. The position of the two lines at that point were only about a hundred yards apart with a comparatively deep ravine intervening. In the bottom of this ravine the work commenced. The position was unfavorable in this particular: that the enemy's line at that point was re-entering, so that its front was commanded by their own lines both to the right and left. Then, too, the ground was sloping upward back of the Confederate line for a considerable distance, and it was presumable that the enemy had, at least, a detached work on this highest point. The work progressed, and on the 23d of July the mine was finished ready for charging; but I had this work of charging deferred until we were ready for it."

Since Grant wasn't confident Burnside could make a successful attack after exploding the mine, he decided to take action in a way that would clear as many Confederates in Burnside's front as possible:

"On the 17th of July several deserters came in and said that there was great consternation in Richmond, and that Lee was coming out to make an attack upon us the object being to put us on the defensive so that he might detach troops to go to Georgia where the army Sherman was operating against was said to be in great trouble. I put the army commanders, Meade and Butler, on the lookout, but the attack was not made.

I concluded, then, a few days later, to do something in the way of offensive movement myself, having in view something of the same object that Lee had had. Wright's and Emory's corps were in Washington, and with this reduction of my force Lee might very readily have spared some troops from the defences to send West. I had other objects in view, however, besides keeping Lee where he was. The mine was constructed and ready to be exploded, and I wanted to take that occasion to carry Petersburg if I could. It was the object, therefore, to get as many of Lee's troops away from the south side of the James River as possible."

On the night of July 26, Grant put the plan in motion by marching Hancock's men and Sheridan's cavalry north across a pontoon bridge. Grant wanted the cavalry to tear up railroad while Hancock's II Corps covered them and allowed them to return, but Lee had no way of knowing that. To Lee, it looked like a considerable force was marching north toward Richmond. That would compel Lee to counter the perceived threat by marching infantry to deal with them. Lee complied by first sending a division to counter Hancock and then sending even more reinforcements.

Sheridan's cavalry were blocked by strong defenses, and the Confederates attacked Hancock's men from July 27-28, engaging in mostly inconsequential fighting that left about 500 casualties on each side. For all intents and purposes, Grant had successfully distracted Lee, paving the way for Burnside's corps to explode the mine and follow it up with an attack on July 30. As Horace Porter noted, "Now that Grant had satisfied himself that more than half of Lee's command had been sent to the north side of the James, he made preparations to throw Hancock's corps again in front of Petersburg, and carry out his intended assault upon that front... On the morning of the 30th Lee was holding five eighths of his army on the north side of the James, in the belief that Grant was massing the bulk of his troops near Deep Bottom, while he had in reality concentrated his forces in the rear of Burnside at a point fifteen miles distant, ready to break through the defenses at Petersburg."

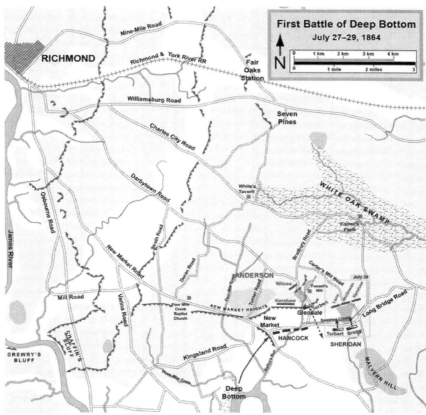

The First Battle of Deep Bottom

### Planning the Attack

"Meade's instructions, which I, of course, approved most heartily, were all that I can see now was necessary. The only further precaution which he could have taken, and which he could not foresee, would have been to have different men to execute them." – Ulysses S. Grant

On July 24, Grant issued the following orders to Meade and the Army of the Potomac in an attempt to describe how he wanted the attack to follow up the explosion of the mine:

> "CITY POINT, VA., July 24, 1864.
>
> MAJOR-GENERAL MEADE,
>
> Commanding, etc.
>
> The engineer officers who made a survey of the front from Bermuda Hundred report against the probability of success from an attack there. The chances they think will be better on Burnside's front. If this is attempted it will be necessary to concentrate all the force possible at the point in the enemy's line we expect to

penetrate. All officers should be fully impressed with the absolute necessity of pushing entirely beyond the enemy's present line, if they should succeed in penetrating it, and of getting back to their present line promptly if they should not succeed in breaking through.

To the right and left of the point of assault all the artillery possible should be brought to play upon the enemy in front during the assault. Their lines would be sufficient for the support of the artillery, and all the reserves could be brought on the flanks of their commands nearest to the point of assault, ready to follow in if successful. The field artillery and infantry held in the lines during the first assault should be in readiness to move at a moment's notice either to their front or to follow the main assault, as they should receive orders. One thing, however, should be impressed on corps commanders. If they see the enemy giving away on their front or moving from it to reinforce a heavily assaulted portion of their line, they should take advantage of such knowledge and act promptly without waiting for orders from army commanders. General Ord can co-operate with his corps in this movement, and about five thousand troops from Bermuda Hundred can be sent to reinforce you or can be used to threaten an assault between the Appomattox and James rivers, as may be deemed best.

This should be done by Tuesday morning, if done at all. If not attempted, we will then start at the date indicated to destroy the railroad as far as Hicksford at least, and to Weldon if possible.

\*\*\*\*\*\*\*\*\*\*\*\*\*\*\*\*\*\*\*\*\*\*\*\*\*\*\*\*\*\*\*\*\*\*\*\*\*\*\*\*\*\*

Whether we send an expedition on the road or assault at Petersburg, Burnside's mine will be blown up....

U. S. GRANT,

Lieutenant-General."

After the mine had been finished, the Pennsylvania miners had placed 320 kegs of gunpowder totaling 8,000 pounds inside the T shaped mine, which was just 20 feet below the Confederate line. They had the charge to detonate the powder ready by July 28, and they also had to seal the gunpowder off from the rest of the mine and then seal the entrance to the mine itself to avoid blowback. Sandbags were placed around the kegs to help direct the blast upward.

With the work complete, the plan was to detonate the mine around 3:30 a.m. on July 30, and Grant had Hancock and Sheridan return to the lines on July 29. Grant had given the different corps commanders instructions for what to do the second the mine detonated, as he explained in his memoirs:

"Warren was to hold his line of intrenchments with a sufficient number of men and concentrate the balance on the right next to Burnside's corps, while Ord, now commanding the 18th corps, temporarily under Meade, was to form in the rear of Burnside to support him when he went in. All were to clear off the parapets and the abatis in their front so as to leave the space as open as possible, and be able to charge the moment the mine had been sprung and Burnside had taken possession. Burnside's corps was not to stop in the crater at all but push on to the top of the hill, supported on the right and left by Ord's and Warren's corps.

Warren and Ord fulfilled their instructions perfectly so far as making ready was concerned. Burnside seemed to have paid no attention whatever to the instructions, and left all the obstruction in his own front for his troops to get over in the best way they could."

Meade issued orders to the army on July 29:

"At 3.30 in the morning of the 30th Major-General Burnside will spring his mine and his assaulting columns will immediately move rapidly upon the breach, seize the crest in the rear, and effect a lodgment there. He will be followed by Major-General Ord, who will support him on the right, directing his movement to the crest indicated, and by Major-General Warren, who will support him on the left. Upon the explosion of the mine the artillery of all kinds in battery will open upon those points of the enemy's works whose fire covers the ground over which our columns must move, care being taken to avoid impeding the progress of our troops. Special instructions respecting the direction of fire will be issued through the chief of artillery."

As Grant noted, Burnside may not have had obstacles in his front cleared, but he was well aware that the explosion of the mine would make the battle operations unlike anything the soldiers had ever seen before. For that reason, he decided to have his men practice the assault. Burnside had 4 divisions, and he picked Edward Ferrero's division to lead his corps' assault. Ferrero's division had two brigades and over 4,000 men, making it the largest division in Burnside's corps. Burnside had it train for the attack. One of the brigades would go to the right of the crater, the other to the left, and a regiment from each brigade would march perpendicular to the crater, helping extend the breach in the Confederate line while the other men charged forward and into the rear of the Confederates. Burnside's other divisions would then support Ferrero's flanks and push for Petersburg itself. This training was considered so important that Burnside pulled Ferrero's division out of the lines at Petersburg and had them practice the attack for nearly two weeks in the rear.

**Burnside**

**Ferrero**

Despite the training Burnside had Ferrero's division do before the Battle of the Crater, General Meade changed the attack plan the very day before the mine was set to explode. What was the problem? Though Meade's exact reasons remain unclear, it seems he was uncomfortable with Ferrero's division leading the assault because the division consisted of black soldiers. Meade explicitly stated he was worried that the deaths of black soldiers during the fight would be a political problem in the North, but it seems just as likely that he was doubting the ability of the black soldiers to succeed. Thus, the division that had been specially trained to lead the assault would no longer do so.

Making matters worse, Burnside had his other three divisions (led by white generals) draw straws to pick which division made the attack, because nobody would volunteer for fear the attack wouldn't work. Thus, instead of being proactive and picking the division he thought would be best, Burnside left it to chance. The result was the worst possible, because Ferrero's division was replaced with James Ledlie's division. Ledlie was the same general who drunkenly walked his men into a needless slaughter at the Battle of North Anna two months earlier, and he was also drunk during the Second Battle of Petersburg the previous month. Ledlie was simply the worst possible choice of the 4 divisions, and Grant himself noted, "Ledlie besides being otherwise inefficient, proved also to possess disqualification less common among soldiers."

However, it was Grant who had the final say on letting Ledlie lead the assault, because Burnside was so taken aback by the change in plans that he protested to the commander himself. Grant took Meade's side. Months later, Grant explained the decision before the Joint Committee on the Conduct of the War: "General Burnside wanted to put his colored division in front, and I believe if he had done so it would have been a success. Still I agreed with General Meade as to his objections to that plan. General Meade said that if we put the colored troops in front (we had only one division) and it should prove a failure, it would then be said and very properly, that we were shoving these people ahead to get killed because we did not care anything about them. But that could not be said if we put white troops in front."

**General Ledlie**

**The Battle of the Crater**

**A.R. Waud's sketch of the explosion of the mine**

"It was the saddest affair I have witnessed in the war." – Ulysses S. Grant

The Battle of the Crater may have been the most unique battle of the Civil War, and it may also have been the most controversial and tragic of the entire war too.

The plan went haywire before the battle even started. Pleasants lit the fuse at 3:15 a.m. on the morning of the 30th, which should have set off the explosion at 3:30. Ledlie's men had taken up advanced positions that would've left them exposed in daylight, so as time passed and no explosion went off, the Army of the Potomac grew more nervous. Horace Porter captured the atmosphere around Grant's headquarters as they waited for the mine to explode without results:

> "Now came the hour for the explosion-half-past 3 o'clock. The general-in-chief was standing, surrounded by his officers, looking intently in the direction of the mine; orderlies were holding the saddled horses near by; not a word was spoken, and the silence of death prevailed. Some minutes elapsed, and our watches were anxiously consulted. It was found to be ten minutes past the time, and yet no sound from the mine. Ten minutes more, and still no explosion. More precious minutes elapsed, and it became painfully evident that some neglect or accident had occurred. Daylight was now breaking, and the formation of the troops for the assault would certainly be observed by the enemy. Officers had been sent to find out the cause of the delay, and soon there came the information that the match had been applied at the hour designated, but that the fuse had evidently failed at some point along the gallery. Another quarter of an hour passed, and now the minutes seemed like ages; the suspense was agonizing; the whole movement depended upon that little spark

which was to fire the mine, and it had gone out. The general-in-chief stood with his right hand placed against a tree; his lips were compressed and his features wore an expression of profound anxiety, but he uttered few words. There was little to do but to wait. Now word came that the men of the 48th Pennsylvania were not going to permit a failure."

When it was obvious something had gone wrong, two of the Pennsylvania soldiers offered to crawl into the mine and investigate. The two soldiers found that the fuse had burned out where they had spliced it a few days earlier. They lit the fuse again at 4:15 a.m. and scurried back out of the mine.

Around 4:45 a.m., the mine exploded, producing a blast unlike anything the soldiers had ever seen before. Almost instantly, the unfortunate Confederates who happened to be positioned above the mine were blown to smithereens, with nearly 300 of them instantly killed or badly wounded. The ground shook across the battlefield as men on both sides watched dirt, body parts and pieces of artillery go flying high up into the air. Some sleeping Confederates in the lines and shelters nearby were buried alive by falling debris.

Meade's aide, Theodore Lyman, described the sight and sound from the Union lines:

"At ten minutes before five there was a distant, dull-sounding explosion, like a heavy gun, far away; and, in an instant, as if by magic, the whole line of batteries burst forth in one roar, and there was nothing but the banging of the guns and the distant hum of the shells! My back was turned at the moment, but those that had a good view say that a mass of earth about 50 feet wide and 120 long was thrown some 130 feet in the air, looking like the picture of the Iceland geysers."

Horace Porter's description was far more colorful:

"The general had been looking at his watch, and had just returned it to his pocket when suddenly there was a shock like that of an earthquake, accompanied by a dull, muffled roar; then there rose two hundred feet in the air great volumes of earth in the shape of a mighty inverted cone, with forked tongues of flame darting through it like lightning playing through the clouds. The mass seemed to be suspended for an instant in the heavens; then there descended great blocks of clay, rock, sand, timber, guns, carriages, and men whose bodies exhibited every form of mutilation."

One Confederate soldier who miraculously survived the explosion humorously joked about his experience to a Union surgeon after being treated at a Union hospital: "I'll jest bet you that after this I'll be the most unpopular man in my regiment. You see, I appeared to get started a little earlier than the other boys that had taken passage with me aboard that volcano; and as I was comin' down I met the rest of 'em a-goin' up, and they looked as if they had kind of soured on me, and yelled after me, 'Straggler!'"

The explosion of the mine had created a crater that measured about 170 feet long, 70 feet wide, and 30 feet deep in some places. The crater was so large that visitors to the battlefield can still see it today.

An 1865 picture of the Crater with a Union soldier standing in it.

**A picture of part of the Crater today**

More importantly at the time, the explosion immediately produced a large breach in the Confederate lines. The mine exploded nearly 90 minutes late, but it had the precise effect Grant had hoped, as he noted in his memoirs, "When it did explode it was very successful, making a crater twenty feet deep and something like a hundred feet in length. Instantly one hundred and ten cannon and fifty mortars, which had been placed in the most commanding positions covering the ground to the right and left of where the troops were to enter the enemy's lines, commenced playing." Grant later told Army Chief of Staff Henry Halleck, "Such an opportunity for carrying fortifications I have never seen and do not expect again to have." Grant explained his optimism in his memoirs:

"I somewhat based my calculations upon this state of feeling, and expected that when the mine was exploded the troops to the right and left would flee in all directions, and that our troops, if they moved promptly, could get in and strengthen themselves before the enemy had come to a realization of the true situation. It was just as I expected it would be. We could see the men running without any apparent object except to get away. It was half an hour before musketry firing, to amount to anything, was opened upon our men in the crater. It was an hour before the enemy got artillery up to play upon them; and it was nine o'clock before Lee got up reinforcements from his right to join in expelling our troops."

Unfortunately for Grant and the Union, things went wrong as soon as Ledlie's division started marching forward to lead the attack. This was due in no small part to the fact that General Ledlie himself was nowhere to be found. He and General Ferrero decided to find a safe bunker in the rear and start drinking instead. Moreover, the Union soldiers were so awed by the explosion that the start to their advance was delayed by 10 minutes. And on top of that, they hadn't cleared the obstacles in their front as they marched toward the crater. In defense of the soldiers, Horace Porter noted, "It appeared as if part of the debris was going to fall upon the front line of our troops, and this created some confusion and a delay of ten minutes in forming them for the charge."

All of that gave the Confederates precious time to start regrouping themselves. The Confederate soldiers in the vicinity of the crater were so stunned that it took them a whole 15 minutes to start firing their muskets and artillery in an organized manner. Had Ledlie's division moved faster and with a proper purpose, the Confederates might have been overwhelmed before they had recovered their senses.

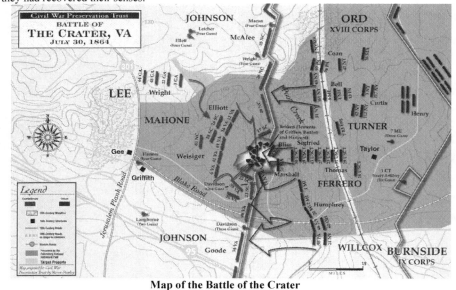

**Map of the Battle of the Crater**

Without Ledlie leading them, and with no practice or training for the attack like Ferrero's division had, the soldiers in Ledlie's division began to lose their way almost immediately upon reaching the crater. The soldiers who came to the lip of the crater were so amazed by what they saw that many of them initially stopped to look at the carnage instead of continuing to move. Some were so horrified by the sight that they actually stopped to help injured Confederates in the area; Horace Porter wrote, "Some stopped to assist the Confederates who were struggling out of the debris, in which many of them were buried up to their necks."

The plan had called for the attacking division to have its soldiers march around the crater on both sides, spreading out to help enlarge the breach in the Confederate lines and make room for reinforcements to pour through. However, Ledlie's division hadn't trained for this kind of action. The soldiers had been engaged in trench warfare for most of the last three months, including during the Overland Campaign. Perhaps not surprisingly, their first instinct was to find cover, and the crater seemed like an awfully inviting place to seek shelter, since it was so deep in places. As if that wasn't enough, the lead brigade in Ledlie's division was Elisha Marshall's brigade, which had been formed out of dismounted cavalry and artillerists. In other words, the infantry assault was being led by men who weren't originally infantry soldiers.

When Ledlie's division reached the crater, some of Ledlie's men spaced out to the left and right of the crater properly, but a lot of them headed into the crater instead of around it. With so many going into the crater, it meant that the Union soldiers were not advancing forward and into the rear of the Confederate lines. This had two important results. First, it meant that when Union reinforcements rushed forward, they could not advance past the crater. And more importantly, it gave Lee the time to order two brigades under General Mahone to reinforce the breach formed by the crater around 6:00. It would still take Mahone's brigades nearly 2 hours to reach the crater.

When the Confederates began to rally and Mahone's men arrived to fight, they found Union soldiers literally stuck in the crater. Since the plan had been to go around the crater, there were no ladders or equipment on hand to help Union soldiers get out of the crater if they went into it. With the crater nearly 30 feet deep and more men piling in, the soldiers literally trapped themselves in it. The Confederates who arrived at the edge of the crater were shooting fish in a barrel, and Mahone himself would call it a "turkey shoot". Horace Porter wrote, "The crater was soon filled with our disorganized men, who were mixed up with the dead and dying of the enemy, and tumbling aimlessly about, or attempting to scramble up the other side. The shouting, screaming, and cheering, mingled with the roar of the artillery and the explosion of shells, created a perfect pandemonium, and the crater had become a cauldron of hell."

Despite the difficulties, the reinforcements from Burnside's corps kept pouring in, and by 8:30 about 15,000 Union soldiers were engaged in and around the crater. By then, Mahone's men were pouring in musket fire, and Confederate batteries were bombarding the soldiers in the crater. At one point, the Confederates rolled up mortars to within 50 yards of the crater and fired shells.

Meanwhile, some of Burnside's soldiers had managed to push around and ahead of the crater: Ferrero's black division. This was no doubt accomplished because of their training and the familiarity with the plan, but the failure of the other divisions essentially left them without support. Horace Porter noted, "When the confusion was at its worst Burnside threw in his division of colored troops, who rushed gallantly into the crater, but only added greater disorder to the men already crowded together there." The advanced parts of Ferrero's division were able to push the Confederates several hundred yards back, and even engaged in hand-to-hand fighting, but Mahone's men eventually swept them back toward the crater. When the advanced parts of Ferrero's division were forced to retreat, they had no choice but to fall into the crater along with the other Union soldiers.

Grant was monitoring the situation, and within the first few hours he had determined that the assault was a failure. He began to ride to find Burnside, as Horace Porter recalled:

"As the shots shrieked through the air, and plowed the ground, I held my breath
in apprehension for the general's safety. Burnside was in the earthwork for which
we were heading, and was not a little astonished to see the general approach on
foot from such a direction, climb over the parapet, and make his way to where the
corps commander was stationed. Grant said, speaking rapidly: 'The entire
opportunity has been lost. There is now no chance of success. These troops must

be immediately withdrawn. It is slaughter to leave them here.' Burnside was still hoping that something could be accomplished; but the disobedience of orders and the general bungling had been so great that Grant was convinced that the only thing to do now to stop the loss of life was to abandon the movement which a few hours before had promised every success…

Instructions were reiterated to Burnside to withdraw the troops; but he came to Meade in person and insisted that his men could not be drawn out of the crater with safety; that the enemy's guns now bore upon the only line of retreat; and that there must be a passageway dug to protect them in crossing certain dangerous points. Both of these officers lost their tempers that morning, although Burnside was usually the personification of amiability, and the scene between them was decidedly peppery, and went far toward confirming one's belief in the wealth and flexibility of the English language as a medium of personal dispute. Meade had sent Burnside a note saying: 'Do you mean to say your officers and men will not obey your orders to advance? If not, what is the obstacle? I wish to know the truth.' Burnside replied: 'I have never, in any report, said anything different from what I conceive to be the truth. Were it not insubordinate, I would say that the latter remark of your note was unofficerlike and ungentlemanly.' It was quite evident that the conference was not going to resolve itself into a 'peace congress.'"

Although Burnside's men couldn't advance, Burnside didn't want to give up the ground his men had already captured at the crater either. He began arguing with Edward Ord, who commanded the 18 Corps adjacent to his men. Meade's aide Theodore Lyman was on hand to witness the argument, writing:

"10.30 A. M. Burnside and Ord came in. The former, much flushed, walked up to General Meade and used extremely insubordinate language. He afterwards said he could advance, and wished of all things to persist; but could not show how he would do it! Ord was opposed to further attempts. Meade ordered the attack suspended. As Ord and Burnside passed me, the latter said something like: 'You have 15,000 men concentrated on one point. It is strange if you cannot do something with them.' Ord replied angrily, flourishing his arms: 'You can fight if you have an opportunity; but, if you are held by the throat, how can you do anything?' Meaning, I suppose, that things were so placed that troops could not be used. Burnside said to one of his Staff officers: 'Well, tell them to connect, and hold it.' Which was easy to say, but they seem to have had no provision of tools, and, at any rate, did not connect with the old line. Poor Burnside remarked, quite calmly: 'I certainly fully expected this morning to go into Petersburg!'

While Burnside was bickering with Meade and Ord, Lee was making plans to counterattack in a way that would clear the Union soldiers out of the crater. The Union assault had failed miserably, but they still held the crater nearly 100 yards in advance of the rest of their lines, and Lee couldn't afford to give a single inch. Mahone's reinforcements had already done good work, but Lee called on them again to sweep Burnside's soldiers out of the crater once and for all.

Mahone's attack commenced around 1:00 p.m., 8 hours after the mine had been detonated. Burnside had insisted to Meade that his men couldn't safely leave the crater, but they certainly would have fared better trying to flee without being attacked by Mahone's men. Naturally, they didn't put up much of a fight against the Confederates since they were trying to leave the crater in the first place, even without the Confederates trying to push them out. Some of Mahone's

Confederates placed their caps on their bayonets and stuck them over the lip of the crater, waiting for Union soldiers to shoot. Then, before they could reload, the Confederates jumped into the crater and began fighting the Union soldiers in hand-to-hand combat.

It was during this time that the most memorable and controversial fighting of the Battle of the Crater took place. Both black and white Union soldiers had been fighting for hours or had been stuck in the crater for hours, and they were understandably tired and not willing to fight anymore. But according to soldiers who fought and witnessed it, the Confederates began slaughtering the black soldiers of Ferrero's division after they surrendered, shooting them point blank or stabbing them with bayonets after they had already given up. This enraged other black soldiers, who put up a fierce but futile resistance. Many of them suffered a similar fate. Despite the fact black soldiers comprised only one of Burnside's 4 divisions, 40% of the Union soldiers killed in the battle were black and 35% of all casualties were black. One of the officers in Ferrero's division said after the battle, "I felt like sitting down & weeping on account of our misfortune..."

The Battle of the Crater ended in the middle of the afternoon with Mahone's successful counterattack. The Union had lost over 4,000 casualties, many of them captured, and they had nothing to show for it. The Confederates lost less than half that number. As he usually was when something went wrong, Grant was remarkably circumspect about the Battle of the Crater in his memoirs, merely writing, "The effort was a stupendous failure. It cost us about four thousand men, mostly, however, captured; and all due to inefficiency on the part of the corps commander and the incompetency of the division commander who was sent to lead the assault."

According to Horace Porter, Grant was circumspect after the battle as well. Porter wrote:

"When the general-in-chief and staff rode back to Petersburg that day, the trip was anything but cheerful. For some time but little was said by him, owing to his aversion to indulging in adverse criticisms of individuals, which could not mend matters. He did not dwell long upon the subject in his conversation, simply remarking: 'If I had been a division commander or a corps commander, I would have been at the front giving personal directions on the spot. I believe that the men would have performed every duty required of them if they had been properly led and skillfully handled.'"

Although the Battle of the Crater didn't change the strategic situation in front of Petersburg, there were plenty of recriminations in the wake of the Union's failure. Since the top generals had believed everything was in place for a critical success, the decisive loss ensured that important changes would be made. Within 2 weeks, Grant removed Burnside from command of the IX Corps, and Meade brought charges against him. The Joint Committee on the Conduct of the War fully investigated the debacle, and 3 of Burnside's 4 division commanders were censured. The Committee, which was a heavily partisan body that frequently and controversially played political favorites, eventually exonerated Burnside and pinned the blame on Meade. Both generals deserved a fair share of the blame, and by then Burnside's reputation had been permanently tarnished anyway.

Incredibly, General Ledlie, who was ultimately cashiered out of the army several months later than he should have been, blamed Ferrero's black division for the calamity. The man who had stayed behind the lines and got drunk wrote a report of the battle that claimed:

"At this time the enemy was holding the same line of intrenchments with my own troops, starting from the point where the right of my division rested and extending thence to the left (our right). It was impossible for my line to advance from this position, as no troops had come up on my right to dislodge the enemy, and had I moved my line forward the enemy would merely by filing to the right in the same trench have occupied my position and poured a deadly fire into my rear. I reported this fact to one of the corps staff officers and soon after received peremptory orders to move my troops forward. I immediately gave the necessary orders, and the brigade commanders had barely got their men into proper position for a charge when the colored troops came running into the crater, and filing through passed into the rifle-pits to the left (our right) of the fort, where my troops now formed for the charge. The colored troops then made a feeble attempt at a charge, but before they accomplished anything the enemy made a fierce attack, and they retreated precipitately into the rifle-pits, breaking my line and crowding the pits to such an extent that it was impossible to reform my line. The enemy seeing the advantage gained by this attack, shortly afterward made another attack, fiercer and more determined than the first, and owing to the crowded condition of the troops a panic was created among the colored regiments and they broke and fled in disorder to the rear, pressing back with them a large portion of my line..."

The Battle of the Crater spelled the end of Ambrose Burnside's controversial Civil War career, and it finally led to Ledlie being removed from command for good. But more importantly, the failure of the IX Corps that day meant the siege of Petersburg would continue.

**Tightening the Grip**

The Battle of the Crater was a controversial disaster for the Union, but the siege lines of Petersburg kept Lee completely pinned down and stretched his army. As Lee continued to maintain a tenuous grip there, Sherman's men in the West defeated Joseph E. Johnston and John Bell Hood in the Atlanta Campaign and then marched to sea, capturing Savannah by Christmas. Sherman's successes helped ensure Lincoln was reelected, ensuring the war would go on.

Searching for some way of breaking the stalemate, Lee decided to detach Jubal Early with an independent command and send him through the Shenandoah Valley to make a feint toward Washington D.C., hoping that would force Grant to detach some of his own men from the siege lines of Petersburg. Thus, it would be Early who commanded the Confederacy's last invasion of the North. Lee certainly expressed faith in Lieutenant General Early, who he publicly lauded as his "best on-the-battlefield commander, rivaled only by Stonewall Jackson."

As Confederate territory was rapidly being captured (or slashed and burned) by Grant and Sherman, Lee sent Early's corps in to mount an offensive against Washington, and by late June, with the Union Army closing in on Lee's Army of Northern Virginia, Early led an army of 14,000 through the Valley, then marched into Maryland, headed for Washington. Proving to be an effective tactic, Grant (who characterized Early as "redoubtable") was forced to divert troops to stop Early, allowing Lee to further consolidate his forces and entrench his men at Petersburg.

On July 9, 1864, Early defeated an aggressive Union force at Monocacy, Maryland, and then advanced to the outskirts of the heavily defended Washington. --vigorously bombarding the Union Capital. Although initially successful (reaching the outskirts of the Union stronghold with a full head of steam) he met serious resistance from Union Generals Franz Sigel and Lew Wallace and was unable to seize control. Even after reinforcements arrived, Early was forced to withdraw, retreating into the Shenandoah Valley where he attempted to delay Union General Sherman's advance. On July 12, Early dispatched a communique to Lee stating, "We haven't taken Washington, but we've scared Abe Lincoln like hell!" Subsequent reports, however, reveal that some of the resistance he encountered actually came from state militia, non-combat soldiers from the quartermaster corps, and other civilians who were mustered out to resemble a combat unit. Had Early persisted, he may well have been able to do more damage.

On July 30, 1864, while retreating from Washington and pursued by Union forces, Early dispatched his cavalry to Chambersburg, Pennsylvania, demanding the town pay more than one half-million dollars restitution for Union destruction of Virginia farms and communities or be burned to the ground. When city officials refused to pay, Early did as threatened, reducing the city to ashes. "On the 30th of July McCausland reached Chambersburg and made the demand as directed, reading to such of the authorities as presented themselves the paper sent by me. The demand was not complied with, the people stating that they were not afraid of having their town burned, and that a Federal force was approaching. The policy pursued by our army on former occasions had been so lenient that they did not suppose the threat was in earnest this time, and they hoped for speedy relief. McCausland, however, proceeded to carry out his orders, and the greater part of the town was laid in ashes."

Just as Grant had used Sheridan to rid the war of Jeb Stuart, in early September, President Lincoln began sending missives to Grant to direct Sheridan (who he typically referred to as "Little Phil") to deal with General Jubal Early in Virginia. He wrote, "Sheridan and Early are facing each other at a dead lock. Could we not pick up a regiment here and there, to the number of say 10,000 men, and quietly, but suddenly concentrate them at Sheridan's camp and enable him to make a strike?"

After a bad start during which the Confederates nearly won an unexpected victory (and Sheridan's army suffered heavy casualties) at the Battle of Third Winchester/Opequon (fought on September 19, 1864 in Winchester, Virginia), Sheridan managed to drive General Jubal Early out of Winchester, followed by another Union victory at the Battle of Fisher's Hill (fought on September 21–22) near Strasburg, Virginia. But Lincoln was still displeased with General Early's progress toward Washington D.C., writing to Grant on September 29, "I hope it will lay no constraint on you, nor do harm any way, for me to say I am a little afraid lest Lee sends reinforcements to Early, and thus enables him to turn upon Sheridan."

Intending to increase the odds in the Union's favor, General Sheridan began his systematic destruction of the "breadbasket" of the Shenandoah, destroying crops and any other resources he found in his path, assuring with cold, methodical effectiveness that the Valley would never again serve as a base for Confederate armies. For his own part, Sheridan stated, "I would rather win by burning a man's farm than by killing his sons." He would later claim to have destroyed over 2,000 barns filled with wheat, hay, and farming implements, 70 mills filled with flour and wheat, appropriated over 4,000 head of livestock; and killed and distributed to his men no fewer than 3,000. The hatred the South now bore for him would be exceeded only by that for General Sherman.

By the fall of 1864, Union forces under Grant had three key pieces of their victory puzzle in place: General Lee was stuck without initiative at Petersburg, Sherman was occupying and set to destroy Atlanta, and Sheridan was carving a path of destruction that was sending terror through the Southern psyche. This set the stage for one of Sheridan's most celebrated engagements of the war.

When fighting broke out at Cedar Creek, northeast of Strasburg, Virginia on October 19, 1864, Sheridan was still at Winchester. During what would prove to be the culminating battle of the Valley Campaigns, Early had launched a surprise attack against Sheridan's encamped army, and the Confederates not only caught Sheridan's army off-guard -- Sheridan himself was not there.

Upon receiving word of the attack, Sheridan set out on an 11 mile trek to reassume command of his men, who had by then been driven back four miles and were on the verge of defeat. (The famous poem by Thomas B. Read, "Sheridan's Ride," incorrectly states that he rode twenty miles.) According to cavalry corps division commander Maj. General Wesley Merritt (who was serving under Maj. General Alfred T. A. Torbert), upon arrival, Sheridan "took his colors in hand and where the fire was hottest, led his men on, his horse plunging wildly under him." Rallying even the stragglers, Sheridan managed to not only turn the tide of the battle, his forces gave General Early's Confederates such a vicious beating that after the battle's end, they would no longer pose a danger as a combat force. For this astonishing victory, Sheridan even received an official thanks from Congress. Grant paid him the highest of praise, writing to Secretary of War Edwin Stanton,""Turning what bid fair to be a disaster into glorious victory stamps Sheridan, what I have always thought him, one of the ablest of generals."

**Sheridan's Ride, a chromolithograph by Thure de Thulstrup**

Though Early had made it to the outskirts of Washington D.C. and Lincoln famously became the only president to come under enemy fire during fighting near Fort Stevens, "Little Phil" Sheridan pushed Early back through the Valley and was now ready to fully scorch it. With his sites now set on Louden Valley, Virginia (where he would conduct his infamous "burning raid" throughout November and December of 1864), Sheridan wrote, "I will soon commence of Louden County and let them know there is a God in Israel."

On March 2, 1865, the Union Army managed to finally corner Early at Waynesboro, Virginia, and by now his forces were severely reduced. While Early himself and a few of his staff were able to escape, the remainder of his army surrendered or was killed. By the time of this battle, Early, who'd once been respected in the North and lionized in the South, was now vilified in the

North for destroying Chambersburg and cursed in the South for presumably causing Sheridan to retaliate.

As it turned out, the Battle of Waynesboro would be Early's last fight. After that disaster, he was relieved of command. Lee tried to explain the decision and soften the blow in a letter to Early, "While my own confidence in your ability, zeal, and devotion to the cause is unimpaired, I have nevertheless felt that I could not oppose what seems to be the current of opinion, without injustice to your reputation and injury to the service. I therefore felt constrained to endeavor to find a commander who would be more likely to develop the strength and resources of the country, and inspire the soldiers with confidence. ... [Thank you] for the fidelity and energy with which you have always supported my efforts, and for the courage and devotion you have ever manifested in the service..."

## The End of the Siege of Petersburg

"At the end of February, some 68,000 Confederate soldiers answered the roll behind the line of works, barely 56,000 of whom would have been ready to go into a fight. At that same moment, the two Union armies under Grant reported 118,000 present for duty. At the end of March, Grant would gain another 5,700 cavalry when Phil Sheridan came to him from the Shenandoah Valley, while Sheridan's departure from the Valley freed fewer than 1,300 cavalry and artillery for Lee's use." - William Marvel, *Lee's Last Retreat: The Flight to Appomattox*

By the beginning of 1865, the Confederacy was in utter disarray. The main Confederate army in the West under John Bell Hood had been nearly destroyed by General Thomas's men at the Battle of Franklin in late 1864, and Sherman's army faced little resistance as it marched through the Carolinas. Although Confederate leaders remained optimistic, by the summer of 1864 they had begun to consider desperate measures in an effort to turn around the war. From 1863-1865, Confederate leaders had even debated whether to conscript black slaves and enlist them as soldiers. Even as their fortunes looked bleak, the Confederates refused to issue an official policy to enlist blacks. It was likely too late to save the Confederacy anyway.

In February of 1865, Sheridan volunteered his men to join Grant at Richmond to take Lee down once and for all. In his *Memoirs* he would later write, "Feeling that the war was nearing its end, I desired my cavalry to be in at the death." By the time Lincoln delivered his Second Inaugural Address in March 1865, the end of the war was in sight. That month, Lincoln famously met with Grant, Sherman, and Admiral David Porter at City Point, Grant's headquarters during the siege, to discuss how to handle the end of the war.

Joining Grant near the end of March 1865, Sheridan took his troops south and west of Petersburg, severing General Lee's rail communications. As it turned out, it would be Sheridan's men that would finally break Lee's line. After destroying what was left of Early's cavalry near Waynesborough, Virginia, Sheridan moved 12,000 men into position on General Lee's right flank near the crossroads known as Five Forks, effectively threatening Lee's supply line. Without unfettered access to men and supplies, Lee knew that his army and Richmond could not maintain the status quo and that battle was now imminent, so he sent what infantry and cavalrymen he could muster to hold the crossroads known as Five Forks, including General George Pickett's troops.

**Pickett**

Having already suffered tens of thousands of casualties in 1864, and with an army fatigued by the daily grind of siege warfare, Grant might have overseen a wounded army, but it still had a dangerous lock on its foes. The Union had not scored any remarkable victories of late, but Northern engineers and laborers had managed to create a vast network of trenches across the Virginia countryside, and the earthworks bound the Army of the Potomac to the Army of Northern Virginia. Neither seemed able to move, but more importantly, Lee could not escape. Only the promise of the cessation of spring rains suggested that one side or the other would finally move out of their fortifications. Which one would be the first to brave the muddied roads and strike out across the earthwork lines of forces? Since Grant knew Lee could not indefinitely stretch his defensive lines, it was Grant who moved first.

Union general Philip Sheridan, one-time commander of the Army of the Shenandoah and fresh from success in the Valley of the same name, was now tasked as the vanguard of a cavalry force to strike at Lee's extreme right flank. Grant intended for Lee to witness the buildup of forces, expecting the Confederate commander to respond by the adjustment of lines against the concentration of the Union strike force. Lee, however, intended to do much more than defend; characteristically, Lee would go on the offensive. Perhaps Lee knew he would face Sheridan, who had scorched the Shenandoah Valley and made it wholly ineffective as a region, but either way, he intended to hit hard, fast, and ruthlessly, sensing the urgency of the moment against the opponent his right flank faced.

However, while Lee's creation of a mobile force, 10,000 strong comprised mostly of the division of Pickett's Virginians, seemed adroit in its position to attack the Union armies, Lee's army was the one in a desperate position. Grant, with his ability to mix-and-match numerically superior forces from one army to the other, demonstrated his advantages, while Lee could barely respond with risky gambles. Perhaps aware of the difficulty of the objective of challenging the Union buildup, Lee did not give command of the force to Pickett but instead entrusted the leadership with his nephew, Major General Fitzhugh Lee.

The chain of command would lead to another set of problems later on, mainly in the memory of the Confederacy and how the South would explain the last days of the Confederacy within the larger narrative of the Lost Cause. Pickett's loss of nerve to capitalize on early successes made Lee part of the narrative that enshrined him as a symbol of Southern resoluteness, and as with the criticism of James Longstreet at Gettysburg, a scapegoat was necessary to make Lee appear blameless. That said, Pickett definitely had his chance at some type of substantial glory, for while he was not in command of the larger force, his first actions did prove successful on March 31, when his men had stopped Sheridan's first probes of the right flank. However, when reinforcements arrived, coming from the Union V Corps led by Major General Gouverneur K. Warren, Pickett withdrew and headed back to the Southern entrenchments, feeling it wiser to fight there than possibly be flanked on his left by the V Corps. Lee was horrified that the earlier successes came up with nothing. Sheridan had not only driven back Pickett's Virginians, but he was gifted the field by the Virginians' move to entrenchments, exposing the entire right flank of the Confederate lines. Lee's disappointment with the results of that fighting, now known as the Battle of Dinwiddie Court House, was evident in his dispatch to Pickett: "Hold Five Forks at all hazards. Protect road to Ford's Depot and prevent Union forces from striking the Southside Railroad. Regret exceedingly your forces' withdrawal, and your inability to hold the advantage you had gained."

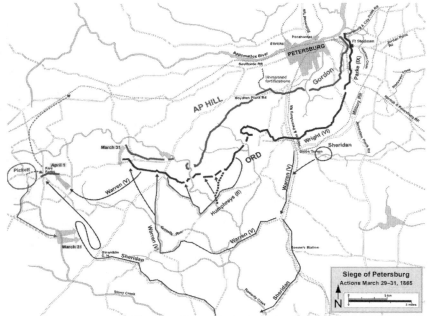

**The siege lines at the end of March**

While similar in approach to earlier contests during the Overland Campaign, the Battle of Five Forks on April 1, 1865 was markedly different than the static nature of the siege of Petersburg in early 1865. Most notably, the battle that Lee gambled the fortunes of his army (if not the war) on did not have any of the hallmarks of his earlier attempts to change the fortunes of his army outright. Instead, his plan for the Battle of Five Forks was the result of the earlier failure of General George Pickett to conclude an earlier fight that might have actually produced a decisive outcome. Lee planned the battle to complete what Pickett did not accomplish. The battle forced him into a position where Southern positions were their most vulnerable.

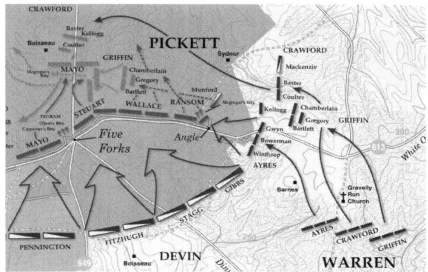

**The lines at the Battle of Five Forks on April 1**

As if March 31 wasn't bad enough, when the Battle of Five Forks finally commenced on April 1, Pickett was two miles away, reportedly enjoying a shad bake with Fitz Lee and General Thomas L. Rosser, and didn't hear the fighting. By the time the generals reached the battlefield, it was too late; Union troops had already overrun Pickett's lines and pushed them away from Five Forks. Historians have attributed it to unusual environmental acoustics that prevented Pickett and his staff from hearing the battle despite their close proximity, not that it mattered to the Confederates at the time.

After Five Forks, Grant could now order an attack along all lines, which he did the following day, and Lee now helplessly watched those simultaneous federal assaults stretch his already weakened defensive lines. In the early morning of April 2, Lee, A.P. Hill and Longstreet were all conferring when news reached that their lines were breaking. Hill immediately mounted a horse and rode toward his lines, moving so quickly that Lee actually sent his own aide after him to warn him to be careful.

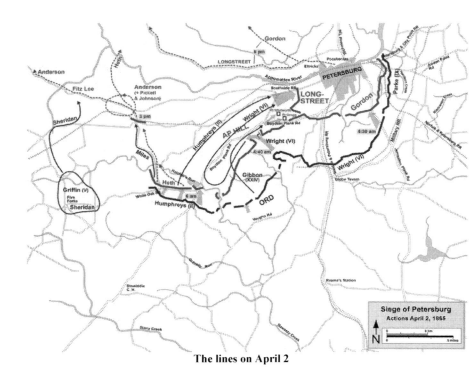

The lines on April 2

**Hill**

Hill and the aide, Colonel Venable, came upon two Union soldiers and convinced them to surrender, and after securing their surrender, Hill kept riding until he reached Lt. Col. William Poague's artillery, which he personally ordered to fire. Leaving Venable there, Hill now rode with just one aide as he headed southwest in an attempt to reach General Heth. During the ride, hill turned to him and said, "Sergeant, should anything happen to me, you must go back to General Lee and report it."

Along the Boydton Plank Road, the two Confederates came upon a couple of Union soldiers from the 138th Pennsylvania Infantry, Daniel Wolford and William Mauk. Seeing the two riders approaching, the two Union soldiers ducked behind a tree and took aim at their targets, now a mere 20 yards away. Hill's aide yelled at them to surrender, shouting, "If you fire you will be swept to hell... our men are here -- surrender!" Hill echoed the demand, shouting at them, "Surrender!" In response, Mauk turned to Wolford and said, "Let us shoot them." Wolford's shot at Hill's aide missed, but Mauk's shot struck Hill directly, passing through his gauntlet and into his chest, clean through his heart and out his back. As Hill fell to the ground mortally wounded, his aide grabbed his horse's bridle and raced away. As news of Hill's demise began to spread, men like Lee and Hill's chief of staff, Colonel Palmer, openly wept. Upon hearing the news, Lee moaned, "He is at rest now, and we who are left are the ones to suffer."

By the end of April 2, Petersburg had lost its connection to the South Side Railroad, and the writing was on the wall. With that loss, there was no reason to hold Petersburg, and without Petersburg, it meant Richmond could not be defended either. On April 2, Lee wrote to President Davis to inform him that the capital of the Confederacy, Richmond, must be abandoned.

After the Battle of Five Forks, Pickett had few soldiers left to command, and Lee ordered Pickett and two other generals to transfer their remaining men to other units and return to base. While this order was regarded by many Confederate insiders as the logical reorganizational move in last-ditch efforts to muster a cohesive, resistant force, others saw it as reflective of Lee's disappointment in Pickett's performance and diminished capacity to command effectively. In either regard, the reasons behind Lee's decision would soon prove moot as Confederate forces faced their final attempts to defend their "cause."

**Some of the ruins of Richmond on April 3 after Union occupation**

## The Escape from Petersburg and Richmond

By the end of April 2, the Confederate lines held by a thread, while in other places, like where the destruction of the Norfolk Light Infantry took place at the epicenter of the Union attack, the defenses collapsed and the refugees of the fighting began to collide with the remnants of those who fought at the battle at Five Forks. As a result, Lee planned for nighttime moves along the last railroad, the Richmond & Danville line, while General Longstreet's fresh troops were brought from Richmond to hold back the Union advances along all lines. While smoke rose from the tobacco warehouses of Petersburg, set fire in the course of the Southern retreat, Longstreet's forces held their ground. Part of the reason the Union attack did not aggressively pursue was out of fear of Lee's intentions; no one knew where he meant to go, and a counterattack by the Southern commander was not entirely ruled out.[4]

While the Confederate government of President Jefferson Davis left the capital aboard a single train, the long-planned course of retreat took four paths out of the trenches around Petersburg and Richmond, which they had protected for almost nine and one-half months. "General James Longstreet's First Corps, along with General Richard S. Ewell's Reserve Corps, would leave the Richmond defenses and cross to the south side of the James River. General William Mahone, whose division held the Howlett Line between the James and Appomattox Rivers across Bermuda Hundred, moved inland to Chesterfield Court House. General Lee, with General John B. Gordon's Second Corps and the remnants of Hill's Third Corps, passed through the "Cockade City" and crossed to the north bank of the Appomattox. Finally, those cut off at Five Forks and by the breakthrough in the lines west of the city, would stay south of the Appomattox River."[5]

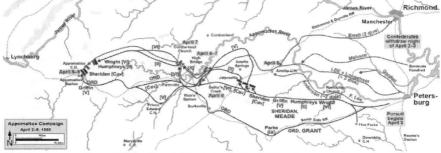

**The course of the retreat from Petersburg**

While Lee had long prepared for his army to escape the trenches and head west to unite with Joseph E. Johnston's army in North Carolina, the lines of retreat his army would take still needed to overcome two major obstacles logistically: crossing the Appomattox River and acquiring supplies via train. If the river crossings could be forded, if the footbridges could be held, and if the pontoon bridges worked as planned, the branches of the Army of Northern Virginia would reunite at the Amelia Court House, where a train with loaded supplies would await them. On paper, the exercise merely meant a 30 mile march, but in reality, it required an expert handling of materials to make the march possible. Under Lee's leadership, and the trained experience of his quartermasters, the Army of Northern Virginia could previously be counted on to complete coordinated actions of troop-and-supply movements, but Lee had just witnessed how inactivity in the trenches worked against his mobile forces at Five Forks, and he now would see how nearly 10 months of sedentary life would work against his army's ability to move and be supplied.

Supporters of Robert E. Lee, as well as historians, have long maintained that the subsequent chain of events were not the fault of the heroic Southern leader, but if the ultimate defeat of the Confederacy belonged to the Northern industrial advantages and Southern politicians like Davis, then the narrative of the Lost Cause has problems when confronted with the early stages of the Appomattox Campaign, for while Lee was not responsible for the weather, he surely was obligated to keep abreast of operations within his general staff. For example, the fact that he did not know of the failure to get a pontoon bridge at Genito Road in order to cross the Appomattox

[4] William Marvel, *Lee's Last Retreat: The Flight to Appomattox*, 17-26.

[5] Calkins, Chris, "The Battle of Little Sailor's Creek," *Civil War Trust*, 207-213;
http://www.civilwar.org/battlefields/sailorscreek/sailors-creek-history-articles/sailorscreekcalkins.html

says much about Lee's condition as a leader during the week. He could not be blamed for the high waters on the river, with the last rains of the spring having heightened the levels of the Appomattox and making it difficult to cross in places, but he could have modified the places to cross.

All of this was a byproduct of the fact that Lee was relying on an old plan of escape, and it proved inflexible to the demands of the moment. Apologists would suggest that Lee had no other choice. If so, he had more control over his quartermaster staff than anything else in this campaign, and he did not know that the absence of his chief of staff, Walter Taylor, on the first day of the retreat would impact the ability to move supplies to the Amelia Court House.[6]

Two things are clear about this early delay that would impact the Army of Northern Virginia. First, the delay of Lieutenant General Ewell's Richmond column across the Appomattox at Genito Road was the major reason for the delay at Amelia, wasting the Confederates' one day head start and allowing Grant to position the Army of the Potomac and the Army of the James in the path of the Confederate retreat from the capital. Second, Lee's quartermaster staff never successfully communicated the need for the transport of supplies to Amelia, so the reserve stores in Richmond never received the information.

The pontoon bridge at Genito Road can be partly blamed on Lee; for a man with a reputation of remarkable feats of military engineering, he could have been aware of the failure to have a pontoon bridge sent to Genito Road. However, the fiasco at the Amelia Court House that forced him to wait another day in the hope of getting future supplies was the fault of staff under his control, and that staff failed to address the most basic of needs for an army: military supplies.[7]

**Grant Chases Lee**

Grant could not ascertain what Lee intended to do with the Army of Northern Virginia, but Grant could accomplish one thing, and in doing so, he could doom Lee's army. By positioning forces well ahead of Lee, mainly in an effort to block any progress to unite Lee's Confederate forces with those in North Carolina, Grant could defeat Lee right there and then. Grant was not wholly worried about where Lee intended to consolidate his spread out army, which had been dispersed by the chaos of retreat and the drubbing at Five Forks and further confused by the desertions that had begun to afflict the Army of Northern Virginia. Instead, he was preoccupied with keeping the Army of Northern Virginia away from Johnston in North Carolina. "Sheridan's riders led the way, pressing closely on the cavalry and infantry that had escaped from the collapsed right flank. Supporting Sheridan were foot soldiers from the Fifth Corps, now led by Brevet Major General Charles Griffin in the place of Gouverneur K. Warren, who had been relieved of command by Sheridan immediately after Five Forks. Closing up behind these were the Second and Sixth Corps, also with the Army of the Potomac, along with units from the Army of the James's all-white Twenty-fourth and all-black Twenty-fifth Corps. Taking up the rear was the Ninth Corps, which had orders to garrison Petersburg and to secure the supply lines reaching westward to keep pace with the hard-marching troops."[8]

While Grant soon learned from Sheridan's scouts that Lee's disparate forces were on their way to Amelia Court House, he did not command the federal pursuers to cross the Appomattox River and follow immediately after them. Instead, the best route was to follow a parallel course, so as to keep the remnants of Lee's army from taking a southern course. Major General George G.

---

[6] Marvel, William, *Lee's Last Retreat: The Flight to Appomattox,*

[7] William Marvel, *Lee's Last Retreat: The Flight to Appomattox*, 207-213.

[8] "The Campaign to Appomattox," *Civil War Series* (National Park Service: History E-Library), http://www.nps.gov/history/history/online_books/civil_war_series/6/sec2.htm#1

Meade, commander of the Army of the Potomac, argued against this course, but Grant's mind was made up, and with some luck, his plan proved the correct one. When the Confederates led by General Ewell were prevented from crossing at Genito Road -- along with other causes of delays across the risen river -- the head start of a full day for the Confederates was entirely lost, making Grant's plan not just possible but ideal.

The final positioning of Union troops to block all Confederate progress at the railroad junction at Jetersville took place while a paralysis, as one of Lee's staff called it, afflicted the Army of Northern Virginia's leader. The Confederates had reached Amelia Court House on April 4, but for lack of supplies that would ultimately never come, Lee kept his men in place all day, which he later called a "fatal delay."

At this point in the campaign, it was discipline that dictated cohesion during pursuit and retreat. General Ewell tried to solve the problem at Genito by using planks to cross Goode's Bridge Road, which Longstreet's rearguard forces used to cross the Appomattox. This at least held together an orderly retreat towards the pre-arranged point of consolidation at Amelia, but General Sheridan and the Union cavalry were aggressive in attack and pursuit. Sheridan worked coolly to seize the advantage against Lee by keeping one of his three divisions to take up position to block the railroad near Jetersville, south of Amelia. He was also able to motivate a fast-charging V Corps that followed behind his command; having been given discretion by Grant to replace the cautious General Warren with Charles Griffin, Sheridan was able to demonstrate to his troops that regardless of who was in command, he expected aggressiveness in the field.

Both sides, North and South, faced similar conditions in that they were fighting in terrain that had been little fought over in the years of the war and charging far ahead of their lines of supply, where the ability to forage food and other materials from the countryside became crucial. Lee did so out of desperation, issuing a proclamation that read, "Citizens of Amelia County, Va...meat, beef, cattle, sheep, hogs, flour, meal, corn, and provender in any quantity that can be spared."[9] For the Union forces, the fast pursuit of Confederate retreaters meant that foraging, not supply wagons, would supply their armies. Amidst the trials of living off the land, Sheridan, perhaps following the example set forth by Grant and General William Tecumseh Sherman, continued to act aggressively, not only when it came to stripping Confederate lands of supplies but also harassing the rear of the crippled Confederate army.

Ultimately, Lee's decision to remain at Amelia Court House on April 4 allowed Sheridan to strip cavalry from his command, led by the young Ranald Mackenzie, and get closer to Confederate General Anderson's lagging corps. At the same time, Sheridan's knowledge of Lee's scattered forces gave him the confidence to follow Grant's plan to get men ahead of the Army of Northern Virginia. Sheridan pushed Union Major General George Crook's cavalry, as well as the V Corps' infantry and artillery, west to the railroad junction at Jetersville, where they could block Lee's plan to follow the railroad and take away all Confederate hopes of immediate supplies. At this point, Lee allowed himself to be outgeneraled; he knew not only the position of his own strung-out soldiers but also the location of Mackenzie's forward cavalry, which made clear the Union objective of getting to Jetersville before the Confederate army. Nonetheless, Lee's decision to stay at Amelia Court House meant that by the morning of April 5th, "three corps of the Army of the Potomac and four divisions of Union cavalry slept near Jetersville that night."[10]

---

[9] "The Campaign to Appomattox," *Civil War Series* (National Park Service: History E-Library), http://www.nps.gov/history/history/online_books/civil_war_series/6/sec2.htm#1
[10] William Marvel, *Lee's Last Retreat: The Flight to Appomattox*, 47-51, 65.

Sheridan's rapid decisions and aggressive movements would inevitably lead to Lee's surrender, and much of it was made possible by quick thinking scouts: "During the Appomattox Campaign the scouts proved to be of invaluable assistance to General Sheridan and the Federal cavalry. They began the campaign by capturing General Rufus Barringer, a Confederate cavalry commander from North Carolina, and his staff as they were looking for a comfortable camp for the night near Namozine Church. The scouts then proceeded to capture a dispatch from General Robert E. Lee requesting supplies to be sent to his army at Amelia Court House. Sheridan had the scouts send the message, but his cavalry were to capture the supplies for themselves. The scouts, even though they worked in groups of three or four, were responsible for leading numerous rebels to capture."[11]

## The Battle of Sailor's Creek, April 6

By now, desperate maneuvers on the part of both Union and Confederate commanders were being made, albeit for different reasons fueling their anxiety. As President Lincoln believed, Lee could be defeated if the "thing was pressed," and the Army of the Potomac was frantically trying to press the issue. Meanwhile, even though the Army of Northern Virginia had not won a major strategic victory in nearly two years, it was willing to trust Lee however he challenged their old nemesis. Lee's knowledge that he had been checked at Jetersville meant he would make decisions that started the events around Sailor's Creek, a tributary of the Appomattox to the north, which was deemed unfordable by Lee's admission. The two sides would ultimately make decisions that brought them to the Battle of Sailor's Creek on April 6.

Naturally, without the supplies arriving at Amelia Court House, Lee was still desperate to provision his army, which now required getting his army near Farmville. Farmville was located near the South Side railroad line, where supplies could be transported, and on the morning of the sixth, Longstreet, Lee's "old war horse, drove his four divisions hard in the direction of Deatonville. "In the van of Lee's column was General James Longstreet's combined First and Third Corps, followed by Richard Anderson's small corps of Generals Pickett and Bushrod Johnson's divisions, then General Richard S. Ewell's Reserve Corps made up of Richmond garrison troops, the main wagon train, and finally General John B. Gordon's Second Corps acting as rearguard."[12]

Sheridan's forward forces, probing and witnessing this large movement, suspected that Lee was moving his entire infantry, a belief that set up an engagement between the forces at Amelia Springs. That was an inconclusive engagement that merely prolonged the agony of the Army of Northern Virginia, but Sheridan still feared the presence of Lee's corps on the Deatonville Road, seeing in their movements a threat against Major General Ord's rear. Since they would be threatened if Longstreet did swing back to Burkesville Junction, Sheridan's response guaranteed two things about the coming battle at Sailor's Creek: "It would be the Federal II Corps that spied Gordon's troops passing near Amelia Springs at daybreak on the 6th and set out in immediate pursuit. Following on a parallel road to the south of the one that the Confederates were moving on was fast riding blue cavalry under General Sheridan. Close behind them would be [Union] General Horatio G. Wright's VI Corps leaving from their trenched position at Jetersville."[13]

---

[11] "The Campaign to Appomattox," *Civil War Series* (National Park Service: History E-Library), http://www.nps.gov/history/history/online_books/civil_war_series/6/sec2.htm#2
[12] Calkins, Chris, "The Battle of Little Sailor's Creek," *The Civil War Trust*, http://www.civilwar.org/battlefields/sailorscreek/sailors-creek-history-articles/sailorscreekcalkins.html
[13] Calkins, Chris, "The Battle of Little Sailor's Creek," *The Civil War Trust*, http://www.civilwar.org/battlefields/sailorscreek/sailors-creek-history-articles/sailorscreekcalkins.html

Ultimately, the battle would be three separate engagements, as the nature of the spread-out forces of the Army of Northern Virginia allowed the Union to defend and then attack the Confederates in a piecemeal action. Lee knew he only had two places to cross at – Farmville and High Bridge – and seeing the need to cross at selected spots, he gave orders to hold up the movements of soldiers, losing time. Furthermore, thinking the Union could not cross anywhere else on the river was a misconception of Lee's that Longstreet warned him about and Sheridan would prove wrong at various times.

On April 6, Lee watched his divided army struggle to move while simultaneously deal with the Union forces' efforts to weaken its cohesion, and with his army's back to a river, Lee had to fight now, even though there were major gaps between the corps making up the Army of Northern Virginia. Indeed, Sheridan's cavalry made sure that the Confederates never fully united; as the Confederates attempted to march west, the Union cavalry kept pace with them, running parallel to their position and launching hit-and-run attacks the entire time.

The Confederate generals Richard Anderson, Ewell, and John Gordon all commanded their divisions to halt their marches to come together and make preparations for a large Union assault, but they could never unite their forces. When they proved unable to unite, they resumed their marches, but that created an even larger gap between Anderson and the Confederate forces further west. This gap was exploited by General George Custer, who swiftly moved his cavalry division into the gap, effectively separating Anderson and two other corps from the rest of the Army of Northern Virginia. Lee's "black day," as historians call this event, was about to begin.[14]

---

[14] "10 Facts about Sailor's Creek," *The Civil War Trust*,
http://www.civilwar.org/battlefields/sailorscreek/sailors-creek-history-articles/ten-facts-about-sailors.html

Custer

CIVIL WAR TRUST

BATTLE OF
SAILOR'S CREEK, VA
HILLSMAN HOUSE/MARSHALL CROSSROADS – APRIL 6, 1865
Civilwar.org

**The lines at Sailor's Creek, with Union cavalry cutting off the Confederates from the west**

At Holt's Corner, Ewell made another fateful decision. After waiting for the federal assault that never came and fearing more delays, Ewell ordered his supply wagons to separate from his own to head northwest to arrive at Danville, the next of Lee's objectives after Farmville. However, while Ewell took his time at Holt's Corner, mindful of maintaining a defensive perimeter and fearful of a federal attack, Gordon's artillery went along with the baggage trains, so Ewell would not have artillery when he needed it the most. The Union's II Corps would move northwest in chase of the supply trains, leaving the VI Corps to deal with Ewell.

With the Union forces never breaking contact with the Confederate retreat, it meant Union cavalry confronted Anderson and infantry faced off against Ewell, effectively boxing in both rebel commands. Anderson and Ewell would have to fight back-to-back, with neither able to support the other. "Ewell had no artillery with him and so was unable to reply when, at 5:15 P.M., a row of 20 Yankee cannon lined up along the ridge opposite his position opened a concentrated fire that lasted for more than 30 minutes. A Maryland officer on the receiving end of the barrage recalled the 'shot sometimes plowing the ground, sometimes crashing through the trees, and not infrequently striking in the line, killing two or more at once.' Behind the curtain of powder smoke Federal battle lines took shape. At 6:00 P.M. the guns fell silent and the infantry formations began to advance.[15]

---

[15] "The Campaign to Appomattox," *Civil War Series* (National Park Service: History E-Library), http://www.nps.gov/history/history/online_books/civil_war_series/6/sec3.htm#2

**Anderson**

**Ewell**

As Longstreet arrived at Rice's Depot, he was separated from the rest of the Confederates to his east, so he and Lee were unaware about the impending fight at Sailor's Creek. Battle began at Sailor's Creek with the aggressive move of Custer into the gaps between the three separated Confederate corps. Anderson, having realized his predicament, chose to make a stand at a crossroads of two farms, while Ewell maneuvered his force to the southwest side of the creek. Back to back, the two corps and their adjuncts would fight. The Union artillery under the command of General Horatio Wright fired on Ewell immediately, and Ewell's men were forced to take cover, unable to return a fusillade of shells on the Federals. Simultaneously, Sheridan gave his subordinates the chance to attack Anderson through the use of three cavalry divisions - Custer would partially get the honor, along with generals Thomas Devin and George Crook – but Anderson's men still had their artillery to use point blank against any frontal charge.[16]

General Wright, in command of the Union VI Corps, was satisfied by a bombardment lasting a half hour and then ordered his men for a charge across the swollen creek. Their ragged line tentatively reformed across the difficult terrain and ran into Ewell's men, who, having dug themselves in, now rose and gave a volley that caused the Union line to break and fall back.

---

[16] Calkins, Chris, "The Battle of Little Sailor's Creek," *The Civil War Trust*,
http://www.civilwar.org/battlefields/sailorscreek/sailors-creek-history-articles/sailorscreekcalkins.html

When the Federals finally reformed and re-assaulted Ewell with great difficulty, only the use of hand-to-hand fighting brought the fighting to an end. In addition to being victorious against Ewell's shattered corps, the Union soldiers captured 6 rebel generals (including Ewell and Lee's son, Curtis Lee) and 3,000 ragged Confederate soldiers.

With Ewell cut off and forced to surrender, Anderson's command eventually broke, but they were able to retreat as a disorganized mob, along with what was left of Ewell's corps, to the northwest towards Rice's Depot and down the valley of Big Sailor's Creek. Lee stood on a knoll to oversee the creek, and with the knowledge coming late about the battle, he was confronted with the sight of the refugees of the Confederate defeat. Upon seeing the chaotic retreat, he exclaimed, "My God! Has the army been dissolved?"[17]

In a fight defined by big and little creeks and taking place on the compact parcels of family farms, Gordon, in charge of the supply train that had sped Ewell's much-needed artillery away, was now forced to defend his line of wagons on the high ground above Lockett's farm, knowing that the Union II Corps under command of General Humphreys would soon attack. Gordon was able to hold his ground until the overwhelming numbers of Union soldiers accomplished a flanking movement against his position and presented Gordon with only one option: retreat. By the time Gordon's men retreated, 1,700 prisoners and 200 wagons belonged to the Union.

Gordon's corps, in their retreat, chose another route, one that would figure importantly into the ultimate surrender of the Army of Northern Virginia. The retreat over High Bridge, an untouched railroad bridge upon stone columns that crossed the Appomattox River, would serve as an important place in the campaign. While the segments of the Army of Northern Virginia attempted to consolidate on the northwest bank of the river, attempting all the time to hold off Federal cavalry in pursuit, the supply trains were sent down the line to Appomattox Station 30 miles away. Lee had thought if he could get his army across the river and destroy all four bridges, the Union pursuers would be stalled and his army could escape and gain a reprieve, making the action at High Bridge crucial as a potential crossing for the Union forces.[18]

### High Bridge

"The roving representative of (Union) Signal Corps befriended an ailing, lice-infested South Carolinian with whom he reached the approach to High Bridge, begged a meal, and collapsed on the ground. Hundreds like them wandered in shadows around the army's campfires, beyond the calls of their captains but unwilling, yet, to forsake the army altogether."[19]

After the fighting of April 6, a great many Confederate soldiers now hovered around the camps of their army, following along but hardly obeying orders. At this point, many were remaining just close enough to hope that supplies might arrive so they could eat. The shattering defeat at Sailor's Creek had demonstrated that the Army of Northern Virginia could no longer stand and fight, a loss that not only resulted in the capture of a huge part of the army but one that put an end to any Confederate soldier's belief in the army's invincibility.

When the first divisions of Lee's army retreated across High Bridge, the ragged remnants of the army followed, but since the majority could no longer be considered soldiers but refugees, the mishandling of the burning of High Bridge makes more sense. Lee knew what Grant intended to do, and the realization must have chilled him; Grant would do all he could to get ahead of Lee,

---

[17] Calkins, Chris, "The Battle of Little Sailor's Creek," *The Civil War Trust*, http://www.civilwar.org/battlefields/sailorscreek/sailors-creek-history-articles/sailorscreekcalkins.html
[18] Calkins, Chris, "The Battle of Little Sailor's Creek," *The Civil War Trust*, http://www.civilwar.org/battlefields/sailorscreek/sailors-creek-history-articles/sailorscreekcalkins.html
[19] Marvel, *Lee's Last Retreat*, 93.

obstruct his western escape, and end the war in Virginia. Everything counted on the ability to get across the river, and more importantly, how well the Confederates could destroy those same bridges. If that was completed, then Lee could get as far as Lynchburg or Roanoke, then link up with Johnston in North Carolina. At the same time, Lee knew he faced great odds, as the Union army only needed to use one wing of its army to block the Confederates at their intended destination, and with the other wing, pin the army down north of the river.

With the Union pursuit continuing to harass them, Confederate generals had to deal with logistical issues and worry about the only thing keeping the army intact: the promise of supplies. Of course, there was a high level of disorganization that undercut the Confederate commands; even ignoring the starvation plaguing the Confederate soldiers, the state of demoralization that caused desertion now meant that most of the rebels' time was spent policing its own. Efforts to stop deserters also worked against the Confederates at High Bridge, watering down the urgency of the retreat across the bridge. The constant halt, identification, and appraisal of the intents of every soldier that crossed the bridge dangerously slowed all traffic.

The increasingly hopelessness felt by Confederate leaders also worked to undermine attention to their retreat and reunion at Appomattox, a situation not helped by Grant's own knowledge of his foes' desperation and his own willingness to use diplomatic channels to weaken the Confederate resolve to fight. Even as the Confederate leaders began to consider surrender, the Army of Northern Virginia was also trying to deal with the destruction of the bridges. To plan for a potential surrender while simultaneously planning to fight on are not two things that can take place together without one getting in the way of the other, and conflicting thoughts only reinforced the disorganized nature of the Army of Northern Virginia. No matter the reasons, when the time came to destroy the bridges, the army failed.

Meanwhile, the Union officers under Grant were not confused in their determination to catch up with Lee. The pursuit hectically continued, to the extent that Federal officers who could not keep pace were removed and replaced with officers who would continue to apply the pressure. The goal was all haste, and the Union commanders began to operate with the belief that if they could even get one corps across the river, Lee's army would have no rest.

Humphreys' II Corps was chosen to make the crossing at High Bridge, and the first brigades made it across the bridge and acted to prevent it from going up in flames after it was set on fire by Confederate engineers. When the Confederates realized that the bridge was captured, Mahone's men counterattacked the Union soldiers. Pressed against the burning bridge, Union artillery fired back at the desperate rebel charge, and Union general Francis Barlow's 3rd brigade crossed the bridge en masse and smashed the Confederate counterattack, which retreated along Longstreet's lines. The bridge was now secure, and the Union armies could continue to pursue and pressure.

If the officers in the Army of Northern Virginia had not known about inevitability of collapse, they knew it now. Grant would not let up, nor would his officers. Lee's army still fought, even at times inflicting great harm on the Union pursuers, but the news of a possible truce overtook the minds of the Confederate soldiers.

## Moving Towards Appomattox

While news of the failure at High Bridge made surrender seem inevitable, it would be the arrival of Sheridan and Ord at Appomattox Station that forced Lee to accept it.[20] The exhausted nature of the Confederate retreat and Lee's obsessive drive to cross the river both worked to form

---

[20] Welch, Richard F, "Burning High Bridge: The South's Last Hope," *Civil War Times*, http://www.historynet.com/burning-high-bridge-the-souths-last-hope.htm

an illusionary image of the reality of the campaign. Getting over the river would not solve all his problems, nor prevent the Union pursuers from continuing their plan to entrap the Army of Northern Virginia. Along with Sheridan's success at commanding forces across water obstacles, the loss of High Bridge merely mocked Lee's mistaken picture of the situation. The presence of various Federal brigades and corps, across the river in multiple directions and preparing to converge on Lee again, further worked to taunt the Army of Northern Virginia's leader and convince him that the end was near.

With High Bridge secure, Grant commanded his armies to pursue, which took the form of three columns. The II Corps under Humphreys, infantry from Ord's Army of the James, and Union cavalry all headed west, with the Army of the James just south of Farmville and Sheridan's horsemen prepared to take up a blocking position in front of Danville. The rebel forces they immediately faced belonged to Gordon and Mahone, who took a defensive position around Cumberland Church, with the right flank covered by Longstreet and Lee's nephew, Fitzhugh Lee, who were also responsible for screening the supply wagon en route to the northwest.

Fighting immediately took place in this desperate position around Cumberland Church, and the II Corps encountered concentrated rebel resistance in the early afternoon of April 7. The Southerners must have sensed the urgency of the hour, as their lines never broke under the pressure of a series of relentless attacks. Perhaps inspired by the sight of continued resistance that looked more haphazard and broken upon every viewing of battlefields, or perhaps inspired by the loss of more northern soldiers – 571 casualties occurred at Cumberland Church - Grant would say upon his arrival at Farmville that the time had come to offer Lee terms of surrender. Later that day, a note was composed with Grant's typical straightforward delivery: "The results of the last week must convince you of the hopelessness of further resistance on the part of the Army of Northern Virginia in this struggle. I feel that it is so, and regard it as my duty to shift from myself the responsibility of any further effusion of blood by asking of you the surrender of that portion of the Confederate army known as the Army of Northern Virginia."

Passing the note to General Longstreet, one of his few remaining advisors, Longstreet replied, "Not yet."[21] Lee may have heeded that advice, but he was at least willing to continue the dialogue with Grant, and his reply spoke to the one issue both commanders agreed on: avoiding needless bloodshed. Lee replied, "I have rec'd your note of this date. Though not entertaining the opinion you express of the hopelessness of further resistance on the part of the Army of N. Va.— I reciprocate your desire to avoid useless effusion of blood, & therefore before considering your proposition, ask the terms you will offer on condition of its surrender."

When knowledge came of Grant's first letter to Lee, an appeal to the sanity of surrender began being passed to lower levels of the Confederate army. For example, one was given to General William Mahone by Union Brigadier General Seth Williams, assistant general to Grant. Perhaps helped by knowledge of the letter, more and more officers under Lee began to see the futility of continuing to hold out. Mahone, Anderson, and Gordon all broached the idea of surrendering, no doubt because they saw capitulation as likely if not inevitable. In much stronger terms, the majority of them saw the war's hopelessness, and the junior generals put a plan in play to approach Lee with the proposal. Since Anderson had previously served under Longstreet, he went to Longstreet to go to Lee.

---

[21]     Davis, Kenneth C. *The Civil War: Everything You Need to Know About America's Greatest Conflict but Never Learned.* Page 402.

Still, Lee had no intent of surrendering yet, and the fighting at Cumberland Church was a sideshow to the important tasks at hand: escaping along the Lynchburg Stage Road and facing the predictable bottleneck of traffic that would result from all the different parts of the Confederate army marching. To pull off an organized retreat and move with all haste towards a supply depot yet-to-be determined, Lee needed his soldiers to be able to move quickly, but they also couldn't give up the ability to instantly fight the Union pursuit on a moment's notice. Of course, regardless of what Lee may have thought, by this time the Army of Northern Virginia could barely accomplish either of those tasks, let alone retreat and fight simultaneously. "Many of his men were moving in a dull fog, barely conscious of their surroundings. A cavalryman assigned to straggler patrol was aghast at the sight of the soldiers "who had thrown away their arms and knapsacks [and were] lying prone on the ground along the roadside, too much exhausted to march further, and only waiting for the enemy to come and pick them up as prisoners."

The next chain of events involved Lee's last attempt to fix the morale of his struggling army, and his decisions would attract future criticism among detractors who vociferously complained about Lee relieving Anderson, Johnson, and Pickett of their commands. It must be noted that around this time, Lee's judgment of the future of the conflict looked suspiciously muddled, as his belief in the cause seemed to have clouded his own perspective. While he removed generals, other senior officers had already approached him about the idea of listening to Grant's peace proposals. After listening to Brigadier General William Pendleton explain his reticent position, Lee answered, and quite differently than he had before: "I trust it has not come to that! We certainly have too many brave men to think of laying down our arms. They still fight with great spirit, whereas the enemy does not. And, besides, if I were to intimate to General Grant that I would listen to terms, he would at once regard it as such an evidence of weakness that he would demand unconditional surrender—and sooner than that I am resolved to die. Indeed, we must all determine to die at our posts."[22]

Lee may have been trying to take hard stands, but tremors of capitulation in the Army of Northern Virginia did not bode well for Lee's promise that his army could fight a brave Union opponent, for their determination to pursue the Confederates at least showed a willingness to confront their enemies. By April 8, the VI Corps had moved across the Appomattox River, and its skirmishers may have been able to glimpse the sight of officers of the II Corps looking for any sign of the westward direction of the Army of Northern Virginia.

As these movements continued, to Grant's credit, he personally realized that Lee's response was enough of an opening for him to write again. Thus, he continued the dialogue: "Your note of last evening in reply of mine of same date, asking the condition on which I will accept the surrender of the Army of Northern Virginia is just received. In reply I would say that, peace being my great desire, there is but one condition I would insist upon, namely: that the men and officers surrendered shall be disqualified for taking up arms again against the Government of the United States until properly exchanged. I will meet you, or will designate officers to meet any officers you may name for the same purpose, at any point agreeable to you, for the purpose of arranging definitely the terms upon which the surrender of the Army of Northern Virginia will be received."

As the dialogue continued between the two leaders, the action itself potentially lay in the hands of junior officers, albeit for different reasons. Lee's commands were in flux due to his release of

---

[22] "The Campaign to Appomattox," *Civil War Series* (National Park Service: History E-Library), http://www.nps.gov/history/history/online_books/civil_war_series/6/sec4.htm#2

generals, while Grant relied on subordinates like Sheridan to capably box in the Army of Northern Virginia. Sheridan's excellent intelligence scouts told of the supply trains at Appomattox Station waiting for the hungry Southern soldiers. Knowing this, Sheridan raced on, knowing that he could finally trap Lee and force his army's capitulation. Ord's command of the Army of the James, joined by the V Corps under Griffin, must have sensed the opportunity too, as Ord implored his men to march hard, promising that with long, hard marches, victory would come and the campaign would end.[23]

On top of all this, Grant was aware of the desertions that leaked from Longstreet's vanguard, which no officers prevented, and the Union commander could see plenty of evidence of a desperate opponent when he traveled up the road to meet General Meade. As the two men met, the path was littered with the detritus of the Confederate retreat, "in the roadway lay pistols, rifles, cooking utensils, personal baggage, camp equipment of every description, and frequently the carcasses of horses and mules that had succumbed to hunger, overwork, or the bullets of sympathetic soldiers."[24] Meanwhile, the Union forces left their own supply lines and sent foragers into the land to procure food, supplies, and mounts. With the countryside suddenly swarming with blue-jacketed skirmishers, Lee could only have been aware of the Union's attempt to intercept his army at Appomattox Station. The stage was set for the last series of fights around Appomattox Station and Lee's final decision.

**The Battle of Appomattox Station and the Battle of Appomattox Courthouse**

As it turned out, the first Union soldiers to arrive at Appomattox Station consisted of Sheridan's mounts, with Custer in the lead. Upon seeing the four supply trains that awaited Lee's starved army, Custer gave orders to engineers to spirit the trains away before a suspected large Confederate force appeared. The nearby rebels did not disappoint, and when they appeared, they rained shells down on the Federal horsemen at the station. With cries of "The Yankees are coming," the Reserve Artillery of Brigadier General Reuben Lindsay Walker was suddenly alert and prepared to scare off Custer's intrusion. The battle quickly began to take shape, and at the same time, another supply train arrived, with Walker joined by Talcott's Engineers serving as infantry, General Martin Gary's Cavalry Brigade alongside them, and nearly 100 artillerymen, now with guns pressed into their hands to hold a semi-circle defensive line.

Neither side could operate well in the poor terrain. The Confederates were stymied by a lack of organization that was characteristic of an ad hoc defense by engineers and artillerymen, while Custer's ordered charges moved clumsily over the grounds. The condition of opposing lines explained the sequence of battle, as Custer ordered charge after charge into artillery grapeshot, each one repulsed only to be attempted again because the Confederates could not mount any type of organized counteroffensive to capture the field.

The Union sides got the worst of things, taking massive shots of canister, vainly moving forwards against walls of iron they feared to fully approach. While the success of the Confederate artillery did not lead to a full retreat of their foes, the rebels could themselves escape the federal envelopment of their position. However, as darkness fell upon the field of battle, the Union cavalry continued to organize, persistent in their determination to seize the station and trap the Army of Northern Virginia. The Union soldiers continued to attack, and eventually, through the blast of cannons, they were able to capture the artillery guns. While the death toll of

---

[23] "The Campaign to Appomattox," *Civil War Series* (National Park Service: History E-Library), http://www.nps.gov/history/history/online_books/civil_war_series/6/sec4.htm#2

[24] Marvel, *Lee's Last Retreat*, 141.

the Southerners is not known, the reduction of their forces by 1,000 soldiers taken prisoner severely depleted numbers of an army that could ill afford any losses.

Of course, the worst part of the battle was the Union's capture of the station, which was completely overrun by the 15th New York Cavalry. Under the directions of Lieutenant Colonel August Root, the 15th New York gained the Lynchburg-Richmond Stage Road and captured more of the supply wagon of the Army of Northern Virginia. The successful assault ended badly for Root, who died in a hail of bullets fired by desperate Alabamians, and the rest of his New Yorkers were eventually forced to retreat, but they continued to seize prisoners and supplies during their retreat, further reducing the ability of the Confederates to supply an army that was already chronically undersupplied.

The five hour battle at Appomattox Station on April 8 did more than take away Lee's supplies too, because the capture of the Richmond-Lynchburg Stage Road meant the Union commanded the high ground west of Appomattox Court House, directly across the planned line of Lee's western march. After a council of war, Lee decided that an assault along the stage road would open up his army's escape, but he made that decision in the belief that only cavalry blocked the way. What Lee did not know was that the forced nighttime march of Ord's Army of the James had brought plenty of infantry nearby.

Lee was ready to move and took the last steps to consolidating forces, trading out soldiers from one brigade to make another and removing the last commands from the generals who no longer possessed viable battle-ready commands. In a sense, the Confederate desertions that sapped the strength of the Confederates should not be viewed as a sudden development that doomed the Army of Northern Virginia but instead looked at as the final outcome of Lee's mistakes to fully prepare his staff for the army's escape. Part of the problem was Lee's orders to wait for supplies to reach his soldiers, because his army dwindled immediately when that failed.

Some sources estimate that nearly 75% of the army's Virginians abandoned Lee,[25] and the moves he would make against former lieutenants such as Pickett would endure long after the arguments about the nature of Lee's surrender, but for what Lee had planned - a last desperate breakout - he still possessed an army of 30,000. Even with the Virginians' willingness to desert for their nearby homes, the remainder of these men most likely did not desert, not for belief in final Confederate victory but for the fact many hailed from the Carolinas, Georgia, Alabama, and Florida. They stayed with Lee in hopes of finding food, and by failing to secure a place to get supplies, Lee let them down. Now he was asking them to attack and break the Union stranglehold on their position.

Even as Lee planned for this assault, he and Grant continued their dialogue. Early on April 9, Grant wrote to Lee, "Your note of yesterday is received. As I have no authority to treat on the subject of peace, the meeting proposed for ten A.M. to-day could lead to no good. I will state, however, General, that I am equally anxious for peace with yourself, and the whole North entertains the same feeling. The terms upon which peace can be had are well understood. By the South laying down their arms they will hasten that most desirable event, save thousands of human lives and hundreds of millions of property not yet destroyed. Sincerely hoping that all our difficulties may be settled without the loss of another life, I subscribe myself, etc."

The Union commander had rebuffed his offer for a general truce covering the entire war, but Grant had only insisted that Lee disband his own army. With knowledge that Grant would probably accept a surrender under those same conditions at a subsequent point, one that would

---

[25] Marvel, *Lee's Last Retreat*, 206.

stop the bloodshed and likely deliver supplies to his starved soldiers, Lee chose to make one last attempt at a breakout.

Union cavalry continued to show up to block Lee's passage, defended by breastwork positions at dirt and fence rails. They were led by Brevet Brigadier General Charles Smith, who also directed Lieutenant James H. Lord's cannons to fire into the enemy camps, but the barrage did not prevent the Confederates from forming lines to attack. Major General John B. Gordon created a line of battle with General Clement Evans on the left, General James Walker in the center, and General Bryan Grimes on the right, while General Fitz Lee's cavalry divisions of Rooney Lee, Thomas Rosser, and Thomas Mumford prepared themselves. These forces were supported by General Armistead Long's artillery.

Before 8:00 a.m. on April 9, the lines moved forward in a left wheel motion, with everyone along the line giving the notoriously eerie rebel yell, and almost immediately, Smith's line began to collapse in slow motion, allowing Confederates to capture guns and for a brief time look upon an open road. Knowing that Smith's line faced the reality of being flanked, the rebel cavalry charged forward to fully gain the rear of the stage road.

Behind the Union lines, events took place quickly. McKenzie's small division of cavalry moved forward, along with Colonel Samuel B. Young's move to support Smith's left. However, the rebels, thoroughly emboldened by the knowledge that the road seemed to be in their grasp, drove back the Union cavalry, and with that, the road was open to Confederate soldiers. A North Carolina brigade commanded by William Cox began advancing along the road in a western direction.

Unfortunately for the Confederates, a corps from Ord's Army of the James arrived at this point in time, and the full weight of the Union numbers began to make itself felt as they fell upon the Confederate assault and changed the course of the battle. Brigadier General John Turner's Division from the XXIV Corps and Colonel William Woodward's brigade of Colored Troops supported Foster's right, and they began to move in concert against the rebel assault. The Confederates began to unravel, and upon seeing this, Gordon sent a message to Lee, one Lee might have been anticipating even before the battle: "Tell General Lee that my command has been fought to a frazzle and unless Longstreet can unite in the movement, or prevent these forces from coming upon my rear, I can not long go forward."

Gordon learned quickly how much more would threaten to disintegrate his ranks as he moved against the presence of more corps, first coming against him from the south (from Major General Charles Griffin's V Corps) and also to Gordon's right (the approach of the 185th New York and 198th Pennsylvania infantries, both commanded by Brigadier General Joshua Chamberlain). Gordon left what he could in the field, barely 25 men, to delay the Federal pursuit, while the remainder of his corps reformed on the east side of the Appomattox River.

At this moment, white flags of truce began to appear along the line. Some skirmishing continued, as both sides prepared for the resumption of battle, but a profound event had begun to take shape. Soldiers yelled up and down the line about the sight of white flags, and all seemingly came from the Confederates. As it turned out, aside from the ongoing skirmishing, the dreaded final battle that would spell the complete end of the Army of Northern Virginia would be averted. Instead, by the actions of April 8-9 and the ongoing dialogue between Grant and Lee, surrender was imminent without a final dramatic battle. For the 500 total already killed and wounded during the fighting around Appomattox, the hour came too late, and perhaps nobody was aware of it other than Lee and Grant, but the last senseless battles at the Appomattox Station and Court House would be the last major engagements between the two sides.[26]

## Lee Surrenders

Gordon's inability to open the road was the last straw for Lee. Lee sent word to initiate a conversation with Grant, and as Lee put it to some of his own men on the way to meet the Union commander, "There is nothing left me but to go and see General Grant, and I had rather die a thousand deaths."[27]

For Grant, the headache that had long afflicted him on April 9 went away when Lee contacted him. He sent back a letter to Lee: "General, Your note of this date is but this moment, 11:50 A.M. rec'd., in consequence of my having passed from the Richmond and Lynchburg road. I am at this writing about four miles West of Walker's Church and will push forward to the front for the purpose of meeting you. Notice sent to me on this road where you wish the interview to take place." Once the location was clear, Grant made sure to hurry with all haste to Lee's position at Appomattox Court House, and Sheridan, who had done so much to force Lee's surrender, now completed the task through the notification of all commands that Grant was en route to Lee to formally discuss surrender. The truce was obeyed by all sides. Sitting in sight of one another, little fanfare greeted the fact that the guns of the Army of Northern Virginia and Army of the Potomac had fired at each other for the final time after several years of constant warfare. Stunned silence filled the fields.

Of course, the surrender in the parlor of the McLean House at Appomattox is still better known than the actual campaign itself. Grant appeared in his typically disheveled manner, while Lee was impeccably dressed in uniform, a stark contrast between two men who hadn't seen each other since they fought on the same side during the Mexican-American War. Grant explained in his memoirs, "I had known General Lee in the old army, and had served with him in the Mexican War; but did not suppose, owing to the difference in our age and rank, that he would remember me, while I would more naturally remember him distinctly, because he was the chief of staff of General Scott in the Mexican War. When I had left camp that morning I had not expected so soon the result that was then taking place, and consequently was in rough garb. I was without a sword, as I usually was when on horseback on the field, and wore a soldier's blouse for a coat, with the shoulder straps of my rank to indicate to the army who I was… General Lee was dressed in a full uniform which was entirely new, and was wearing a sword of considerable value, very likely the sword which had been presented by the State of Virginia; at all events, it was an entirely different sword from the one that would ordinarily be worn in the field. In my rough traveling suit, the uniform of a private with the straps of a lieutenant-general, I must have contrasted very strangely with a man so handsomely dressed, six feet high and of faultless form. But this was not a matter that I thought of until afterwards."

After discussing that war for a bit, they set to the task of negotiating, and Grant referred to his previous terms as he dictated out the surrender: "In accordance with the substance of my letter to you of the 8th inst., I propose to receive the surrender of the Army of N. Va. on the following terms, to wit: Rolls of all the officers and men to be made in duplicate. One copy to be given to an officer designated by me, the other to be retained by such officer or officers as you may designate. The officers to give their individual paroles not to take up arms against the Government of the United States until properly exchanged, and each company or regimental

---

[26] Patrick Schroeder, "The Battles of Appomattox Station and Courthouse," *The Civil War Trust*, http://www.civilwar.org/battlefields/appomattox-station/appomattox-station-history/the-battles-of-appomattox.html

[27] Davis, Kenneth C. *The Civil War: Everything You Need to Know About America's Greatest Conflict but Never Learned*. Page 402.

commander sign a like parole for the men of their commands. The arms, artillery and public property to be parked and stacked, and turned over to the officer appointed by me to receive them. This will not embrace the side-arms of the officers, nor their private horses or baggage. This done, each officer and man will be allowed to return to their homes, not to be disturbed by United States authority so long as they observe their paroles and the laws in force where they may reside."

Grant was unsure of what Lee was thinking as they worked on the surrender, as he noted in his memoirs: "What General Lee's feelings were I do not know. As he was a man of much dignity, with an impassible face, it was impossible to say whether he felt inwardly glad that the end had finally come, or felt sad over the result, and was too manly to show it. Whatever his feelings, they were entirely concealed from my observation; but my own feelings, which had been quite jubilant on the receipt of his letter, were sad and depressed. I felt like anything rather than rejoicing at the downfall of a foe who had fought so long and valiantly, and had suffered so much for a cause, though that cause was, I believe, one of the worst for which a people ever fought, and one for which there was the least excuse. I do not question, however, the sincerity of the great mass of those who were opposed to us."

Lee formally accepted the surrender terms: "GENERAL:—I received your letter of this date containing the terms of the surrender of the Army of Northern Virginia as proposed by you. As they are substantially the same as those expressed in your letter of the 8th inst., they are accepted. I will proceed to designate the proper officers to carry the stipulations into effect." With that, a campaign that was so heavily influenced by Confederate attempts to draw supplies would end with the Army of Northern Virginia being supplied by the victorious Army of the Potomac in the wake of the surrender.

**The McLean House at Appomattox**

A few days later, the Army of Northern Virginia was formally surrendered and processed. It was a solemn moment for all involved, and it was poignantly captured in an account written by Joshua L. Chamberlain, one of the heroes of Gettysburg. "The momentous meaning of this occasion impressed me deeply. I resolved to mark it by some token of recognition, which could be no other than a salute of arms. Well aware of the responsibility assumed, and of the criticisms that would follow, as the sequel proved, nothing of that kind could move me in the least. The act could be defended, if needful, by the suggestion that such a salute was not to the cause for which the flag of the Confederacy stood, but to its going down before the flag of the Union. My main reason, however, was one for which I sought no authority nor asked forgiveness. Before us in proud humiliation stood the embodiment of manhood: men whom neither toils and sufferings, nor the fact of death, nor disaster, nor hopelessness could bend from their resolve; standing before us now, thin, worn, and famished, but erect, and with eyes looking level into ours, waking memories that bound us together as no other bond;—was not such manhood to be welcomed back into a Union so tested and assured? Instructions had been given; and when the head of each division column comes opposite our group, our bugle sounds the signal and instantly our whole line from right to left, regiment by regiment in succession, gives the soldier's salutation, from the "order arms" to the old "carry"—the marching salute. Gordon at the head of the column, riding with heavy spirit and downcast face, catches the sound of shifting arms, looks up, and, taking the meaning, wheels superbly, making with himself and his horse one uplifted figure, with profound salutation as he drops the point of his sword to the boot toe; then facing to his own command, gives word for his successive brigades to pass us with the same position of the manual,—honor answering honor. On our part not a sound of trumpet more, nor roll of drum; not a cheer, nor word nor whisper of vain-glorying, nor motion of man standing again at the order, but an awed stillness rather, and breath-holding, as if it were the passing of the dead!"

## The Aftermath and Legacy of Appomattox

In the American Civil War, one of the most charged images is that of the surrender of Lee to Grant on April 9, 1865. What is forgotten, or at least glazed over in the moment, is the campaign that preceded Lee's surrender, when Grant chased his foe across western Virginia and forced the Army of Northern Virginia's surrender. So much of the myth of Lee – a symbol of a noble, righteous South – is supported by the way he fought during the last campaign, yet he was ultimately compelled to give up the fight.

In many ways, the image of the impeccably dressed Lee and the disheveled Grant sticks out when discussing the Lost Cause and the way it shaped the legacy of the war as a whole. Indeed, the heroic qualities of Lee are used to support the myth of the Lost Cause, a concept explained by the Georgia Encyclopedia: "The argument of the Lost Cause insists that the South fought nobly and against all odds not to preserve slavery but entirely for other reasons, such as the rights of states to govern themselves, and that southerners were forced to defend themselves against Northern aggression. When the idea of a Southern nation was defeated on the battlefield, the vision of a separate Southern people, with a distinct and noble cultural character, remained. The term *culture religion* refers to ideals that a given group of people desires to strengthen or restore, and Lost Cause religion sought to maintain the concept of a distinct, and superior, white southern culture against perceived attacks. Major components of religion include myth, symbol, and their expressions through rituals. The Lost Cause culture religion manifested all three."[28]

Of course, that myth relies on an account of the Appomattox Campaign and Lee's actions that is mistaken, or at least partially inaccurate. The Confederate Army of Northern Virginia did not surrender due solely to overwhelming numbers; decisions and mistakes made by Lee and others played vital roles. While Lost Cause advocates sought to make Lee blameless for everything, the Appomattox Campaign hardly represented Lee's first or only mistakes, as the decisions at Gettysburg make clear. Instead, they are proof that Lee, who is universally recognized as a capable general, was still human.

The focus on Lee and the Lost Cause has also helped popularize Appomattox as the end of the Civil War, even though fighting continued for several weeks after Lee surrendered. In fact, Jefferson Davis was adamant that the Confederates keep fighting on, even as he was in full flight away from Richmond and receiving news of Lee's surrender. Joseph E. Johnston, a man who had been at odds with Davis throughout the war, still had an army opposing Sherman, and ironically, he was now the Confederacy's last hope. But as made clear in his memoirs, given the surrender of Lee's army and his hopeless position in the Carolinas, Johnston proposed to negotiate terms of surrender with Sherman against Davis' explicit orders:

"Mr. Mallory came to converse with me on the subject, and showed great anxiety that negotiations to end the war should be commenced, and urged that I was the person who should suggest the measure to the President. I, on the contrary, thought that such a suggestion would come more properly from one of his "constitutional advisers," but told Mr. Mallory of my conversation with General Breckenridge.

That gentleman fulfilled his engagement promptly; and General Beauregard and myself were summoned to the President's office an hour or two after the meeting of his

[28] Williams, David S, "Lost Cause Religion," *New Georgia Encyclopedia*, http://www.georgiaencyclopedia.org/articles/history-archaeology/lost-cause-religion

cabinet there, next morning. Being desired by the President to do it, we compared the military forces of the two parties to the war: ours, an army of about twenty thousand infantry and artillery, and five thousand mounted troops; those of the United States, three armies that could be combined against ours, which was insignificant compared with either-Grant's, of a hundred and eighty thousand men; Sherman's, of a hundred and ten thousand, at least, and Canby's of sixty thousand-odds of seventeen or eighteen to one, which in a few weeks could be more than doubled.

I represented that under such circumstances it would be the greatest of human crimes for us to attempt to continue the war; for, having neither money nor credit, nor arms but those in the hands of our soldiers, nor ammunition but that in their cartridge-boxes, nor shops for repairing arms or fixing ammunition, the effect of our keeping the field would be, not to harm the enemy, but to complete the devastation of our country and ruin of its people. I therefore urged that the President should exercise at once the only function of government still in his possession, and open negotiations for peace.

The members of the cabinet present were then desired by the President to express their opinions on the important question. General Breckenridge, Mr. Mallory, and Mr. Reagan, thought that the war was decided against us; and that it was absolutely necessary to make peace. Mr. Benjamin expressed the contrary opinion. The latter made a speech for war, much like that of Sempronius in Addison's play. The President replied to our suggestion as if somewhat annoyed by it. He said that it was idle to suggest that he should attempt to negotiate, when it was certain, from the attempt previously made, that his authority to treat would not be recognized, nor any terms that he might offer considered by the Government of the United States. I reminded him that it had not been unusual, in such cases, for military commanders to initiate negotiations upon which treaties of peace were founded; and proposed that he should allow me to address General Sherman on the subject. After a few words in opposition to that idea, Mr. Davis reverted to the first suggestion, that he should offer terms to the Government of the United States--which he had put aside; and sketched a letter appropriate to be sent by me to General Sherman, proposing a meeting to arrange the terms of an armistice to enable the civil authorities  to agree upon terms of peace. That this course might be adopted at once, I proposed that he should dictate the letter then to Mr. Mallory, who was a good penman, and that I should sign and send it to the Federal commander immediately. The letter, prepared in that way, was sent by me with all dispatch to Lieutenant-General Hampton, near Hillsboroa, to be forwarded by him to General Sherman. It was delivered to the latter next day, the 14th, and was in these terms: "The results of the recent campaign in Virginia have changed the relative military condition of the belligerents. I am therefore induced to address you, in this form, the inquiry whether, in order to stop the further effusion of blood and devastation of property, you are willing to make a temporary suspension of active operations, and to communicate to Lieutenant-General Grant, commanding the armies of the United States, the request that he will take like action in regard to other armies — the object being, to permit the civil authorities to enter into the needful arrangements to terminate the existing war."

Ironically, what followed would result in both Johnston and Sherman being subjected to ludicrous charges of treason. As soon as Lee surrendered on April 9, 1865, Grant dispatched a boat from his headquarters at City Point, Virginia with a message to Sherman announcing the surrender and authorizing him to offer the same terms to Johnston. On April 18, Sherman entered into an agreement with Johnston which addressed political and military considerations conditionally, the understanding being that the armistice was subject to approval by superior authority. Moreover, Sherman drafted the terms of surrender consistent with what he thought Lincoln had conveyed to Grant and him at City Point in March. General Sherman sent a staff officer to Washington to hand-deliver the terms of the agreement to Grant, which reached him on April 21.

Thus, on April 26, 1865, after all the confusion, General Johnston ignored President Davis's orders and surrendered his army and all the Confederates under his command in the Carolinas, Georgia, and Florida. However, even as Johnston's surrender was secured, Secretary Stanton continued to denounce Sherman, calling for his formal "dressing down." And although Sherman was never officially charged with treason and the public finally came to understand the circumstances of Sherman's so-called "act of treason," the riff between Sherman and Stanton continued throughout Stanton's tenure as Secretary of War until 1869.

Johnston telegrammed Southern leaders to explain his surrender. "The disaster in Virginia, the capture by the enemy of all our workshops for the preparation of ammunition and repairing of arms, the impossibility of recruiting our little army opposed to more than ten times its number, or of supplying it except by robbing our own citizens, destroyed all hope of successful war. I have made, therefore, a military convention with Major-General Sherman, to terminate hostilities in North and South Carolina, Georgia, and Florida. I made this convention to spare the blood of this gallant little army, to prevent further sufferings of our people by the devastation and ruin inevitable from the marches of invading armies, and to avoid the crime of waging a hopeless war."

In his surrender address, General Order Number 22, Johnston exhorted his men: "Comrades: In terminating our official relations, I earnestly exhort you to observe faithfully the terms of pacification agreed upon and discharge the obligations of good and peaceful citizens, as well as you have performed the duties of thorough soldiers in the field. By such a course, you will best secure the comfort of your families and kindred and restore tranquility to our country. You will return to your homes with the admiration of our people, won by the courage and noble devotion you have displayed in this long war. I shall always remember with pride the loyal support and generous confidence you have given me. I now part with you with deep regret – and bid you farewell with feelings of cordial friendship and with earnest wishes that you may have hereafter all the prosperity and happiness to be found in the world."[29]

After Johnston surrendered, Sherman made the magnanimous decision to give 10 days' rations to the Confederate soldiers, as well as horses and mules that they could use for farming. Sherman even distributed foodstuffs to civilians across the South. Though this is all forgotten in the name of demonizing Sherman across the South even 150 years after the start of the Civil War, Johnston was both impressed and exceedingly grateful. Johnston wrote to Sherman that his generosity "reconciles me to what I have previously regarded as the misfortune of my life, that of having you to encounter in the field."

In the immediate aftermath of Johnston's surrender, the remaining Confederate forces would surrender or quit. The last skirmish between the two sides took place May 12-13, ending ironically with a Confederate victory at the Battle of Palmito Ranch in Texas. Two days earlier, Jefferson Davis had been captured in Georgia.

Of course, one of the Civil War's most important events had happened in the meantime, and

---

[29] Bennett Place State Historic Site website.

one that happened after Lee surrendered at Appomattox. The assassination of Lincoln on April 14 had thrown the government into flux and strengthened the positions of Radical Republicans and men like Secretary of War Edwin Stanton, who sought to take a harder stance against the defeated rebels. Lincoln's assassination would shape the future of the Reconstruction Era and the direction in which the United States went from there.

**A centennial stamp commemorating Appomattox and the reunification of the country**

**Online Resources**

Other books about the Civil War by Charles River Editors

Other books about Petersburg

**Bibliography**

Beringer, Richard E., Herman Hattaway, Archer Jones, and William N. Still, Jr. Why the South Lost the Civil War. Athens: University of Georgia Press, 1986. ISBN 0-8203-0815-3.

Calkins, Chris. The Appomattox Campaign, March 29 – April 9, 1865. Conshohocken, PA: Combined Books, 1997. ISBN 978-0-938289-54-8.

Davis, Burke. To Appomattox: Nine April Days, 1865. New York: Eastern Acorn Press reprint, 1981. ISBN 0-915992-17-5. First published New York: Rinehart, 1959.

Davis, William C. An Honorable Defeat: The Last Days of the Confederate Government. New York: Harcourt, Inc., 2001. ISBN 978-0-15-100564-2.

Greene, A. Wilson. The Final Battles of the Petersburg Campaign: Breaking the Backbone of the Rebellion. Knoxville: University of Tennessee Press, 2008. ISBN 978-1-57233-610-0.

Hess, Earl J. In the Trenches at Petersburg: Field Fortifications & Confederate Defeat. Chapel Hill: University of North Carolina Press, 2009. ISBN 978-0-8078-3282-0.

Kennedy, Frances H., ed. The Civil War Battlefield Guide. 2nd ed. Boston: Houghton Mifflin Co., 1998. ISBN 0-395-74012-6.

Longacre, Edward G. The Cavalry at Appomattox: A Tactical Study of Mounted Operations During the Civil War's Climactic Campaign, March 27 – April 9, 1865. Mechanicsburg, PA: Stackpole Books, 2003. ISBN 978-0-8117-0051-1.

Marvel, William. Lee's Last Retreat: The Flight to Appomattox. Chapel Hill: University of North Carolina Press, 2002. ISBN 978-0-8078-5703-8.

Sommers, Richard J. Richmond Redeemed: The Siege at Petersburg. Garden City, NY: Doubleday, 1981. ISBN 978-0-385-15626-4.

Stoker, Donald. The Grand Design: Strategy and the U.S. Civil War. Oxford and New York: Oxford University Press, 2010. ISBN 978-0-19-537-305-9.

Trudeau, Noah Andre. The Last Citadel: Petersburg, Virginia, June 1864–April 1865. Baton Rouge: Louisiana State University Press, 1991. ISBN 0-8071-1861-3.

Weigley, Russell F. A Great Civil War: A Military and Political History, 1861–1865. Bloomington and Indianapolis: Indiana University Press, 2000. ISBN 0-253-33738-0.

Winik, Jay. April 1865: The Month That Saved America. New York: HarperCollins, 2006. ISBN 978-0-06-089968-4. First published 2001.

Made in the USA
San Bernardino, CA
05 March 2018